ACCOUNTING IN EUROPE

MICHAEL LAFFERTY, A.C.A.

Published by
Woodhead-Faulkner Ltd
in association with
National Westminster Bank

Woodhead-Faulkner (Publishers) Ltd
7 Rose Crescent
Cambridge CB2 3LL

First published September 1975

ISBN 0 85941 013 7

The opinions expressed in this book are those of the author and do not necessarily coincide with those of National Westminster Bank Limited.

Printed in Great Britain by Galliard (Printers) Ltd,
Great Yarmouth, Norfolk

Foreword

by Gerhard G. Mueller
Professor and Chairman,
Department of Accounting,
University of Washington

International affairs of accounting are exciting and challenging. When the history of the twentieth century comes to be written, important spaces of it must be reserved for the growth of truly international financial capital markets, the emergence of the multinational enterprise as a key factor in world affairs, the regional integration and harmonisation of widely divergent national systems, and the growth of economic citizenship for countries of the so-called Third World. The dichotomy between "domestic" and "foreign" is slowly becoming old-fashioned. Dreams of multinationalism are turning into reality at a fair speed.

What does all this have to do with accounting? More than meets appearances at first glance! Accounting, as the language of business, serves international capital markets and the world-wide operations of multinational enterprises in a great many respects. It is sure to make contributions to economic and social regionalisation and assist materially in processes of economic development. The United Nations Group of Eminent Persons appointed to study the role of multinational corporations on development and on international relations has gone so far as to propose recently the creation of a world-wide accounting data bank and the convening of a group of experts to make recommendations on international accounting standards. Of course, the accounting profession itself has already created an International Accounting Standards Committee based in London for the express purpose of establishing world-wide standards. The work of this International Accounting Committee is proceeding so well that the International Federation of Stock Exchanges, at its meeting in Madrid on 8 to 10 October 1974, adopted a resolution which calls for member exchanges in countries whose professional accountancy bodies are either founders or associate members of the International Accounting Standards Committee to take steps to include in their respective listing requirements reference to compliance with standards issued by that committee. A development of such scope and impact would have been unthinkable only ten years ago!

It is not surprising, then, that every single day a new periodical article, government regulation, research study or book comes across my desk dealing with some aspect of international accounting. The book before us is one item in this procession. But it is a singularly noteworthy item because it makes several unique contributions.

In the first place, it has a broad foundation that embraces academic, professional accounting, financial management and general business viewpoints. It is more than an accounting recipe book or a dry, scholarly treatise. Its aim is to promote an understanding and appreciation of European accounting as opposed to the "how they do it" objective of other publications on the same subject. A director or financial executive should find this book just as valuable as the practising professional accountant or the educator and researcher.

A second and particularly refreshing characteristic of Michael Lafferty's work is his frankness and honesty in dealing with a subject that is by nature controversial. So long as there are important national differences between the accounting standards and practices of individual countries, we shall have plenty of people claiming that theirs are better than any others. And, in reality, some things are better than some others in accountancy when measured against the needs and expectations of those using accounting reports. So why not attempt to assess things openly and frankly, even if it means that some value judgements have to be made? As an academic, I welcome and respect the honesty of this book. It is sure to be controversial and therefore engender considerable discussion.

The book's innovative nature is its third major characteristic. I know of no other publication which directly tackles the subject of the international professional accounting firms and devotes a full chapter to the history of their respective evolutions and the nature of their international organisation. This chapter alone will be of major interest to those concerned with international accounting matters.

Accounting in Europe exhibits careful preparation and obvious help from professional accounting bodies in each of the nine EEC countries. It is probably as authoritative as one can make a study of this kind. It is a book for desks and worktables rather than for library shelves. With the United Kingdom now firmly committed to membership of the EEC, I would like to take this opportunity to welcome it to a special place among the literature on international accounting.

Professor G. G. Mueller
University of Washington

Author's Preface

This book has been written to cater for the needs of accountants, financial analysts, bankers, businessmen and all those other individuals who require to know a lot—or even a little—about accounting in the context of the European Economic Community.

The book has been written to fill a gaping hole in the literature of accounting and I hope that its publication will encourage more people to join in the debate on the harmonisation of company and professional laws in the EEC.

Accounting in Europe is meant to be used again and again. It is no academic treatise; indeed, if it were it would probably be worthless to those for whom it is written. *Accounting in Europe* is intended to inform and help people in any way concerned with financial statements—be they in London or Paris, Copenhagen or Milan—but it is by no means the last word.

I wrote this book because I could find no source with adequate answers to all the questions I was asking. While it was easy enough to find an accountant or analyst who had some familiarity with accounting in France, or Germany, or Holland, the chances of finding one person with a reasonable knowledge of all three were decidedly remote. I believe that no such person existed.

I first became actively interested in the subject of accounting in Europe when I acted as chairman at a conference organised by the Chartered Accountant Students' Society of London in December 1972, not long after I qualified as a chartered accountant. There I was amazed to find that although a few of the distinguished speakers had heard of the proposed fourth EEC company directive on annual accounts (and at least one speaker said he had seen a copy of the document) no one knew very much about it.

I might well have forgotten about that obscure fourth directive if my good friend Christopher Hill had not asked me to try to write an article on what he called "EEC accounting" for his new magazine.

It was the research for that article which really opened my eyes to the incredible lack of knowledge, both written and unwritten, which existed in the United Kingdom, and indeed, as I soon discovered, in every other European country, on the whole area of accounting in the other EEC countries. How, I wondered, could anyone even begin to understand the implications of the European Commission's proposals to harmonise accounting practices in the EEC if he had no knowledge of the state of the art in the other Member States? I started to dig and before long I was commissioned to write a series of articles for "The Executive's World" page of the *Financial Times*, a newspaper to which I am still privileged to contribute.

The next step was obvious. Suddenly, European accounting was "in". Publishers could hardly wait to have a book on the subject but they were reluctant to pay for the intensive "in the field" research which I considered essential. Then Woodhead-Faulkner contacted me and with the backing of the National Westminster Bank we were able to get the project off the ground.

Yet now as I read through the page proofs of this book I am, like J. M. Keynes, "acutely conscious of its defects". Like him, "I feel like someone who has been forcing his way through a confused jungle. Now that I have emerged from it, I see that I might have taken a more direct route and that many problems and perplexities which beset me during the journey had not precisely the significance which I supposed at the time."

My research took me to every country in the EEC but what I present here is far from being all my own work. It is the work of literally hundreds of people—from bankers, financial journalists and trade unionists, to government officials and, of course, accountants—from all over Europe. In particular it is also the work of those distinguished gentlemen in each of the countries covered who were kind and generous enough with their time to review the individual chapters dealing with their own countries. To all those people I owe an eternal debt of gratitude. I list their names here in the order in which the chapters appear in the book.

France
Roger Marron, Partner in Deloitte, Haskins & Sells, Paris
David Adamson, Technical Consultant to the Paris region of the Cie National des Commissaires aux Comptes
Germany
Herbert Schnitzler, Partner in Touche Ross & Co., Frankfurt
Dr Friedrich Ziehm, Partner in Deloitte, Haskins & Sells, Düsseldorf

The Netherlands
Henk Volten, Director of the Nederlands Instituut van Register-accountants
J. M. Vecht, Onderdirecteur, AMRO Bank
Belgium
J. J. Schellekens and P. E. Berger, Partners in Berger, Block, Kirschen, Schellekens & Co. and Presidents (1972–73) of the Institut des Reviseurs d'Entreprises and the Institut des Reviseurs de Banque respectively
Denis M. Constant and F. Hendrickx, Partners in Whinney Murray Ernst & Ernst, Brussels and Antwerp offices respectively
Luxembourg
Manu Khosla of Price Waterhouse & Co., Luxembourg City
Denmark
B. Niemann Olsen, Secretary of the Foreningen af Statsautoriserede Revisorer
Arthur L. Swanson, Partner in Arthur Andersen & Co., Copenhagen
Italy
John Anderson, Partner in Arthur Young & Co., Rome
David Coombs, Partner in Deloitte, Haskins & Sells, Milan
Michael Stilwell, Partner in Coopers & Lybrand, Milan
United Kingdom
Shirley Bevan, Partner in Binder Hamlyn Singleton Fabian, London
John Norton, Partner in Arthur Andersen, London
Ireland
Roger Hussey, Director of the Institute of Chartered Accountants in Ireland
David Rowe, Partner in Stokes Kennedy Crowley & Co., Dublin
Harmonisation of EEC Company Law
Paul Rutteman of Arthur Young McClelland Moores & Co., London
The European Method
David Gibson-Moore, now in international banking and formerly of Coopers & Lybrand and DAFSA.

In addition the whole book was reviewed by David Gibson-Moore, who is one of those few people with extensive knowledge of the subject.

Other names which cannot be omitted include John Trafford, former Management Editor and now Property Editor of the *Financial Times* and all my other friends in Bracken House. I must also thank Michael Bywater, Deputy Librarian at the Institute of Chartered Accountants in England and Wales, who, in my opinion, must be the best business librarian in the world; Pauline M. Katborg, with the British Embassy, Copenhagen, who kindly provided me with a free advance copy of her translations of the new Danish company laws when everyone else had to pay a very high price, and Mary Waite, who took time off from her many marketing trips overseas to translate the *avant-projet* of the proposed new Belgian law on company accounts into English. The index is the excellent work of Kathleen Morris, the librarian of the Institute of Chartered Accountants in England and Wales.

Accounting in Europe is thus the result of true, unselfish, almost unbelievable, European co-operation.

Having said all this, I must emphasise that the responsibility for all opinions and errors is mine alone. Indeed, there have been many instances where my reviewers have disagreed with me but I have nevertheless decided to leave the text unchanged.

June 1975 M.J.L.

Contents

Chapter 1

France

BACKGROUND

French industry has always been dominated by small and medium-sized family-controlled businesses. The Bourse has not, until recently, played an important part in company financing and the consequent absence of a large body of shareholders is probably the most important reason for the present relatively underdeveloped state of the French accounting profession. The importance of an active equity market playing a leading role in corporate finance needs no emphasis and it is interesting to observe the way in which the French profession has recently begun to find its wings under active Bourse encouragement.

According to Valéry Giscard d'Estaing, Paris enjoys in the 1970s, for the first time in its history, the essentials necessary for it to play the role of an international financial centre: "an industrially buoyant economy, abundant savings, a large financial market and a sound currency".

Although the recent period of Gaullist prosperity is seen by some Frenchmen as just another respite in the cycle of development and recession which has characterised the French economy since the eighteenth century, there seem to be reasonable grounds for optimism. In 1972 French *per capita* GNP exceeded by 50 per cent that of the United Kingdom, which it had overtaken in the early 1950s. The Hudson Institute calculates that it will equal that of Germany in the mid 1980s. Economic growth is the Government's primary goal and an average post-war growth of just under 6 per cent in GNP seems to pose no problem.

These remarkable achievements have taken place against a background of national economic plans and a high degree of central government control. The presence of the Government is felt everywhere and it is estimated that approximately 80 per cent of all medium- and long-term finance passes at some stage through Government hands. The authorities control the capital market via the Bank of France and the credit agencies, thereby ensuring that capital flows to investments with the highest priority. The bond market, which accounts for some 70 per cent of new capital (Table 1.1), is dominated by annual issues from nationalised institutions while the private sector is subject to a queue system regulated by the Government.

Although the household sector, on average, accounts for over 40 per cent of total gross savings, the typical investor has a marked liquidity preference, and, of necessity, the re-employment of savings via the State-dominated banking system is highly developed. In the past, individuals have not been encouraged to invest in the equity market, and, according to a recent survey, only 1½ million Frenchmen think it worth their while to become shareholders and their average age is almost 60. The institutions have also taken little interest in equities and the reason most often advanced for this is twofold—bad financial reporting, and the fact that the bulk of shares is still privately controlled.

TABLE 1.1. GROSS NEW ISSUES (in F billions)

	1968	*1969*	*1970*	*1971*	*1972*
1 Fixed-interest securities					
Government—Post Office Motorways Fund	0.91	0.67	1.04	1.74	2.29
Local authorities	0.73	0.71	1.04	1.13	3.57
Public sector financial institutions	4.63	5.40	6.52	7.19	7.51
Nationalised industries	2.33	1.81	2.12	2.74	3.26
Private sector	1.64	2.86	4.96	8.88	8.95
Overseas borrowers	—	—	—	0.25	0.10
Total 1	**10.24**	**11.45**	**15.68**	**21.93**	**25.68**
	73.8%	60.3%	64.4%	73.3%	70.8%
2 Equities	**3.63**	**7.54**	**8.68**	**7.97**	**9.18**
	26.2%	39.7%	35.6%	26.7%	29.2%
Total	**13.87**	**18.99**	**24.36**	**29.90**	**34.86**

Source: La Bourse in 1972, Compagnie des Agents de Change.

With firm economic expansion well under way, however, the Government has turned its attention to the development and popularisation of the Bourse. In 1968 the Commission des Opérations de Bourse (COB) was established, primarily to control all information provided to shareholders and published by quoted companies and to check and ensure their compliance with financial reporting requirements. It is the activities of this "stock exchange commission with SEC powers" which have been largely responsible for the transformation which has taken place over the past few years. Reforms are now under way to introduce an Anglo-Saxon jobber-broker system and to provide more protection for minority shareholders.

BUSINESS ORGANISATIONS

The generic term for a business organisation in France is *société*. Under French law, there is a basic distinction between *sociétés commerciales*, which are concerned with commercial operations, and *sociétés civiles*, which include all other forms. Furthermore, *sociétés commerciales* are subject to the jurisdiction of the commercial courts and the Commercial Code whereas *sociétés civiles* are subject to the civil courts and the Civil Code.

TABLE 1.2. STATISTICS OF FRENCH BUSINESS ORGANISATIONS (as at 31 December 1969)

Sociétés anonymes	87,474
Sociétés à responsibilité limitée	118,372
Sociétés (all forms)	252,000

Source: Ministère de l'Economie et des Finances.

The law of 24 July 1966 deals with *sociétés commerciales* (Fig. 1.1) and states that the following, each with a statutory maximum life of 99 years, qualify:

1. General partnerships (*sociétés en nom collectif*).
2. Limited partnerships (*sociétés en commandite simple*).
3. Private limited liability companies (*sociétés à responsibilité limitée*).
4. Limited liability companies (*sociétés anonymes*) } *sociétés par actions*.
5. Limited partnerships with shares (*sociétés en commandite par actions*) } *sociétés par actions*.

Companies

The *société à responsibilité limitée* (SàRL) is an exact copy of the German *Gesellschaft mit beschränkter Haftung* (GmbH) and was introduced into French law in 1925 as a result of the return of Alsace-Lorraine (which had many GmbH companies) to France after the First World War.

Both SA and SàRL companies are by far the most popular forms of business organisation (Fig. 1.1) and the significant features of each may be compared as follows:

	SA	*SàRL*
Shareholders	Minimum of 7, and no restrictions on nationality or residence.	Minimum of 2, maximum of 50 and no restrictions on nationality or residence.

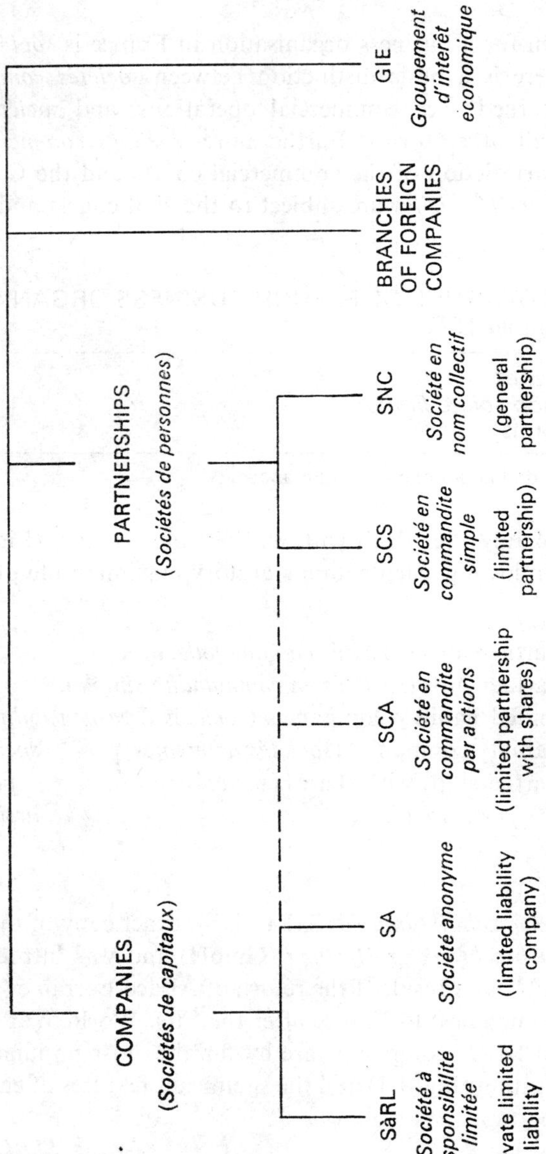

Fig. 1.1. Forms of business organisation in France

	SA	*SàRL*
Securities	Shares can be bearer,[1] except that the following shares must be registered: directors' qualifying shares; shares issued in exchange for contributions of assets for the first two years; and shares not fully paid. The minimum nominal value of shares is F 100 or F 10 in the case of quoted companies following a decree of 18 October 1973. Shares cannot be issued for consideration of less than par value.	Registered shares only (*parts sociales*). Transfers must be approved by majority of members representing 75 per cent of capital and effected with a registered agreement, which is inscribed in an official ledger kept by the "Administration de l'Enregistrement", and requires the payment of registration duties. A private agreement is binding between the parties, but does not have full legal effect on third parties. But transfers to other shareholders or to stated family members may be made freely. There are no formal certificates and shares have a minimum nominal value of F 100.
Capital	At least F 500,000 for quoted companies; F 100,000 for other companies. Shares must be fully subscribed and issued, and capital contributions in cash must be at least 25 per cent paid in with balance due within 5 years. Capital contributions in kind must be fully paid up before shares are issued. Cannot purchase its own shares except as part of a capital reduction or under very specific limited conditions.	F 20,000 minimum. Capital must be fully subscribed, issued and paid up. Cannot purchase its own shares except in the case of a capital reduction.

	SA	*SàRL*
Capital impairment	If accumulated losses result in net assets being reduced to less than a quarter of capital, an extraordinary general meeting must be held to determine whether the entity should be liquidated or continued, and the decision must be published and filed at the Commercial Register. If the entity is to continue, net assets must be restored to a figure at least equal to a quarter of the share capital by the end of the third following year.	
Annual general meeting	General meeting required at least annually, and within 6 months of the closing date.	

An SA may be managed by either (1) a president and board of directors or (2) a supervisory board (shareholders' council—*conseil de surveillance*) and a directorate (*directoire*). Under the first, classical-style, structure, the board of directors, numbering three to twelve, is elected by the shareholders, and the board, in turn, elects a Président Directeur Général (PDG). The PDG may not be president of more than two companies simultaneously; nor may any other director hold more than eight directorships. Subject to the by-laws of the company, directors are appointed for up to a maximum of six years, or three years if named in the articles of incorporation, and are remunerated by means of attendance fees (*jetons de présence*). They may also receive salaries for performing particular functions but no more than one-third of the directors may have employment contracts with the company at any one time. Although the practice is dying out, directors may also receive a share of profits (*tantièmes*) if this is provided by employment contracts subject to (1) the payment or allocation of dividends and (2) the reserves set aside by the shareholders in general meeting.

According to the 1966 law, the board is "vested with the broadest powers to act in any circumstance in the name of the company". In particular the directors are responsible for the administration of the company, the preparation of the annual accounts and the calling of shareholders' meetings.

The alternative, German-style, two-tier board was introduced by the 1966 law, but it is not yet widely used. Under this system, the function of control is separated from that of management, and the supervisory board appoints the members of the directorate who are responsible for the day-to-day running of the company. The supervisory board comprises between three and twelve members, each of whom must hold a minimum number of shares in the company, and its tenure, functions and remuneration are broadly similar to those of directors. The members of the supervisory board are appointed for terms of three to six years and are vested with the same broad powers as directors. Members of the directorate, one to five in number, are appointed for terms of four years which are renewable, and it is not permitted to serve on the *directoire* of more than two companies simultaneously.

It is interesting to observe that, although bankers have traditionally had major interests, including equity holdings, in French companies, they have not followed German example but have refrained from participation in management.

An SàRL is managed by one or more managers (*gérants*) who need not be shareholders and whose powers and responsibilities are similar to those of directors or members of the directorate.

Partnerships

The *société en nom collectif* (SNC) is the nearest French equivalent to the UK general partnership, except that it has a separate legal personality. The partners (*associés*) are jointly and severally liable for the debts of the company.

The *société en commandite simple* is similar to the SNC with the addition of one or more sleeping partners (*commanditaires*) whose liability is limited to the amount of capital which they contribute.

Limited Partnerships with Shares

Although few limited partnerships with shares (*sociétés en commandite par actions*) exist today, this form of business organisation was frequently used in the nineteenth century before SAs were developed. It is described as being half-way between the limited partnership and the *société anonyme* and comprises at least one general partner (*commandité*) and a minimum of three limited partners (*commanditaires*) who are treated as shareholders. The minimum capital is fixed at F 500,000 where public offerings are made and F 100,000 for all others. Management is in the hands of one or more managers chosen from the general partners or third parties. A limited partner cannot participate in management. The managers are subject to a supervisory board which consists of at least three people none of whom can be a limited partner.

Groupements d'Interêt Économique (GIE)

This form of "group for the furtherance of common economic interests" (*i.e.* a form of joint venture) is used by companies or individuals wishing to "co-operate on particular projects" which need not necessarily be profit-making. It is registered and has a legal status.

Branches of Foreign Companies

The branch of a foreign company is not considered to be a separate entity although it must be registered, and its debts and obligations are considered to be those of its parent.

Employee Participation

All employers with more than 50 employees are required to have a works committee (*comité d'entreprise*) elected. The works committee must send two representatives to board or shareholders' council meetings, but these representatives have no voting rights. Companies must supply the *comité* with copies of the annual accounts, and the *comité* is allowed to appoint an independent auditor to assist it in understanding the accounts and, if the *comité* considers it necessary, to carry out an independent audit.

Under an ordinance of 17 August 1967, all employers with more than 100 employees are required to set up a special employee profit-sharing fund. Funds may be invested in distributable shares or bonds, special outside deposits or savings schemes. Reduced taxation usually means that the cost to the employer is negligible although the 1974 finance law has created a situation whereby part of the cost will be borne gradually by employers. Employees are not allowed to receive the benefit for at least five years.

ACCOUNTING AND FINANCIAL REPORTING

The development of accounting and financial reporting standards has been a relatively recent affair in France, where annual accounts have generally been prepared for the use of the Government and tax authorities. It is not surprising, therefore, in a country where *dirigisme* is so dominant that reform has been mainly the prerogative of Government rather than that of the accountancy profession.

Prior to the Second World War the principal accounting regulations were contained in the Commercial Code and company laws of 1867. During the war the Germans introduced the French to uniform accounting, and, although Germany abandoned uniformity after the war,[2] the French embraced it and found it to be a most effective instrument for the planning and control of the economic growth which they now enjoy.

In 1947 a committee, set up in 1945 under the Ministry of Finance and Economic Affairs to propose a uniform accounting system, produced the Plan Comptable Général—a national uniform chart of accounts. A permanent official body, the Conseil National de la Comptabilité (National Accounting Committee) was set up later in 1947 to supervise the introduction of *le plan*. This body was also charged with responsibility to review and revise the original plan. The plan was last revised in 1957 and another version has been in the process of preparation since 1970.

The French law on commercial companies was considerably reformed and codified in the law of 24 July 1966. This law did not affect the Plan Comptable, but it did require further disclosures from companies and laid down more demanding requirements for statutory auditors. The advent of the Commission des Opérations de Bourse in 1968 heralded a new era in the history of French financial reporting. The COB believes that it has an important role to play in the improvement of accounting and auditing standards and already it has a record to prove this.

Le Plan Comptable Général

By a law of 1959 and a decree of 1962 the Government has secured universal progressive adoption of the Plan Comptable, with variations to suit particular industries. Currently there are about 75 variations on the general plan and the ultimate aim is to have a particular plan for each major class of industrial and commercial activity.

Generally the Plan Comptable includes:

1. A detailed chart of accounts (Fig. 1.2) according to economic and legal considerations numbered on a decimal system from which the periodic accounts of the enterprise may readily be prepared.
2. Recommendations on the valuation of assets and determination of costs, expenses and results: the text includes a general discussion of the functions of the financial accounts in Classes 1–8 and indicates the content of each account.
3. Model financial statements and statistical reports.
4. A discussion of the cost accounting procedures relevant to Class 9 of the plan.

The plan is said to be flexible but such judgements are relative, as will soon be discovered. Accounts prepared in accordance with the Plan Comptable have, to quote one commentator, "a seductive uniformity which masks a multitude of differences"!

BALANCE SHEET ACCOUNTS

Class 1	Class 2	Class 3	Class 4	Class 5
Capital and long-term liabilities	Fixed assets	Inventories	Third party accounts	Financial accounts
10 Capital	20 Formation expenses	30 Purchased finished goods	40 Accounts payable (suppliers)	50 Loans payable (less than one year)
11 Reserves	21 Fixed assets	31 Raw materials	41 Accounts receivable (customers)	51 Loans receivable (less than one year)
12 Prior year's profit and loss account balance	22	32 Consumable supplies	42 Personnel	52 Bills and warrants payable
13	23 Fixed assets in construction (or in course of acquisition)	33 Scrap and defective work	43 State	53 Bills and warrants receivable
14 Equipment subsidies received	24 Fixed assets destroyed by war	34 Semi-finished products	44 Accounts with shareholders or partners	54 Cheques to be cashed
15 Provisions	25 Loans receivable (more than one year)	35 Finished goods	45 Branches, subsidiaries, holding company or head office	55 Marketable securities
16 Loans payable (more than one year)	26 Investments	36 Work in progress	46 Miscellaneous debtors and creditors	56 Banks and Post Office accounts
17 Intercompany accounts	27 Deposits guarantees	37 Packaging materials	47 Accrued liabilities	57 Cash
18	28	38	48 Accrued assets	58 Imprest funds and other advances to be accounted for
19	29	39	49 Suspense	59 Cash in transit

Fig. 1.2 French national uniform chart of accounts

OPERATING ACCOUNTS		PROFIT AND LOSS	COST ANALYSIS	SPECIAL ACCOUNTS
Class 6	Class 7	Class 8	Class 9	Class 0
Expenses	Revenues	Profit and loss	Cost analysis	Special accounts
60 Purchases	70 Sales of goods and finished products	80 Trading account	90 General cost control accounts	00 Contingent liabilities
61 Wages and salaries	71 Government subsidies for operating expenses	81	91 & 92 Cost reclassifications	
62 Taxes	72 Scrap and reject sales	82		
63 Services and supplies	73 Selling price reductions	83	93 Cost of sales analysis	
64 Transportation and travel	74 Rebates, reductions and allowances received	84	94 Permanent inventory	
65	75	85	95	
66 Miscellaneous	76 Miscellaneous income	86 Exchange of products and services without charge	96 Cost variances	
67 Financial	77 Financial income	87 Profit and loss account	97 Differences between costs charged and actual	
68 Depreciation and provisions	78 Products manufactured for own use; expenses applicable to other periods	88 Results in suspense	98 Cost operating statements	
69	79	89 Balance sheet	99 Internal transfers	

Fig. 1.2—(continued) French national uniform chart of accounts

The stated objectives of the plan are, nevertheless, impressive, and are well worth consideration:

1. To propose more reliable national economic and fiscal policies.
2. To assist in eliminating fiscal inequalities.
3. To minimise social misunderstandings by informing the public of the true distribution of national wealth.
4. To provide data for the study of market trends.
5. To improve healthy competition.
6. To aid in the development of fairer taxation.
7. To provide shareholders, suppliers and bankers with an opportunity to exercise their judgement more satisfactorily.
8. To aid governmental authorities in exercising controls.
9. To provide a clear and prompt view of financial results.
10. To permit analysis and comparison of manufacturing costs.

These objectives are indeed laudable and in his book A. J. H. Enthoven states his belief that "the French Plan Comptable may serve as a useful example for international economic co-operation and integration (and prove particularly useful for developing countries), making accounting a more effective instrument in the economic process".[3]

The model financial statements included in the plan (Figs. 1.3 and 1.4) must be followed by all French companies. Unfortunately the large majority of companies tend to publish the minimum necessary to satisfy the legal requirements; consequently corresponding figures and notes to the accounts are still rare. The reluctance of many French companies, and notably the Michelin Group, to make additional disclosures apart from those required by law is one of the major problems facing the COB. The tradition of secrecy in business affairs is still very strong and it is probable that only the force of law will eventually solve the problem of adequate disclosure.

Tax evasion and the falsification of accounts are said to be one of the other reasons for the introduction of the Plan Comptable. Whatever the truth of this, it is fair to say that tax law has had a significant influence on the plan. The absence of any effective regulatory authority, apart from the tax authorities, to ensure compliance with the plan has resulted in a situation whereby accounting aspects of tax law have come to be regarded as amendments to the Plan Comptable.

Accounting Principles

France does not yet have accounting standards similar to those now being defined by the UK accountancy profession. However, the Plan Comptable

ACTIF (ASSETS)

	Montant brut (Gross amount)	*Amortissements ou provisions pour dépréciations* (Depreciation)	*Montant net* (Net amount)
Frais d'établissement (Formation expenses)			
Primes de remboursement des obligations (Redemption premium)			
Autres frais d'établissement (Other deferred charges)			
Immobilisations (Fixed assets)			
Terrains (Land)			
Constructions (Buildings)			
Matériel et outillage (Machinery and tools)			
Matériel de transport (Transportation equipment)			
Mobilier, aménagements, installations (Furniture and fixtures)			
Immobilisations incorporelles (Intangibles)			
Autres immobilisations (Others)			
Autres valeurs immobilisées (Other non-current assets)			
Prêts à plus d'un an (Long-term receivables)			
Titres de participation (Investments)			
Dépôts et cautionnements (Guarantee deposits)			
Valeurs d'exploitation (Inventory)			
Marchandises (Merchandise)			
Matières premières et fournitures (Raw materials and supplies)			
Produits semi-ouvrés (Work in progress)			
Produits finis (Finished goods)			
Emballages commerciaux (Packing materials)			
Valeurs realisables à court terme ou disponibles (Current assets other than inventory)			
Fournisseurs—advances et acomptes sur commandes (Advances to suppliers)			
Clients (Accounts receivable)			
Autres débiteurs (Other receivables)			

Fig. 1.3 Example of *bilan* (balance sheet)

	Montant brut (Gross amount)	*Amortissements ou provisions pour dépréciations* (Depreciation)	*Montant net* (Net amount)
Comptes de régularisation—actif (Prepaid expenses)			
Prèts à moins d'un an (Short-term loans receivable)			
Effets à recevoir (Notes receivable)			
Chèques et effets à encaisser (Cheques and notes to be collected)			
Titres de placement (Marketable securities)			
Banques et chèques postaux (Cash at bank)			
Caisses (Cash in hand)			
Total de l'actif (Total assets)	—	—	—

PASSIF (LIABILITIES)

	Avant repartition (Before distribution)	*Aprés repartition* (After distribution)
Capital propre et réserves (Capital and reserves)		
Capital social (Capital)		
Primes d'émission d'actions (Premium on shares)		
Réserve légale (Legal reserve)		
Autres reserves (Other reserves)		
Report à nouveau (Retained earnings)		
Situation nette (avant résultats de l'exercice) (Total reserves and retained earnings before net earnings for the year—which are shown at the foot of the page)		
Provisions pour pertes et charges (Provisions for losses and expenses)		
Provisions pour risques (Provisions for contingencies)		
Provisions pour charges à répartir sur plusieurs exercices (Provisions for expenses to be spread over several years)		
Dettes à long et moyen termes (Long-term and medium-term debts)		
Obligations et bons à plus d'un an (Bonds and notes)		

Fig. 1.3—(continued) Example of *bilan* (balance sheet)

	Avant repartition (Before distribution)	*Aprés repartition* (After distribution)
Autres dettes à plus d'un an (Other long-term debts)		
Dettes à court terme (Current liabilities)		
Fournisseurs (Accounts payable)		
Clients—avances et acomptes reçus (Customers' advances)		
Comptes courants d'associés (Accounts payable to associates)		
Versements restant à effectuer sur titres de participation non libérés (Investments—not yet paid)		
Autres créanciers (Other accounts payable)		
Comptes de régularisation—passif (Accrued expenses and deferred credits)		
Obligations et bons à moins d'un an (Bonds due within one year)		
Autres emprunts à moins d'un an (Other loans due within one year)		
Effets à payer (Notes payable)		
Resultats (Net earnings)		
Bénéfice de l'exercice (Net earnings for the year)		
Total du passif (Total liabilities)	—	—

Fig. 1.3—(continued) Example of *bilan* (balance sheet)

contains some general recommendations for the valuation of assets and the Ordre[4] issues occasional statements for the guidance of its members.

According to Article 342 of the 1966 law, even in the absence of sufficient profits, the accounts must include "such depreciation and reserves as may be necessary for the balance sheet to be true [*sincère*]". There does not appear to be much difference between this and the UK concept of a "true and fair view", but in practice the combined effects of tax law and a prescriptive Plan Comptable result in accounts which often give anything but an overall true and fair view, particularly where adequate disclosures are not clearly made in notes to the accounts. The same law also provides that "the general operating account, the profit and loss statement and the balance sheet shall be drawn up for each fiscal year according to the same

I COMPTE D'EXPLOITATION GENERALE (TRADING ACCOUNT)

Debit

Stock au debut de l'exercice (Opening stock)
Achats de matières et marchandises (Purchases of raw materials and goods)
Frais de personnel (Salaries, wages, social and fiscal charges on salaries)
Impots et taxes (Taxes [including VAT])
Travaux, fournitures et serves extérieurs (Supplies and services)
Transports et déplacements (Transport and travel)
Frais divers de gestion (Administrative expenses)
Frais financiers (Bank charges and interest)
Dotation de l'exercice aux amortissements (Depreciation for the year)
Dotation de l'exercice aux provisions (Provisions for the year)
Bénéfice d'exploitation (Trading profits)

Credit

Stock en fin d'exercice (Closing stock)
Ventes de marchandises et produits finis (Sales of products and goods (including VAT)
Subventions d'exploitation reçues (Subsidies)
Ventes de dechets et d'emballages recuperables (Sales of scrap, etc.)
Ristournes, rabais et remises obtenus (Discounts and allowances)
Produits financiers (Interest, etc.)
Travaux faits par l'entreprise pour elle-même (Self-constructed assets)
Perte d'exploitation (Trading losses)

II COMPTE DE PERTES ET PROFITS (PROFIT AND LOSS ACCOUNT)

Debit

Perte d'exploitation de l'exercice (Year's operating losses)
Pertes sur exercices antérieurs (Losses in prior years)
Pertes exceptionnelles (Exceptional losses)
  moins-value résultant de la cession d'éléments de l'actif immobilisé (loss on disposal of fixed assets)
  autres pertes exceptionnelles (other exceptional losses)
Dotation de l'exercice aux comptes de provisions hors exploitation ou exceptionnelles (Year's allocation to reserves and exceptional provisions)
Impôt sur les bénéfices (Tax on profits)
Bénéfice net (Net earnings for the year)

Credit

Bénéfice d'exploitation de l'exercice (Year's operating profit)
Profits sur exercices antérieurs (Profits in prior years)
Profits exceptionnels (Exceptional profits)
  plus-values réalisées a l'occasion de la cession d'éléments de l'actif immobilisé (gains on disposal of fixed assets)
  autres profits exceptionnels (other exceptional profits)
Perte nette (Loss for the year)

Fig. 1.4 Example of *compte d'exploitation et de pertes et profits* (operating and profit and loss account)

forms and methods of valuation as in previous years". A change in accounting bases must therefore be disclosed if this has a material effect on the result although it is not clear in practice whether such disclosures should be made in accompanying notes forming part of the accounts or whether it is sufficient to have them spelled out in the separate board or statutory auditors' report.

Accounting Practices and the Annual Accounts

Although there is much justification for caution when dealing with French accounts, these problems can be overcome to a large extent by an appreciation of the particular considerations which apply in each case. What follows is intended to provide a basis for critical review.

Consolidated Accounts

The preparation of consolidated accounts is one area where the COB has been very active. Equity accounting is not obligatory in France, although the 1966 law did require important disclosures of interests in first-tier subsidiaries (*filiales*) and associated companies (*participations*)[5] (Fig. 1.5). Furthermore, companies are given the alternative of preparing consolidated accounts provided that the basis of consolidation is disclosed, but few companies have opted for this. Companies seeking new quotes on the Bourse must now consolidate and the COB claims significant success in its efforts to encourage all quoted companies to prepare consolidated accounts. Twenty-three companies published consolidated accounts in 1972.

The Balance Sheet

Fixed assets. Generally fixed assets are stated at historical cost apart from those acquired before 1959 when a revaluation was required.

Although there is no legal obligation for tax and book depreciation to be the same, the situation is such that, since depreciation must be booked to be allowable for tax purposes, the rates acceptable to the tax authorities are generally followed. Until 1965 a straight-line basis was usual, but since then the reducing-balance method has been recognised for a basic range of certain new plant and equipment. Although there was a tendency in the past to limit depreciation provisions to profit availability, since 1965 companies have been required to provide an annual charge at least equivalent to that amount which would apply on a straight-line basis.

Intangible assets. Goodwill is not usually amortised and tax relief is not granted for any write-off; patents are amortised over their useful lives (the legal life of French patents is 20 years) and such deductions are allowable for tax purposes. Discount and expenses on the issue of long-term debt are written off over the term of the debt.

Setting-up expenses, such as legal fees, advertising, etc., incurred when the company was first established tend to be written off within a time limit of five years depending on profits.

Long-term (one year plus) loans. Long-term loans repayable after one year or more can include loans to employees or to certain Government-sponsored or approved schemes for the purpose of housing employees (repayable after 20 years), intercompany loans, etc. They should not include loans to directors, which are illegal.

Trade investments. These investments, whether quoted or unquoted, are shown at purchase cost with a provision for any loss of value (gains are ignored). If not fully paid up the shares are stated at their gross amount with the corresponding liability for calls shown under current liabilities. Quoted companies must publish in their accounts an annual list of all transferable securities held.

Guarantee deposits. Normally these are deposits paid for rent, returnable containers, gas, electricity, etc.

Inventories. Tax rules require that inventories be valued at the lower of cost or net realisable value. Cost may be calculated by any reasonable method although the FIFO and LIFO methods are not officially permitted. Average cost is often used in practice, as are variations of FIFO. If the realisable value is less than cost, a provision is required. In addition there may be "tax-free" inventory reserves such as the *réserve pour fluctuation des cours* (a reserve for certain raw materials whose world market price is subject to significant fluctuation), the creation of which is determined by tax law.

Other current assets. Most of the items under this heading are self-explanatory and do not require further amplification. Marketable securities are subject to the same rules as trade investments; the largest item in prepaid expenses is likely to be recoverable VAT on purchases. Certain of the receivables may be used as security for loans as the UK concept of a floating charge does not exist in France.

Capital and reserves. The amount shown is the par value of issued share capital—any uncalled capital appears as an asset. Share premiums are

Fig. 1.5 Statement of information concerning subsidiaries and interests (Articles 247 and 295 of the Decree on Commercial Companies)

Source: French Law on Commercial Companies as at January 1, 1971 (Commerce Clearing House Inc.)

Companies or groups of companies	*Capital*	*Reserves*	*Percentage of capital held*	*Inventory value of securities held*	*Loans and Advances by the company outstanding*	*Amount of security and guaranties given by the company*	*Turnover for previous fiscal year*	*Net profit or loss for previous fiscal year*	*Dividends received by the company during fiscal year*	*Comments*[1]
I. Information to be supplied if company has not attached to its balance sheet a balance sheet and consolidated statements drawn up in accordance with Article 248.										
A. *Detailed information on interests whose inventory value is more than 1 per cent of the capital of the company subject to publicity.*										
1 Subsidiaries (At least 50 per cent of capital held by the company):										
Company *A* (name, registered office)										
Company *B*										
2 Interests (10 to 50 per cent of capital held by the company):										
Company *X*										
Company *Y*										
B. *Information on other subsidiaries or interests.*										
1 Subsidiaries not shown under item A:										
(*a*) French subsidiaries (all)										
(*b*) Foreign subsidiaries (all)										
2 Interests not shown under item A:										
(*a*) In French companies (all)										
(*b*) In foreign companies (all)										
II. Information to be supplied if company has attached to its balance sheet a balance sheet and consolidated statements drawn up in accordance with Article 248										
1 Subsidiaries:										
(*a*) French subsidiaries (all)										
(*b*) Foreign subsidiaries (all)										
2 Interests:										
(*a*) In French companies (all)										
(*b*) In foreign companies (all)										

1. Show in this column, under I-A, the opening and closing dates of the years of the companies in which interests are held when such dates do not coincide with the opening and closing dates of the company's fiscal year.

not considered to be part of permanent capital and are sometimes used to set up the legal reserve, to set up reserves for contingencies or to write off share issue and organisation expenses although more restrictive uses of such premiums are being considered; they may also be distributed as dividends.

All companies must set up a legal reserve by annual profit transfers of at least 5 per cent of annual taxed profits until this reaches 10 per cent of share capital. Other reserves may include equipment grants which are taken to profit under the deferred credit method.

Provisions for losses and expenses. The number and nature of these provisions are unlimited, but the most common is that relating to employees' profit-sharing schemes. This latter provision applies generally to companies with over 100 employees and it is set up for the benefit of employees who have worked for at least three months in the year when the profits were earned.

Long- and medium-term debts. All such debts are repayable in more than one year. The due dates and interest rates are not required and rarely given.

Current liabilities. All of these items are self-explanatory and comment is necessary only to point out what may be missing from this total—provision is not always made for accrued pension rights and vacation pay as these are not allowable tax deductions.

Net earnings. This results from the French practice of preparing the AGM accounts with profits not yet appropriated. If the balance sheet is prepared after allocation of profits, this item will, of course, disappear.

The Trading and Profit and Loss Account

The French trading and profit and loss account contains considerably more detail than the minimum required in the United Kingdom. The items in both sections of the account are taken directly from Classes 6–8 of the Plan Comptable with the result that no indication of the destination of the expenses is given.

Turnover and cost of sales. The disclosure of the cost of sales is not required, although it can easily be calculated for non-manufacturing companies.

Profits and losses of prior years. Usually this caption refers to various provisions no longer necessary. It may include surplus bad debt provisions, although only specific provisions are allowable for tax purposes.

Dividends. Dividend rates are decided at the AGM; however, the board of directors or supervisory board has authority to distribute interim dividends under certain limited conditions. If the company is quoted, the interim dividend may not be less than five francs per share. Bank of France permission must be obtained for the transfer of interim dividends to a parent company outside France.

Share of profits. Companies are not obliged to disclose the value of shares of profits, attendance fees or other remuneration received by members of the board or by the supervisory board and directorate. However, the total remuneration received by the five or ten highest-paid persons in companies having, respectively, less than or over 200 employees must be disclosed to shareholders upon demand.

Taxation. It is not customary to agree the tax liability at the end of each year and companies submit annual returns and accounts and make payments on account. The tax authorities may carry out a "tax audit" if they feel this is justified and visits are generally made at four-yearly intervals when the books of account for the previous four years may also be investigated. Contingent liabilities relating to any additional liabilities arising from such inspections are naturally not disclosed in the accounts.

Deferred tax accounting is not practised, but, bearing in mind that tax and book depreciation are usually similar, this may not be significant when judged by UK standards.

Publication and Filing of Financial Statements

All SA[6] and SàRL companies must, at least 15 days before the AGM, supply their shareholders with the management report[7] on the operations of the year, the auditors' report where applicable, and the annual financial accounts comprising:

1. The balance sheet drawn up in accordance with the model set forth in Article 1 of Decree No. 65.968 of 28 October 1965 (Fig. 1.3).
2. The general operating account for the year with details of inventories, principal costs and sources of income (Fig. 1.4).
3. The profit and loss statement for the year showing the amount of tax attributable to the year's income (Fig. 1.4).
4. A table of information concerning subsidiary and associated companies (Fig. 1.5).

The AGM must be held within six months of the year end and every company is obliged to file the accounts in duplicate with the clerk of the local court within one month of their approval by the general shareholders' meeting. One copy of the accounts is then entered on the Commercial Register, and, within 15 days following the month of filing, the other copy must be entered on the National Commercial Register in Paris.

The filed accounts do not have to include the statutory auditors' report; nor is it normal practice to have detailed accompanying notes to the accounts. Accounts filed with the Commercial Register are available for public inspection.

Management Report

The contents of the management report of every SA company are laid down in Decree No. 67.236 of 23 March 1967. Article 148 of the decree states that the management report must describe clearly and precisely the activities of the company and of its subsidiaries, if any, during the past year, the results of such activities, the progress made or the difficulties encountered, and the prospects for the future.

The report must be accompanied by a table drawn up in accordance with a model laid down in the decree (Fig. 1.6) showing the results attained by the company in each of the last five years, or in each year since the company was established or since it acquired another company if there are less than five.

Large Quoted Companies

Quoted companies with assets in excess of F 10 million are bound to publish their accounts in the *Bulletin des annonces légales obligatoires (BALO)* within 45 days of the approval of the general meeting. The following should also be published with the accounts:

1. An inventory of transferable securities held at the end of the year, indicating the number of certificates and value of each category.
2. A statement of the value of undertakings (guarantees) entered into by the company and not shown in the balance sheet.
3. A table of information concerning subsidiary and associated companies according to a prescribed model (Fig. 1.5).

The above quoted companies are also required to publish the following interim figures in the *BALO*:

1. *Turnover*. Within 45 days the amount of turnover net of tax for the past quarter, and, where applicable, for each of the previous quarters of the current year and for that full year, as well as corresponding information for the previous fiscal year. Companies with distinct divisions are obliged to publish the turnover for each division along with the same comparative data.
2. *Balance Sheet*. Within four months following each half of the fiscal year a provisional balance sheet drawn up at the end of the previous half-year.

INFORMATION	19...	19...	19...	19...	19...
I. *Financial condition at end of fiscal year:*					
(*a*) Corporate capital.					
(*b*) Number of shares issued.					
(*c*) Number of bonds convertible into shares.					
II. *Over-all results of actual operations:*					
(*a*) Turnover after taxes.					
(*b*) Profit before taxes, depreciation, and reserves.					
(*c*) Taxes on earnings.					
(*d*) Profit after taxes, depreciation, and reserves.					
(*e*) Amount of distributed profits.[1]					
III. *Results of operations per share:*[2]					
(*a*) Profit after taxes, but before depreciation and reserves.					
(*b*) Profit after taxes, depreciation and reserves.					
(*c*) Dividend per share.[1]					
IV. *Employees:*					
(*a*) Number of employees.					
(*b*) Salaries and wages.					
(*c*) Total of amounts paid for social benefits (social security, welfare, etc.).					

1. For the year for which the financial statements will be submitted to the general shareholders' meeting, show the amount of profits which the board of directors, the directorate, or the managers propose be distributed.
2. If there has been a change in the number of shares during the period covered, the results shown must be adjusted and the operations in which the amount of the capital was changed must be indicated.

Fig. 1.6 Statement of financial results of the company for the last five years (Articles 133, 135 and 148 of the Decree on Commercial Companies)

Source: French Law on Commercial Companies as at January 1, 1971 (Commerce Clearing House Inc.)

If 50 per cent or more of the capital of any unquoted SA is held by one or more quoted companies with balance sheet totals of more than F 10 million, that company is subject to the same rules as a quoted company with assets in excess of F 10 million, provided that the balance sheet of the subsidiary is at least F 10 million or its portfolio of investments amounts to at least F 1 million.

Small Quoted Companies

Quoted companies with assets of less than F 10 million have to send copies of the last approved annual accounts and details of the additional information published by large quoted companies ((1)–(3) above), within 15 days of being requested to do so, to any shareholder.

Stock Exchange Listing Requirements

Bank sponsorship is essential in order to obtain a Bourse quote. An application must receive approval from the Commission des Opérations de Bourse, the COB having first consulted the Chambre Syndicale des Agents de Change (Stockbrokers' Committee). At a time when every effort is being made to popularise the Bourse, there are no definite requirements for acceptance, but the following factors are considered:

1. A minimum capital of F 10 million.
2. Profit record for the previous five years.
3. Adequate dividend distribution.
4. Free negotiability of shares.

Business Records

Many of the regulations governing business records are contained in the tax code and consequently the books of account are principally fiscal records. The Commercial Code requires every business to keep a general journal (*journal général*)—usually maintained in the form of monthly summaries of transactions—and a "total balance book" (*livre d'inventaire*) which must contain copies of the annual accounts. The Labour Code requires a payroll book (*livre de paie*). These three official books must be prenumbered and bear the stamp of a judge or mayor; in practice they are registered and stamped at the local town hall (*mairie*). All books and records should be retained for 10 years and must be written in French.

THE ACCOUNTANCY PROFESSION

The development of the French accountancy profession reflects to a large extent the overall pattern of development of French industry and the capital market. The educational prejudice of the French against commerce and industry has not helped recruitment, with the result that the profession has never attained the status and influence which it enjoys in other countries.

The Government, however, is now committed to establishing a strong profession, and it has played a leading role in bringing about changes which have helped to clothe the profession with some status and a degree of respectability in recent years.

L'Ordre des Experts Comptables et des Comptables Agréés

Although many small bodies of accountants existed before the Second World War, it was not until l'Ordre des Experts Comptables et des Comptables Agréés was formed in 1942 that the French profession achieved any kind of national organisation. Immediately after the war, the Ordre received official recognition by parliamentary decree on 19 September 1945. It was charged with "assuring the defence of the honour and the independence of the profession" which it represented. A long period of consolidation followed until the law of 31 October 1968 when the French parliament adopted radical measures to unify the profession and terminate recruitment of the lower grade of *comptable agréé*. Transitional measures ending on 23 February 1975 provide for *comptable agréés* with 10 years' experience in the profession being classified as *experts comptables*. This law was a major step forward, showing that the French at least were not satisfied with a two-tier profession. According to the new law, both categories of accountant are defined as follows:

> *Expert comptable*
>
> One who regularly carries out the professional work of auditing and of forming an opinion on the accounting of businesses and other entities to which he is not bound by a contract of employment. He is also qualified to express an opinion on the truth and fairness of balance sheets and profit and loss accounts. . . . An *expert comptable* can also organise the accounting procedures and analyse, by the use of accounting techniques, the states of affairs and operations of businesses under their economic, legal and financial heads.
>
> *Comptable agréé*
>
> A professional man who regularly keeps, centralises, opens, closes and supervises accounting and accounts of every kind, and in the course of such work rectifies the accounting of businesses and other entities to which he is not bound by a contract of employment. . . . The *comptable agréé* is qualified to express an opinion on the truth and fairness of balance sheets and profit and loss accounts of businesses whose accounts he draws up.

The law of 31 October 1968 also provides for the admission under specific conditions to the Ordre of individuals who do not hold the necessary diplomas but who can claim a technical competence which provides them with "experience equivalent to an *expert comptable*".

Membership of the Ordre is restricted to *experts comptables* or *comptables agréés* working in public practice and is lost when members enter industry or commerce (Table 1.3). Members may work for each other and for companies provided that they do not relinquish absolute responsibility for the work undertaken. Another factor which, in the past, inhibited the growth of the profession was the limitation to five of the number of professional assistants who could be employed by a member in public practice. The limit was raised to 10 assistants per principal in 1970 and this does not include *stagiaires* (articled clerks), of which each principal can have five.

TABLE 1.3. MEMBERSHIP OF PROFESSIONAL ACCOUNTANCY BODIES (as at 1 October 1973)

L'Ordre des Experts Comptables et des Comptables Agréés	
Experts comptables	3,739
Comptables agréés	6,290
	10,029
Stagiaires	2,750
Sociétés d'expertise comptable[1] (companies of *experts comptables*)	1,073
Sociétés d'entreprise de comptabilité (accounting companies—mainly *comptables agrées*)	755
La Compagnie Nationale des Commissaires aux Comptes	
Total number of members of the various regional companies of *commissaires aux comptes*	6,132
Of which *experts comptables* are estimated to number	3,500

1. It should be noted that every *société d'expertise comptable* will normally also have a parallel accounting company of *comptables agréés.*

Traditionally, French accountants have been sole practitioners although they can form companies[8] provided these are registered with the Ordre. Since 1966 it has not been possible to form new SA or SàRL companies to carry out statutory audits, but the new form of company provided for this, the *société civile professionnelle*, has not proved popular for tax reasons.

The following are among the best-known and are certainly among the largest of the French accounting firms (*sociétés d'expertise comptable*):

1. Société d'Expertise Comptable Fiduciaire de France.
2. Société d'Etudes Economiques et Comptables.

3. Fiduciaire Economique et Financière.
4. Société Fiduciaire de l'Est Paris.
5. Cabinet Frinault & Cie.

The Ordre is organised on a regional basis, with 19 regions, but overall control rests with the Conseil Supérieur in Paris. Government officials participate in sessions of the Ordre and, if they think fit, they can take Ordre decisions before the court. Furthermore, the Ordre is encouraged to engage in international technical studies provided that it keeps the Government informed.

Foreign accountants practising in France are subject to the supervision and disciplinary control of the Ordre although they cannot become members. Foreigners may be given authority to practise as *experts comptables* or *comptables agréés* on condition that a treaty or agreement of reciprocity has been made with the foreign country, and the applicant:

1. Fulfils a residential qualification of at least five years in France. If there is no such treaty, application can be made on individual merit. This is revocable at any time.
2. Has qualifications equivalent to the diplomas required from French professionals.

So far, only one such agreement has been signed—with Switzerland—although plans for reciprocity with the United Kingdom reached advanced stages before being shelved in view of UK entry to the EEC and the plan of the European Commission for joint EEC action on freedom of establishment. This means that the international accounting firms although tolerated since 1953 are not officially permitted to carry on the practice of accounting in France. One of the major factors influencing the decision to "tolerate" these firms is section 161(b)(1) of the 1948 UK Companies Act, which permits the Department of Trade to authorise individuals with similar qualifications, obtained outside the United Kingdom, to recognised UK accountants to act as auditors of UK companies. Over the years, a number of *experts comptables* have been so recognised. Furthermore, as one senior COB member admitted, "For France, the international accounting firms are an unfortunate necessity but they must not, and will not, be allowed to take advantage of the French profession." Although these firms are still mainly occupied with servicing UK and US subsidiaries they report that an increasing number of French companies now seek their help. This is particularly true in the case of prominent French companies who wish to obtain quotes in leading markets, and especially in London, where French accounts are not yet considered to be "prepared and audited in accordance with generally accepted accounting and auditing standards". The furore which resulted from this has not been to the advantage of the international firms and the Ordre now refuses to allow *stagiaires* to train with these firms.

La Compagnie Nationale des Commissaires aux Comptes

The 1966 law on commercial companies provided for the establishment of a roll of authorised auditors to carry out statutory audits. As a result of this, La Compagnie Nationale des Commissaires aux Comptes was formed by decree on 12 August 1969 to serve as an independent regulatory body for French auditors under the jurisdiction of the Ministry of Justice. All existing authorised auditors, many of them retired bankers and income-tax inspectors, were admitted to the new body and their names are inscribed on the roll kept in each region by the regional commission established at the Appeal Court in whose jurisdiction they live or, in the case of companies, have their headquarters. Although many of those enrolled in 1970 were not members of the Ordre or necessarily skilled in accounting, the Compagnie is committed to the rapid development of auditing in France along lines generally accepted in other leading countries and the entry requirements now laid down represent a major step forward. Only the following candidates are considered for admission:

1. *Experts comptables* listed on the roll of the Ordre.
2. *Comptables agréés* under certain conditions.
3. Auditing and accounting companies under very restrictive conditions.
4. Holders of the Certificat Supérieur de Revision Comptable—*see* below under "Education and Training".
5. Candidates passing the examination of competence in the functions of auditor (at a level equivalent to that of the Higher Certificate mentioned above).
6. Persons having carried out for 10 to 15 years a private or public activity which allowed them to acquire sufficient experience in financial accounting and legal questions, relating to commercial companies, notably in an auditor's office.

To be listed in future it will be necessary to serve three years' articles followed by an examination, unless the candidate is already an *expert comptable*.

Education and Training

In order to qualify for membership of l'Ordre des Experts Comptables et des Comptables Agréés (Fig. 1.7), candidates (*stagiaires*), having attained a minimum age of 19, must serve three years' articles during which they take two examinations. Following this, they must submit a thesis on a relevant subject; until a recent decree the time limit for submission of this thesis was five years, a fact which may be taken as an indication of the standard demanded. Indeed, few qualify before the age of 30, although the minimum age is 25.

Stagiaires do not necessarily have to spend their complete term of articles in public practice, and, with the agreement of the Conseil Régional of the Ordre, the three-year term may be served as set out below:

1. In the office of an *expert comptable*.
2. With an official of the Ministry of Finance and Economic Affairs designated to control the economic and financial interests of the State.
3. Up to one year with a *comptable agréé*, or with a foreign practitioner authorised to practise as an *expert comptable* or *comptable agréé*.
4. Up to one year with a commercial enterprise, in which the accounting is controlled by a member of the Ordre.
5. Up to one year with the Conseil Nationale de la Comptabilité.
6. Up to one year abroad, with the agreement of the Conseil Supérieur of the Ordre, with a foreign practitioner of a standing comparable to that of an *expert comptable* or with a French firm of accountants or with one or several private enterprises whose accounting is controlled by the said practitioners.

The first examination is generally taken after one year, or less in the case of graduates who are granted exemption in the subject of their degrees. The examination includes three papers (written and oral) on Financial and Management Accounting, Mercantile, Industrial and Company Law, and Economics.

The second examination is taken at the end of the period of articles and includes a paper on Auditing (Le Certificat Supérieur de Revision Comptable) and one other paper which may be on any of the following: Law and Taxation; Organisation and Management; International Relations, including knowledge of an overseas language.

The profession is now attracting many graduates from the commercial colleges and universities, in particular those with diplomas in Economics and others such as HEC, ESC and *licencié en droit*.

Unlike their UK and Irish colleagues, French *stagiaires* have never had to pay premiums and have always been remunerated while undergoing training. On the other hand, they do not normally receive pre-examination study leave.

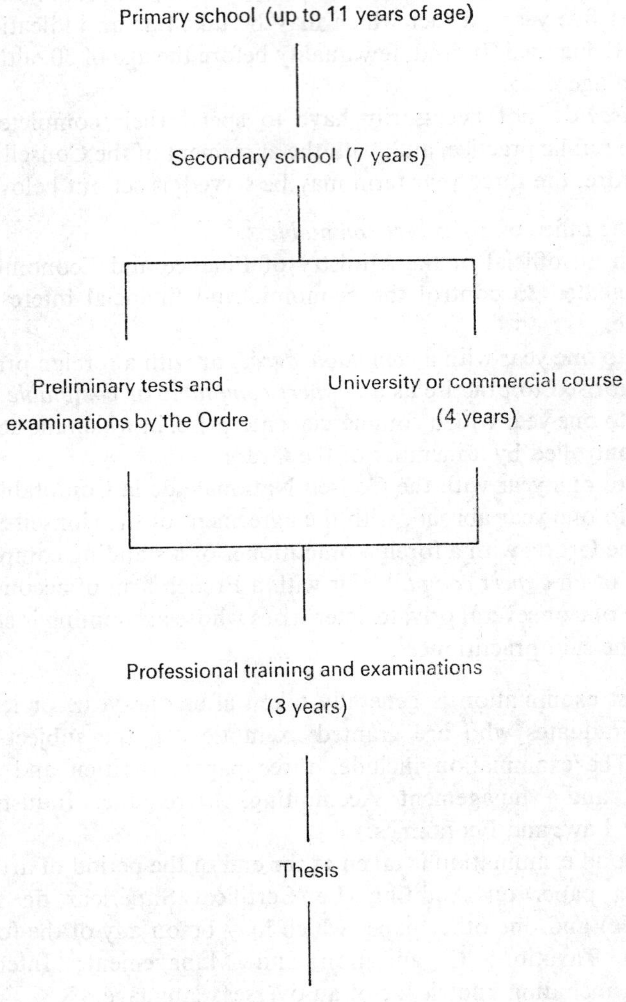

Fig. 1.7 The way to become a French *expert comptable*

Ethics

Ethical standards of the French accountancy profession are of a high standard and include some principles established by law and others laid down by the professional bodies. Generally members of the Ordre:

1. Are required to take the following oath: "I swear to exercise my profession with conscience and honesty, to respect and make others respect the laws in connection with my work."
2. Must consult with the previous *expert comptable* before taking on a new client.
3. Cannot engage in other business transactions beyond the scope of their professional duties.
4. Cannot advertise their services.
5. Must insure against liability for professional negligence.
6. Cannot charge fees on the basis of financial results.

Services Provided

The absence of any reference to management consultancy in the ethical rules is evidence of the ground which the French accountancy profession has yet to cover, if it is to achieve the status of, for instance, the Institutes of Chartered Accountants.

The main services provided by accountants in public practice include accountancy and book-keeping services, acting as *commissaires aux comptes*, tax advice and management services.

AUDITING

The notion of an annual statutory audit is an experience which many French companies have enjoyed only since the 1966 law on commercial companies. Prior to that date, only quoted companies had to appoint officially listed statutory auditors (*commissaires aux comptes*) and the great majority of companies were free to choose almost anyone for the post. It is easy to be critical of such a situation but to do so is to ignore the many important factors, discussed earlier in this chapter, which make the French position somewhat unique. Most important of all, perhaps, is the pattern of corporate development in France, and the fact that even today the vast majority of companies, including many of the largest, are still family controlled. Had the situation been different, with bigger companies, a thriving equity market and a wide body of shareholders, then in all probability France would today boast a body of accountants with a competence and reputation second to none. As matters stand, however, the French accountancy profession seems to be labouring under too much Government control and is thus unable to develop into an independent self-regulatory body playing a leading role in business affairs, while the very young auditing profession represented by La Compagnie Nationale des Commissaires aux Comptes founded in 1969 still lacks individuality and weight.

The *commissaire* is not generally received with open arms by businessmen, who feel that they can manage well enough without his help. The fact that he has been imposed by law means that he is sometimes seen to be a semi-state official under court regulation, and, most of all, the fact that he is bound to inform the State prosecutor of certain offences of which he has knowledge has not made his introduction any easier. The *commissaire aux comptes* takes his duties very seriously, regarding his most important function as ensuring that his client has complied with French tax and company law; he tends to put an emphasis on the statutory aspect of a company's activities and to concern himself particularly with the company's financial tax declaration and the analysis and disclosure of direct or indirect transactions between the company and any of its directors.

Appointment of Auditors

Every limited liability company (SA), limited partnership with shares and every private limited liability company (SàRL) with a share capital in excess of F 300,000 is required to appoint at least one *commissaire aux comptes* for a term of six years which is renewable. If a company is quoted, it must appoint two *commissaires aux comptes*, as must any SA or limited partnership with shares with a share capital in excess of F 5 million. An SàRL with share capital of less than F 300,000 need not appoint a statutory auditor unless one-fifth of the shareholders petition the court to have an auditor designated. Only those on the official list of La Compagnie Nationale des Commissaires aux Comptes can act as statutory[9] auditors and they may therefore be individual *commissaires aux comptes, sociétés civiles professionnelles* composed of *commissaires aux comptes*, or companies, whatever their constitution, which were registered with the Ordre on 24 July 1966, provided that at least 75 per cent of the members of the Ordre in these companies are themselves *commissaires aux comptes.*

The auditor must receive the accounts for the past year not less than 45 days before the ordinary general meeting and the management report must be made available for audit at least 20 days before the general meeting. This means that the year-end audit may be limited to 30 days' work since shareholders should receive the accounts with management and auditors' reports at least 15 days before the AGM.

Duties of Auditors

According to Article 228 of the 1966 law:

> The auditors shall certify the correctness [*régularité*] and truth [*sincérité*] of the account balances, the general operating account, the profit and loss statement and the balance sheet.
>
> The auditors' permanent duties, excluding any intervention in the management, shall be to verify the books and assets of the company and to examine the financial statements for correctness and truth. They shall also verify the truth of the information furnished in the management report and in the documents addressed to the shareholders concerning the company's financial condition and the corporate accounts.

In addition, the auditor is charged with ensuring that the shareholders receive equal treatment, and also with calling the general meeting where the directors or supervisory board fail to do so, subject to the proviso that he may not at any time intervene in management. *The commissaire aux comptes* should be present at the board meeting held immediately before the AGM to agree the accounts for the year. At this meeting his advice may be sought as to provisions and closing entries and he will also report any irregularities or inaccuracies. He need not attend the AGM.

The Auditors' Report

The auditor is required to make the following reports on the results of his work:

1. To the board of directors or directorate and supervisory board. The auditor must report orally or verbally on the extent of his work, dealing with:
   (a) Any adjustments which he considers necessary to the accounts.
   (b) Any irregularities and inaccuracies that he may have discovered.
   (c) His conclusions, following his findings or suggested adjustments, on the results for the year compared with the previous year's results.
2. To the annual general meeting of shareholders. There is no standard audit report, but the following form is gaining acceptance with leading practitioners:

> We have examined the balance sheet as of 31 December 19— and the general operating and profit and loss statements for the financial year ended on that date, of ABC SA. Our examination, which was made in accordance

with generally accepted auditing standards, included such verifications as we considered necessary in view of the rules of normal diligence.

In our opinion, according to generally accepted accounting principles, the accompanying balance sheet and general operating and profit and loss statements fairly reflect, on a basis consistent with that of the preceding year, the financial position of ABC SA as of 31 December 19— and the results of its operations for the financial year then ended.

The following are the official English texts of the auditors' reports on the 1972 consolidated accounts of the Total Group and the accounts of the parent company:

Auditors' report on Total consolidated accounts for the year ended 31 December 1972

Ladies and Gentlemen,

Acting as auditors of the Compagnie Française des Pétroles, we have examined the TOTAL Group consolidated Balance Sheet and operating accounts for the year 1972, together with the accompanying notes and financial statements as shown on pages 51 to 53 of the brochure issued for this meeting.

Our verifications were made in accordance with principles, methods and procedures applicable to international groups, including the review of the principles followed by the parent company in preparing the consolidated accounts and the examination of the records kept by the Consolidating Department based on the figures received from the Group companies. We have received all the information and explanations which we required.

We also verified that the accounts prepared by each Group company have been examined by the auditors appointed by the shareholders; furthermore, and in accordance with the requests we sent to the auditors, we obtained from them such confirmations and explanations as we considered necessary in order to form our opinion.

Based on the examinations performed by ourselves and by the auditors of the Group companies, we report that in our opinion the 1972 consolidated statements present fairly the operations of the TOTAL Group for the year ended 31 December 1972 and the financial position in conformity with the French accounting principles, applied on a basis consistent with that of the preceding year.

June 5, 1973 F. Angleys M. Neveux
(Members of the Compagnie de Paris)

Auditors' general report on the accounts of Compagnie Française des Pétroles

Ladies and Gentlemen,

In accordance with the instructions given us at the General Shareholders'

Meetings of 1969 and 1972 we have pleasure in presenting you our report on your Company's accounts for the 1972 financial year.

In line with our permanent function, we have checked, during the year, the transactions carried out as they were booked. When the accounts were closed and in line with effective French regulations, we audited your Company's books and accounts. With the assistance of supporting documents and vouchers issued by your Head Office Management and your foreign Branch Offices, we were able to perform spot and collation checks at your Head Office and to reach the conclusion set forth in this report. Moreover, we were called upon to certify the Group's consolidated accounts and carried out a special check of these accounts, relying on controls performed to that end by our colleagues, the external and internal auditors of your affiliates and/or affiliated companies.

We appreciated both the assistance of your services for carrying out our auditing procedures and your efficient bookkeeping.

The 1972 accounts have been established according to the same procedures and evaluating methods as for the previous years, except for details set forth below for the various provision items.

After having shown in its Report your Company's and your affiliates' operations for 1972, your Board has presented to you the corresponding accounts.

In line with our assignment, we checked that information set forth in this Annual Report and in documents reflecting your Company's financial position and accounts—communicated to the shareholders according to French legal dispositions—is sincere.

In line with Article 356 of the Law on business corporations, we inform you that your Company set up four new affiliates with a capital of F 100,000 each, in which it has a 99·4 per cent holding. These affiliates are the following: "TOTAL Exploration", "TOTAL Exploration Tunisie", "TOTAL Perou" and "TOTAL Compagnie Minière et Nucléaire".

Moreover, in the scope of restructuration of the Group's interests, your Company acquired a 60 per cent holding in Omnium de Recherches et d'Exploitations (OMNIREX) through purchase of shares from its affiliate, Omnium Français de Pétroles, at the price of F 79.13 each. With this transaction, your holding in Compagnie Générale Doris and part of your holding in Compagnie Générale de Géophysique were transferred to OMNIREX; conversely, your control of TOTAL North America (TOPNA) was increased through acquiring 30,000 TOPNA common shares from Omnium Français de Pétroles and 90,000 shares from Compagnie Générale d'Interêts Pétroliers (COGIP) at the average rate of F 29.76 per share.

A 20 per cent holding was subscribed in Société d'Exploitation Pétrolière de Gabès Oriental, *i.e.*, 3999 shares of 10 Tunisian Dinars as well as a one third holding in the BP Kimberlé Company with a capital of £100.

Apart from these acquisitions of new holdings, the largest share of 1972 investments as set forth in your Board's report and broken down according to nature of operations were made through subscriptions in your affiliates' and affiliated companies' capital increases, and through long-term loans and advance loans on capital increases.

Allocation to provision for loss in the value of investments and loans was deducted according to the same method as last year.

Dry hole expenses incurred by both your Company and its affiliates were fully depreciated.

In other areas, depreciation is applicable for quoted investment stocks when the company's stock market value for December 1972 is lower than the value reflected in your list; and for unquoted stocks, when your share in the company's net assets is lower than your investment in the concerned company.

When the value of TOTAL Chimie and of SOCANTAR was assessed, good will for those companies' affiliates and/or interests in the petrochemical industry and for SOCANTAR's affiliates and/or interests in the oil industry, was maintained without applying corresponding depreciation on the value of your share in the companies' net assets.

Adjustment of aggregate provisions for depreciation thus deducted on each Balance Sheet item justifies allocation of F 257.78 million entered under that heading in operating expenses. Actually, as compared to provisions deducted in the 1971 Balance Sheet, some of the items reflect an increase in provision of F 329.6 million and other items a reduction of F 71.92 million.

Moreover, an amount of F 25 million was allocated to General reserve so as to increase it to F 355 million.

As far as accounting procedure is concerned, we would draw your attention to the fact that, this year, when stocks and shares were realized, the "FIFO" method was replaced by an evaluation of the cost of the stocks and shares sold at average price of each share held by your Company.

SNPA shares now representing for your Company only a 3.87 per cent holding in the capital of this company, were entered this year as marketable securities instead of investments as previously.

As for the provision for exchange fluctuations, which was made up on 31 December 1971 with an amount drawn from General reserve, it was kept unchanged at F 190 million on account of the present monetary situation; the foreign exchange differences reflected for 1972 representing a F 83.19 million amount, were entered as losses for the year under the heading "Exceptional losses".

As concerns the Employees' Investment Program, the agreement submitted for government approval at the end of 1971 was ratified after several adjustments. Consequently, no cost was incurred in 1972 for this item: a F 4.46 million amount drawn from the F 6.5 million provision made up at the end of

1971 was used for the employees' rights for 1970 and 1971, the balance being used for a provision entered in the 1972 accounts.

Finally, this year, only the taxes paid by your Group in 1971 were considered for restitution of taxes made by the Tax Authorities in line with the worldwide consolidated profit system to which your Group is subject. This restitution was entered as a deduction from the item "Taxes and share of the French State in excess profit". In our opinion, after examination of the accounts made in accordance with generally accepted auditing standards and such tests and controls we considered necessary, the Inventory, Statement of Income, Profit and Loss, and Balance Sheet accounts present fairly the financial position of your Company.

May 21, 1973 Ferdinand Angleys Marcel Neveux
(Members of the Compagnie de Paris)

The auditor should also draw the shareholders' attention to any irregularities and inaccuracies discovered in the course of his work.

In addition to the general audit report, the auditor makes a special report (*rapport spécial*) whereby:

1. He is obliged to disclose all transactions between directors, etc., and the company and between companies with common directors.
2. He certifies the remuneration of the 10 highest-paid persons in companies having more than 200 employees and of the five highest-paid persons in companies having less than 200 employees.

Fieldwork

The difficulty of attaining a satisfactory client relationship is one of the major problems facing the French auditor. The frequent lack of client co-operation and the existence of a minimum fee scale (*barème*) have tended to result in sporadic visits, often designed to cause the least disturbance, from the *commissaire*, who in turn is prone to severe staff shortages. What all this means in practice is that "generally accepted auditing standards" are not yet common and this fact is recognised by La Compagnie Nationale des Commissaires aux Comptes, which is now attempting to introduce Anglo-Saxon auditing methods to France. The appointment of a Scottish chartered accountant, David Adamson, as technical consultant of La Compagnie Régionale de Paris is significant. Every effort is now being made to achieve a higher degree of competence by means of regular courses, particularly pilot audits, for *commissaires aux comptes*, and by encouraging the formation of larger units either through straight mergers or by the setting up of common auditing firms whereby staff can be lent back and forth. At present these auditing units are set up in the form of Groupements d'Intérêt Economique (GIEs) (*see* page 7) and in 1973 one such group could call on 250 auditors from some 15 different member firms.

It may be assumed that the *commissaire* is an individualist possessed with great flair. He does not normally use an audit programme and does not concern himself unduly with internal control problems. It has also been said that the *commissaire* has a tendency to judge the credibility of the accounts by the standard of morality which he attributes to management in general and to the chief accountant in particular. The 1966 law specifically states that there is no limit to the extent of an auditor's work. His investigation may cover parent and subsidiary companies, and he can obtain any information which he considers necessary from third parties[10] who have had dealings with the company. However, the *commissaire* does not usually confirm receivables or bank balances, attend stock-takes or perform many of the other audit procedures which are considered essential in other countries. The *commissaire* is thus subject to great practical limitations in his work, but, to counterbalance this, his attitude and approach are different. His primary exercise with the accounts is one of comparison with explanations being sought for significant fluctuations. On the other hand, his review of the turnover tax accounts, profit-sharing bonuses and the tax aspects of all fixed-asset transactions is extensive. The company's income-tax declaration and other tax documents also receive a thorough examination.

Remuneration of Auditors

The law lays down a minimum fee scale (*barème*) for *commissaires aux comptes* based on the net worth and turnover of the company (Article 120, decree 12 August 1969).

Removal of Auditors

Although the *commissaire* is appointed for six years, he cannot rely on reappointment. Moreover, shareholders representing one-tenth of the share capital can petition the court for his removal, but this will be granted only in cases of gross negligence.

Liability of Auditors

Article 234 of the law of 24 July 1966 states that "auditors shall be liable, both to the company and to third parties, for the detrimental consequences of any faults and negligent acts committed by them in the exercise of their duties". There have been very few cases until now involving charges of professional negligence; civil charges against the auditor are statute-barred after three years except where the auditor is held liable for criminal offences, in which case such charges become statute-barred after a lapse of 10 years.

Independence of Auditors

The independence rules for French auditors are strict and complex, and are therefore reproduced below.

The following may not act as statutory auditors in the case of:

1. *Sociétés à responsibilité limitée* (Article 65, law 24 July 1966).
   (a) Managers and their spouses.
   (b) Persons from whom assets in kind have been taken over, persons receiving special advantages and persons receiving periodic remuneration from the company or its managers and the spouses of managers.
   (c) Persons who have previously acted as statutory auditors may not become managers for five years following the termination of their duties.
2. *Sociétés anonymes* and *Sociétés en commandite par actions* (Article 220, law 24 July 1966).
   (a) Directors or members of the supervisory board of a company or its subsidiaries.
   (b) Founders, persons from whom assets in kind have been taken over, persons receiving special advantages.
   (c) Blood relatives and relatives up to the fourth degree of the persons referred to in (a) and (b).
   (d) Directors, members of the directorate or supervisory board, the spouses of directors or the spouses of the members of the directorate or the supervisory board of companies owning one-tenth of the capital of the company or of which the company owns one-tenth of the capital.
   (e) Persons and their spouses who receive from the persons referred to in (a) and (b), from the company or from any company listed in (d) any salary or remuneration whatsoever for services other than those of an auditor.
   (f) Auditing companies of which one of the members is in one of the situations described in the above paragraphs. In practice, however, members of auditing firms are generally, at the same time, practising public accountants for the same client.

CONCLUSION

The French auditing profession must be highly commended for its enthusiastic efforts to improve the competence of auditors but there is a limit to what can be achieved with a profession whose median age is over 50. Recruitment of more and better-educated people can be the only long-term solution. In the meantime, *commissaires aux comptes* can expect regular jolts from the COB, and this, combined with the ever-present foreign firms eager to improve their local/foreign client ratio, will help to keep the profession on its toes.

The long-term plans of the Government appear to contemplate the eventual dominance of a highly qualified auditing profession with the Ordre serving as a co-ordinator for this and the two other streams of industrial and Government accountants.

REFERENCES

1. Bearer shares may be deposited with a central depository—SICOVAM, similar to the German Kassenverein.
2. *Cf.* Chapter 2, page 51.
3. *Accountancy and Economic Development Policy*, p. 227, published by North Holland Publishing Company, Amsterdam, 1973.
4. Ordre des Experts Comptables et des Comptables Agréés, see p. 25.
5. An associated company is defined by Article 355 of Law No. 66.537 as an interest of between 10 and 50 per cent of the capital of another company.
6. In the case of SA companies, registered shareholders may request the company, at any time from the date of calling the shareholders' meeting until the fifth day inclusive prior to the date of the meeting, to send them copies of the accounts as specified above. Registered shareholders may also, at a single request, have the company send them the above-mentioned documents for every subsequent meeting. Holders of bearer shares have similar rights provided their ownership can be proved.
7. The term "management report" refers, in the case of an SA, to the report of the supervisory board or that of the board of directors, and in the case of an SàRL, to the report of the managers.
8. The permitted forms of companies are:

   Sociétés civiles professionnelles.
   Sociétés à responsibilité limitée.
   Sociétés en commandite par actions.
   Sociétés anonymes.

   In order to adopt either of the last two forms the company's most important objective must be to practise the profession of *expert comptable* or *comptable agréé*. Furthermore, at least three members of the Ordre must be shareholders and hold the majority of shares; the company cannot be dependent directly or indirectly on any other person or group; nor can it have any financial interest in any industrial, commercial, agricultural or banking enterprise or in any *sociétés civiles*.

9. Transitional arrangements ending on 1 April 1975 permit those companies which are obliged to appoint only one auditor to appoint a *commissaire aux comptes* who is not on the official list.
10. This right of information, however, does not extend to the transmittal of any instruments, contracts and documents in the possession of third parties unless authorised by court order.

Chapter 2
Germany

BACKGROUND

The all-purpose nature of the commercial banks is the most significant feature of the German financial system. These banks provide the complete range of finance and financial services. They not only are engaged in the conventional lending and deposit business like Anglo-American banks, but also act as issuing houses underwriting new issues, and handle all stock exchange dealings.

The commercial banks fall into two main groups—those regulated under private law, known as the credit banks, and those incorporated under public law, being savings banks, central giro institutions and co-operative institutions (Table 2.1). The banking system is supervised by the Bundesbank (central bank) and all banking operations are controlled by a federal bank supervisory agency. The credit banks include the "Big Three" (Deutsche Bank, Dresdner Bank and Commerzbank), which each have an extensive branch network throughout the whole of Germany together accounting for 12 per cent of bank business; all other commercial banks incorporated as limited liability companies[1] (these banks have clear regional focal points) and private bankers operating as partnerships or sole proprietorships tend to specialise more in industrial and investment business. Overall the credit banks account for some 26 per cent of banking business—only half of that of the public banks. Apart from the commercial banks there are also a number of specialist banks, including the private and public mortgage banks which engage almost exclusively in granting long-term loans against liens on freehold property or other security afforded by local authorities.

Three particular features of the "universal" banking system are the participation of the banks in industrial and commercial companies, the proxy voting rights which they exercise on behalf of individual shareholders and the fact that, as a result, numerous major bank representatives sit on the supervisory board of large industrial undertakings. As far as the holding function is concerned, the "Big Three" banks alone hold a series of participations in excess of 25 per cent in well-known companies, as

TABLE 2.1. THE BANKING GROUPS IN THE FEDERAL REPUBLIC OF GERMANY (as at 30 June 1972)

Banking groups	*Total number*	*Number*	*Capital and published reserves*	*Total assets*
		of banks reporting under the monthly statistics[1]		
			DM millions	*DM millions*
Commercial banks	**7,468**	**3,209**	**26,566**	**723,475**
Private commercial banks	*313*	*313*	*10,951*	*238,515*
of which:				
The big banks[2]	6	6	4,438	98,430
Regional and other commercial banks	146	146	5,126	117,603
of which foreign banks	30	30	—	—
Private bankers	161	161	1,387	22,482
Public banks	*795*	*795*	*11,079*	*373,716*
of which:				
Savings banks	783	783	7,724	221,715
Central giro institutions	12	12	3,355	152,001
Co-operative banks	*6,360*	*2,101*	*4,556*	*111,244*
of which:				
Credit co-operatives	6,348[3]	2,089	3,332	78,576
Central institutions	12	12	1,224	32,668
Specialist banks	**374**	**282**	**9,549**	**288,293**
of which:				
Private mortgage banks	29	29	1,929	69,142
Public mortgage banks	16	16	2,228	61,375
Banks with special functions	18	18	2,998	72,793
Instalment sales financing houses	178	178	710	11,003
Private building and loan associations	14	14	1,030	33,114
Public building and loan associations	12	12	654	21,279
Postal giro and postal savings bank offices	15	15	—	—
Other credit institutions [4]	92[3]	—	—	—
All banks outside the Central Bank system	**7,842**	**3,491**	**36,135**	**1,011,862**

1. Of which some 10 in process of liquidation.
2. Including their Berlin subsidiaries.
3. On 31 December 1971.
4. Credit guarantee institutions, investment trusts, central depository banks for securities.

Source: The Banking System of the Federal Republic of Germany, Bank Verlag GmbH, Koln, September 1972.

for example in Daimler Benz AG, Karstadt and other large department stores, Süddeutsche Zucker (the largest sugar company), Hapag Loyd (the biggest shipping company), as well as in major building undertakings and breweries, etc. While estimates of the overall power of the banks, based upon their direct and indirect participations, vary and are generally overstated, Herr Ulrich of Deutsche Bank stated at the 1974 World Banking Conference that only 4 per cent of the share capital of all AG (*Aktiengesellschaft*) companies is held by banks, whereas 15 per cent is owned by the Federal and State governments and another 15 per cent by non-residents.

The banks' proxy voting right arises from the shares (in bearer form) which they hold in safe custody on behalf of the vast majority of individual shareholders.[2] Section 135 of the AG Law lays down that every proxy must be in writing, that it may be given only for a maximum of 15 months and that the authorised bank may exercise the voting right only to the extent that the shareholder has expressly given directives for the individual subjects on the agenda. However, sub-section 4 of the same section then goes on to say that:

> if the shareholder has not given directives to the bank for exercising the voting right, then the bank shall exercise the voting right in accordance with its own proposals as communicated to the shareholders . . . unless the bank can assume from the circumstances that the shareholders would, with the knowledge of the facts, approve of deviating in the exercise of the voting rights.

The result of this system may well be better representation of shareholders, particularly at general meetings, but, on the other hand, there may well be serious conflicts of interest for a banker who can be a creditor, a director and a shareholder at the same time. Not surprisingly, there is strong criticism of the power of the banks and their influence on the economy generally, especially from the trade unions, with the result that there is an increasing possibility of Government intervention.

Frankfurt and, to a lesser extent, Düsseldorf are the most important of the German stock exchanges, together accounting for over 75 per cent of total turnover. The stock exchanges are controlled by the Government, and, although all dealing is restricted to the banks, at least 50 per cent of the membership committees must be persons who cannot deal in securities. The admission of bonds is controlled by the authorities and priority is given to Government bonds. All bonds are allocated by quota to the banks and are sold through their branches to the public; there are no secondary institutions of a similar size to the UK insurance companies, investment trusts, unit trusts or pension funds.

Industrial bonds suffer from the prevailing high interest rates and restrictions imposed on non-residents in order to control currency speculation. At the end of 1972 industrial bonds in circulation amounted to a mere DM 10,000 million out of a total of DM 214,315 million. Traditionally the mortgage banks were the most important borrowers on the fixed-interest market but in recent years communal bonds, many of which are issued by the central giro institutions and taken up by the savings banks, have taken over both in terms of new issues and also in circulation (Table 2.2).

TABLE 2.2. SALES OF SECURITIES (in DM billions)

	1969	*1970*	*1971*	*1972*
Bonds				
1 Net sales of domestic bonds[1]	*12.38*	*14.31*	*20.58*	*34.07*
Bank bonds	12.26	11.93	14.86	26.07
of which:				
Mortgage bonds	3.14	1.90	4.37	7.99
Communal bonds	7.26	7.65	7.12	12.90
Other bank bonds	1.85	2.38	3.37	5.18
Public authority bonds	0.29	2.16	4.28	7.21
Industrial bonds	−0.16	0.22	1.44	0.79
2 Net acquisition of foreign bonds	*5.37*	*1.04*	*−1.18*	*−4.31*
Total capital raised (1 + 2)	**17.75**	**15.35**	**19.40**	**29.76**
Shares				
1 Sales of domestic shares (market value)	*2.80*	*3.59*	*4.74*	*4.13*
2 Net acquisition of foreign shares by residents	*5.78*	*2.67*	*2.13*	*1.78*
Total capital raised in equity market (1 + 2)	**8.58**	**6.26**	**6.87**	**5.91**

1. Gross sales at market value less redemptions.

Source: Report of the Deutsche Bundesbank for the year 1972.

With only 500 quoted companies, many of which are closely controlled, the equity market is narrow. Equity issues are not an important source of industrial finance, although they rose to some 5 per cent of enterprises' funds in 1971, and it is very likely that businesses will continue to generate about half of their financing needs internally with the other half coming from short- to medium-term loans from the banks.

BUSINESS ORGANISATIONS

The various forms of business organisation generally used in Germany are shown in Fig. 2.1. Companies and partnerships are separate legal entities. All commercial enterprises must be registered in the Commercial Register (*Handelsregister*) which is kept at the local court, and become members of their local Chamber of Commerce which normally also keeps copies of the Commercial Register. In order to carry on a business, a minimum annual turnover must be expected, which (according to court decisions) in the case of retail firms is between DM 125,000 and DM 130,000 and in the case of wholesale firms ranges from DM 200,000 and DM 400,000.

Companies

The separate form of private limited liability company, now in almost universal use throughout the EEC, is based on the German GmbH (*Gesellschaft mit beschränkter Haftung*) company which was first introduced by an enactment in 1892. The GmbH company is by far the most popular form of limited liability company in Germany (Table 2.3) and the

TABLE 2.3. STATISTICS OF GERMAN COMPANIES (as at 31 December 1972)

	AG	*GmbH*
Agricultural	9	495
Energy, water and mining	147	420
Manufacturing	886	25,155
Construction	48	6,181
Trading	147	23,175
Transportation	125	3,721
Credit and insurance	407	1,789
Services	502	39,754
Total	**2,271**	**100,690**

Source: Statistical Yearbook, 1973.

number of those registered increased from 50,275 in 1965 to 100,690 at the end of 1972. The GmbH law is now subject to reform.

The other form of company, the *Aktiengesellschaft* (AG), often called a "stock corporation", is governed by the provisions of the 1965 *Aktiengesetz* and is rather more exclusive than the GmbH. Since 1965 the number

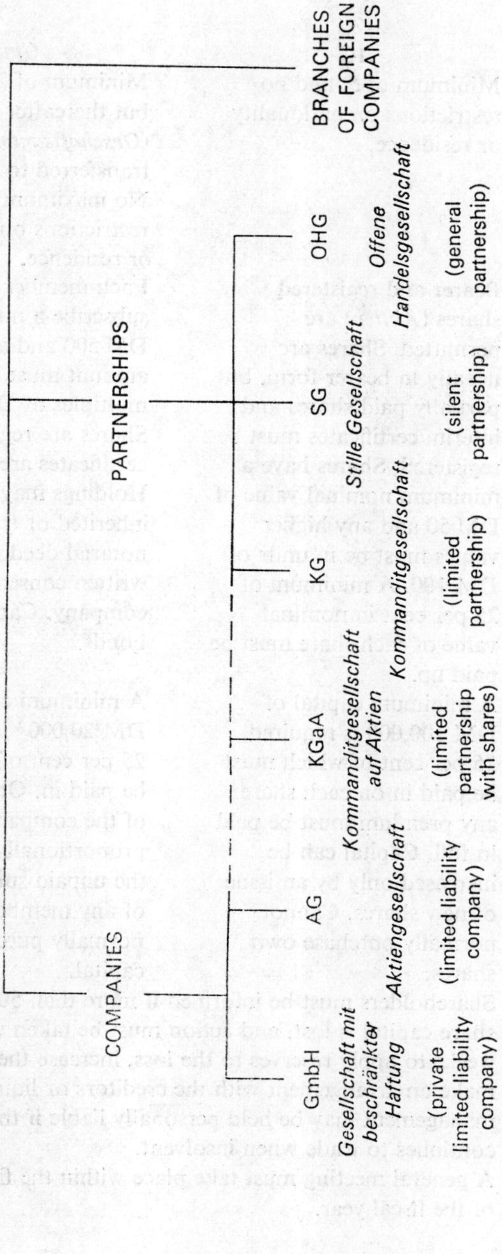

Fig. 2.1 Forms of business organisation in Germany

of AGs has dropped from 2530 to 2271, largely as a result of mergers. The main features of both forms of company may be compared as follows:

	AG	*GmbH*
Shareholders	Minimum of 5, and no restrictions on nationality or residence.	Minimum of 2 founders but thereafter all shares (*Geschaftsanteile*) may be transferred to one party. No maximum and no restrictions on nationality or residence.
Securities	Bearer and registered shares (*Aktien*) are permitted. Shares are usually in bearer form, but partially paid shares and interim certificates must be registered. Shares have a minimum nominal value of DM 50 and any higher values must be in units of DM 100. A minimum of 25 per cent in nominal value of each share must be paid up.	Each member must subscribe a minimum of DM 500 and any additional amount must be in multiples of DM 1000. Shares are registered and certificates are never issued. Holdings may be inherited or transferred by notarial deed with the written consent of the company. Cannot issue bonds.
Capital	A minimum capital of DM 100,000 is required, 25 per cent of which must be paid in on each share; any premium must be paid in full. Capital can be increased only by an issue of new shares. Cannot normally purchase own shares.	A minimum capital of DM 20,000[3] is specified, 25 per cent of which must be paid in. Other members of the company are proportionally liable for the unpaid subscriptions of any members. Cannot normally purchase own capital.
Capital impairment	Shareholders must be informed if more than 50 per cent of share capital is lost, and action must be taken within three weeks to apply reserves to the loss, increase the capital, make an arrangement with the creditors or liquidate. The management may be held personally liable if the company continues to trade when insolvent.	
Annual general meeting	A general meeting must take place within the first 8 months of the fiscal year.	

Germany was the first country to provide for compulsory two-tier boards and employee participation in company management. All AGs are managed by a board of management (*Vorstand*) which in turn is under the general surveillance of a supervisory board (*Aufsichstrat*). The classical management structure is not permitted.

The members of the board of management are appointed by the supervisory board[4] for a period not exceeding five years and are concerned with day-to-day matters subject to any limits set by the statutes (*Satzung*), shareholders or the supervisory board. Each member of the board of management has distinct areas of responsibility and a chairman is generally appointed; each must hold service contracts with the company.

The supervisory board consists of representatives of the shareholders (but not necessarily shareholders) and, with minor exceptions, of elected workers' representatives. One-third of the members (or 50 per cent in the case of the coal, iron and steel industries) must be elected by the employees. Members of the supervisory board must be independent of the board of management and a member cannot hold seats on the supervisory board of more than 10 independent companies. Membership of the supervisory board ranges from 3 to 21 depending on the share capital of the company, but the number must be divisible by 3. The supervisory board is primarily responsible for the appointment, removal and supervision of the board of management as well as final determination of the annual accounts and the authorisation of certain transactions and contracts as stipulated by the articles. The chairman of the supervisory board presides at the general meeting. As for the remuneration of the supervisory board, this is usually specified in the articles but it may be fixed by the shareholders.

In the case of GmbHs, a supervisory board is optional unless the company has more than 500 employees, when the same provisions as those for AGs apply. GmbHs are managed by one or more managers (*Geschäftsführer*) who need not be shareholders and they may be appointed by the members for any length of time. Their remuneration is fixed by the shareholders.

Partnerships

In a general partnership (*Offene Handelsgesellschaft*—OHG) all the partners must take part in the management unless the partnership agreement states otherwise. The OHG is a separate legal entity and is automatically wound up on the death of a partner unless the agreement states otherwise.

The *Kommanditgesellschaft* (KG) is a typical form of limited partnership in which only the general partners can manage the firm. It is a separate legal entity.

The *Stille Gesellschaft* (SG) is a silent partnership which arises from the participation of a single person or company in the profit of an active firm. The silent partner is not liable for the debts of the partnership.

Limited Partnerships with Shares

The limited partnership with shares (*Kommanditgesellschaft auf Aktien*—KGaA) is an association with at least one general (unlimited) partner and others whose interest is limited to the amount of share capital which they contribute. The KGaA is a separate legal entity, requires at least five shareholders and is generally subject to the same provisions as the AG.

Branches of Foreign Companies

Branch offices must generally be registered in the Commercial Register and are called *Zweigniederlassungen*. Very small offices which could not operate in their own right without head office assistance may not need to be registered. The same applies to branches of domestic undertakings.

Works Councils

Since 1952 works councils (*Betriebsrat*) have been a compulsory feature of German business. The law was considerably revised in the Shop Constitution Act which came into force in 1972. All enterprises with more than five employees are required to form works councils, the representatives of which are elected from among the employees by secret ballot for three-year terms.

The council is mainly concerned with the representation of employees' interests towards the management and the settlement of grievances. In addition its approval is necessary for changes in terms of conditions of employment, safety and health measures, employee housing, training procedures, production methods, changes in payment rates and procedures, and the engagement, relocation and dismissal of workers. Any disputes not settled between the employees and management are submitted to arbitration. Enterprises with more than 100 employees are also required to elect a committee with responsibility to discuss with the management general economic and social matters relating to the company.

ACCOUNTING AND FINANCIAL REPORTING

Legal prescription is the chief characteristic of German accounting, a factor which may be ascribed more to native personality than to anything else. The primary consideration of the law has always been to protect the creditor, and this, combined with the influence of the tax regulations, has given German accounting a reputation for conservatism involving understated assets and secret reserves, which all too often masks its other, more commendable, features.

Uniform accounting has been a feature of the German accounting tradition ever since it was first introduced in the 1920s by the late Professor Eugen Schmalenbach, whose book *Der Kontenrahmen* (*The Framework of Accounts*) was published in 1927 (*see* Fig. 2.2). Uniformity found particular favour with the Nazis and the *Reichskontenrahmen* of 1937 made some 200 uniform charts of accounts compulsory for the different branches of German industry and commerce. Thereafter uniform accounting was enforced in every occupied country including France (*see* Chapter 1, page 8) until peace in 1945, when compulsory charts ceased to be binding. Following the war, in 1949, several German business organisations subscribed to a new uniform chart of accounts, the *Gemeinschaftskontenrahmen*, and today almost every German industry has its own particular chart based on this which, like that of 1937, is very much a copy of the Schmalenbach original (Fig. 2.3). Today the Bundesverband der Deutschen Industrie (the business organisation of German industry) encourages the use of the so-called *Industriekontenrahmen* (IKR) which continues the tradition of the former developments in this area.

In Germany, as in almost every other continental European country, the impact of taxation on accounting is significant. In contrast with Italy the Germans believe that taxable profits must be derived from the commercial accounts; they then go on to confound this piece of logic by insisting that, if a particular accounting treatment is to be claimed for tax purposes, that treatment must also be followed in the commercial accounts. Accordingly tax concessions such as accelerated depreciation or the roll-over of capital gains can be claimed for tax purposes only when charged in the accounts. Indeed, the AG Law of 1965 even goes so far as to state specifically in Section 154 (2) that fixed assets may be depreciated at tax rates even if this is excessive in relation to the utilisation of the assets. Furthermore the lower valuation can be retained even when the reasons for the accelerated depreciation have ceased to exist.

Accounting Principles

Under the German tradition accounting principles have to a large extent been prescribed by legislation and the accountancy profession has generally confined itself to the interpretation of the law. Section 149 of the AG Law

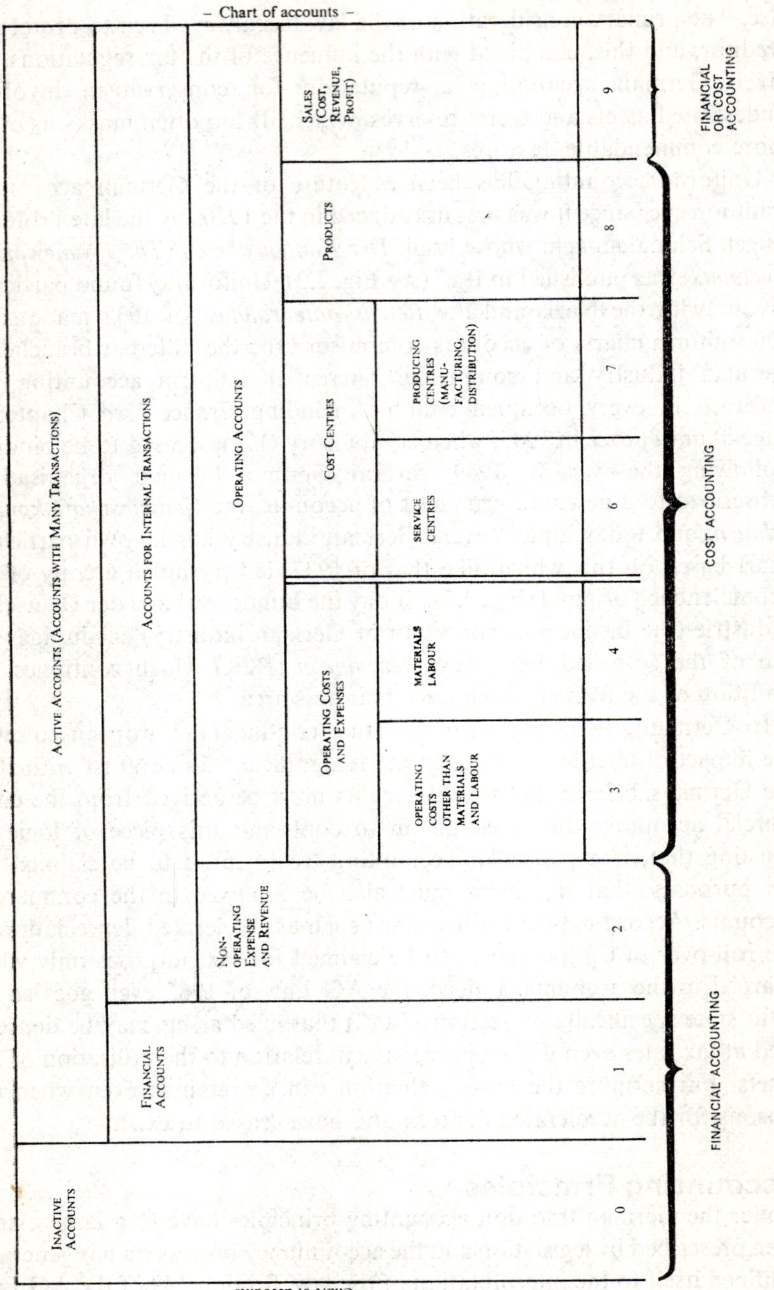
– Chart of accounts –
Inactive Accounts
Active Accounts (Accounts with Many Transactions)
Financial Accounts
Accounts for Internal Transactions
Non-operating Expense and Revenue
Operating Accounts
Operating Costs and Expenses
Operating costs other than materials and labour
Materials Labour
Cost Centres
Service centres
Producing centres (manu-facturing, distribution)
Products
Sales (Cost, Revenue, Profit)
0
1
2
3
4
6
7
8
9
Financial Accounting
Cost Accounting
Financial or Cost Accounting
– Chart of accounts –

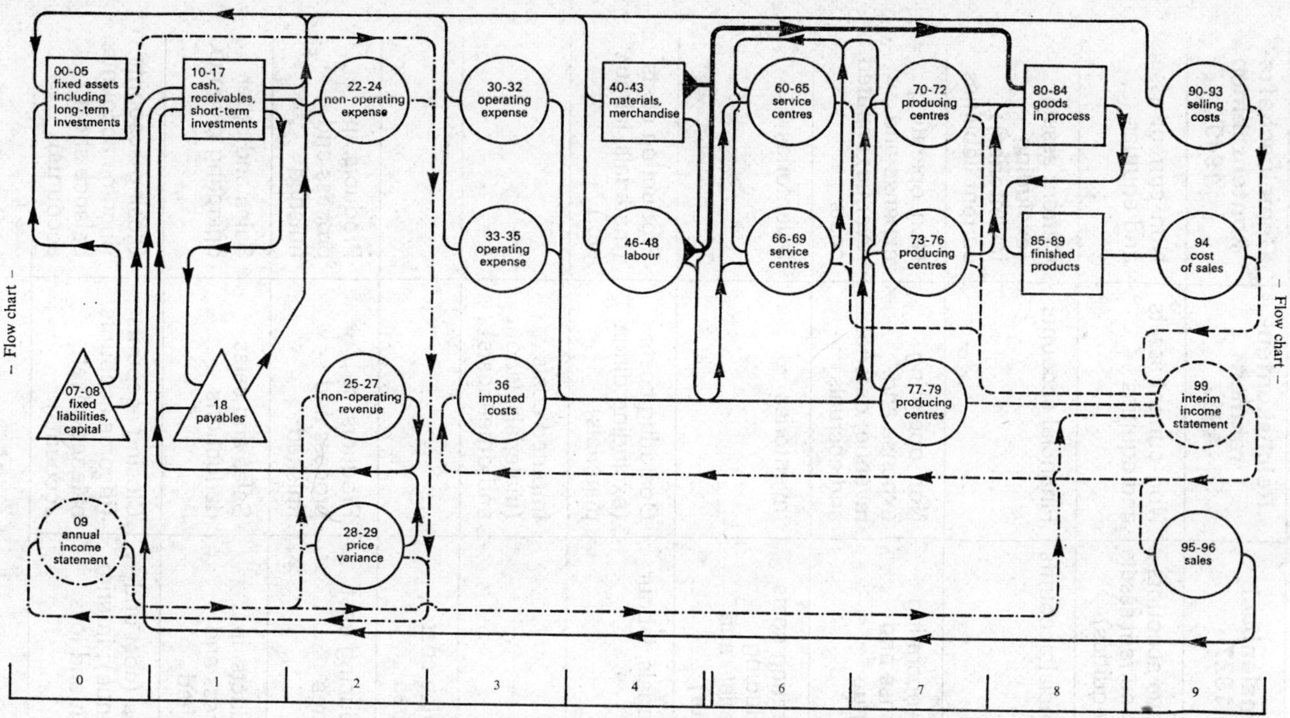

Fig. 2.2. Schmalenbach's standard chart of accounts and flow chart

Source: Karl Kafer, "European National Uniform Charts of Accounts", *International Journal of Accounting* (University of Illinois), Vol. 1, No. 1, pages 70–71

□ = asset accounts; Δ = liability and proprietorship accounts; ○ = income and expense accounts, and summary accounts. → = credit entry; ← debit entry; – –; –.– = to summary and income accounts for closing entries.

	Schmalenbach 1927	Reichskontenrahmen 1937	Gemeinschaftskontenrahmen 1949
Class 0	Inactive accounts (non-current assets and equities)	Non-current assets and equities	Non-current assets and equities
Class 1	Financial accounts	Financial accounts	Current assets (excluding inventories); current liabilities
Class 2	Non-operating expense and revenue	Non-operating expense and revenue; deferrals and accruals	Non-operating expense and revenue; imputed costs
Class 3	Operating costs (excluding materials and labour)	Inventories	Inventories
Class 4	Materials, labour	Operating costs (excluding direct materials)	Production costs (materials, labour, etc.)
Class 5		Imputed costs (materials, labour and other costs)	
Class 6	Service cost centres		
Class 7	Producing cost centres	Products, in process and finished	Products, in process and finished
Class 8	Products, in process and finished	Sales and sales deductions	Sales and other operating revenue
Class 9	Sales (cost and revenue); interim profit and loss	Closing accounts (income accounts, balance sheet accounts)	Closing accounts (income accounts, balance sheet accounts)

Fig. 2.3 The development of uniform accounting in Germany

states that "the annual financial statement shall conform to proper accounting principles [*Grundsätzen ordnungsmässiger Buchführung*]". The accounts must be clear and well set out and give "as true a view of the company's financial position and of its operating results as is possible pursuant to the valuation provisions".

Non-AG companies and particularly those "large enterprises"[5] also obliged by the 1969 Publicity Law (*Publizitätsgesetz*) to publish their accounts must follow "proper accounting principles" but this occasionally means that they apply the provisions of the old and superseded AG Law of 1937 which permitted a much broader range of alternative valuation methods than the 1965 law. There is, nevertheless, a strong trend towards complete application of the AG valuation rules to all companies.

Apart from the prescribed rules there are also certain unwritten but generally accepted accounting principles which according to one writer[6] can be summarised as follows:

1. *Fundamental conventions*
   - (a) The concept of accounting for an economic entity for a definite period of time.
   - (b) The concept of continuity (conformity of the opening and closing balance sheets).
   - (c) The concept of historical costs.
2. *Basic concepts*
   - (a) Completeness—all accountable business transactions must be accounted for.
   - (b) Truthfulness and clarity—the financial statements must not be misleading and should truly reflect the financial position.
   - (c) Prudence—the financial position must not be overstated; this may be better described as the principle of imparity—the lowest value must be attributed to assets, but liabilities must be accounted for at their nominal values.

Accounting Practices and the Annual Accounts

The annual accounts of all AG companies and large enterprises are required to follow the same format as the model set out in the 1965 AG Law (Figs. 2.4 and 2.5) unless the business concerned is of a special nature (*i.e.* banking, insurance and transportation). Additional headings are possible within the basic framework and those which are not applicable can be omitted. The offsetting of assets and liabilities is generally forbidden. Corresponding figures, although not obligatory, are usually given,

AKTIVA (ASSETS)

I Ausstehende Einlagen auf das Grundkapital—davon eingefordert (Share capital not yet paid in—of which there has been called)

II Anlagevermogen (Fixed assets—at net book value)

A *Sachenlagen und immaterielle Anlagwerte* (Property, plant and equipment, intangible assets)

1 *Grundstücke und grunstücksgleiche Rechte mit Geschäfts-, Fabrik- und anderen Bauten* (Land and equivalent rights with office, factory and other buildings erected on such land)

2 *Grundstücke und grundstücksgleiche Rechte mit Wohnbauten* (Land and equivalent rights with dwelling structures erected on such land)

3 *Grundstücke und grundstücksgleiche Rechte ohne Bauten* (Land and equivalent rights without buildings erected on such land)

4 *Bauten auf fremden Grundstücken, die nicht zu Nummer 1 oder 2 gehören* (Buildings erected on leasehold land not included in Nos. 1 and 2)

5 *Maschinen und maschinelle Anlagen* (Machinery and installations)

6 *Betriebs- und Geschäftsausstattung* (Factory and office equipment)

7 *Anlagen in Bau und Anzahlungen auf Anlagen* (Construction in progress and advances paid for construction work (advances to suppliers relating to fixed assets would also be shown here))

8 *Konzessionen, Gewerbliche Schutzrechte und ahnliche Rechte sowie Lizenzen an solchen Rechten* (Intangible assets (franchises, patents, copyrights, trademarks, licences, etc.))

B *Finanzanlagen* (Financial assets)

1 *Beteiligungen* (Investments (participations))

2 *Wertpapiere des Anlagevermögens, die nicht zu Nummer 1 gehören* (Securities held for investment purposes which are not included in No. 1)

3 *Ausleihungen mit einer Laufzeit von mindestens vier Jahren: davon durch Grundpfandrechte gesichert* —— (Loans granted for at least four years; amount of such loans secured by mortgages ——)

III Umlaufvermogen (Current assets)

A *Vorräte* (Inventories)

1 *Roh-, Hilfs- und Betriebstoffe* (Raw materials and supplies)

2 *unfertige Erzeugnisse* (Work in progress)

3 *fertige Erzeugnisse, Waren* (Finished products, merchandise)

B *Andere Gegenstände des Umlaufvermögens* (Other current assets)

1 *geleistete Anzahlungen, soweit sie nicht zu II A Nr. 7 gehören* (Advances other than paid for construction work (II A No. 7))

2 *Forderungen aus lieferungen und Leistugen, davon mit einer Restlaufzeit von mehr als einem Jahr* —— (Trade accounts receivable; amount of such receivables due in more than one year——)

3 *Wechsel—davon bundesbankfähig* (Notes receivable and bills of exchange (trade acceptances), those acceptable for discount by Bundesbank)

4 *Schecks* (Cheques)

5 *Kassenbestand, Bundesbank- und Postcheckguthaben* (Cash on hand and deposits with Bundesbank and postal cheque office)

6 *Guthaben bei Kreditinstituten* (Deposit with banks)

7 *Wertpapiere, die nicht zu Nr. 3, 4, 8 oder 9 oder zu II B gehören* (Securities not classified under No. 3, 4, 8 or 9 nor under II B)

8 *Eigene Aktien unter Angabe des Nennbetrages* (Holding of own shares (note their nominal amount))

Fig. 2.4 Example of *Bilanz* (balance sheet)

9 *Anteile an einer herrschenden oder an der Gesellschaft mit Mehrheit beteiligten Kapitalgesellschaft oder bergrechtlichen Gewerkschaft unter Angabe ihres Nennbetrages, bei Kuxen ihrer Zahl* (Shares of a controlling corporation or of a corporation holding the majority (note their nominal amount). Shares of a controlling mining association or of a mining association holding the majority (note their number))

10 *Forderungen an verbundene Unternehmen* (Amounts receivable, due from affiliated enterprises)

11 *Forderungen aus Krediten, die* (Accounts receivable, due from)
(a) *unter 89* (members of the board of managers)
(b) *unter 115—fallen* (members of the board of supervisors)

12 *Sonstige Vermögensgegenstähande* (Other assets)

IV Rechnungsabgrenzungsposten (Prepaid expenses)

V Bilanzverlust (Accumulated deficit)

PASSIVA (LIABILITIES AND CAPITAL)

I Grundkapital (Share capital)

II Offene Rücklagen (Capital reserves)

1 *Gesetzliche Rücklage* (Legal reserve)

2 *Andere Rücklagen (freie Rücklagen)* (Other reserves (free reserves))

III Wertberichtigungen (Allowances (such as for doubtful accounts))

IV Rückstellungen (Liability reserves (accrued liabilities))

1 *Pensionsrückstellungen* (Pension reserve)

2 *Andere Rückstellungen* (Other accrued liabilities)

V Verbindlichkeiten mit einer Laufzeit von mindestens vier Jahren (Long-term borrowings for at least four years)

1 *Anleihen—davon durch Grundpfandrechte gesichert* (Loans (indicate whether secured by mortgage))

2 *Verbindlichkeiten gegenüber Kreditinstituten, davon durch Grundpfandrechte gesichert* (Bank loans (indicate whether secured by mortgage))

3 *Sonstige Verbindlichkeiten* (Other liabilities (indicate whether secured by mortgage))
davon durch Grundpfandrechte gesichert von Nummer 1 bis 3 sind vor Ablauf von vier Jahren fallig (Amount of No. 1, 2 and 3 due before expiration of four years)

VI Andere Verbindlichkeiten (Other liabilities)

1 *Verbindlichkeiten aus Lieferungen und Leistungen* (Trade accounts payable)

2 *Verbindlichkeiten aus der Annahme gezogener Wechsel und der Ausstellung eigener Wechsel* (Liabilities from acceptances and of promissory notes issued)

3 *Verbindlichkeiten gegenüber Kreditinstituten, soweit sie nicht zu V gehören* (Bank loans and overdrafts—liabilities apart from those of V)

4 *erhaltene Anzahlungen* (Advances received)

5 *Verbindlichkeiten gegenüber verbundenen Unternehmungen* (Accounts payable, due to affiliated enterprises)

6 *Sonstige Verbindlichkeiten* (Accounts payable, other)

VII Rechnungsabgrenzungsposten (Deferred income)

VIII Bilanzgewinn (Retained earnings)

Fig. 2.4—(continued) Example of *Bilanz* (balance sheet)

1 *Umsatzerlöse* (Proceeds from turnover)
2 *Erhöhung oder Verminderung des Bestandes an fertigen und unfertigen Erzeugnissen* (Increase or decrease of inventories of finished products and work in progress)
3 *Andere aktivierte Eigenleistungen* (Capitalised costs of assets constructed or extensive repairs made by company personnel)
4 *Gesamtleistung* (Total output)
5 *Aufwendungen für Roh-, Hilfs- und Betriebsstoffe sowie für bezogene Waren* (Cost of raw material, supplies and purchased goods)
6 *Rohertag/Rohaufwand* (Gross operating profit or loss)
7 *Erträge aus Gewinngemeinschaften, Gewinnab/führungs- und Teilgewinn-abführungsverträgen* (Income from profit pools and profit and loss pooling contracts relating to whole or partial transfer of profit (or loss))
8 *Erträge aus Beteiligungen* (Income from investments)
9 *Erträge aus den anderen Finanzanlagen* (Income from other financial assets)
10 *Sonstige Zinsen und ähnliche Erträge* (Other interest earned and similar income)
11 *Erträge aus dem Abgang von Gegenständen des Anlagevermögens und aus Zuschreibungen zu Gegenständen des Anlagevermögens* (Income from disposals of fixed assets and from appreciation of fixed assets)
12 *Erträge aus der Herabsetzung der Pauschalwertberichtigung zu Forderungen* (Income from a decrease of the global allowance for doubtful accounts receivable)
13 *Erträge aus der Auflösung von Rückstellungen* (Income from provisions no longer required)
14 *Sonstige Erträge davon auberordentliche* (Other income, non-recurrent)
15 *Erträge aus Verlustübernahme* (Income resulting from loss transferred to contracting party in a profit and loss pooling contract)
16 *Löhne und Gehälter* (Wages and salaries)
17 *Soziale Abgaben* (Social security charges)
18 *Aufwendungen für Altersversorgung und Unterstützung* (Old age relief and social aid expenses)
19 *Abschreibungen und Wertberichtigungen auf Sachanlagen und immaterielle Anlagewerte* (Depreciation/amortisation of property, plant and equipment and intangible assets)
20 *Abschreibungen und Wertberichtigungen auf Finanzanlagen mit Ausnahme des Betrages, der in die Pauschalwertberichtigung zu Forderungen eingestellt ist* (Write-down and adjustment of financial assets excepting the amount added to the global allowance for doubtful accounts receivable)
21 *Verluste aus Wertminderungen oder dem Abgang von Gegenständen des Umlaufvermögens auber Vorräten (*151 Abs. 1 Aktivseite III B) und Einstellung in die Pauschalwerberichtigung zu Forderungen* (Losses from the decrease in value or the disposal of current assets except inventories (assets III B) and additions to the global allowance for doubtful accounts receivable)
22 *Verluste aus dem Abgang von Gegenständen des Anlagevermögens* (Losses on disposals of fixed assets)
23 *Zinsen und ähnliche Aufwendungen* (Interest and similar expenses)
24 *Steuern* (Taxes)
   (a) *vom Einkommen, vom Ertrag und vom Vermögen* (on income, on earnings and on net worth)
   (b) *sonstige* (other)

Fig. 2.5 Example of *Gewinn-und Verlustrechnung* (profit and loss account)

25 *Aufwendungen aus Verlustübernahme* (Losses assumed according to profit and loss pooling contracts)
26 *Sonstige Aufwendungen* (Other expenses)
27 *Auf Grund einer Gewinngemeinschaft, eines Gewinnabführungs- und eines Teilgewinnabführungsvertrags abgeführte Gewinne* (Profits transferred in accordance with profit pools and profit and loss pooling contracts relating to whole or partial transfer of profit (or loss))
28 *Jahresüberschug/Jahresfehlbetrag* (Profit/loss for the year)
29 *Gewinnvortrag/Verlustvortrag aus dem Vorjahr* (Profit/loss retained from previous year)
30 *Entnahmen aus offenen Rücklagen* (Reduction of capital reserves)
(a) *aus der gesetzlichen Rücklage* (legal reserve)
(b) *aus freien Rücklagen* (free reserves)
31 *Einstellungen aus dem Jahresüberschub in offene Rücklagen* (Appropriation of profit for the year to capital reserves)
(a) *in die gesetzliche Rücklage* (to legal reserve)
(b) *in freie Rücklagen* (to free reserves)
32 *Bilanzgewinn/Bilanzverlust* (Total profit/loss indicated in the balance sheet)

Fig. 2.5—(continued) Example of *Gewinn-und Verlustrechnung* (profit and loss account)

especially by AG companies. The standard accounts include a great deal of information which for clarity would normally appear as notes in the accounts of UK companies; moreover, the management report of German companies also contains much information in connection with the accounts.

Consolidated Accounts

Consolidated accounts first became compulsory in Germany under the 1965 *Aktiengesetz*. Rather strangely, there is no rule to consolidate foreign subsidiaries. Some AGs do, however, prepare "world accounts" but the AG Law specifically forbids the inclusion of any accounts, domestic or foreign, which would "impair the value of the disclosures on the consolidated financial statement". AGs and large enterprises must consolidate all domestic holdings in excess of 50 per cent and all other domestic group participations the inclusion of which "leads to a different judgement of the financial position and operation of the group". Partially consolidated accounts are necessary where a group includes an AG or large enterprise, but where the controlling entity is not an AG or "large enterprise". Under German law a group relationship exists when companies come under the unified management or control of another (holding) company. A company is deemed to be controlled when it is majority owned, or when for other reasons it is dependent on another company. The 1965 law prescribes a simplified form of consolidated profit and loss account, which may be used in the case where intergroup sales have been eliminated

1 *Außenumsatzerlöse* (Proceeds from external turnover)
2 *Nicht gesondert auszuweisende Aufwendungen nach Verrechnung mit Bestandsänderungen und Eigenleistungen* (Expense which need not be shown separately after set off against changes in inventory and own performances)
3 *Erträge aus Beteiligungen an nicht in den Konzernabschluß einbezogenen Unternehmen* (Income from participations in enterprises not included in the consolidated financial statements)
4 *Erträge aus den anderen Finanzanlagen* (Income from the other financial assets)
5 *Sonstige Zinzen und ähnliche Erträge* (Other interest and similar income)
6 *Erträge aus Zuschreibungen* (Income from appreciation)
7 *Erträge aus der Auflösung von Rückstellungen* (Income from release of provisions for accrued liabilities)
8 *Sonstige Erträge* (Other income)
9 *Abschreibungen und Wertberichtigungen auf Sachanlagen und immaterielle Anlagewerte* (Depreciation and provisions for diminution in value of fixed assets and intangible assets)
10 *Abschreibungen und Wertberichtigungen auf Finanzanlagen* (Depreciation and provisions for diminution in value of financial assets)
11 *Zinzen und ähnliche Aufwendungen* (Interest and similar expenses)
12 *Steuern* (Taxes)
   (a) *Vom Einkommen, vom Ertrag und vom Vermögen* (On income, on yield and on net assets)
   (b) *Sonstige* (Other)
13 *Aufwendungen aus der Übernahme des Verlustes eines nicht in den Konzernabschluß einbezogenen Unternehmens* (Expenses resulting from the assumption of a loss of an enterprise not included in the consolidated financial statements)
14 *Jahresüberschuß/Jahresfehlbetrag* (Profit for the year/loss for the year)
15 *Gewinnvortrag/Verlustvortrag aus dem Vorjahr* (Profit carried forward/loss carried forward from the previous year)
16 *Entnahmen aus offenen Rücklagen* (Withdrawals from disclosed reserves)
17 *Einstellungen in offene Rücklagen* (Transfers to disclosed reserves)
18 *Konzernfremden Gesellschaftern zustehender Gewinn* (Profit attributable to partners outside the combine)
19 *Auf konzernfremde Gesellschafter entfallender Verlust* (Loss attributable to partners outside the combine)
20 *Konzerngewinn/Konzernverlust* (Consolidated profit/consolidated loss)

Fig. 2.6 Example of *Konzern-Gewinn-und Verlustrechnung* (consolidated profit and loss account)

(Fig. 2.6). The valuation rules of the AG Law have precedence over the stipulation that the accounts must give as true a view as possible of the financial position and results. A similar clause in the first draft of the EEC's proposed Fourth Directive was withdrawn in the face of strong opposition from the United Kingdom and Ireland in favour of a provision that accounts are subject to the overriding requirement of giving "a true and fair view". The valuation rules of the AG Law and other practices commonly followed in German accounts are discussed in the following sections.

The Balance Sheet

Fixed assets. Fixed assets, defined as those assets intended for permanent use, must be carried at acquisition or construction cost less depreciation. Construction cost includes reasonable wear and tear and, normally, a reasonable proportion of factory and administrative expenses; it cannot include selling expenses. Additions, disposals, depreciation and other adjustments are stated separately in the annual accounts but it is usual practice for companies to report only the net amount of fixed assets at the beginning and end of a period. The other adjustments (*Zuschreibungen*) (*see* Fig. 2.5, Item 11) generally result from a realignment of fixed asset accounts to amounts acceptable for tax purposes, normally as a result of a tax audit which led to the disallowance of the depreciation or the addition of other items which have not been capitalised. The law lays down that those fixed assets "the utilisation of which is limited by time must be written down by methodical depreciation in accordance with proper accounting principles over the life of the assets". However, the law immediately goes on to contradict this eminently acceptable provision by stating that:

> irrespective of whether or not their utilisation is limited by time, extraordinary depreciation or provision for diminution in value may be provided for fixed and financial assets in order to carry the assets
>
> 1. at the lower value which is to be attributed to them at the closing date, or
> 2. at the lower value which is held permissible for purposes of taxation of income and yield.
>
> The lower valuation may be retained even if the reason for the extraordinary depreciation or provision for diminution in value have ceased to exist.

Problems arise from the higher tax allowances granted to encourage certain investments. Otherwise the disparity between actual depreciation and that allowed for tax purposes might not be very significant since the tax authorities do go to considerable lengths to try to accommodate all types of fixed assets and the guideline depreciation rates which they issue are intended to write off assets over their estimated useful life. Apart from depreciable fixed assets, proper accounting principles require the depreciation of freehold buildings in accordance with the rates permitted for tax purposes. Depreciation provisions may be deducted from fixed assets in the balance sheet and can also appear among liabilities.

Long-term investments with the intention of influencing the policies of the companies concerned are termed *Beteiligungen* and each of those representing at least a 25 per cent participation must be stated under this item. Disclosure of capital commitments is not necessary. *Wertpapiere* refers to any other investment held for a long or short period. Long-term non-interest-bearing debts are usually discounted but the same procedure does not apply to similar liabilities. Any investments in other group companies must be separately disclosed under *Beteiligungen*.

Intangible assets. Intangibles can appear only when they have been acquired for consideration. Goodwill must be written off within five years of acquisition, but write-offs are allowable for tax purposes where there has been an actual loss. Costs of the formation and procurement of capital as well as start-up expenses have to be expended in the first year. Prepaid expenses can be carried forward only to the extent that they constitute expenses for a definite period after the balance sheet date. If the amount repayable for liabilities or loans is in excess of the original amount, the difference is shown as a special item under prepaid expenses subject to full amortisation over the outstanding period.

Current assets. Current assets are valued at the lower of cost and market value and may even be valued at less than this "to the extent that the lower valuation (1) is necessary in accordance with reasonable business judgement in order to prevent the valuation of the assets from being changed in the near future as a result of fluctuations of values or (2) is held permissible for purposes of taxation of income and yield". As in the case of fixed assets, the lower valuation may be retained even if that value is no longer applicable.

Inventories. The AG Law permits any basis of cost which is in accordance with proper accounting principles; the most common method is average cost since this is specifically allowed for tax purposes.

Inter-company accounts. Accounts receivable from and liabilities to group companies are required to be separately stated.

Capital. The aggregate nominal amount of each class of shares must be stated.

Reserves. AGs are obliged to set up a legal reserve by annual transfers of 5 per cent of the annual profit decreased by losses from previous years, until the reserve equals one-tenth of the share capital or a higher amount as laid down by the articles. Premiums on the issue of shares or convertible bonds must also be transferred to the legal reserve; this legal reserve may be used only as follows:

1. When it does not exceed 10 per cent of the capital or a higher proportion in accordance with the articles:
   (a) to compensate a loss for the year to the extent it is not covered by a profit carried forward from the previous year and cannot be compensated by a release of free reserves;

(b) to compensate a loss carried forward from a previous year to the extent it is not covered by a profit for the year and cannot be compensated by a release of free reserves.

2. When it exceeds the necessary proportion determined by (1) above, the surplus amount may be applied:
   (a) to compensate a loss for the year to the extent it is not covered by a profit carried forward from the previous year;
   (b) to compensate a loss carried forward from the previous year to the extent it is not covered by a profit for the year;
   (c) to an increase of the capital of the company by transfer (subject to specific conditions) from reserve.

Movements in all other disclosed reserves have to be specified and "reserve accounting" is not allowed. The law also states that any reserves which are taxed on being released must be stated separately under balance sheet item II.2. Provisions may be made only for imminent losses from uncompleted business in accordance with reasonable business judgement.

Liabilities. Liabilities are stated at the amount due on maturity apart from those of a long-term nature (four years or more) such as pensions provisions, which are discounted actuarially. Section 159 demands the disclosure by way of note of all pension payments made during the year as well as the anticipated payments in percentages of that amount for each of the following five years.

The following contingencies should be disclosed even when there are equivalent claims of recourse:

1. Liabilities from the negotiations and transfer of promissory notes and drafts.
2. Liabilities from sureties, and guarantees of promissory notes, drafts and cheques.
3. Liabilities from warranty contracts.
4. Liabilities from the granting of collateral security for another's liabilities. If the liability or responsibility exists towards group companies this fact must be disclosed and the amount stated.

The Profit and Loss Account

Generally companies are obliged to follow the layout of the profit and loss account as shown in Figs. 2.5 and 2.6. However, unquoted companies (1) with balance sheet totals not in excess of DM 3 million, or (2) which are family companies defined as those companies owned by a natural person or persons who are related or related by marriage, need not disclose the first five items shown in Fig. 2.5 subject to the proviso that this information is available to the shareholders.

Any change in the allocation of income or expenses from the previous year must be stated and quantified. Turnover is stated net of rebates and refunds. Any extraordinary or prior-year items are shown separately under "other incomes" or "other expenses".

Since income, profit and property taxes are grouped together, the tax charge on the income for the year is not normally apparent. Furthermore, the German split-rate system of taxation under which distributions are subject to a lower rate means that the reserves may have been set up before the amount of the distribution has been finally determined. Not surprisingly deferred tax accounting is seldom applied.

After receiving the auditors' report the board of management is required, without undue delay, to present its proposals for the appropriation of profit to the supervisory board in the following form:

1. *Verteilung an die Aktionäre* (distribution to the shareholders).
2. *Einstellung in offene Rücklagen* (transfer to disclosed reserves).
3. *Gewinnvortrag* (profit carried forward).
4. *Zusätzlicher Aufwand bei Beschlussfassung nach dem Vorschlag des Vorstands* (additional expense if the resolution is passed pursuant to the proposals of the board of management).
5. *Bilanzgewinn* (retained earnings).

The boards may determine the accounts or may leave this to the shareholders' meeting. In the case of the shareholders' meeting determining the annual financial statements, a maximum of 50 per cent of the profits for the year may be transferred to the free reserve (Item II.2) after the legal reserve requirement and any losses carried forward have been met. The shareholders have an absolute right to the retained earnings subject to any special provisions in the law or the articles and they may also make further appropriations from retained earnings to reserves. Otherwise the board of management and supervisory board may also transfer a similar amount to free reserve; the articles of association may authorise the management to transfer a greater amount to free reserve subject to the limitation that the free reserves cannot exceed more than 50 per cent of the share capital. Interim dividends are strictly forbidden but the board of management may make an interim payment on the basis of the preliminary annual accounts subject to a maximum of 50 per cent of the amount remaining after transfers required by law and the articles of association; moreover, any interim payment cannot exceed 50 per cent of the previous year's retained earnings and the consent of the supervisory board is necessary for all payments. Such payments are not common.

Publication and Filing of Financial Statements

The annual financial statements, the report of the executive managers, the report of the supervisory board and the appropriation proposals of all AG companies must be made available for inspection by shareholders at the premises of the company as from the date of calling the general meeting. The company has to give copies on request to each shareholder without undue delay. Within 12 days of calling the shareholders' meeting by announcement in the *Federal Gazette* (*Bundesanzeiger*) the board of management of every AG company publishes the agenda for the meeting. This communication normally including copies of the above documents must be sent to the following:

1. Banks holding shares on behalf of shareholders. The banks then distribute copies to each individual shareholder together with their voting proposals.
2. Other organisations exercising voting rights on behalf of shareholders.
3. Shareholders who have deposited a share with the company.
4. Registered shareholders.
5. Any shareholder who so requests.

The following have a statutory duty to file (for public inspection) their annual financial accounts, auditors' attestation and the report of the board of management and supervisory board with the Commercial Register "without undue delay" after the shareholders' meeting:

1. All AG companies.
2. All other "large enterprises". A large enterprise is defined as one which for three years at least two of the following criteria are met: balance sheet totals exceed DM 125 million; net sales exceed DM 250 million; more than 5000 persons have been employed on average during the year.

Partnerships and small traders are exempt from the rules to prepare and file an annual report by the executive managers and need not publish and file a profit and loss account provided the following minimum information is disclosed as an appendix to the balance sheet:

1. Net sales revenues.
2. Income from group companies.

3. Wages and salaries, including social and pension charges.
4. Valuation and depreciation methods and any material changes of bases.
5. Number of employees.

The accounts should include a copy of the shareholders' resolution on the appropriation of retained earnings containing at least the following details:

1. Retained earnings.
2. The amount to be distributed to the shareholders.
3. The amount to be transferred to disclosed reserves.
4. The profit carried forward.
5. The additional expense resulting from the resolution.

The accounts and the auditors' attestation are also published in the *Federal Gazette* and in any newspaper named in the articles of association; as well as this, a copy of the published financial statements is filed with the Commercial Register. The court is charged with supervision of the financial reporting regulations.

GmbH Companies

Proposals for the reform of the GmbH law being considered at the time of going to press would demand that larger GmbHs have their annual accounts audited and published. Small companies would be exempted while medium-sized companies would be permitted to follow less demanding publication rules.

Management Report

Section 160 of the AG Law specifically mentions that in every report of the management statements must be made regarding:

1. The holding of and additions to shares to which a shareholder acting for the account of the company or of a dependent enterprise or of an enterprise the majority of which the company holds, or to which a dependent enterprise or an enterprise the majority of which the company holds, have subscribed as founder or subscriber or by exercising a conversion or pre-emptive right granted at a conditional capital increase. If such shares were disposed of in the year, then the disposition shall also be reported by stating the proceeds and the application of the proceeds.

2. The holding of the company's own shares which it, or a dependent enterprise or an enterprise the majority of which the company holds, or

another person for the account of the company or of a dependent enterprise or of an enterprise the majority of which the company holds, have acquired or taken as a pledge. If such shares were acquired or disposed of in the year, there must also be reported the acquisition or disposal by stating the price of the acquisition or disposal and the application of the proceeds.

3. The existence of a mutual participation by stating the enterprise.

4. Shares which were issued in the year pursuant to a conditional capital increase.

5. The authorised capital.

6. Rights of usufruct, rights from bonus certificates and similar rights by stating those newly issued in the fiscal year.

7. Liabilities not evident from the annual balance sheet including the granting of security for its own liabilities.

8. The aggregate compensation (salaries, profit sharing, reimbursement of expenses, insurance premiums, commissions and fringe benefits of any kind) of the members of the board of management, of the supervisory board and of an advisory council or similar body, in each case separately by stating the individual body. The aggregate compensation also includes compensation which is not paid out but converted into claims of another nature or applied to the increase of other claims. Apart from the compensation for the fiscal year, there should be stated the additional compensation which was granted in the fiscal year but was not previously stated in any report of the management. If members of the board of management of the company receive compensation from connected enterprises for their services for the company or for their services as legal representatives or employees of the connected enterprises, then this compensation should be stated separately.

9. The aggregate compensation (indemnities, pensions, compensation to surviving dependants and consideration of similar nature) of former members of the board of management and their surviving dependants. No. 8 sentences 2 and 3 apply accordingly. If former members of the board of management of the company or their surviving dependants also receive indemnities or pensions from connected enterprises, then this compensation must be stated separately.

10. The legal and business relations to connected enterprises with domestic domicile, in addition statements regarding business events at these enterprises which may have a substantial influence on the company's situation.

11. The existence of a participation in the company which has been communicated to it; thereby must be stated to whom the participation

belongs and whether or not it exceeds one fourth of the aggregate shares of the association or constitutes the holding of a majority.

The report must also detail all members of the board of management and of the supervisory board, also those who retired in or after the end of the year, with the family name and at least one full Christian name. The chairman of the supervisory board, his deputies and, if applicable, the chairman of the board of management must be indicated as such.

Where consolidated accounts are prepared, Section 334 of the Aktiengesetz requires that all enterprises with domestic domicile belonging to the company must be listed individually. Separate mention must be made of domestic enterprises included in the consolidated accounts and detailed reasons should be given if domestic enterprises which are more than 50 per cent owned by the group are not consolidated. If the unconsolidated enterprises are AGs or GmbHs their individual accounts are required to be attached to the management report. The inclusion of enterprises domiciled outside Germany must be stated.

The management report of the group must deal with the course of the business and the situation of the group and that of the consolidated enterprises. If major losses have been incurred or are to be expected by any group company domestic or foreign, that fact must be disclosed. In addition to explaining the consolidated financial statements the management report must also contain statements on:

1. The causes and the nature of differences arising where the values at which the participations in the consolidated enterprises are stated higher or lower than the amounts of capital and disclosed reserves of the enterprises relating to the participation.
2. Liabilities not evident from the consolidated financial statements including the granting of security for liabilities of the enterprises included in consolidated financial statements.
3. The legal and business relation with enterprises with a domestic domicile which do not belong to the group but are connected with one of the group enterprises, as well as on business merits in their enterprises which may have a material influence upon the situation of the group.

When a company is dependent on another company, but a group relationship does not exist, the board of management of that company prepares a dependency report listing and explaining all relevant legal transactions during the year "in accordance with the principles of conscientious and faithful accounting". This report should also state that all business transactions between the companies were at "arm's length".

The supervisory board is obliged to report in writing on its work during the year, also giving its opinion of the result of the audit and stating at the end of the report whether or not it approves the annual financial statement as prepared by the board of management.

Stock Exchange Listing Requirements

Applications for a listing on a German stock exchange have to be submitted through a bank which is a member of the stock exchange concerned. Applications are generally handled by consortiums of the banks, the banks being responsible for the content of the prospectus which is necessary. Applications are submitted to the Listing Committee (*Zulassungsstelle*) of the stock exchange, and, for an application to succeed, the offer must be sufficiently large to create a real market; in the case of shares, there is a minimum of DM 500,000.

The prospectus should include the last annual or group accounts of the company made up to a date normally not more than 13 months earlier including the opinion paragraph of the auditors' report; if it is made up more than nine months previously, a statement of the latest position, which need not be audited, must be added.

Business Records

Section 38 of the 1861 *Handelsgesetzbuch* (Commercial Code) requires every businessman to keep books of accounts recording therein his business transactions and financial situation in accordance with proper accounting principles. The Commercial Code rules that proper bookkeeping implies among other principles: (1) up-to-date double-entry accounting records; (2) the maintenance of fixed asset records; (3) physical stock-taking; and (4) the preparation of annual accounts. Accounting records are subject to periodic scrutiny by tax officials who are entitled, if dissatisfied with the form or completeness of the books, to make estimated assessments. Any alterations or erasures in records are forbidden.

THE ACCOUNTANCY PROFESSION

The official history of the German accountancy profession dates from the introduction of statutory auditing by the Company Law of 1931. As a result the Institut der Wirtschaftsprüfer eV was established in 1932 incorporating the already existing Institut für das Revisions und Treuhandwesen eV. The first accounting firms emerged at the end of the nineteenth century and were staffed by recruits from the accounting and trustee departments of the banks.

The Institut der Wirtschaftsprüfer remained the sole professional organisation for *Wirtschaftsprüfer* with responsibility for the profession under the supervision of the Minister of Economy of the Reich until the establishment in 1943 for this purpose of the Reichskammer der Wirtschaftstreuhänder. In the immediate post-war period the profession operated on a provincial level up to 1951 when it was reformed into the present Institut der Wirtschaftsprüfer in Deutschland eV.

Wirtschaftsprüferkammer

Under a law dated 24 July 1961 (*Wirtschaftsprüferordnung*) the profession was reorganised and new professional rules were instituted. A new body, the Wirtschaftsprüferkammer (Chamber of Accountants), was established as the governing body of the profession under the supervision of the Federal Minister of Economy. Every *Wirtschaftsprüfer* (WP) has to be a member of the Kammer, whereas membership of the Institut is optional, although in fact almost all practising WPs belong. Both bodies share the same offices.

Also regulated by the 1961 Law is the *Steuerberater* (tax consultancy) profession and many WPs qualify as *Steuerberater* (StBs) in the course of their long training. The unification of the tax consultancy profession was agreed in 1973, as a result of which the *Steuerberater* and the *Steuerbevollmächtigte* (tax assistants) are to merge with effect from January 1975. StBs are organised on a regional basis and the regional chambers form the Bundessteuerberaterkammer (Federal Chamber of Tax Consultants). Under the 1961 law recruitment of other accountants known as *vereidigte Buchprüfer* (vBPs) was suspended and vBPs were given the choice of becoming members of the Wirtschaftsprüferkammer on passing an oral examination.

Apart from education and training, the Institut is primarily concerned with improving professional standards and in the period from 1951 to 1972 has issued no fewer than 267 recommendations (*Fachgutachten*) and opinions (*Stellungnahmen*) for the guidance of its members.

The pronouncements are generally intended for the guidance of members in the carrying out of audits. The Institut has not attempted to define accounting principles in the same way as the UK profession but has limited its efforts to the interpretation of the rather comprehensive accounting regulations set out in the legislation.

TABLE 2.4. THE LEADING NINE GERMAN AG ACCOUNTING FIRMS BASED ON TURNOVER FOR THE YEAR 1972

	Turnover in DM '000	*International associate*
1 Treuarbeit AG,[1] Berlin/Bonn	86,021	Interfides
2 Vereinigte Deutsche Treuhandgesellschaft AG, Berlin	43,224[2]	Turquands Barton Mayhew & Co.
3 Schitag, Schwabische Treuhand-AG, Stuttgart	28,150	
4 Wibera Wirtschaftsberatung AG, Düsseldorf	26,559	
5 Treuhand-Vereinigung AG, Frankfurt	21,950	Coopers & Lybrand
6 Treuverkehr AG, Frankfurt	18,046	Touche Ross & Co.
7 Deutsche Warentreuhand AG, Hamburg	13,238	Binder Dijker Otte
8 Süddeutsche Treuhand-Gesellschaft AG, Munich	10,378	Chalmers Impey & Co.
9 Datag Deutsche Allgemeine Treuhand AG, Munich	7,567	

1. To all the names of these firms, the words *Wirtschaftsprufungsgesellschaft* (auditing company), *Steuerberatungsgesellschaft* (tax-consultation company) should be added.
2. In the second half of 1972 Vereinigte Deutsche Treuhandgesellschaft AG took over four other accounting firms. The turnover of these four firms is included in the figure of DM 43,224,000 for a shorter period than a year, because their financial years ended at 30 June and 31 March respectively. The combined turnover amounted to DM 48,382,000 for 1971. For 1972 a 13 per cent increase in turnover on average was reported.

Wirtschaftsprüfer may practise in any business form and almost all of the larger firms are AGs, which means that members of the board of management must be WPs or StBs. The shares of WP–AG companies must be registered and cannot be listed on a stock exchange. WP–GmbH companies must have a minimum capital of DM 500,000. Members may be employed only by other members or by WP firms. On accepting employment outside the profession, a member ceases to be a *Wirtschaftsprüfer*. WPs are permitted to practise in association with other professionals such as *Steuerberater* and lawyers. Following the general trend of German business, accountancy firms tend to concentrate in regions as can be seen from Table 2.4. In common with other main European countries, the leading German firms tend to grow constantly larger. As well as this, almost all of these firms have international links. Apart from those referred to in the table the following large firms which are not organised in AG form are considered to be among the leading 10 German accounting firms: Karoli-Wirtschaftsprüfung GmbH, Essen (associated with McLintock Main Lafrentz & Co.); Kontinentale Treuhand-Gesellschaft GmbH, Düsseldorf (associated with Arthur Young & Co.); Dr Wollert–Dr Elmendorff KG, Düsseldorf (associated with Deloitte, Haskins & Sells); Dr HcH Rätsch, Düsseldorf.

One of the most striking features of the German accountancy profession is the fact that the practising firms need not be owned by WPs. Indeed, the largest firm, Treuarbeit AG, is 100 per cent owned by the Federal and State Governments and Wibera AG is 100 per cent owned by communal organisations. Furthermore, banks have retained links with many accounting firms and hold the majority in Schitag, Süddeutsche Treuhand–Gesellschaft AG, and Datag. A 25 per cent share of the capital of Deutsche Warentreuhand AG is held by a bank and a few banks have a small holding in Vereinigte Deutsche Treuhandgesellschaft AG.

The profession is still very small (Table 2.5) by UK standards, and it is significant that negotiations have been entered into with the tax-consultancy profession whereby experienced tax consultants will be allowed to join the accountancy profession under certain conditions before 1979.

The admission of foreign accountants to practise in Germany is subject to authorisation by the Kammer and must be announced to the profession. Several international accountancy firms are members of the Kammer. Generally foreign accountants prefer association arrangements with German WP firms, in which case the German firm has to ensure that the foreign accountants meet the necessary requirements. Reciprocity for such co-operation must be guaranteed.

Education and Training

The education and training requirements for *Wirtschaftsprüfer* are probably more arduous (Fig. 2.7) than those for accountants in any other country. This factor has no doubt affected recruitment, since the WP qualifies on average between the ages of 30 and 35. In view of this, it is hardly surprising that the German accountancy profession enjoys a very high status, ranking as one of the so-called "legally bound liberal professions" on a par with, for instance, lawyers and notaries.

On the way to qualification, it is normal for prospective WPs to pick up one, two or even three other qualifications—some 60 per cent of *Wirtschaftsprüfer* are also *Steuerberater* and a few actually possess a super-qualification of accountant, tax consultant, lawyer and notary.

TABLE 2.5. MEMBERSHIP OF THE GERMAN ACCOUNTANCY PROFESSION (as at 1 April 1973)

1 Wirtschaftsprüfer		
Sole practitioners		1,431
Wirtschafteprüfergesellschaften		
Principals	400	
Employees	891	
	—	1,291
Steuerberätergesellschaften		
Principals	36	
Employees	—	
	—	36
Co-operative auditing associations		
Principals	28	
Employees	55	
	—	83
		2,841
Qualifications of WPs		
Wirtschaftsprüfer		1,080
Wirtschaftsprüfer/Lawyer		50
Wirtschaftsprüfer/Steuerberäter		1,654
Wirtschaftsprüfer/Steuerberäter/Lawyer		57
		2,841
Number of firms		
Head offices		354
Branch offices		217
		571
2 Vereidigte Buchprüfer		
Sole practitioners		282
Buchprüfergesellschaften		
Principals	1	
Employees	–	
	—	1
Wirtschaftsprüfergesellschaften		
Principals	2	
Employees	4	
	—	6
Steuerberätergesellschaften		
Principals	3	
Employees	–	
	—	3
		292
Qualifications of vBPs		
Vereidigte Buchprüfer		148
Vereidigte Buchprüfer/Steuerberäter		144
		292

Source: WP Yearbook, 1973.

Elementary school (*Grundschule*)
(age 6—10 years)

↓

Gymnasium
(9 years)

↓

University degree course
(4 years)

↓

Practical experience
(6 years : 4 in the profession)

↓

Professional examination
(oral and written plus a thesis)

↓

Entry to the profession

Fig. 2.7 The way to become a German *Wirstchaftsprüfer*

Prospective entrants to the profession must satisfy the following conditions:

1. Be of German nationality or a national of another country granting reciprocity.
2. Hold a degree from a German university (or its foreign equivalent) in Business, Economics, Law, Engineering or Agriculture, or, alternatively, have completed 10 years' experience with a *Wirtschaftsprüfer*, but this is unusual. In fact approximately 75 per cent of entrants hold degrees in Business and 25 per cent in Economics or Law.
3. Have completed six years of business experience, at least four of which have to be spent in the office of a *Wirtschaftsprüfer* or the equivalent foreign experience.
4. Have successfully completed the professional examination.

The professional examination is in two separate written and oral sections. The written section comprises three unseen papers and a thesis on the technical subject (*Hausarbeit*) for which the candidate is given eight weeks to complete. The unseen papers cover Mercantile Law, Tax Law, Business Economics, Auditing, Accounting and Professional Ethics. It is expected that the *Hausarbeit* will be dropped in the near future, with the result that the candidate will have to sit for six unseen papers.

The *Wirtschaftsprüfer* is publicly appointed and sworn in by the supreme official of the Ministry of Economics of the *Land* concerned. At the time of his public appointment, the *Wirtschaftsprüfer* has to swear the following professional oath:

> I swear to almighty God that I will responsibly and carefully execute the duties of a *Wirtschaftsprüfer*; particularly I will observe the duty of secrecy and I will conscientiously and impartially give audit reports and opinions. So God may help me.

When executing his specific tasks the *Wirtschaftsprüfer* is entitled and obliged to use an official seal similar to that used by a notary.

Ethics

The *Wirtschaftsprüfer* profession is bound by the following ethical standards:

1. Clients' affairs must be kept secret.
2. Advertising and the solicitation of clients is prohibited.

3. A WP must refuse to accept any appointment which might prejudice his independence or impartiality. This principle does not apply in the case of consultancy services and the representation of clients' affairs in taxation matters; however, a WP cannot prepare and audit the same accounts.
4. The practice of incompatible occupations is prohibited but consultancy services, teaching and freelance writing are stated to be compatible.
5. Each WP must be insured against possible risk arising from his professional activities to a minimum of DM 500,000 for each single case of damage.

Services Provided

Wirtschaftsprüfer are principally auditors normally looking after clients' tax affairs at the same time. At present their monopoly of auditing is limited to statutory audits, but, although non-WPs can carry out other audits, these also tend to be the province of WPs. In addition, *Wirtschaftsprüfer* are qualified to act in the consultation and representation of clients in tax matters, including representation before the financial courts. Members of the profession may also act as trustees. Management consultancy services are offered by practically all accounting firms in Germany.

AUDITING

German auditing standards are generally considered to be as high as any in the world and, as leading German accountants point out, procedure has been substantially influenced by international and particularly US practice since the last war. The 1965 AG Law dropped an unused clause in the 1937 law which gave the Minister of Economics power to issue auditing rules and the accountancy profession was encouraged to codify its own standards. This the Institut did on 15 March 1967 by issuing comprehensive "guidelines for the execution of a regular examination" which the Kammer has decreed cannot be departed from without due cause.

Appointment of Auditors

Each enterprise required to prepare and file annual accounts (*see* page 65) must also appoint a statutory auditor who may only be a *Wirtschaftsprüfer* or *Wirtschaftsprüfergesellschaft*. As already mentioned, the proposed reform of the GmbH law will probably demand statutory audits for at least the majority of GmbH companies. The first statutory auditor is appointed by the supervisory board, but thereafter he is reappointed on an annual basis by the shareholders.

On the application of shareholders holding at least one-tenth of the share capital or a nominal amount of DM 2 million the court must replace an auditor after hearing all the parties concerned if this appears to be necessary, especially if there is a danger of partiality.

Under the AG Law an auditor may in certain conditions be engaged by the court to examine events leading to the formation of an AG or certain transactions in connection with the formation or management of a company, notably when capital is contributed in kind. Such auditors need only be adequately trained and experienced in book-keeping.

Duties of Auditors

The auditor is obliged to examine the annual financial statements including the book-keeping and the financial section of the management report. The audit extends to the specific items in the management report and to the complete report which must not "create a misconception of the situation of the company". Under Section 176 (2) of the AG Law an auditor must attend the annual general meeting and give explanations to members if the accounts need the approval of the members as the result of a difference of opinion between the supervisory board and the executive managers. If the financial statements are altered by the board and audit reports have been given, they must be re-examined and any previous attestation becomes ineffective. The Institut pronouncement points out that the foremost objective of an audit is to determine that the accounts "have been prepared in accordance with the law and proper accounting principles".

The Auditors' Report

The German auditor must report to the supervisory board, stating in particular whether or not the "book-keeping, annual financial statements and the report of the management to the extent that it explains the annual financial statement are in accordance with the legal provisions" and whether or not the board of executive managers have provided the necessary explanations and evidence (AG Law, Section 166.1). The auditor must further specify any facts in this report which "endanger the existence of the company or which may substantially affect its development, or which make apparent significant violations of the law or of the articles of association by the board of executive managers" (Section 166.2). This report is signed and submitted to the board of executive managers which should in turn submit it, together with the annual financial statement and the management report, to the supervisory board without undue delay. The report is in most cases a lengthy document; its contents are as follows:

Main section	Engagement and performance.
	Legal situation of the company.
	Financial position.
	Classification and valuation.
	Financial analysis.
	Major items of balance sheet.
	Earnings position.
	Book-keeping.
	Management report.
	Final remarks and attestation.
Appendix	Comments to the individual items of the balance sheet.
	Comments on the individual items of the profit and loss statement.
Schedules	Balance sheet.
	Profit and loss statement.
	Auditors' General Terms.

The wording of the so-called attestation or short form of report—the only part of the auditors' report which is published with the annual accounts—is laid down in Section 167 of the AG Law: "The book-keeping, the annual financial statement and the report of the management accord with the law and the articles of association on the basis of my (our) dutiful examination." If the auditor has objections he can qualify or refuse the attestation. Since the accounts cannot be approved without the auditors' report the threat of refusing or qualifying a report is a strong weapon. The most common qualifications are believed to relate to the valuation of assets.

The auditor may be called upon to give two further reports. When consolidated accounts are prepared, the following attestation is necessary: "The consolidated financial statements and the report of the management for the group are in accordance with the legal provisions on the basis of my (our) dutiful examination."

The content of the second report, required when a dependency report has been prepared by the board of management, is prescribed thus:

> On the basis of my (our) dutiful examination and judgement I (we) confirm that:
>
> 1. the factual statements of the report are correct;

2. the consideration of the company for the legal transactions stated in the report was not inadequately high;
3. the measures stated in the report must not be judged pursuant to the circumstances to be essentially different from the opinion expressed by the board of management.

A standard form of auditors' contract entitled the "Auditor's General Terms" has been published by the Institut. As mentioned above, the auditor normally sends a copy of this to his clients together with his audit report. The following is the complete text of the recommended terms:

Auditor's general terms
for *Wirtschaftsprüfer* and *Wirtschaftsprüfungsgesellschaften* (auditors and auditing companies)
18 October 1971

1. *Scope and application*

(1) These terms are applicable to agreements between *Wirtschaftsprüfer* or *Wirtschaftsprüfungsgesellschaften* (hereafter uniformly referred to as "Wirtschaftsprüfer") and their clients concerning audits, advisory work and any other services, as far as these terms are not excluded by special written agreements or non-discretionary legal provisions.

(2) If, in exceptional cases, contractual relations also exist between the *Wirtschaftsprüfer* and a third party, the provisions of Section 9 below are likewise applicable for the relations with such third party.

2. *Scope and execution of engagement*

(1) The *Wirtschaftsprüfer*'s obligations under the engagement include only the performance of agreed services but not the achievement of success.

(2) The engagement does not extend to an investigation into due adherence to tax laws or other special provisions, *e.g.* to laws of price control, laws of limitation of competition and other controls, unless such is the nature of the engagement or unless this has otherwise been agreed in writing. The execution of an engagement in accordance with generally accepted professional standards does not include the application of auditing procedures aimed at the disclosure of bookkeeping frauds and other irregularities unless this has been expressly agreed in writing.

(3) The engagement is executed in accordance with generally accepted professional standards.

(4) The *Wirtschaftsprüfer* is entitled to use qualified assistants for the execution of his engagement.

3. *Information to be given by the client*

(1) The client has the responsibility, even without specific request on the part of the *Wirtschaftsprüfer*, of furnishing him in due time with all the

documentary evidence necessary for the execution of the engagement and of informing him of all events and circumstances which may have a bearing on the execution of the engagement. This also applies to any evidence, events and circumstances which come to light during the course of the *Wirtschaftsprüfer*'s work.

(2) Upon request of the *Wirtschaftsprüfer*, the client is obliged to confirm in a written statement drafted by the *Wirtschaftsprüfer* that the evidence information, and explanations provided by him are complete.

4. *Safeguard of independence*
The client undertakes to ensure that no action is committed which might endanger the independence of the *Wirtschaftsprüfer*'s staff. This applies especially to offers for employment and offers to perform professional work on the staff member's own account.

5. *Reporting and oral information*
If the *Wirtschaftsprüfer* summarizes the results of his work in a written report, oral explanations, given either by himself or by his staff, are not binding. In the case of an audit the report is, unless otherwise agreed, submitted in writing. Oral explanations and information given by the staff of the *Wirtschaftsprüfer* outside the scope of the engagement are never binding.

6. *Protection of the Wirtschaftsprüfer's interests*
The client undertakes to prevent the use of opinions, organization plans, drafts, sketches, tabulations and calculations, particularly quantity and cost computations, produced by the *Wirtschaftsprüfer* within the scope of the engagement, for purposes other than his own.

7. *Release of a Wirtschaftsprüfer's professional statements to third parties*
The release to third parties of professional statements made by the *Wirtschaftsprüfer* (reports, opinions, etc.) requires the *Wirtschaftsprüfer*'s written consent, unless the terms of the engagement allow release thereof to a designated person.

8. *Correction of deficiencies*
(1) The client is entitled to have any deficiencies in the *Wirtschaftsprüfer*'s work corrected. Claims for refund or reduction of fees as well as claims for refund of expenses incurred in the effort of achieving adequate performance are not allowed. Claims for additional compensation are dealt with under Section 9.

(2) The client is obliged to submit his claim for correction of deficiencies in writing without delay. The claim expires six months after the *Wirtschaftsprüfer*'s submission of the statement to which the client takes exception or—if no statements have been made in writing—six months after the completion of the *Wirtschaftsprüfer*'s work to which the client takes exception.

(3) Obvious errors, such as typing and arithmetical errors and deficiencies of form contained in a *Wirtschaftsprüfer*'s professional statements (report,

opinion, etc.), may be corrected by the *Wirtschaftsprüfer* any time with effect not only against the client but against any other person as well. Errors which are apt to question the conclusions to be drawn from the *Wirtschaftsprüfer*'s professional statements, entitle the *Wirtschaftsprüfer* to withdraw such statements with effect not only against the client but against any other person as well. In such cases the *Wirtschaftsprüfer* should, if practicable, contact the client before taking any action.

9. *Liability*

(1) The extent of the *Wirtschaftsprüfer*'s liability is, unless the law provides for a larger or smaller amount, limited to DM 500,000 for each single case of damages; this also applies to the exceptional cases where a *Wirtschaftsprüfer* may be held liable by persons other than the client. A single case of damages is defined as the sum total of the damage claims of all persons entitled to claim which arise from one and the same offence; a single case of damages is also defined as the total of all offences committed in performing an audit or other coherent service (a specifiable professional service which technically represents an undivisible performance) by a single person or by several persons. However, in case of damages suffered from several offences brought about by the same technical error within the scope of several audits of the same kind or several coherent services of similar nature a *Wirtschaftsprüfer* can be held liable only up to an amount of DM 2.5 million without regard to whether the damages were caused by offences committed within one year or within several consecutive years.

(2) A *Wirtschaftsprüfer* cannot be held liable for infringement or non-observance of foreign law unless the engagement is concerned with an audit or a special investigation.

(3) If the client has been informed that the work is being carried out with the aid of a sub-contractor, *e.g.* a data-processing firm, it is understood that all and any warranty and damage claims against the sub-contractor, whether arising under the applicable law or the sub-contractor's engagement terms, are deemed to have been transferred to the client. The *Wirtschaftsprüfer* can be held responsible only for negligence in selecting the sub-contractor.

(4) Unless statutory limitations provide for an earlier date of expiration, a claim for damages can only be lodged within six months after the damage and the event giving rise to has come to the knowledge of the person entitled to the claim, but in no case later than five years after the event which gave rise to the claim. The claim expires unless legal action is taken within six months after the claim for damages has been rejected in writing. Special statutory provisions, if any, governing the limitation periods resulting for statutory audits continue to apply.

(5) In regard to persons other than the client, the *Wirtschaftsprüfer* may be held liable only if he had consented in writing to the release of his professional statements (reports, opinions, etc.) to such other persons.

10. *Supplementary provisions relating to audits*

(1) The provisions and principles applicable to statutory audits apply to voluntary audits *mutatis mutandis*, with the proviso that the auditor's certificate shall be worded so as to comply with the professional reporting standards applicable to the particular type of business.

(2) The client is entitled to five copies of the report. Additional copies are charged for separately.

(3) A subsequent amendment or abridgement of the audited and certified financial statements or management report requires the written consent of the *Wirtschaftsprüfer* even if these documents are not published. In cases where the *Wirtschaftsprüfer* has not issued an audit certificate, reference in the management report or other publications to the *Witschaftsprüfer*'s examination must not be made without his written consent and then only in a wording authorized by him.

(4) If the *Wirtschaftsprüfer* withdraws his certificate, it must no longer be used.

11. *Supplementary provisions relating to tax advisory work*

(1) When advising the client on a particular problem of taxation or when furnishing continuous tax advice, the *Wirtschaftsprüfer* is entitled to assume that all facts, especially figures provided by the client, are correct. He is, however, obliged to inform the client of errors discovered by him.

(2) The client is obliged to supply the *Wirtschaftsprüfer* with all documents essential for meeting deadlines, especially with tax assessments, sufficiently early for the *Wirtschaftsprüfer* to give them adequate treatment.

(3) In the absence of other written agreements, a continuous tax advice engagement covers the following work arising during the period of the agreement:

(a) Drafting of the annual income, corporation and trade tax returns as well as property tax returns on the basis of financial statements and other records and evidence required for tax purposes, as submitted by the client.
(b) Review of assessments concerning the taxes mentioned in (a).
(c) Negotiations with the tax authorities in regard to the returns and assessments mentioned in (a) and (b).
(d) Participation in tax audits and evaluation of the results of tax audits concerning the taxes mentioned in (a).
(e) Participation in protests and complaints filed with the Inland Revenue Office ("Einspruchsverfahren" and "Beschwerdeverfahren"), concerning the taxes mentioned in (a).

In cases where the *Wirtschaftsprüfer* receives a global consideration for continuous advice, the work mentioned in (d) and (e) will be charged for separately unless otherwise agreed in writing.

(4) A special agreement is required to engage the *Wirtschaftsprüfer*'s service for the treatment of particular problems in regard to income, corporation, and trade tax, the valuation procedures for property taxation, the property

tax proper, as well as any problems concerning turnover tax, wages tax and any other taxes and dues. This applies to:

(a) The treatment of non-recurring tax matters, *e.g.* in the field of estate tax, capital transactions tax, real estate acquisition tax.
(b) Participation and representation in proceedings before tax and administrative courts and in criminal proceedings concerning taxes.
(c) Granting of advice and expert opinions in connection with changes in legal status, mergers, capital increases and reductions, financial reorganizations, admission and retirement of partners or shareholders, sale of businesses, liquidations, etc.

(5) If, in addition to the above, the *Wirtschaftsprüfer* is requested to prepare the annual turnover tax return, he is not obliged to control adherence to special accounting requirements, if any, or to determine whether the client has taken full advantage of all benefits offered under the turnover tax law. No guarantee is assumed that the evidence compiled in substantiation of the credit against the client's turnover tax liability for his suppliers' turnover tax charges is complete.

12. *Professional discretion towards third parties*

(1) The *Wirtschaftsprüfer* is, as provided by law, obliged to treat all matters which come to his knowledge as a result of his engagement as confidential irrespective of whether these matters concern the client himself or his business connections, unless the client discharges him of this obligation.

(2) The *Wirtschaftsprüfer* is not allowed to release reports, opinions, and other written statements concerning the results of his work to third parties without the consent of his client.

13. *Termination of engagement*

In the absence of other written agreements or non-discretionary legal provisions, the termination of the agreement is subject to the following rules:

(1) Either party may terminate the agreement by notice at any time. A permanent engagement against a global consideration can, failing an important cause, be terminated only at 3 months' prior notice as of the end of a month.

(2) (a) If the client terminates the agreement without important cause, the *Wirtschaftsprüfer* is entitled to the full fee as determined either by specific agreement or by custom reduced, however, by the amount of expenses actually saved by the termination of the agreement; the *Wirtschaftsprüfer* need not allow a reduction of his fees for the amount of income he has earned, or has refrained from earning, by use of his and his staff's professional skill under other engagements.
(b) If the client terminates the agreement for important cause other than violation of the agreement by the *Wirtschaftsprüfer*, the *Wirtschaftsprüfer* is entitled to that portion of his fee which is the equivalent consideration for the services rendered by him prior to termination.

(c) If the client terminates the agreement for important cause arising from the *Wirtschaftsprüfer*'s violation of the agreement, the *Wirtschaftsprüfer* is not entitled to a fee to the extent that the services rendered by him are, as a result of the termination, of no interest to the client; Section 9 is applicable to the claiming of damages by the client.

(3) (a) If the *Wirstschaftsprüfer* terminates the agreement without important cause, he is entitled to that portion of his fee which is the equivalent consideration for the services rendered by him prior to termination unless these services are, as a result of the termination, of no interest to the client. If the termination of the agreement by the *Wirtschafts-prüfer* is untimely, he is obliged to compensate the client for the resulting damage in accordance with Section 9.

(b) If the *Wirtschaftsprüfer* terminates the agreement for important cause, and if the client is responsible for such cause, paragraph (2) (a) shall apply accordingly. In all other cases of termination by the *Wirtschaftsprüfer* for important cause, paragraph (3) (a), 1st sentence, shall apply accordingly; this does not affect the *Wirt-schaftsprüfer*'s rights, if any, for additional damages.

14. *Default of acceptance and lack of co-operation on the part of the client*

If the client is in default of accepting the services offered by the *Wirtschafts-prüfer* or if the client refrains from the co-operation incumbent on him in accordance with Section 3 or otherwise, the *Wirtschaftsprüfer* is entitled to terminate the agreement without notice. His rights are governed by Section 13, paragraph (2) (a) above. The right of the *Wirtschaftsprüfer* for compensation of additional expenses and damages caused by default or by the client's refraining from co-operation continues to hold, even if the *Wirtschaftsprüfer* does not exercise his right to terminate the agreement.

15. *Sundry*

(1) In addition to his fees or remuneration, the *Wirtschaftsprüfer* is entitled to reimbursement of his expenses. He may request adequate advances on account of his remuneration and expenses and may withhold the results of his services until full payment of his claims has been made.

(2) Exceptions taken to the work of the *Wirtschaftsprüfer* do not entitle the client to withhold payment of fees and disbursements. The *Wirtschaftsprüfer*'s claims must not be set off against other amounts.

(3) After settlement of his claims emanating from the engagement, the *Wirtschaftsprüfer*, on request of the client, is obliged to return all documents received from the client or from a third party on his behalf by reason of his engagement. This does, however, not apply to correspondence exchanged between the *Wirtschaftsprüfer* and his client or to any documents which the client has on his files or of which he has obtained a copy. The *Wirtschaftsprüfer*

is entitled to prepare and retain on his files copies or photostatic copies of any documents which he returns to the client.

(4) The *Wirtschaftsprüfer* shall, for a period of seven years, retain the documents submitted to him or prepared by himself in connection with the engagement as well as copies of his correspondence concerning the engagement.

16. *Applicable law and court of competent jurisdiction*

(1) The engagement of the *Wirschaftsprüfer*, the execution thereof and the resulting claims are solely governed by German law.

(2) The court of competent jurisdiction is determined by the place of the *Wirtschaftsprüfer*'s German professional domicile at the time legal action is brought against him, and failing such German professional domicile at the time being, by the place of the last German professional domicile maintained prior to the time legal action is brought against him.

Fieldwork

Section 165 of the AG Law asserts that the auditor is permitted "to examine the books and records of the company as well as the assets, especially the company's cash on hand and the inventory of securities and merchandise". The auditor may demand all explanations and evidence "necessary for a diligent examination" from the board of management, besides having similar rights towards any group or dependent or dominating enterprise.

The Institut "guidelines" stress the importance of an evaluation of the system of internal control, and most German auditors give this considerable attention in their audits. The Institut remains undecided about the necessity for a physical inventory and only advises that, as well as carrying out a normal examination of the inventory, the auditor "must also investigate the planning and performance of the employees taking the physical inventory". However, the practice is gaining ground.

On the question of independent confirmations the Institut emphasises that "it is the duty of the auditor to obtain proper evidence by confirmation from the custodians if such assets have not been physically counted by the enterprise being audited." As far as it appears necessary to verify accounts receivable and payable, the "guidelines" maintain that "confirmation of account balances must be resorted to". At present, however, with the exception of the leading firms it is not general practice to obtain confirmation for receivables, payables or bank balances.

The auditor should plan the audit by dividing "the accounting to be audited into areas, and he may also shift the emphasis on certain details to be audited from year to year". However, the Institut also emphasises that an examination of the system of internal control is of paramount importance and this, except for small enterprises, has replaced the previous detailed tests. The WP should provide adequate supervision on an audit; the *Wirtschaftsprüferordnung* actually stipulates that the ratio of WPs to non-WPs cannot exceed 1 to 5.

Remuneration of Auditors

An auditor is entitled to a fee for his services and a refund of all his expenses. These are normally based on time spent or on a combination of time spent and balance sheet totals. A scale of fees in accordance with Section 55 of the *Wirtschaftsprüferordnung* has recently been promulgated but has been prohibited by the cartel authorities (*Bundeskartellamt*).

Removal of Auditors

An auditor may be reappointed from year to year at the annual general meeting and he may be removed in the manner already described, namely, by shareholders representing 10 per cent of the share capital or a minimum nominal amount of DM 2 million.

Liability of Auditors

As can be seen from the "Auditor's General Terms" it is customary for an auditor to limit his liability to DM 500,000 in each single case of damages—the same amount for which he is compelled to hold liability insurance. In the case of several offences ("Auditor's General Terms", No. 9) the liability is limited to DM 2.5 million. Accordingly insurance cover is generally increased to between DM 1 million and DM 2 million. Under the AG Law the auditor is liable to pay compensation not exceeding DM 500,000 per audit when either himself or his assistants have wilfully or otherwise neglected their duties. An auditor cannot easily be held liable for damages to third parties. All claims are statutorily barred after five years. Liability under criminal law arises when anyone who is an auditor or an auditor's assistant (1) makes a false report of the results of an audit or conceals important facts in his report (such a person is liable to imprisonment for up to three years and/or a fine); (2) without authority reveals a secret, particularly a business or trade secret, of which he has been apprised in his professional capacity (in which case he is liable to imprisonment for up to one year and/or a fine).

Independence of Auditors

Apart from the ethical regulations the AG Law stipulates that:

1. A *Wirtschaftsprüfer* may not become an auditor:
   (a) if he is or was in the last three years before his appointment a member of the board of executive managers or supervisory board or an employee of the company to be examined;
   (b) if he is a legal representative or a member of the supervisory board of a legal entity, partner of a partnership or owner enterprise if the legal entity, the partnership or the single trader is connected with the company to be examined;
   (c) if he is an employee of an enterprise which is connected with the company to be examined.
2. A firm of *Wirtschaftsprüfer* may not become an auditor:
   (a) if it, or an enterprise connected with it, is connected with the company to be examined;
   (b) if a legal representative of the company of *Wirtschaftsprüfer* which is a legal entity or partner of other firm of *Wirtschaftsprüfer* could not become an auditor pursuant to (1) above;
   (c) if a member of the supervisory board of the association of *Wirtschaftsprüfer* could not become an auditor pursuant to (1) (a) above.

CONCLUSION

The quality of German accounting must be measured against the considerable handicap imposed by the legal prescription of accounting rules and the provisions of tax law—a situation in which "true and fair view" accounting hardly flourishes.

On the other hand, the German accounting profession is one of the most highly qualified in Europe.

REFERENCES

1. This group comprises every bank (except the "Big Three") incorporated as an *Aktiengesellschaft* (limited liability company), a *Kommanditgesellschaft auf Aktien* (limited partnership with shares) or a *Gesellschaft mit beschränkter Haftung* (private limited liability company).
2. While no statistics are available for shares, an indication of the extent to which securities are deposited with the banks may be had from a survey by the Deutsche Bundesbank of all fixed-interest securities of domestic and

foreign borrowers in circulation at end 1970–71 within the Federal Republic and West Berlin. The survey found that out of an aggregate nominal value of DM 204 billion, some DM 100 billion were in customers' safe-custody accounts with the commercial banks.

3. The draft reform of the GmbH Law proposes to raise the minimum capital of the GmbH to DM 50,000, 50 per cent of which must be paid up on formation.
4. In the coal, iron and steel industries the employees have the right to nominate one member of the board of management.
5. "Large enterprises" are defined on page 65.
6. Rudolf J. Niehus, "Generally accepted accounting principles in Germany and the consistency and accruals concepts" *Journal UEC*, July 1973, pages 214–222.

Chapter 3

The Netherlands

BACKGROUND

The Netherlands alone among all the founder members of the European Community stands out as a nation of free enterprise with conventions and institutions very similar to those of the United Kingdom and where industry and the financial bodies are largely self-governing. As a trading and seafaring nation the Dutch have always had a strong tradition in banking and international finance: indeed, Amsterdam was the financial centre of Europe until London assumed this role after the Napoleonic era. The Amsterdam Wissel Bank, founded in 1609, is one of the oldest in the world, while the Dutch East India Company, founded in 1602, was the first-ever company to issue shares to the public.

Since the Second World War, the Netherlands has pursued a policy of industrial expansion and some 40 per cent of national income now comes from industry. The Dutch are highly dependent on international trade and exports represent over 50 per cent of GNP. The balance of payments has been mostly in surplus and the guilder remains one of the strongest currencies in the world.

Foreign investment in the Netherlands has always been high and the recent fall-off in US interest has been countered by increasing UK and Japanese investment. The Amsterdam Stock Exchange possesses particular attractions for UK companies seeking a base for Continental operations, but on a broader scale the ASE ranks as one of the most prestigious stock exchanges in the world. In view of the Dutch preference for bearer securities, virtually all foreign equities are in the form of CDRs (Continental Depository Receipts), thereby avoiding the necessity to register individual shares.[1]

The private loan sector is the principal source of industrial finance (Table 3.1), and companies tend to use the commercial banks as intermediaries for placing debt, usually between 15 and 25 years, with the institutions.[2] The banks are principally providers of short- and medium-term credit, and, although their equity participations are limited to 5 per cent, Dutch bankers normally hold non-executive board appointments.

TABLE 3.1. SUPPLY AND DEMAND ON THE CAPITAL MARKET
(in Fl millions)

	1961	*1966*	*1971*
Net supply			
Domestic	*4,519*	*7,316*	*14,261*
Foreign	*580*	*173*	*1,584*
of which:			
Shares }	1,605	1,614	1,345
Bonds and mortgage bank loans }			3,016
Private loans	2,460	3,864	8,313
Mortgage loans	826	1,515	2,105
Real property	208	496	1,066
Total	**5,099**	**7,489**	**15,845**
Net demand			
Domestic	*4,202*	*7,627*	*14,437*
Foreign	*897*	*−138*	*1,408*
Total	**5,099**	**7,489**	**15,845**

Source: De Nederlandsche Bank NV, Report for the year 1972.

The Stock Exchange, dominated by the five multinationals—Royal Dutch, Unilever, Philips, AKZO and Hoogovens (now merged with Hoesch)—which represent some 50 per cent of total capitalisation, is not an effective vehicle for new issues (Table 3.2). The Dutch prefer bonds, which because of the tax deductibility of interest have higher yields than shares, and the institutions, reflecting the lack of choice in domestic shares, have been turning to foreign equities and property investment. Of greater

TABLE 3.2. PUBLIC NEW ISSUES
(in Fl millions)[1]

	1956	*1961*	*1966*	*1971*	*1972*
Bonds	**777**	**1,528**	**2,153**	**3,606**	**3,307**
Central government	396	643	448	1,191	549
Local authorities and Bank for Netherlands Municipalities	233	258	834	924	1,095
Private and public enterprises	142	80	804	1,043	1,343
Churches and charities	5	11	67	268	270
Parties abroad	—	537	—	179	50
Shares	**146**	**134**	**8**	**74**	**62**
Total issues	**922**	**1,662**	**2,161**	**3,680**	**3,369**

1. Differences due to rounding.

Source: Amro Bank Economic Quarterly Review.

importance to the equity market, however, is the widespread apprehension felt at the power of the unions. Against a background of rapidly changing national social priorities and a Government committed to the redistribution of wealth, wage costs have escalated and profits have fallen (Fig. 3.1).

Since 1950 the Netherlands has had a social and economic council (SER) consisting of representatives from labour, industry and Government which plays a leading role in national economic affairs. In 1970 the SER

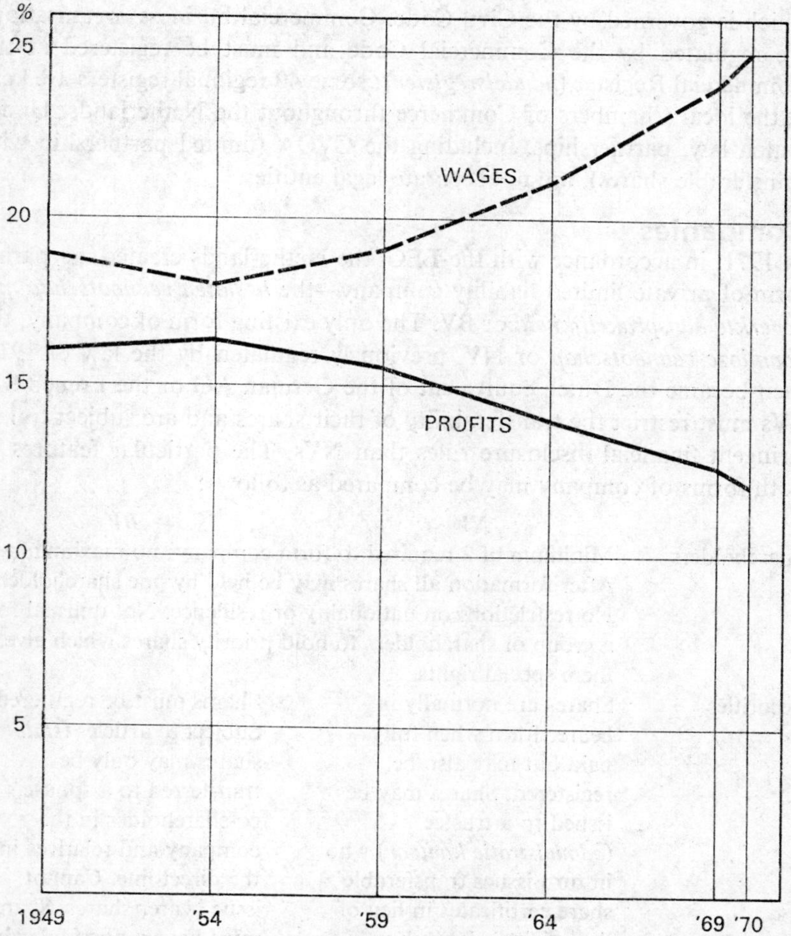

Fig. 3.1 Wages and net profits as percentage of Dutch companies' turnover

Source: Nederlands Credietbank NV, *Annual Report, 1970*

produced a merger code containing rules of conduct for mergers which, unlike the United Kingdom's "City Code", places great emphasis on the protection of employees.

BUSINESS ORGANISATIONS

Figure 3.2 shows the various forms of business organisation available in the Netherlands including the *maatschap* or professional partnership which is governed by the Civil Code. Commercial business organisations are regulated by the Commercial Code and must be registered at the Commercial Register (*handelsregister*); some 40 regional registers are kept at the local Chambers of Commerce throughout the Netherlands. Under Dutch law, partnerships, including the CVOA (limited partnership with transferable shares), are not separate legal entities.

Companies

In 1971, in accordance with the EEC, the Netherlands created a separate form of private limited liability company—the *besloten vennootschap met beperkte aansprakelijkheid* or BV. The only existing form of company, the *naamloze vennootschap* or NV, previously regulated by the law of 1928, then became the Dutch equivalent of the German AG or the French SA. BVs must restrict the transferability of their shares and are subject to less stringent financial disclosure rules than NVs. The particular features of both forms of company may be compared as follows:

	NV	*BV*
Shareholders	Minimum of 2 required to form company; no maximum. After formation all shares may be held by one shareholder. No restrictions on nationality or residence. Not unusual for a group of shareholders to hold priority shares which give them special rights.	
Securities	Shares are normally in bearer form when fully paid but may also be registered. Shares may be issued to a trustee (*administratie kantoor*) who in turn issues transferable share certificates in lieu of the original shares but retains voting control. Shares must have a nominal value.	Shares must be registered. Subject to articles (*statuten*) shares may only be transferred to a spouse, co-shareholder in the company and relatives in the direct line. Cannot issue bearer shares. Shares must have a nominal value.

Capital	No minimum. The subscribed capital must be at least 20 per cent of the authorised capital. A minimum of 10 per cent of the subscribed capital must be paid up before formation. Can purchase own shares in accordance with the articles up to a maximum of 50 per cent of the subscribed capital.
Capital impairment	The law contains no stipulations for action in the event of losses exceeding a stated proportion of the capital.
Annual general meeting	Shareholders' meetings must be held once every year not later than 6 months after the financial year end.

The Dutch have not adopted a rigid approach to management and with the exception of "large enterprises" companies are free to choose any suitable form of management structure. Nevertheless, the Commercial Code states that the articles (*statuten*) of any company may provide for the appointment of one or more supervisory directors (*commissarissen*). A supervisory board (*raad van commissarissen*) is obligatory for every "large enterprise" defined as being an NV or BV which for three continuous years:

1. Has had total share capital and reserves of Fl 10 million or more.
2. Has had, with its subsidiaries, 100 or more employees in the Netherlands and which, in consequence, is required to have a works council.
3. Is not the subsidiary of a Dutch parent company which is itself subject to the large enterprise rules.

Day-to-day operations are in the hands of executive managers (*directie*) who need not be shareholders. It is interesting to note that the company may only be represented towards third parties by one or more executive managers in accordance with the *statuten*. Their names are filed with the Commercial Register. Except in the case of large enterprises *directie* are initially appointed in the *statuten* and subsequently at shareholders' meetings; the *statuten* may, however, grant the right to priority shareholders or to the *commissarissen*. The *directie* may be dismissed at any time by the board of *commissarissen* but the shareholders may overrule this decision. In large enterprises, the engagement and dismissal of *directie* is entirely in the hands of the *commissarissen*. Apart from everyday business affairs the *directie* are responsible for the preparation of the annual accounts and are required to make an annual report on the course of the business. The remuneration of the *directie* may be fixed by the shareholders in general meeting.

The *commissarissen* are responsible for the supervision of the *directie* and they should also advise on the general course of business. They are

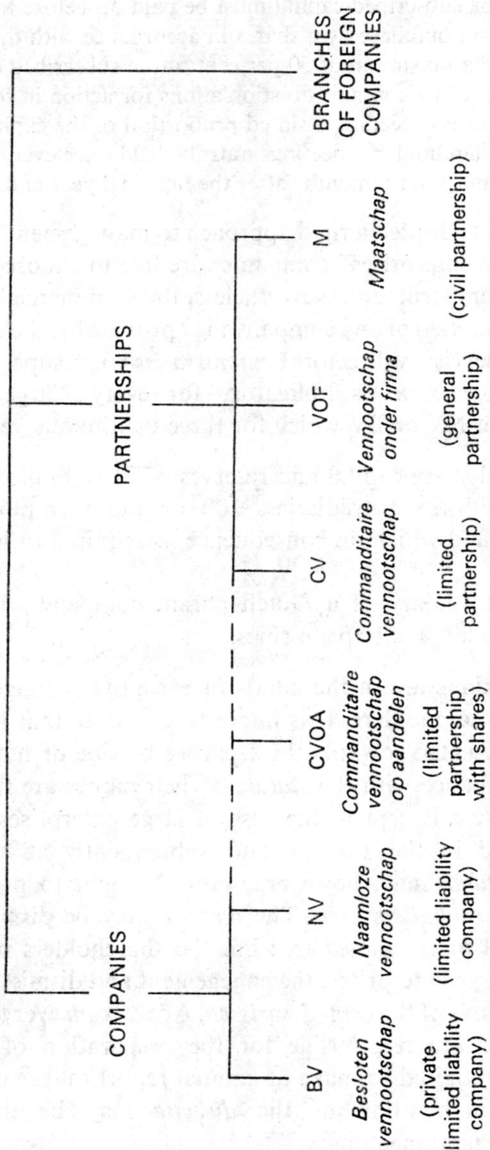

Fig. 3.2 Forms of business organisations in the Netherlands

appointed for four-year terms and may be re-elected subject to the stipulation that all *commissarissen* must retire at the age of 72.

The *commissarissen* of large enterprises are first appointed by the shareholders, but thereafter the board makes its own appointments by co-option on the basis of recommendations from the shareholders, works council and *directie*. In all other cases the *commissarissen* are first appointed by the *statuten* and subsequently by the shareholders in general meeting, who may also remove them. The board of *commissarissen* of large enterprises must consist of at least three members; in other cases no limit is specified.

The board of *commissarissen* of large enterprises has the right to appoint and dismiss the *directie* and must give its approval to such decisions as changes in share capital, issues of share certificates, mergers and take-overs, public issues, major additions to fixed assets[3] and radical changes in the numbers of employees or working conditions. The *commissarissen* are also charged with the finalisation of the annual accounts, and, if not otherwise provided in the *statuten*, both the *directie* and supervisory directors are responsible for calling general meetings. Holders of 10 per cent of the issued capital may call a general meeting and may in the case of an NV request the court to institute an independent enquiry into the company's affairs; the required percentage may be reduced by the *statuten*. In large enterprises an employee of the company or its subsidiary cannot be a *commissaris*, nor may a limited company, nor an official of the trade union of the industry.

Partnerships

The *vennootschap onder firma* (VOF) is a normal general partnership where the partners are jointly and severally liable for the debts of the firm. The VOF requires a written partnership agreement (*vennootschapscontract*).

The Dutch limited partnership (*commanditaire vennootschap*—CV) consists of at least one general partner and one or more silent partners whose liability is limited to their capital contributions. The general partners are liable as in the VOF but the silent partner may also become liable if he allows his name to be included in the partnership (unless he was a former general partner) or takes part in management.

Under Dutch civil law there exists a separate form of general partnership (*maatschap*—M) which is intended for professional firms. The *maatschap* is thus generally used by lawyers, accountants and architects. The liability of the partners is unlimited, but the debts of the *maatschap* are shared equally among the partners.

Limited Partnerships with Shares

The *commanditaire vennootschap op aandelen* (limited partnership with shares) is the Dutch equivalent of the French *société en commandite par actions*, but it is not a separate legal entity. The general partners manage the CVOA and are jointly and severally liable for the debts of the firm. The limited partners are precluded from management and their shares may be in registered or bearer form. Their liability is limited to their capital contributions.

Branches of Foreign Companies

Branches can be formed very easily and, apart from registration with the Commercial Register, no particular regulations apply. A branch operation has certain advantages in the short term since the formation of a company can take over six months to complete.

Although foreign subsidiaries satisfying the requirements for large enterprises must appoint a *raad van commissarissen*, the supervisory board's powers are curbed so as not to have a detrimental influence on foreign investment. Specifically the authority to appoint and dismiss the *directie* and the finalisation of financial statements remains with the foreign parent through its control of the general meeting.

Works Councils

The Dutch introduced their own brand of compulsory works councils for every establishment with 100 or more employees at the same time as they provided for supervisory boards. All members of the works council must be employees who have been elected by secret ballot. The senior executive manager or his equivalent is president of the council. The works council is required to meet at least six times a year; in at least two of the six meetings the company's policy and affairs have to be discussed in the attendance of one or more *commissarissen* or a member of the *directie*. The works council must be consulted on such matters as wage rates, training and promotion schemes and the appointment, dismissal and promotion of staff. It has the same rights as a shareholder or the public prosecutor to request an investigation by an expert into cases of mismanagement. Generally the council must be supplied with the accounts, but these may be in a very condensed form in the case of those BVs which are not obliged to publish financial statements.[4] The works council has power to nominate candidates for co-option to the board of *commissarissen* and it may also object to other nominations subject to the final decision of the Social and Economic Council.

ACCOUNTING AND FINANCIAL REPORTING

The general standard of financial reporting in the Netherlands is among the highest in the world, and the Netherlands emerges as a nation remarkably uninfluenced by Franco–German practices. Traditionally, the Dutch approach to accounting has been flexible and realistic with the result that accounting practices often differ little from those in the United Kingdom.

The international orientation of many Dutch companies has played a significant role in accounting developments; so, too, has a vigilant stock exchange and a high-quality financial press. The accountancy profession has not been found wanting either, and, although small by UK standards, it enjoys a worldwide status for its competence and expertise.

The Dutch approach to accounting is substantially influenced by the ideas of the late Professor Th. Limperg,[5] who believed that accounts should reflect the economic significance of events rather than provide a mere historical record. It was largely under the influence of this professor and his followers that the Dutch developed their theory of business economics, within which accounting is considered to be "integrated with the body of economic knowledge and methodology".[6] The business economics approach has many implications and it is argued that it provides a completely separate conceptual basis for accounting, serving to integrate all the accounting functions into their micro- and macro-economic environment.[7] It may therefore be seen as fundamentally different from conventional accounting and up to now, at least, has remained unfettered by standard rules.

Against this impressive background it must be said that Dutch statutory financial reporting requirements were left extremely inadequate until the Act on the Annual Accounts of Enterprises, dated 10 September 1970, came into force. The old law, enacted on 25 June 1929, contained only one regulation concerning annual accounts and there were no stipulations as to the content of the profit and loss account. Although accounting theory had made great advances in the intervening years, not all companies maintained the same high standards in their annual accounts: thus the reform, initiated in 1960, was received with great approval.

Accounting Principles

The 1970 Act on the Annual Accounts of Enterprises states "that the annual accounts should provide such information that a sound judgement can be formed on the financial position and result of the enterprise and, to the extent to which annual accounts permit, on its solvency and liquidity".

The accounts consisting of the balance sheet, profit and loss account and explanatory notes are required to "reflect fairly and systematically" the size and composition of the enterprise's capital at the end of the financial year and of its result for the year. Herein lies the essence of the Dutch financial reporting rules, the equivalent of the United Kingdom's "true and fair view" which must underlie every set of annual accounts. In its commentary on the Act, the Nederlands Instituut van Registeraccountants (NIvRA) points out that not only should the accounts give a fair picture but the data supplied should be relevant to the purpose of the information and classified in such a manner as to be illuminating and not misleading: "the information must enable the forming of a sound, *i.e.* well-formed, opinion; greatly detailed information is unnecessary, but the financial position of the enterprise taken as a whole must clearly appear therefrom".

The Dutch accept that annual accounts have several users and should, as far as possible, be prepared with this in mind. As the NIvRA maintains: "When judging annual accounts a deplorable financial situation, if any, should immediately be evident to the average reader". However, "it goes without saying that generally it is only an expert informed about the situation in and the prospects for the branch of industry who can derive a really sound judgement from the accounts; it is to him in particular that the accounts must provide adequate and clear information".

The 1970 Act does not attempt to define accounting principles but states that "the bases underlying the valuation of the assets and liabilities and the determination of the result shall comply with standards that are regarded as being acceptable in economic and social life". This reflects back to the traditional Dutch belief that accounting standards should comply with "sound business practice" and emphasises the public accountability aspect of financial reporting.

Tax rules have not influenced Dutch accounting at all although some of the more acceptable tax decisions have endorsed various accounting practices. The Dutch accountancy profession has never considered that it had the sole right or responsibility to define acceptable standards. Over the years the only authoritative guidance available to businessmen, apart from the writings of leading accountants, consisted of certain recommendations published in 1955 and 1962 by the Council of Netherlands Employers' Associations (Raad van Nederlandse Werkgeversverbonden). The matter was put on a much more formal basis in 1971 when the Minister for

Economic Affairs invited the employers' organisations, trade unions and the accountancy profession to set up a joint study group to define standards which are "acceptable in economic and social life". Initially the reports of the study group take the form of recommendations but it is likely that they will eventually assume the same character as the United Kingdom's "Statements of Standard Accounting Practice".

At present, however, the major problem confronting the user of Dutch financial statements is their lack of comparability. Bearing in mind the tenets of business economics, the primary objective of which is to portray the economic significance of each event, it is obvious that the exercise to this extent of individual judgement can only result in considerable diversity both in valuation and in reporting practices. The difficulty is well highlighted by the results of a survey carried out by the Economic Institute of the Free University, Amsterdam, before the 1970 Annual Accounts of Enterprises Act came into force. The survey, covering the period from 1 April 1967 to 31 March 1968 examined the bases of depreciation calculations in the accounts of all industrial and trading companies quoted on the Amsterdam Stock Exchange. The results of the survey (Table 3.3) disclosed that 51 per cent of companies used the historical cost basis with the rest divided between those who compromised on historical cost and others who adopted the replacement-value basis completely.

TABLE 3.3. DEPRECIATION BASES

Net fixed assets of companies (in Fl millions)	*I*	*II*	*III*	*IV*	*Total number of companies*	*Total (%)*
0–10	100	27	21	8	156	*60.2*
10–25	16	10	9	8	43	*16.6*
25–75	12	7	7	11	37	*14.3*
Above 75	3	3	5	12	23	*8.9*
Total	**131**	**47**	**42**	**39**	**259**	**100**
(%)	*50.7*	*18.1*	*16.2*	*15.0*	*100*	

I Historic cost and depreciation.

II Historic cost but depreciation above historic cost.

III Fixed assets at historic cost with depreciation on same basis subtracted; as a charge to income, however, extra depreciation calculated. This extra depreciation credited to an account belonging to equity capital.

IV Fixed assets at replacement value and depreciation on same basis.

Replacement Value Accounting

Within the tenets of business economics Dutch accountants believe that replacement or current values are an essential and logical means of economic valuation. Replacement value accounting was first advocated by Professor Limperg during the 1920s, but although Philips used it before the Second World War it was not until the 1951 Annual Report that current values were applied in their published accounts. The practice is now well known and partially practised in the Netherlands and is endorsed by the second report of the joint study group mentioned above. Replacement value accounting involves the periodic revaluation of, usually, fixed assets and inventories at current prices thereby ensuring that current costs are matched against current revenues in the determination of income. A revaluation surplus is not considered to be profit available for distribution but is credited to capital. A loss on revaluation, however, must be treated as a deduction from trading profits. The theory of current value accounting facilitates the continuity of the firm by providing for the maintenance of capital in real as opposed to historical terms, and, although particularly relevant in times of raging inflation, it has a permanent application as long as price levels change.

Accounting Practices and the Annual Accounts

The 1970 Act does not prescribe particular formats for annual accounts but those shown in Figs. 3.3 and 3.4 may be considered fairly typical. Companies are required to explain the accounting bases adopted in their accounts, a stipulation similar to the United Kingdom's SSAP 2, "Disclosure of Accounting Policies", and any significant change of basis should be clearly disclosed showing its effect on the net equity and result. Corresponding figures for the previous year are essential.

Consolidated Accounts

The 1970 Act lays down that a company owning more than 50 per cent of the capital of other companies (defined as subsidiaries) shall either prepare consolidated accounts or publish "individual or amalgamated annual accounts of these subsidiaries" (Section 13) together with its own accounts. There is, therefore, a strong incentive to consolidate and most companies do so. The publication of consolidated accounts does not exempt a company from publishing its own balance sheet but an individual profit and loss statement is not necessary if the consolidated statement contains all relevant consolidated information. Section 12 of the Act defines a participation as a "direct or indirect holding for an enterprise's own account of shares or

ACTIVA (ASSETS)	*Fl* *Cost*	*Fl* *Afschrijving*	*Fl* *Net*
Duurzame produktiemiddelen (Fixed assets)[1]			
Terreinen en gebouwen (Land and buildings)			
Machines en installaties (Machinery and equipment)			
Kantoorinventaris (Furniture and fittings)			
Immateriële activa (Intangible assets)			
Niet geconsolideerde deelnemingen (Non-consolidated investments)			
Niet direct realiseerbare waarden (Other non-current assets)			
Voorraden (Inventories)			
Grondstoffen (Raw materials)			
Goederen in bewerking (Work-in-process)			
Gereed produkt (Finished goods)			
Vorderingen (Accounts receivable)			
Handelsdebiteuren (Trade debtors)			
Verdisconteerde wissels (Discounted notes)			
Diverse debiteuren (Other debtors)			
Vooruitbetaalde kosten (Prepaid expenses)			
Liquide middelen (Cash and marketable securities)			
Effecten (Marketable securities)			
Deposito's (Short-term investments)			
Kas en banken (Cash on hand and at banks)			

PASSIVA (LIABILITIES)	*Fl*	*Fl*
Eigen vermogen (Capital stock and reserves)		
Aandelenkapitaal (Share capital)		
Reserves (Reserves)		
Agio reserve (Paid-in surplus (share premiums))		
Algemene reserve (General reserve)		
Ingehouden winsten (Retained earnings)		
Vermogensverschillen door herwaardering (Differences in net worth due to revaluations)		
Minderheidsbelang van derden (Minority interests in subsidiaries)		
Diverse voorzieningen (Provisions)		
Op lange termijn (Long-term)		
Op korte termijn (Short-term)		
Latente belastingen (Tax equalisation provision)		
Schulden op lange termijn (Long-term debts)		
Converteerbare obligatieleningen (Convertible debentures)		
Overige obligatieleningen (Other debentures)		
Overige schulden op lange termijn (Other long-term debt)		
Schulden op korte termijn (Current liabilities)		
Bankkredieten (Bank credits)		
Crediteuren (Accounts payable)		
Belasting op de winst (Income tax)		
Nog te betalen kosten (Accrued expenses)		
Winstuitkering (Profit distribution, i.e. dividends payable)		
Signed Directie (Executive managers)		
Commissarissen (Supervisory directors)		

1. If valued at replacement cost, these will be described as *Vervangingswaarde*.

Fig. 3.3 Example of *geconsolideerd vermogensoverzicht* (consolidated balance sheet)

	Fl	Fl
Omzet (Sales)		
Kosten (Cost of sales)		
Kostprijs van de omzet (Cost of goods sold)		
Verkoopkosten en algemene kosten (Selling and general expenses)		
Afschrijvingen (Depreciation)		
Bedrijfsresultaat (Operating income)		
Overige baten en lasten (Other income and deductions)		
Betaalde interest (Interest paid)		
Diversen (Other)		
Ontvangen interest (Interest received)		
Winst vóór aftrek van belasting (Profit before tax)		
Belasting op de winst (Tax on income)		
Winst na aftrek van belasting (Profit after tax)		
Aandeel in de nettowinst van niet geconsolideerde deelnemingen (Share in net profit of unconsolidated subsidiaries)		
Minderheidsbelang van derden (Minority interest in subsidiaries)		
Nettowinst (Net profit)		
Voorstel tot Winstverdeling (Proposed appropriation)		
Signed *Directie* (Executive Managers)		
Commissarissen (Supervisory directors)		

Fig. 3.4 Example of *geconsolideerd resultatensoverzicht* (consolidated profit and loss account)

certificates of shares representing at least 25 per cent of the issued share capital of another enterprise". In UK terms, an "associated" company relationship would therefore appear to exist in the case of all holdings between 25 and 49 per cent: all income from associated companies must be separately stated. The name and domicile[8] of all direct and indirect subsidiaries and of all other direct or indirect participations, where the value of the participation represents at least 15 per cent of the assets of the participating company, must be disclosed in the annual accounts; alternatively companies may omit this information provided that the relevant details are filed at the Commercial Register and the accounts contain a note to this effect.

Companies need not disclose the name and domicile of those subsidiaries and participations (holdings from 15 to 49 per cent) whose aggregate assets do not exceed 15 per cent of the assets of the participating company, after deduction of the value of its holding included in such assets and after addition of the amount of the aggregate assets of its holding. Companies may also appeal to the Minister of Economic Affairs for exemption from the disclosure of names and domiciles of participations; this exemption may be granted for one to five years. If, however, a company has been granted exemption from disclosure this fact must be stated in its annual accounts. Similar provision for exemption is given in the case of disclosure of turnover data, as well as analyses of inventories, receivables and capital.

Section 15 contains a significant exemption for foreign subsidiaries, perhaps influenced by a similar, but more effective, German regulation (*cf.* page 59) whereby their latest annual accounts, prepared in compliance with applicable foreign statutory regulations, may either appear as notes to the accounts or be filed for public inspection at the Commercial Register provided this fact is mentioned in the accounts.

Parts II and III of the Act go on to detail the various items which should be disclosed in the annual accounts and these together with the accounting practices commonly observed are discussed in the following sections.

The Balance Sheet

Fixed assets. The Act directs that the following assets be separately stated:

1. Business plant and premises.
2. Machinery and fittings.
3. Other durable business equipment.
4. Fixed assets not used for business activities.

The variety of practices followed in the valuation of fixed assets is amply illustrated by Table 3.3. The joint study group states that the historical cost basis of valuation is not acceptable and prescribes the disclosure of current values in all cases where replacement value accounting is not applied.

Intangible assets. Intangible assets cannot be valued in excess of cost less accumulated depreciation, and goodwill, patents, licences, copyrights, concessions and exploitation rights, and formation expenses must be shown separately. There is no requirement to write off intangibles over any specific period, but it is not unusual for goodwill arising on the acquisition of subsidiaries to be written off to reserves in the year of acquisition. The expense and discount on raising debt may be spread over several years or written off in the first year depending on the individual case.

Investments. The principal feature of the rules relating to investments is the necessity to classify them according to the degree of control. Various disclosures apply and these are detailed on page 100 under "Consolidated accounts".

Inventories. The Act prescribes that stocks of a differing nature such as raw materials, auxiliary materials, semi-finished products, work in progress and finished products or merchandise must be separately stated. Methods of valuation are numerous within the parameters of the lower of cost or net realisable value. Generally cost includes some overheads and is calculated using any of the FIFO, LIFO, average or (occasionally) base stock methods.

Receivables. The financial statements must distinguish between the major receivables such as trade debtors, instalments due and mortgaged receivables.

Cash and marketable securities. The Act requires the individual disclosure of:

1. Cash, bank and giro balances.
2. The aggregate value of quoted securities.
3. The aggregate values of other securities which are not participations.

It is necessary to distinguish between items at call and those not at free disposal.

Capital and reserves. Companies are obliged to disclose the various classes of share capital in issue, and the extent to which each category is paid up. The nominal value of repurchased but uncancelled shares and the amount at which such shares are included in the balance sheet should also be stated. The names of the holders (or the directors' names if the holder is a legal entity) of any shares granting special powers, apart from those relating to the appropriation of profits or the balance upon winding up, must be given, as well as the number of shares or rights held by each of them; the number of any founders' shares, profit shares or similar shares in issue which entitle the holders to specific rights in connection with the appropriation of profits or of the balance upon winding up is similarly required. The various reserves should be split up, and, in so far as it is necessary to give a fair picture, reserves and movements therein should be separately stated and explained in the annual accounts. Dutch law contains no legal reserve requirement and there are no stipulations regarding the distribution of share premiums.

Provisions. Section 23 defines provisions as "amounts set aside for risks and obligations of which the size is not exactly known at the time of the preparation of the balance sheet". The various provisions should be subdivided "according to the nature of the risks and obligations".

The joint study group favours a precise distinction between reserves as part of equity and provisions as part of liabilities. The study group found that some provisions were unjustified and specified two requirements for the creation of acceptable provisions:

1. The provisions should relate to specific risks rather than normal trade risks.
2. The risks in question should exist at the balance sheet date but cannot be precisely ascertained.

The Act specifically mentions provisions for deferred tax which are as common in the Netherlands as in the United Kingdom. The Dutch have gone a little further and sometimes provide for deferred tax using discount factors.

Long-term debts. All debts of over one year must be classified by type, such as debenture loans, amounts due to creditors and pension liabilities; information must be supplied as to whom and in what form collateral has been assigned, as must details of any debts for which the company has engaged itself not to encumber assets in the future. The duration and interest rates of loans are disclosed as are the conversion terms for any convertible debentures. The total amount of the debt due within the following financial year must also be disclosed.

Current liabilities. This caption refers to amounts payable within one year and the Act specifically mentions amounts due to banks and suppliers as well as trading credits received and amounts payable for pensions and taxation.

Contingent liabilities and capital commitments. Contingent liabilities arising from negotiated bills, guarantees and other obligations must be quantified and disclosed. Capital commitments such as those resulting from long leases, building rights, rentals, leaseholds, purchases by instalment, chartering or leasing agreements and other financial obligations of particular significance such as material investments must be disclosed either in the notes or, Italian-style, on both sides of the balance sheet.

The Profit and Loss Account

The various appropriations of profit should be disclosed in the accounts. In common with other Continental countries the Dutch do not usually maintain a large retained earnings account.

Post-balance-sheet Events

In its commentary on the 1970 Annual Accounts of Enterprises Act the NIvRA states that

> important facts occurring or becoming known after the balance sheet date, but before the preparation of the accounts must be brought into account when evaluating the items, if at the latter moment such facts give another insight into the value of assets or liabilities other than the one existing at the balance sheet date.

Publication and Filing of Financial Statements

The annual accounts comprising the balance sheet, profit and loss account and explanatory notes must be prepared by the *directie* within five months of the financial year end for approval by the general meeting which should be held within six months of the year end unless this term has been extended by the general meeting for special reasons. The accounts have to be signed by the *directie* (executive managers) and by any *commissarissen* (supervisory directors).

The accounts and the auditors' report must be available for inspection by shareholders at the principal office of the company from the day of convening the general meeting until the end of that meeting—a period of at least 15 days. In addition, third parties are entitled to receive copies of these documents on payment of an amount to cover costs.

The Dutch financial reporting rules exempt private (BV) companies so far as possible from having to file their accounts. Accordingly every NV and only those BVs (1) whose business is wholly or partly in the banking or insurance field or (2) that have issued bearer debentures or bearer certificates of issued debentures are required to file their complete financial statements and auditors' report.[9]

A large BV (not to be confused with "large enterprise"), defined as a BV (1) having total assets of at least Fl 8 million and (2) employing at least 100 persons at the balance sheet date including employees of Dutch subsidiaries, need not file its profit and loss statement but instead files its balance sheet with accompanying notes and auditors' report.[10] All other BVs are exempt from filing regulations.

The Commercial Code permits one exception to the filing regulations for NVs and large BVs, whereby a company which is a subsidiary of a Dutch parent company need only file summarised financial statements and is exempt from filing an auditors' report. In order to adopt the summary form it is necessary that the financial statements of the company be consolidated, or combined with the financial statements of its Dutch parent, that the subsidiary's shareholders agree and that the D files a guarantee of its subsidiary's affairs with the Commercial R The guarantee is not essential when the parent company's activities exclusively or mainly outside EEC territory, but this exemption is not permitted in those cases where:

1. The company has issued either bearer shares or bearer debentures, or bearer certificates substituting registered shares or debentures.
2. Shares or debentures of the company or certificates substituting such securities are listed in the official list of a stock exchange.
3. It is the company's business wholly or partly to raise monies from third parties or it is engaged in the insurance business.

The minimum contents of the summarised financial statements are:

Balance sheet
- Total fixed assets
- Total current assets
- Net equity
- Long-term debt
- Current liabilities

Income statement
- Trading result
- Balance of other income and charges

The executive managers (*directie*) are responsible for ensuring that the accounts and auditors' report are filed for public inspection with the Commercial Register within eight days of being passed by the general meeting.

The Act prescribes that if the published accounts "give a misleading presentation of the company's position the supervisory directors next to the executive managers are jointly and severally liable towards third parties for consequent damage suffered".

Management Report

The *directie* have a statutory duty to report to the general meeting on the company's affairs and on their stewardship. Their report, the contents of which are not specified, can be oral or in writing, but the general meeting may stipulate that future reports must be in written form; in practice the report is always given in writing and issued together with the annual accounts. If the report is in writing, it must be made available to shareholders and third parties on the same basis as the accounts and auditors' report.

On the question of the enforcement of the financial reporting regulations the Act states that "each interested party holding the view that the annual accounts of an enterprise do not meet the relevant requirements . . . may take action in law" to force the company to correct the position; this includes the public prosecutor. Legal actions are exclusively within the jurisdiction of the Enterprise Chamber of the Court of Justice in Amsterdam, subject to appeal to the High Court. Legal proceedings are handled by members of the Court of Justice and a *registeraccountant* and his deputy; there is a time limit of two months after approval of the financial statements for proceedings to be initiated, and the claim should specify the adjustments necessary.

Stock Exchange Listing Requirements

The Amsterdam Stock Exchange is governed by a group of banks and brokers who are the only persons who may buy and sell securities. Similar groups, subject to ASE rules, exist in Rotterdam and The Hague. In order to obtain a listing, therefore, it is necessary to contact a bank that is a member of the Association of the Stock Exchange (Vereniging voor de Effectenhandel) which will assist in drawing up the prospectus. The prospectus plays a very important role and it must include copies of the approved accounts and auditors' reports for the last two financial years. The minimum nominal amount offered for subscription must be, in general, at least one-tenth of the amount in circulation after the issue, with a minimum of Fl 500,000.

Business Records

The Dutch regulations for business records are simple and realistic. Article 6(3) of the Commercial Code states that financial records must be maintained in such a way as to enable all assets and liabilities to be determined at any time. The minimum retention period is 10 years and records should be available for inspection by the Government or when needed in the course of judicial proceedings.

THE ACCOUNTANCY PROFESSION

The Dutch accountancy profession has a history dating back to the formation of the Nederlands Instituut van Accountants (NIvA) in 1895, only 15 years after the English Institute received its Royal Charter. The first firm of public practising accountants, Moret & Starke, was established in 1883.

In 1927 the seemingly radical view of Professor Limperg forced a split in the profession and resulted in the formation of the Vereniging van Academisch Gevormde Accountants (VAGA—Association of University-trained Accountants). Both bodies went their separate ways, providing similar services and observing the same ethical rules until the Register-accountants Act of 28 June 1962 provided for the establishment of a unified profession. As a result, the Nederlands Instituut van Register-accountants (NIvRA) was formed in 1967 as the sole accountancy body under public law whose members have the exclusive right to offer written opinions on financial statements and enjoy the title of *registeraccountant* (RA). The unification proposals also admitted members of some of the many other small accountancy bodies, including the Broederschap (Fellowship) and the NUvA (Union of Accountants) as well as other experienced people to the NIvRA. In 1972 a separate law created the title *accountant-administratieconsulenten* (AAC) for those accountants who are primarily concerned with the provision of book-keeping services to small clients. AACs are not formally organised. As from 1979 the title of *accountant* will be legally protected in the Netherlands.

The NIvRA is a self-governing body and has the power under public law to make by-laws which are binding on all RAs. The "Rules of Conduct and Professional Activities of *Registeraccountants*" (CPAR) approved on 8 November 1973 replaced the "Rules of Professional Conduct" which had been in existence, virtually unchanged, since 1946 and are possibly the most advanced professional rules in the world. The rules fall into three main sections:

Section II. Rules for all *registeraccountants*.
Section III. Rules for *registeraccountants* acting as auditors.
Section IV. Rules for *registeraccountants* acting as public accountants.

The rules not only cover professional ethics but also include auditing standards.

Traditionally, RAs have practised as partnerships, both civil and commercial, and sole practitioners (Table 3.4), but the CPAR permit RAs for the first time the option of conducting a public accountancy practice in corporate (BV or NV) form. Likewise the CPAR open the possibility for *registeraccountants* to form partnerships, corporate or other-wise, with members of other liberal professions. Instituut permission is necessary for the new legal form of public practice; partnerships with non-*registeraccountants* will be approved by the Instituut Council only if it is con-vinced that the co-responsibility for the work of the non-*registeraccountant*

TABLE 3.4. MEMBERSHIP OF NEDERLANDS INSTITUUT VAN REGISTERACCOUNTANTS AND NUMBER OF STUDENTS (as at 31 August 1973)

1 Number of registeraccountants	
In public practice	1,628
Internal accountants (industry, banking, etc.)	235
Internal accountants (government)	368
Other posts in industry, banking, etc.	539
Other posts in government	134
In education	31
Retired	373
Miscellaneous	35
	3,343

In public practice

	Number of firms	*Total number of accountants*
100 or more accountants	5	961
51–100	2	120
21–50	4	110
11–20	3	53
6–10	7	58
2–5	58	154
Sole practitioners	172	172
	251	1,628

2 Number of students (approximate)	
Taking NIvRA courses	5,200
University students with master's degree in economics	270
	5,470

which arises from practising under a joint name can be effectively borne by the *registeraccountants*.

Education and Training

The standard of education in the Dutch accountancy profession has always been very high—a fact which has contributed greatly to the considerable status it possesses. University teaching began as far back as 1915 in Rotterdam at the Netherlands School of Economics and continues today at five Dutch universities as one of the two alternative ways of becoming a *registeraccountant* (Fig. 3.5).

As an alternative to university education, the Instituut organises and runs a schedule of courses for NIvRA students (*assistenten*) which take an average of seven and a half years. *Assistenten* work full-time, usually either with a member of the NIvRA in practice or with internal audit departments in industry, banking, the Government service, etc.; they are

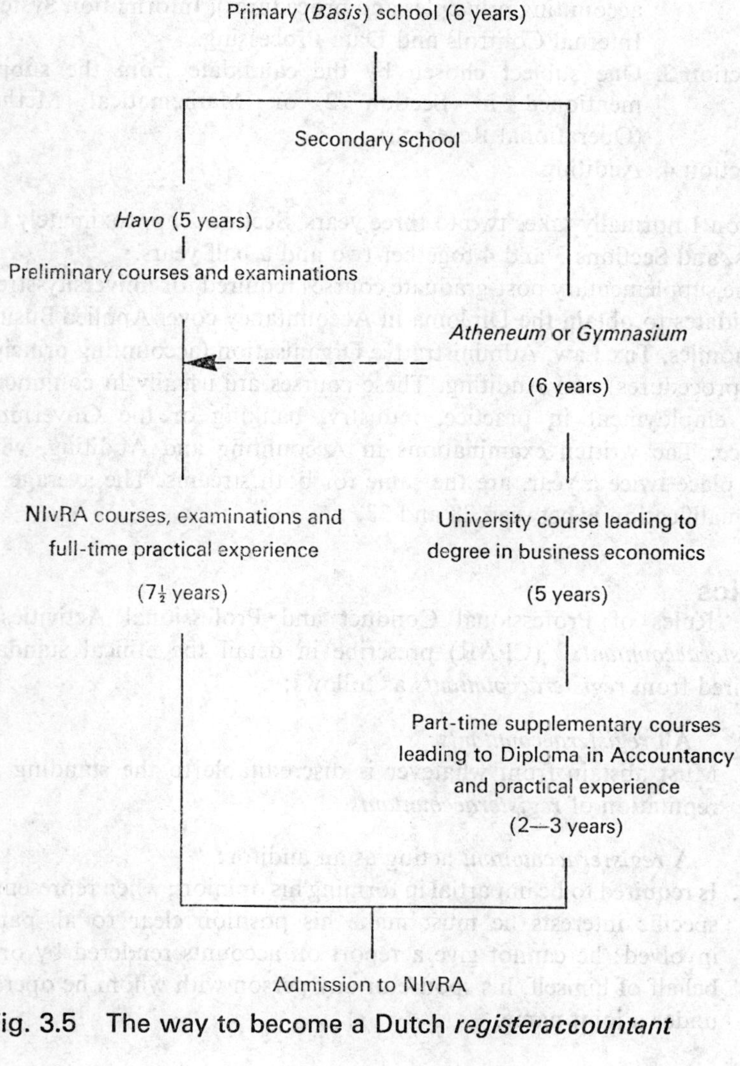

Fig. 3.5 The way to become a Dutch *registeraccountant*

not required to serve a compulsory period of training. At present, courses are attended in the evenings and on Fridays and Saturdays. The courses are divided into four sections:

Section 1. Civil Law, Mathematics, Social Economics, Book-keeping and Statistics, and Business Economics.

Section 2. Tax Law, Business Economics (including practice), Organisational Theory, Administrative Organisation (essentially accounting principles and procedures), Information Systems, Internal Controls and Data Processing.

Section 3. One subject chosen by the candidate from the subjects mentioned in Section 2 or Mathematical Methods (Operational Research).

Section 4. Auditing.

Section 1 normally takes two to three years, Section 2 approximately four years, and Sections 3 and 4 together two and a half years.

The supplementary post-graduate courses required for university-stream candidates to obtain the Diploma in Accountancy cover Applied Business Economics, Tax Law, Administrative Organisation (accounting principles and procedures) and Auditing. These courses are usually in conjunction with employment in practice, industry, banking or the Government service. The written examinations in Accounting and Auditing, which take place twice a year, are the same for both streams. The average age for qualification is between 28 and 33.

Ethics

The "Rules of Professional Conduct and Professional Activities of *Registeraccountants*" (CPAR) prescribe in detail the ethical standards required from *registeraccountants* as follows:

All *registeraccountants:*

1. Must abstain from whatever is discreditable to the standing and reputation of *registeraccountants*.

A *registeraccountant* acting as an auditor:

2. Is required to be impartial in forming his opinion; when representing specific interests he must make his position clear to all parties involved; he cannot give a report on accounts rendered by or on behalf of himself, his spouse or any person with whom he operates under a joint name.

3. Must observe secrecy in all matters and cannot make any further use of confidential data even after he has ceased to act as auditor.

A *registeraccountant* acting as a public accountant:

4. Is required to be independent of his appointor, the parties whose affairs he reports upon as well as parties having an interest in or dependent upon either or both of the two former parties.
5. Must take due care that this independence is not impaired by financial or other interests of third parties.
6. Cannot give an opinion on accounts rendered on behalf of himself or of a private party of which he himself, his spouse, persons with whom he practises under a joint name, or any party subordinate to him, or to whom he is subordinate, is related in such a manner that a material financial interest is involved.
7. Is not allowed to receive remuneration on a commission basis, or contingent on the outcome of his activities.
8. Cannot fulfil any function that might jeopardise the impartiality of opinions formed by himself or by persons with whom he practises under a joint name.
9. May not advertise or tender for services.
10. Must first consult the previously engaged accountant before accepting an appointment.

Services Provided

The profession is led by the "Big Five" accounting firms (Table 3.5) which together with several other firms throughout the Netherlands also provide their clients with a comprehensive service including auditing and

TABLE 3.5. THE "BIG FIVE" DUTCH ACCOUNTANCY FIRMS (as at 31 August 1973)

	Number of registeraccountants	*International associates*
1 Klynveld Kraayenhof & Co.	270	Turquands Barton Mayhew & Co. Vereinigte Deutsche Treuhand-Gesellschaft
2 Moret & Limperg	260	Interfides SA
3 Dijker en Doornbos Accountants	201	Binder Dijker Otte
4 Nederlandse Accountants Maatschap	120	Touche Ross
5 Van Dien & Co.	110	Deloitte, Haskins & Sells

management consultancy. The fact that these and other firms grew up before any statutory auditing requirements existed is an indication of the competence of the profession and the reputation it enjoys among businessmen. Apart from the very small firms, it has been the custom for Dutch accountancy firms to co-operate in clients' tax affairs with specialist firms providing these services, although there is now a tendency to follow UK practice and set up internal taxation departments.

AUDITING

The views of Professor Limperg have penetrated and considerably influenced Dutch auditing. His vision of the auditor as "the trustee of the public", and the man in whom everyone could trust, provided his followers with an ideal which makes the Dutch approach to auditing rather more comprehensive than is the case in most other countries.

Appointment of Auditors

The Commercial Code directs that the following companies appoint an auditor:

1. All *naamloze vennootschap* (NV) companies.
2. Those *besloten vennootschap* (BV) companies satisfying any of the following three conditions:
   (a) Carrying on business wholly or partly in the insurance or banking field or having issued bearer debentures or bearer certificates or registered debentures.
   (b) Having, according to their last balance sheet:
      (i) aggregate assets of at least Fl 8 million and
      (ii) which, at their balance sheet date, employ at least 100 employees, including employees of Dutch subsidiaries.
   (c) Having issued share capital of at least Fl 500,000.

The responsibility for appointing the auditor, who may be either a *registeraccountant*, or authorised foreign accountant, rests with the general meeting of shareholders, or, failing this, the supervisory board. Foreign accountants may be recognised by the Minister of Economic Affairs subject to proof of competence; such permission is revocable and may be granted under specific conditions. The principle of reciprocity is applied when considering foreign applications and such accountants are not limited to the provision of statutory audits. Permission to enter into partnership with non-Dutch public accountants on a restricted basis was first given by an *ad hoc* modification of the old "Rules of Professional Conduct" in 1971. Instituut Council approval is essential in each case.

Duties of Auditors and the Auditors' Report

The Commercial Code simply states that the auditor should "examine the balance sheet, the profit and loss account and the explanatory notes as prepared by the *directie* and report thereon to the general meeting".

A *registeraccountant* is deemed to be acting as an auditor if he "professionally examines the fairness of accounts" (CPAR 1(2)(16)). If an audit has not been carried out this fact must be stated on the relevant documents by using one of the terms "no examination made into the fairness", "unaudited" or "not audited" on each document.

A *registeraccountant* may not report on the outcome of his activities unless his expert knowledge and the work done provide a sound basis for a report. A report must reflect clearly the outcome of his activities and must cover the accounts taken as a whole, "as well as what, with his assent, is disclosed in respect of the accounts in documents submitted therewith". This overall approach to auditing whereby the auditor considers it his responsibility to ensure that the complete annual report and accounts give the necessary insight into the financial position and result of the company is emphasised in Rule 26 of the CPAR, which states that the report of an RA acting as a public accountant "relates to whatever is stated about the accounts in any document published together therewith" and a *registeraccountant* may not give his consent to the publication of his report if:

1. The contents of the documents published jointly with the accounts create a wrong impression of their meaning.
2. What has become known between the issue and publication of the report detracts from the fairness of the accounts.

The substance of the auditors' report must be unequivocably self-evident and cannot be other than approval (with or without qualification), disapproval or witholding of an opinion. For any report which contains less than an unqualified approval, the exact wording to be used is prescribed:

1. Qualification: *"onder voorbehoud"* ("with the qualification").
2. Disapproval: *"niet getrouw"* or *"niet juist"* ("not fair" or "not true").

3. Withholding of an opinion: *"geen oordeel omtrent de getrouwheid van . . . als geheel"* ("no opinion on the fairness of [name of the accounts] taken as a whole").

The CPAR furthermore state what the content or meaning is of each category of report:

1. Unqualified approval means that the *registeraccountant* is convinced that the accounts meet all requirements.
2. Qualified approval means that objections or uncertainties about the accounts exist, which are not of such materiality that they impair the approval, but on the other hand are not immaterial.
3. Disapproval means that the *registeraccountant* is convinced that the accounts do not meet all the requirements.
4. Withholding of an opinion implies that uncertainties continue to exist of a character and scope such that the *registeraccountant* is not in a position either to approve or to disapprove of the accounts taken as a whole. The withholding report cannot be given:
   (a) If the *registeraccountant* has restricted his examination, either of his own accord or on instruction from his client; or
   (b) If his examination has shown that the accounts do not meet all requirements.

The question of a part-audit, implied in the incomplete (no profit and loss statement) disclosure required from "large" BVs is answered by CPAR 17(3) which forbids a *registeraccountant* from agreeing to "an examination into the fairness of only a component part of financial statements".

A *registeraccountant* may use the report of another auditor only "if due care has been exercised in selecting that auditor" (CPAR 15(1)). If the report is made by another auditor who is not a public accountant, the RA must perform a supplementary examination in order to arrive at a sound basis for his report. Where the other auditor is a public accountant, and his report relates to a component part of the accounts, the RA need only review the work done by the other accountant. He must mention in his report that he has used the report of another auditor, if his review is confined to the bases underlying the other auditor's work; such mention should be omitted when the review, if necessary supplemented by an examination, enables the *registeraccountant* to accept undivided responsibility for the complete accounts.

The following is the text of the auditors' report on the annual accounts of Philips for the year 1972.

Philips
Auditors' report

We have examined the accounts for the year 1972 of N.V. Philips' Gloeilampenfabrieken and of N.V. Gemeenschappelijk Bezit van Aandeelen Philips' Gloeilampenfabrieken. With respect to certain subsidiaries and associated companies, mainly outside Europe, we have also made use of the reports of other auditors.

In our opinion, the accompanying accounts of N.V. Philips' Gloeilampenfabrieken and of N.V. Gemeenschappelijk Bezit van Aandeelen Philips' Gloeilampenfabrieken give a true and fair view of these companies' state of affairs as at 31 December 1972 and of their results for the year 1972.

We have also examined the Consolidated Statements of Financial Position and of Results, which combine the consolidated accounts for the year 1972 of N.V. Philips' Gloeilampenfabrieken and of the United States Philips Trust. In conducting our examination we have also made use of the other auditors' reports referred to above.

As regards the consolidated accounts of the United States Philips Trust we have relied on the report, dated 20 February 1973 of Messrs Smith and Harder, Certified Public Accountants, New York.

In our opinion, based on our examination and on the aforementioned report of Messrs Smith and Harder, the accompanying Consolidated Statements give a true and fair view of the combined state of affairs as at 31 December 1972 and of the combined results for the year 1972.

Eindhoven, Klynveld Kraayenhof & Co.
13 March 1973

Fieldwork

Sections 42(a) and 57(s) of the Commercial Code state that the auditor has the right to inspect all books and documents of the company (NV and BV), the appreciation of which is necessary for a proper fulfilment of his task; the company's valuables must be shown to him on request.

The Dutch auditor is very concerned with interrelationships between flows of money and goods: one example of this is the reconciliation commonly carried out to purchases and payments, sales debtors and collections, and the comparison of the closing inventory thus obtained with the physical records. Attendance at physical stocktakes is considered essential and mathematical sampling techniques are increasingly used. Confirmations of receivables and cash balances, though normal with the larger firms, are not generally regarded as essential in view of the cash transfer (giro) systems used.

Where possible the Dutch auditor works in close co-operation with internal auditors, especially where these are *registeraccountants*, and it is not unusual for the executive managers to certify that they have not interfered with the work of the internal auditor.

The CPAR require *registeraccountants* acting as auditors to keep records which make it possible, without undue effort, to arrive at a proper representation of the activities undertaken; such records must be retained for 10 years.

Remuneration of Auditors

The auditor's remuneration is based on the time spent by the various staff in carrying out the audit.

Removal of Auditors

The auditor may be removed at any time by the general meeting, or, if appointed by the supervisory board, by this body.

Liability of Auditors

The auditor may be held liable for negligence where his work is not up to professional standards. He may also be held liable for damage to shareholders and third parties.

Independence of Auditors

The rules governing the independence of auditors are contained in the *Rules of Professional Conduct and Professional Activities of Registeraccountants* (*CPAR*), which are discussed in detail above under "Ethics".

CONCLUSION

In many ways, accounting appears to have found its place in the Netherlands. The business economics approach and the use of current values have earned the Dutch profession an enviable esteem not only in the Netherlands but throughout the world. Although Dutch accountants have a somewhat similar background and tradition to their colleagues in the United Kingdom, they have already achieved many of the aims to which UK accountants are still aspiring.

REFERENCES

1. The system operates on the basis of bearer certificates issued by a depository company against a tranche of shares registered in its own name. The leading Dutch banks have combined to form the Amsterdam Depository Company NV for this purpose.

2. Insurance companies, pension funds and the Nationale Inverestings Bank (Herstelbank) NV.
3. Defined as 25 per cent of net equity.
4. For minimum contents, *see* page 107.
5. Professor Th. Limperg (1879–1961) was Professor of Managerial Economics at the University of Amsterdam, 1922–1949.
6. A. van Seventer, "The Continuity Postulate in the Dutch Theory of Income", *The International Journal of Accounting, Education and Research*, Vol. 4, No. 2, Spring 1969, p. 1.
7. See George M. Scott, "A Business Economics Foundation for Accounting: The Dutch Experience", *Accounting and Business Research*, Autumn 1970, pages 309–17.
8. In the case of domestic investments, the area or town where the registered office is situated must be disclosed.
9. In order to permit BVs to arrange their book-keeping systems in a manner suitable for auditing, the requirement that the auditors' report be filed with the financial statements was delayed until the close of the first financial year ending after 28 June 1974.
10. The requirement for large BVs to file their auditors' report commenced for the first time in respect of the financial year that included 29 June 1974.

Chapter 4

Belgium

BACKGROUND

The most striking feature of the Belgian financial system is the power of "Les Holdings", the notorious holding companies which control or closely influence almost all of the private sector of the nation's economy. Such was their domination even as far back as 1934 that the Government was forced to intervene and as a result the banking activities of "Les Holdings" had to be transferred to subsidiaries under independent management. The oldest and by far the largest of the holding companies is the Société Générale de Belgique, which was formed in 1822 by King William I to industrialise what was then the southern part of the Netherlands. La Générale is followed by the recently merged Cie Bruxelles Lambert. Both have holdings and cross-holdings in other companies and holding companies which make any attempt at disentanglement virtually impossible (Table 4.1). The activities of a holding company are well described in the following extract from an advertisement for the Société Générale:

> Société Générale de Belgique takes an active part in the lives of companies in its group. It provides financial support . . . short term in the form of loans, guarantees, endorsements, new issues and subscriptions, shares and bonds; and takes a direct part in running its subsidiaries, in association with their senior management, as regards general policy and fundamental decisions, though not in the day-to-day management.

Whatever the effect of the 1935 law, however, the holding companies continue to control the banking system. The two largest banks, Société Générale de Banque and the Banque de Bruxelles, are both controlled as their names indicate by the two largest holding companies.

Against this background, as one might expect, the Belgian capital market is a small affair, used more by public institutions than the private sector (Table 4.2). Belgians dislike equities, having instead a traditional preference for property. Although 328 Belgian shares are quoted no more than 25 are considered suitable for institutional investment. Petrofina alone is reckoned to account for 25 per cent of total turnover. The banks are primarily providers of short-term credit; they arrange bond placings and, since they are allowed to deal on their own account for amounts in excess of BF 10 million, effectively control the equity market. In recent years industry has been largely financed by substantial credit from the banks and the semi-public credit institutions as part of the national programme of economic expansion. Predominant among the semi-official credit institutions are Société Nationale de Credit à l'Industrie (SNCI), established in 1919, and Société Nationale d'Investissements (SNI), which was formed in 1962. SNCI aims to promote the development of industry by granting long- and medium-term loans, but in contrast with SNI it never provides capital by way of equity investment; at the end of 1972 its

TABLE 4.1. THE TWO LARGEST BELGIAN HOLDING COMPANIES

1 Société Générale de Belgique **Main interests**	*% of assets*
Companies—24 investments	35.6
Société Générale de Banque (22.2% owned)	
Banque Belge pour l'Etranger (99.8%)	
Banque Belge Ltd, London (93.8%)	
Holding companies	
Union Financière et Industrielle (62.2%)	
Metalchim (74.4%)	
Sofina (27.2%)	
Non-ferrous metals and minerals—8 investments	22.1
Union Minière (18.2%)	
Société Générale des Minerais (77.9%)	
Metallurgie Hoboken-Overpelt (59.1%)	
Energy—10 investments (4 in liquidation)	11.0
Société de Fraction et d'Electricite (41%)	
Petrofina (6.7%)	
Iron and steel—3 investments	9.3
Cockerill (17.4%)	
Arbed (15.1%)	
Sidmar (69.9%)	
Construction and property—7 investments	6.7
Cimenteries CBR (25.8%)	
Electrical—9 investments	5.2
ACEC (10.9%)	
The rest—12 investments	10.1
	100.0

Source: 1973 Annual Report.

TABLE 4.1—(continued) THE TWO LARGEST BELGIAN HOLDING COMPANIES

2 Bruxelles Lambert	
Main interests	
	% of assets
Property and property companies	14.8
Financial—75 investments	24.1
Banque Lambert (100% owned)	
Dewaay, Cortvriendt (stockbroker)	
Banque de Bruxelles (9.7%)	
L'Urbaine (life assurance, 43%)	
William Witter (US stockbrokers, 20%)	
Berliner Handels-Gesellschaft (2%)	
Oil—1 investment	10.3
Petrofina (2.5%)	
Drink—8 investments	8.6
Heineken (2%)	
Bralima (various)	
Utilities—4 investments	8.3
Electrobel (7%)	
Electrogaz (7%)	
Intercom (1%)	
Interbrabant (2%)	
Steel, metal—15 investments	7.3
Cockerill ($2\frac{1}{2}$%)	
Thy-Marcinelle (23%)	
Tourism, coal, distribution, food, engineering, textiles, radio—185 investments	19.8
CLT (Radio Luxembourg, 35%)	
Wagons Lits (9%)	
Short-term assets	6.8
	100.0

Source: The Economist.

total resources amounted to $\$3\frac{1}{4}$ million while outstanding loans stood at \$3 million.

The independence of the Belgian Congo (now Zaire) in 1960 was a tremendous blow to the Belgian economy. Yet thanks to the EEC it has achieved and maintains a high growth rate, with over 45 per cent of GNP exported—the highest percentage in the world.

Apart from through its membership of the EEC, Belgium has close ties with Luxembourg in the form of the Belgian and Luxembourg Union (BLEU) dating from 1921, and with Benelux, first set up in 1948, which also includes the Netherlands. As a founder member of the EEC, Belgium is an enthusiastic supporter of the European ideal and since the old Six

TABLE 4.2. ISSUES OF SHARES AND BONDS (in BF billions)

	1967	*1970*
Public	**52.7**	**70.6**
State	12.2	10.5
Autonomous funds and social security funds	12.2	12.2
Public credit institutions	12.5	21.6
(of which tap issues)	(6.8)	(15.2)
Local authorities	12.8	19.5
(of which tap issues)	(9.0)	(11.0)
Public enterprises	3.0	6.8
Private	**14.4**	**26.9**
Shares:		
Belgian companies	4.6	1.9
Foreign companies and investment trusts	0.2	11.2
Bonds:		
Tap issues	6.8	12.5
Block issues	2.8	1.3
Total	**67.1**	**97.5**
Of which, total tap issues	23.6	38.7

Source: Commission Bancaire.

alone accounted for almost 70 per cent of Belgian trade she has good reason to remain that way.

BUSINESS ORGANISATIONS

The Belgian law on business organisations is contained in the Commercial Code. It dates from 1873, with major amendments in 1935, and really follows the same pattern as French legislation. All business entities must be registered with the Register of Commerce which is kept at the office of each and every Commercial Court and centrally at the Ministry of Middle Classes (Ministère des Classes Moyennes/Ministerie van Middenstand) in Brussels. All of the organisations shown in Fig. 4.1 apart from joint ventures are endowed with separate legal personality apart from their members.

Companies

Both *sociétés anonymes* (SAs) and *sociétés de personnes à responsibilité limitée* (SPRLs) have a statutory life of 30 years which is renewable. At the end of 1970 there were over 30,000 SPRL companies in existence compared

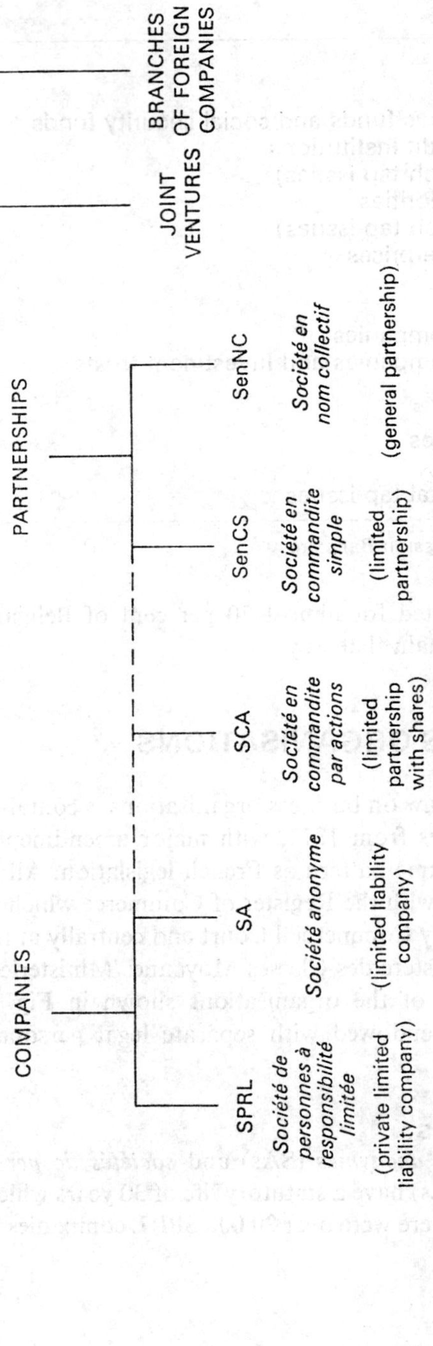

Fig. 4.1 Forms of business organisation in Belgium

with 17,600 SAs (Table 4.3). SPRLs cannot engage in any form of banking, insurance or investment. The particular characteristics of each form of company may be compared as follows:

	SA	*SPRL*
Shareholders	Minimum of 7, and no restrictions on nationality or residence.	Minimum of 2, maximum of 50. Husband and wife count as one, and only physical persons can be members. No restrictions on nationality or residence.
Securities	Can issue shares (*actions*) or sub-shares with or without a par value which may be registered or in bearer form if fully paid. May also issue beneficiary shares (*parts bénéficiares*) which do not constitute capital but entitle holders to a share of profits.	Contributions are represented by registered certificates (*droits sociaux*) all of which must be of the same class with a minimum par value of BF 1000 and are not divisible. Transfers require approval from 50 per cent of the members representing 75 per cent of the capital. Cannot issue beneficiary shares.
Capital	No minimum. Capital must be fully subscribed and 20 per cent paid up in cash or otherwise. Can purchase own shares from the surplus over and above the capital and legal reserve. Issued bonds cannot exceed paid-in capital.	Minimum of BF 250,000, all of which (and a further 20 per cent of any additional amount) must be paid up. Cannot issue bonds.
Capital impairment	If accumulated losses exceed 50 per cent of the share capital the directors are obliged to call a general meeting to decide whether to continue or discontinue the business. When losses exceed 75 per cent of share capital members holding 25 per cent of the capital represented at the general meeting may demand dissolution.	
		If capital falls below BF 200,000, the SPRL can be dissolved at the request of any interested party.
Annual general meeting	An AGM must be held each year.	

TABLE 4.3. STATISTICS OF BELGIAN COMPANIES, 1970

	Belgian	*Foreign*	*Total*
Sociétés anonyme (SA)	17,598	156	17,754
Sociétés en commandite par actions (SCA)	15	1	16
Sociétés de personnes à responsibilité limitée	30,043	14	30,057
Other enterprises	6,896	1,309	8,205
Inactive companies	3,505	30	3,535
Companies in liquidation, etc.	4,143	17	4,160
Total companies	**62,200**	**1,527**	**63,727**

Source: Ministry of Finance.

SAs are managed by a board of at least three directors (*administrateurs*), elected by the shareholders for periods up to six years. The board of directors may delegate the daily management to executive managers (*administrateurs délegués*) or managers (*gérants*). Each director is obliged to pledge a certain number of registered shares to be determined by the articles as a guarantee (*cautionnement*) for the performance of his duties. The directors have the power to perform all acts of management and are responsible for the preparation of the annual accounts. Their remuneration is normally specified in the articles and may be a fixed amount and/or a percentage of profits.

SPRLs are managed by a manager (*gérant*) or board of managers (*collège de gestion*) who need not be shareholders.

Partnerships

Under Belgian law only the names of the partners may form a part of the name of the general partnership (*société en nom collectif* (SNC)/*vennootschap onder gemeenschappelijke naam*).

The limited partnership (*société en commandite simple* (SCS)/*vennootschap bij wijze van eenvoudige geldschieting*) is managed by general partners (*commandités*), one of whose names must be the name of the firm. Limited partners (*commanditaires*) cannot participate in management without becoming fully liable and the names of the limited partners may not form part of the firm name.

Limited Partnerships with Shares

The Belgian limited partnership with shares (*société en commandite par actions* (SCA)/*vennootschap bij wijze van geldschieting op aandelen*) is a replica of a similar French entity of the same name. SCAs are generally subject to the same provisions as SAs and are managed by managing partners (*associés gérants*) named in the partnership agreement. Unless otherwise provided, the SCA terminates upon death of the managing partner.

Joint Ventures

Belgian law recognises two forms of joint venture, *association momentanée/tijdelijke vereniging* (temporary association) and *association en participation/verening in deelneming*. The temporary association is formed by individual or corporate members, without use of a separate name, with the object of performing one or several specific commercial operations. The partners are free to decide on the distribution of profits, but any provision reserving all the profit or loss for one partner is illegal.

The *association en participation* is a joint venture in which individual or corporate partners take a financial interest in the result of business operations undertaken by only one of the partners who manages the association's affairs in his own name. Joint ventures are not separate legal entities.

Branches of Foreign Companies

Apart from the usual establishment requirements foreign companies setting up branch operations in Belgium are obliged to publish their annual accounts in the *Annexe au Moniteur Belge* (Annexe of the Belgian State Gazette). It is also necessary to designate a responsible resident representative for tax purposes and companies must furnish a guarantee for payment of all Belgian taxes. Generally, a branch operation has few advantages and most foreign companies prefer to establish a Belgian subsidiary.

Works Councils

Under a law dated 20 September 1948, Belgium introduced various institutions designed to provide for the participation of employees, namely:

1. A Central Council of the Economy (Comité National d'Expansion Economique) including representatives from labour, management and the Government.
2. Joint labour–management councils for each sector of industry.
3. Works councils (*conseils d'entreprises*).

Works councils are compulsory in all enterprises with 150 or more employees and consist of the employer as president and representatives of the employees.

The works councils are mainly concerned with working conditions and management relations. In contrast with the German works councils their powers are very limited.

ACCOUNTING AND FINANCIAL REPORTING

The standard of accounting and financial reporting in Belgium is almost as poor as that in Italy. Unlike the Italians, however, the Belgians are now making a very determined effort to reform their law on the basis of the draft Fourth Directive of the European Commission and by adopting a national accounting plan similar to the French Plan Comptable Général. In April 1973 the Central Council of the Economy issued its proposal for a Belgian national accounting plan (Plan Comptable Général Belge) but at the time of going to press this has not yet received the Royal Assent. The proposals include:

1. A detailed chart of accounts very similar to that of the French Plan Comptable Général (page 9) but without Class 9 (cost accounts).
2. Model financial statements and rules for the valuation of assets and liabilities and the determination of profit based on the first draft of the EEC's Fourth Directive (page 323).

The proposed chart of accounts (Plan Raymond Mayer), recommended since 1964 by the Collège National des Experts Comptables, has now been adopted by several companies. The Belgians were first introduced to charts of accounts by Hector Blairon in 1926 and in fact many industries had their own charts before German prescription enforced uniform accounting during the Second World War.

Accounting Principles

Belgium has no established accounting principles. The annual accounts are the sole responsibility of the directors, who are supposed to be guided by caution and good faith. Indeed, directors can be held liable for overvaluation and in practice the worst features of conservative accounting prevail. Against this vacuum it is not surprising that tax laws contain many accounting rules, and it is these which have tended to become standard practices, since it is accepted that companies can prepare only one set of accounts for both commercial and taxation purposes.

The detailed valuation rules of the draft law will make a big difference and it is interesting to note that Article 4 of the proposed law contains the following provision:

> On the advice of the most representative professional organisations, the Minister of Economic Affairs can, in a particular field, bring to the provisions of the present bill or its annexes all derogation or changes justified by the character of the particular field in question.

It would thus appear that the Belgians appreciate the need for some flexibility in the establishment of accounting and reporting standards—indeed, the possibility of some derogation to the accountancy profession is also held out by the proposed law which continues: "These measures can be taken when proposed by an official to be designated by the Minister of Economic Affairs."

Accounting Practices and the Annual Accounts

Campaigning annual financial reports are hardly a feature of the Belgian business scene and companies generally tend to disclose the absolute minimum required by law—a fact which is often attributed to the stranglehold of the ubiquitous holding companies.

The Commercial Code stipulates that the management of every company must prepare "an inventory containing a schedule of real and personal property and of all assets and liabilities" (Article 77). A typical set of accounts as published in the Annexe of the *Moniteur Belge* is shown in Figs. 4.2 and 4.3, and these, together with the accounting practices followed, are discussed in the following sections.

Consolidated Accounts

The law makes no reference to consolidated accounts and very few companies including the largest holding company consolidate. Moreover, the draft law contains no provision for consolidation.

The Balance Sheet

Fixed assets. Fixed assets are generally stated at cost less depreciation. Cost may include installation or transport costs in which their ancillary items may be depreciated at a faster rate than the main asset. As far as depreciation is concerned, companies use the rates up to the maximum allowed for tax purposes and less or even no depreciation may be provided

ETABLISSEMENTS ALEX CARTIER
société anonyme, à Forest—Bruxelles
Avenue Van Vromen, 371
Registre du commerce de Bruxelles, n° 14,668
Acte constitutif publié année 1951, n° 1200 aux annexes du Moniteur Belge

BILAN AU 31 DECEMBRE 19—(BALANCE SHEET AS AT 31 DECEMBER 19—)
approuvé par l'assemblée générale ordinaire du 16 avril 19— (Approved by general meeting at 16 April 19—)
Actif (Assets)
Immobilisé (Fixed)
Réalisable (Current)
Disponible (Cash)
Compte de régularisation (Miscellaneous debits)
Passif (Liabilities)
Non exigible (Stockholders' investment)
Capital (Capital stock)
Réserve légale (Legal reserve)
Réserves et provision (Reserves and provisions)
Fonds d'amortissements (Accumulated depreciation)
Exigible (Liabilities)
A court terme (Short-term current liabilities)
Emprunt hypothécaire (Mortgage loan)
Divers créditeurs (Other creditors)
Résultat (Retained earnings)
Bénéfice reporté (Beginning balance)
Bénéfice de l'exercice (Current year's profit)

COMPTES DE PERTES ET PROFITS (PROFIT AND LOSS ACCOUNT)
Débit (Debit)
Frais généraux et divers (Administrative and miscellaneous expenses)
Amortissements (Depreciation)
Solde bénéficiare (Balance)
Crédit (Credit)
Report à nouveau (Balance beginning of year)
Bénéfice brut et divers (Gross and miscellaneous profit)
Répartition bénéficiare (Distribution of profit)
Tantièmes (Directors' fees)
Dividendes (Dividends)
Réserve spéciale (Special reserve)
Report à nouveaux (Carried forward)
Situation de capital: Entièrement libéré (Capital is fully paid)
Liste des administrateurs et du commissaire (List of directors and statutory auditor)

Fig. 4.2 Example of Belgian financial statements in French

Source: The data for this and the following two illustrations are taken from *Business Study: Belgium* (Touche Ross & Co., October 1969)

ETABLISSEMENTEN ALEX CARTIER
nammloze vennootschap te Zelzate
Van Looystraat, 17
Handelsregister van Gent, nr. 15,667
Stichtingsakte verschenen in de bijlagen van het Belgisch Staatsblad, jaar 1949, nr. 18,858

BALANS OP 31 DECEMBRE 19— (BALANCE SHEET AS AT 31 DECEMBER 19—)
Goedgekeurd door de algemene vergadering der aandeelhouders van 13 april 19— (Approved by general meeting at 13 April 19—)
Activa (Assets)
Vastliggend (Fixed assets)
Omzetbaar (Receivables and inventories)
Beschikbaar (Cash)
Divers activa (Miscellaneous debits)
Passiva (Liabilities)
Niet Eisbaar (Stockholders' investment)
Kapital (Capital stock)
Wettelijke reserve (Legal reserve)
Andere reserves (Other reserves)
Eisbaar (Long-term and current liabilities)
Schuldeisers op korte termijn (Short-term current liabilities)
Hypotecaire lening (Mortgage loan)
Verscheidene schuldeisers (Other creditors)
Afschrijvingen (Accumulated depreciation)
Resultaat (Retained earnings)
Overdracht vorig boekjaar (Beginning balance)
Winst van het jaar (Net earnings for the year)

VERLIES—EN WINSTREKENING (PROFIT AND LOSS ACCOUNT)
Debet (Debit)
Bedrijfsonkosten (General and administrative expenses)
Afschrijvingen (Depreciation)
Batig saldo (Balance end of year)
Krediet (Credit)
Overgedragen saldo (Beginning balance)
Brutowinst en verscheidene inkomsten (Gross and miscellaneous income)
Verdeling der winsten (Distribution of profit)
Tantièmes (Directors' fees)
Dividenden (Dividends)
Bijzondere reserve (Special reserve)
Overdracht op nieuw (Carried forward)
Het kapitaal is volstort (Capital is fully paid)
Lijst der in fuctie zijnde beheerders en toezichter (List of directors and statutory auditor)

Fig. 4.3 Example of Belgian financial statements in Flemish

ACTIF	ACTIVA	ASSETS
Immobilisé	**Vastliggend**	**Fixed assets**
Immobilisations industrielles non réévaluées	*Niet herwaardeerd vastliggend*	Non-revalued industrial building and equipment
Amortissements	*Afschrijvingen*	Accumulated depreciation
Immobilisations industrielles réévaluées	*Herwaardeerd vastliggend*	Revalued industrial building and equipment
Immobilisations incorporelles	*Onstoffelijk vastliggend*	Intangible assets
Disponible et réalisable	**Beschikbaar en omzetbaar**	**Current assets**
Caisse, chèques postaux, banque	*Kas, postchecks, bank*	Petty cash, postal accounts, bank
Clients et effets à recevoir	*Klanten en te ontvangen wissels*	Accounts receivable and notes receivable
Portefeuille, titres et participations financières	*Effectenbezit, titels en financiele aandelen*	Investments—financial interests
Timbres divers	*Verscheidene zegels*	Miscellaneous stamps
Débiteurs divers et garanties	*Verscheidene schuldenaars en waarborgen*	Other debts and deposits
Magasins et travaux en cours	*Inventaries en werk aan de gang*	Inventories and work in process
PASSIF	**PASSIVA**	**LIABILITIES**
Non exigible	**Niet eisbaar**	**Stockholders' investments**
Capital	*Kapitaal*	Capital stock
Réserve légale	*Wettelijke reserve*	Legal reserve
Réserve extraordinaire	*Buitengewone reserve*	Extraordinary reserve
Exigible	**Eisbaar**	**Liabilities**
Crédit d'investissement	*Investeringskrediet*	Investment loan
Emprunt hypothécaire	*Hypothecaire lening*	Mortgage loan
Fournisseurs	*Leveranciers*	Trade accounts payable
Effets à payer	*Te betalen wissels*	Notes payable
Dividendes non réclamés	*Niet teruggevorderde dividenden*	Unclaimed dividends payable
Dividendes à payer	*Te betalen dividenden*	Dividends payable
Précompte professionnel à payer	*Te betalen bedrijfsvoorheffing*	Taxes withheld from employees
Charges sociales à payer	*Te betalen sociale lasten*	Social security
Prévision fiscale	*Fiskale provisie*	Tax provision
Créditeurs divers	*Verscheidene schuldeisers*	Other creditors
Solde bénéficiaire	*Batig saldo*	Earnings

Fig. 4.4 List of balance sheet accounts (not typical of those published in the *Moniteur Belge*). The column on the left contains the account name in French, the centre column is in Flemish and the column on the right is the English translation

in years of lower or nil profits; this practice will be forbidden by the proposed law. In the past, companies have been allowed to revalue fixed assets free of tax liabilities on two occasions provided that the surplus would not be distributed. The draft law permits the restatement of fixed assets at replacement values.

Intangible assets. Such assets are stated at cost generally under the heading of fixed assets. Both goodwill and initial expenses can in certain circumstances be amortised for tax purposes. The proposed law specifies the treatment of intangibles in detail:

1. Initial expenses can be capitalised, but they must be depreciated by at least 10 per cent per annum and profits cannot be distributed until

such expenses are fully written off or covered by retained profits.

2. Discount on bond issues can be capitalised and written off over the life of the issue.
3. Goodwill and research and development expenses must be expensed within 10 years.

Inventories. Tax law states that inventories must be valued at the lower of cost or market value. Cost can be calculated on a FIFO or average basis; LIFO and the base stock method are not permitted. Work in progress and finished goods are generally valued at the combined cost of materials, direct labour and factory overheads. Inventories are often written down below the above value by means of provisions—a practice which is encouraged by the tax law since such writebacks can be tax free. The draft law necessitates the valuation of inventory at the lower of cost or market value and permits FIFO and LIFO or any similar method.

Receivables and liabilities. Any amount due to the company by its managers, directors or auditors must be separately stated in a note to the balance sheet. The draft bill provides for an analysis of all receivables and liabilities between those which are due in more than one year and those which are more than six months overdue.

Reserves. Every SA, SPRL and SCA must set up a legal reserve by annual transfers of at least 5 per cent of net profits until the reserve equals at least 10 per cent of capital. Share premiums need not be capitalised. A reserve resulting from revaluation cannot be distributed.

The Profit and Loss Account

The amount of information normally given in profit and loss accounts varies enormously but sales are seldom revealed. Any amount shown as *tantièmes* often refers only to the directors' percentage of profits; their aggregate emoluments are rarely shown. Exceptional and prior-year items are not normally stated.

Publication and Filing of Financial Statements

The annual accounts are sent to the registered members and these, as specified below, must be available for inspection by shareholders at the company's registered offices at least 15 days before the general meeting:

1. The balance sheet and profit and loss statement.
2. Schedule of Government securities (*fonds publics*), shares, bonds and other corporate securities held by the company.
3. A schedule of those shareholders whose shares are not fully paid,

with the number of shares and the domiciles of the shareholders indicated.

4. The auditors' report and, if applicable, the additional report of the *commissaire-reviseur* (*cf.* page 141).

Any member holding bearer shares can also arrange to receive the above documents "upon presentation of his shares 15 days before the general meeting". Having approved the balance sheet (*i.e.* the accounts), the meeting then votes to release (*décharge*) the directors and auditors from liability. The release is valid only "if the balance sheet has no omission and does not contain false information thereby concealing the true situation of the company" (Article 79). Within 15 days of the general meeting the directors of all SAs and SCAs should ensure that the balance sheet and profit and loss account are published by filing them with the Registre du Commerce. Within 10 days of filing, both statements are published in the Annexe to the *Moniteur Belge* and copies are sent to the clerks of the local courts and tribunals where any interested party may examine them. In addition to the balance sheet and profit and loss account, companies should also publish the names, professions and domiciles of the directors and auditors with special mention of any *commissaire-reviseur* and a table indicating the allocation and distribution of profits.

SPRLs need only file their balance sheets within 15 days of approval with the office of the clerk of the local Commercial Court (*greffe du tribunal de commerce*) where it can be examined by any interested person.

Directors' Report

Although the directors are obliged to present a report on the company's operations to the auditors, the contents of this report are not specified; nor is there any obligation that it must be published.

Stock Exchange Listing Requirements

The only important stock exchange is in Brussels and companies seeking a listing of shares or bonds must file an application, generally through a bank, with the Listing Committee (Comité de la Cote). All issues are supervised by the all-powerful Commission Bancaire which can delay an issue for up to two or three months. In order to obtain a quote, the capital and reserves of the company have to total at least BF 10 million and at least 15 per cent of the securities issued by the company must be available to the public. Notice of the intended listing should be published in the *Moniteur Belge* along with accounts for the past two years. Bonds will be listed only if the company has already issued quoted shares and a minimum nominal value of each bond is BF 1000. Foreign companies need the approval of the Minister of Finance and such companies should be listed in their country of incorporation.

Business Records

The Commercial Code lays down that every company should keep a "total balance" book (*livre d'inventaire*) containing copies of the annual accounts and an official journal which is now limited to recording summaries of transactions. These books must be prenumbered and authorised by presentment to a judge at the Commercial Court, the Mayor or a councillor who stamps them. Companies must keep detailed personnel and payroll records under the Labour Law. Registers are necessary for any nominative shares or bonds if issued; the usual books of account are maintained and these, together with the copies of all correspondence, have to be retained for 10 years. Since 1973 companies have had to keep all records including correspondence in either Flemish or French, depending on the areas in which they operate.

THE ACCOUNTANCY PROFESSION

The Belgian accountancy profession is fragmented and disunited. At the time of going to press, the Belgian Government appears determined to resolve the situation once and for all, but several years of discussion have produced little in the way of progress.

Institut des Reviseurs d'Entreprises

The Institut des Reviseurs d'Entreprises was established by the law of 22 July 1953 as a body of highly competent accountants whose members' main function is the auditing of quoted companies. With less than 350 quoted companies to audit, the number of *reviseurs d'entreprises* has remained low, hardly changing from the original 200 admitted in 1953. Members generally practise alone but there are 13 partnerships, of which the largest is that of Berger, Block, Kirschen, Schellekens & Co.

Institut des Reviseurs de Banque

Formed in 1935, the year in which the banking activities of the holding companies were hived off to subsidiaries, the Institut des Reviseurs de Banque is a separate body of bank auditors. Members of this body are appointed by the Commission Bancaire and the banks are free to choose from an annual list. With only 80 banks the number of *reviseurs de banque* is theoretically limited to 36 but in recent years the number has not gone beyond 24 or 25. *Reviseurs de banque* were allowed to become members of the Institut des Reviseurs d'Entreprises on its formation and almost all of them decided to become members.

TABLE 4.4. MEMBERSHIP OF THE BELGIAN ACCOUNTANCY PROFESSION (as at 31 December 1973)

Reviseurs de banque	**24**
Reviseurs d'entreprises	**227**
Experts comptables CNECB	**1,525**
In practice	568
Employees in business	722
Retired (members of honour)	235
Number of students	
Reviseurs d'entreprises	49
Experts comptables CNECB	456

Collège National des Experts Comptables de Belgique

This body was formed on 20 April 1950 as an association of 20 professional groups which still retain their individual identity. Although it lacks legal status the CNECB may be considered as the most representative body of mainstream accountants in Belgium.

The first Belgian accountancy body, the Chambre Syndicale des Experts Comptables, was formed in 1903. Other bodies grew up all over the country and shortly before the Second World War proposals were put before Parliament to give the profession legal status. Unfortunately the war intervened and the proposed law was dropped. In 1942 the Germans made some effort to establish a State body but this proved unsuccessful and was suppressed after the war. With the formation of the Collège in 1950 the Belgian accountancy profession was almost united until the 1953 law set up the more exclusive Institut des Reviseurs d'Entreprises. Almost 50 per cent of the members of the Institut are *experts comptables*. Members of the Collège bear the designation *experts comptables CNECB*. In 1957 the member bodies of the CNECB also set up another body, the Association Nationale des Comptables en Belgique, to represent a second tier of members who did not aspire to become *experts comptables*.

Education and Training

The entry routes to both of the major accounting bodies are shown in Fig. 4.5.

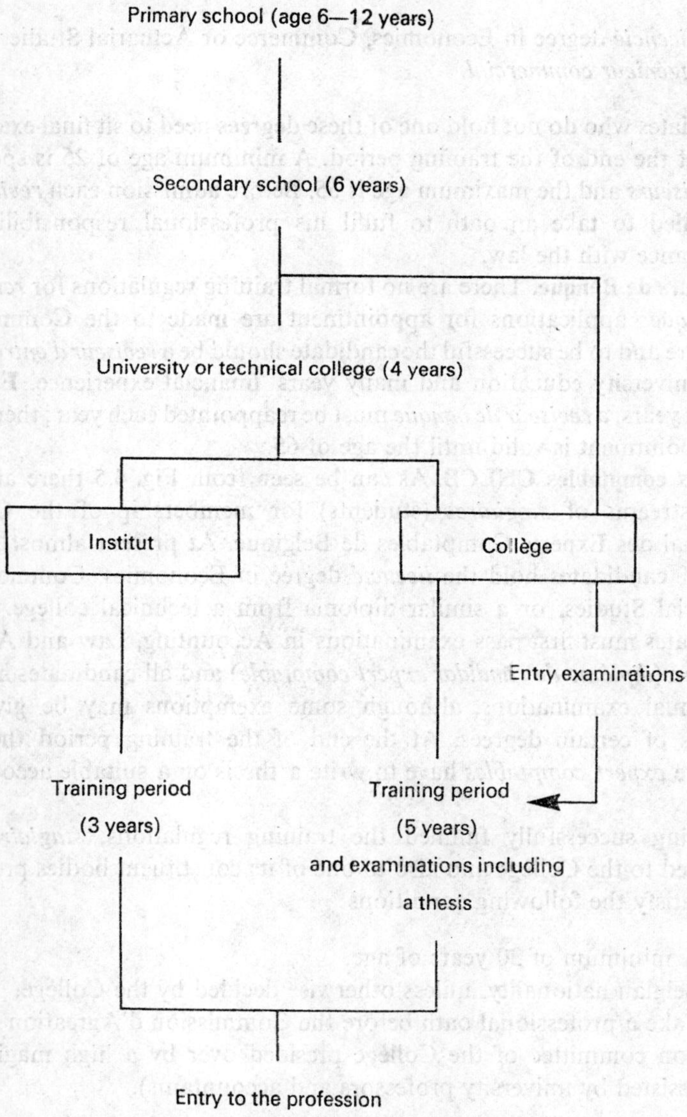

Fig. 4.5 The way to become a Belgian accountant

Reviseurs d'Entreprises. At the end of the training period, the prospective *reviseur* generally holds one of the following degrees:

1. *Licencié* degree in Economics, Commerce or Actuarial Studies.
2. *Ingénieur commercial.*

Candidates who do not hold one of these degrees need to sit final examinations at the end of the training period. A minimum age of 25 is specified for *reviseurs* and the maximum age is 65. Before admission each *reviseur* is compelled to take an oath to fulfil his professional responsibilites in accordance with the law.

Reviseurs de Banque. There are no formal training regulations for *reviseurs de banque*; applications for appointment are made to the Commission Bancaire and to be successful the candidate should be a *reviseur d'entreprises* with university education and many years' financial experience. For the first six years, a *reviseur de banque* must be reappointed each year; thereafter his appointment is valid until the age of 65.

Experts comptables CNECB. As can be seen from Fig. 4.5 there are two main streams of *stagiaires* (students) for membership of the Collège National des Experts Comptables de Belgique. At present almost 50 per cent of candidates hold the *licencié* degree in Economics, Commerce or Actuarial Studies, or a similar diploma from a technical college. Other candidates must first pass examinations in Accounting, Law and Administration (*diplôme de candidat expert comptable*) and all candidates have to sit annual examinations, although some exemptions may be given to holders of certain degrees. At the end of the training period the prospective *expert comptables* have to write a thesis on a suitable accounting topic.

Having successfully fulfilled the training regulations, *stagiaires* are admitted to the Collège and also to one of its constituent bodies provided they satisfy the following conditions:

1. A minimum of 30 years of age.
2. Belgian nationality, unless otherwise decided by the Collège.
3. Take a professional oath before the Commission d'Agreation (selection committee of the Collège presided over by a high magistrate, assisted by university professors and accountants).

There is no obligation for candidates to train in practice; the only condition required by the CNECB is that each *stagiaire* must be attached to a member of the Collège.

Ethics

The Minister of Economic Affairs issued an ethical code for *reviseurs d'entreprise* by Royal Decree on 16 March 1957. The Collège has also issued a similar code.

Reviseurs d'Entreprises. Members of the Institut may not advertise or engage in any form of publicity. A member cannot have financial interests in his clients and in theory cannot act as a book-keeper, tax adviser, management consultant, businessman, insurance broker, etc. Article 7 of the law of 22 July 1953 provides that *reviseurs* may not, except for educational activities:

1. Enter upon a dependent relationship through a contract of employment.
2. Act as director or representative of a commercial company.
3. Do work paid by the State, provincial or local authorities.

Reviseurs de Banque. The activities of each *reviseur de banque* are subject to the strict control of the Commission Bancaire. A *reviseur de banque* cannot have a material financial interest in any bank and can act as a *commissaire-reviseur* of non-banks only with the approval of the Commission Bancaire.

Experts comptables CNECB. The Collège code forbids advertising and demands that the *expert comptable* avoid any situation that might make it difficult for him to fulfil his mission freely. However, members are not barred from holding financial interests in clients.

Services provided

Reviseurs d'entreprise. The Institut des Reviseurs d'Entreprises is a body of auditors and the following specific functions are reserved for its members:

1. Audits of quoted companies (law of 1 December 1953).
2. Audits of organisations of public interest (law of 16 March 1954).
3. Investigations in the case of amendments to the statutes of SAs (law of 30 June 1967) and of SPRLs (law of 26 June 1967).
4. Checking of assets other than cash contributed to SAs or SPRLs.
5. The certifying of the conversion of debentures into capital (law of 23 July 1962).
6. Audit of businesses receiving reimbursable funds from the public (law of 10 June 1964).
7. Investigation in the case of transformation of the companies (law of 23 February 1967).

8. Audit of holding companies (Royal Decree No. 64, 10 November 1967).
9. The *reviseurs d'entreprise* may also audit companies in which the State has a material interest (Royal Decree, 11 November 1967) and may be assigned to missions within the positions of the 1972 law on Economic Expansion (Royal Decree, 25 September 1972).
10. Audit and certification of documents submitted to works councils. In practice this provision is not fully implemented.

Experts comptables CNECB. *Experts comptables* generally practise alone or in small partnerships. They are allowed to enter partnerships with members of other liberal professions, subject to the approval of the Collège, but so far very few such partnerships have been established. Essentially therefore members of the CNECB are concerned with tax matters, auditing and the provision of accounting and book-keeping services.

AUDITING

The general standard of auditing is poor in Belgium and no more than one or two local professional firms have the staff to carry out a UK-style audit. In keeping with the best traditions of conservative accounting, Belgian auditors are generally satisfied with the so-called "minimum position" and do not normally qualify their reports provided at least that the accounts do not overstate the true position. The accountancy bodies have not yet issued any significant audit guidance to their members, although the Commission Bancaire has specified in some detail the minimum work which it expects *reviseurs de banque* to perform. Needless to say, this attitude has led to strong criticism, not least from the trade union movement, and it seems very likely that some Government-inspired effort will soon be made to improve standards.

Appointment of Auditors

Every SA and each SPRL with more than five members is obliged to appoint one or more auditors (*commissaires*) for periods of up to six years. SCAs must appoint three *commissaires* and at least one of the auditors of all quoted SAs and SCAs has to be a member of the Institut des Reviseurs d'Entreprises (*i.e.* a *commissaire-reviseur*). A *commissaire-reviseur* must be appointed for a term of between three and six years. It should be noted that the auditors of all unquoted companies need not have any particular qualifications. The auditors of all SAs and SCAs must deposit shares of the company by way of pledge (*cautionnement*) for the proper fulfilment of their duties. No such pledge is necessary for a *commissaire-reviseur*.

Duties of Auditors

Commissaires are generally charged with auditing (*surveillance*) the annual accounts of the company. At least one month before the general meeting the directors should remit all necessary documents together with a report on the operations of the company to the auditors. The law also stipulates that the directors provide the auditors at least once every six months with a statement summarising the assets and liabilities of the corporation. In addition the law appears to contemplate the appointment of several *commissaires* forming a board of auditors (*conseil de surveillance*) which, in accordance with the articles of the company, are also responsible for the general supervision of the directors, rather like the Italian Collegio Sindicale. Furthermore the Commercial Code states that the articles "may provide that the directors and auditors shall constitute a general council" (Article 68). In the case of SAs and SCAs this council has the right to appoint provisional directors in the event of any vacancies. As far as SCAs are concerned, the law provides that the board of auditors "may give its advice on matters which are submitted to it by the management and may authorise those acts specifically reserved for it" (Article 112).

The Auditors' Report

Article 65 of the Commercial Code directs that the "auditors must submit the results of their findings as they shall deem appropriate to the general meeting and shall advise the general meeting of the method adopted for auditing the inventory". Where the auditors include one or more *reviseurs d'entreprise*, they must submit a separate report. The typical report does not contain an opinion on the fairness of the accounts. The following reports are taken from the English version of the 1973 annual report of Société Générale de Belgique:

Société Générale de Belgique
Report of the board of auditors
Ladies and Gentlemen,

We were much affected to learn of the death of M. Jules Dubois-Pelerin, Honorary Vice-Governor, on 29 August last.

The contacts we have had with him in the course of our various duties were always marked by his intellectual gifts, his thorough knowledge of business and his great competence.

We shall retain an affectionate and appreciative memory of his engaging personality, and we would wish to associate ourselves with the tribute paid to his memory by the Board of Directors of our Company.

As required by law, and by the Articles of Association of your Company, we have the honour to report to you on the exercise of our mandate during the year 1973.

At the monthly meetings of the General Council, the Board of Directors kept us informed of the progress of the Company's affairs.

In July, we held a special meeting of the Board of Auditors to examine the state of the half-yearly accounts as of the end of June.

In due time after the end of the accounting period, we were put in possession of the accounts and the Report of the Board of Directors.

The verification of these documents was carried out by sampling and counterchecks with the books of account, the Bank statements and other voucher documents.

We are thus satisfied that the Balance Sheet and Profit and Loss Account are a true and sincere picture of the situation and earnings of your Company.

We accordingly recommend that you approve these documents, and the appropriation of profits proposed to you by the Board of Directors.

Brussels, 24 January 1974.

P. Solway — Vicomte Ch de Jonghe d'Ardoye
Reporting Member — Chairman

Société Générale de Belgique

Report of the examining board (*commissaire-reviseur*)

Ladies and Gentlemen,

We would associate ourselves most sincerely with the tribute paid by the Board of Directors and by our fellow auditors, to the memory of M. Jules Dubois-Pelerin, Honorary Vice-Governor, who died on 29 August, 1973.

As required by law, and by your Company's Articles of Association, we have the honour to report to you on the execution of our mandate during the year 1973.

We regularly followed the course of the Company's activity by the examination and checking of periodical accountancy statements. In addition, all further information and all voucher documents which we considered necessary or useful in the accomplishment of our task, were always supplied to us without delay. We would add that our task was greatly facilitated by the courtesy of the Company's management and personnel.

The half-yearly accountancy statement, closed as of 30 June, 1973 was put before us with ample commentary; and, in addition, we subjected it to a thorough verification.

We are convinced of the accuracy of the statement of assets and obligations as of 31 December, 1973. Proceeding by way of sampling, we checked the existence of the shares, bonds, cash notes and public funds recorded in the

Balance Sheet. In addition, we noted that these securities had been valued with all necessary caution. The liquid assets were found to accord with the statements of the bankers concerned and of the postal giro system. Adequate provision was made for depreciation. The items making up the suspense accounts were also subjected to a careful examination.

As a result of these investigations, we are able to state our opinion that the Balance Sheet, Profit and Loss Account and the comments of the Board of Directors thereon, reflect sincerely and in good faith the situation of the Company as of 31 December, 1973 and the profits for the accounting period ending on the same date.

We therefore recommend that the General Meeting approve the Balance Sheet and Profit and Loss Account as drawn up by the Board of Directors.
Brussels, 28 January, 1974.

A. Mas
Examining Auditor

Fieldwork

According to Article 65 of the Commercial Code the auditors "have an unlimited right to inspect and audit all operations of the company. They may examine on the premises all books, correspondence and minutes and generally all papers of the company." *Commissaires* may use assistants only if these are approved by the company. It may in fact be said that the standard of auditing is as high as the accounting standards and staff limitations of auditors allow.

Remuneration of Auditors

An auditor's remuneration is fixed by the general meeting at the beginning and for the duration of his term of office but it may be modified with the consent of both parties. Apart from his remuneration the auditor of an SA or SCA cannot receive any benefits in any form from the company; the company may not specifically grant him any loans or advances or accord him any guarantees.

The remuneration of the *reviseur de banque* is usually fixed in advance by the general meeting and must be approved by the Commission Bancaire; this approval is also essential when a *reviseur de banque* acts as a *commissaire-reviseur*.

Removal of Auditors

An auditor may resign or be removed by a general meeting at any time. When a *commissaire-reviseur* is dismissed, the agenda of the general meeting must clearly mention that the dismissed auditor is a member of the Institut des Reviseurs d'Entreprises.

Liability of Auditors

Auditors are jointly and severally liable towards the company and third parties for all damages resulting from a violation of their duty. As already mentioned on page 133, it is customary for the general meeting to release the directors and auditors from all liabilities in connection with the accounts provided that there are no omissions and that the accounts do not contain false information thereby concealing the truth of the position of the company.

Independence of Auditors

The law forbids auditors of SAs and SCAs from exercising any other function in the company apart from that of auditing. The following persons, if related to a director or manager of the company, may not act as *commissaires-reviseurs*: the spouse, ascendants and descendants as well as persons related by marriage to such spouse, ascendants and descendants up to the fourth degree, collateral relatives as well as persons related by marriage to such persons up to the fourth degree. Furthermore, a *commissaire-reviseur* may not be elected director or manager of a company of which he was auditor until three years have elapsed from the termination of such appointment. Similarly a former officer (*préposé*) of the company cannot be appointed as a *commissaire-reviseur* of that company until at least three years after having terminated his services for the company. This section should be read in conjunction with the ethical rules of *reviseurs d'entreprises* and *experts comptables CNECB*. *Reviseurs de banque* may not hold any office in any bank apart from that of auditor.

CONCLUSION

The Belgian profession has a lot of ground to cover before it can hope to achieve the status of its Dutch counterpart. For too long have the main energies of the recognised bodies been channelled towards the preservation of their own privileged position. In the broader context of Europe, it is to be hoped that wiser counsels will prevail and result in the formation of one strong professional body. Only then will the Belgian profession find itself capable of keeping up with the more progressive professions of the United Kingdom, Ireland, the Netherlands, Germany and Denmark.

Chapter 5

Luxembourg

BACKGROUND

With a total land area of no more than 1000 square miles Luxembourg is, of necessity, a very European-minded country. The only major industry is steel and this is the dominion of one company—Arbed-Hadir—which accounts for 25 per cent of the GNP, 65 per cent of exports and almost 50 per cent of the labour force.

In recent years, however, Luxembourg has achieved much more prominence as an international financial centre largely as a result of taxation

TABLE 5.1. THE STRUCTURE OF OFFICIAL LISTINGS ON THE LUXEMBOURG STOCK EXCHANGE

	1969	*1973*
Debenture loans	**407**	**671**
Luxembourg Government loans	28	46 (for the five lines bracketed)
Loans guaranteed by the State	3	
Local authorities (municipalities)	6	
Luxembourg companies	9	
Foreign companies	9	
European and international institutions	28	57
Eurobonds: international loans	221	410
Convertible loans	103	158
Shares and participation certificates	**59**	**75**
Luxembourg	23	24
Other countries	36	51
Investment funds	**90**	**90**
Luxembourg	54	59
Other countries	36	31
Summary		
Debenture loans	407	671
Shares and participation shares	59	75
Investment funds	90	90
Total	**556**	**836**

Source: Luxembourg Stock Exchange.

and exchange control concessions which have particular attractions for holding companies and investment funds. The Stock Exchange achieved little importance until Luxembourg emerged as an important Eurobond centre in the mid 1960s. Of the 836 securities listed at the end of 1973 (Table 5.1), no fewer than 630 were Eurobonds, while a mere 46 could be considered to be domestic securities.

The number of banks operating in Luxembourg has increased from 13

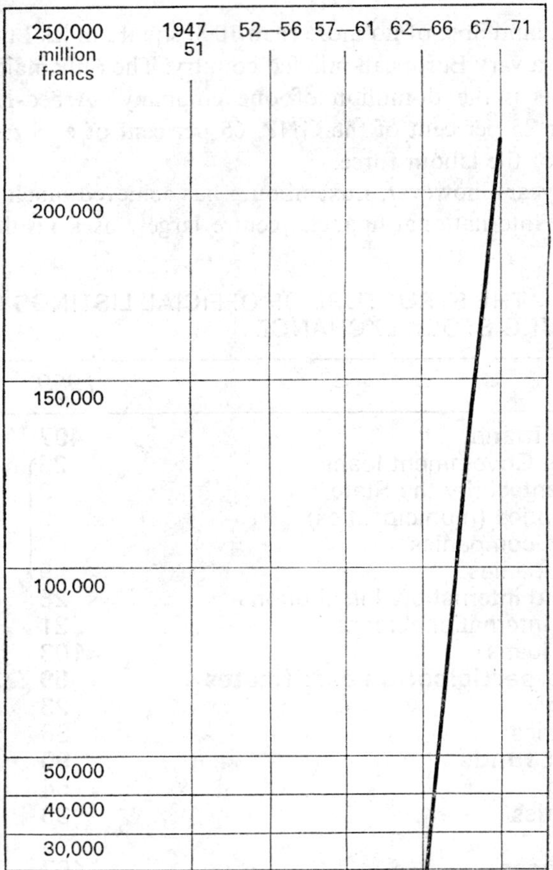

Fig. 5.1 (a) Principal resources of the Luxembourg credit institutions: liabilities against banks

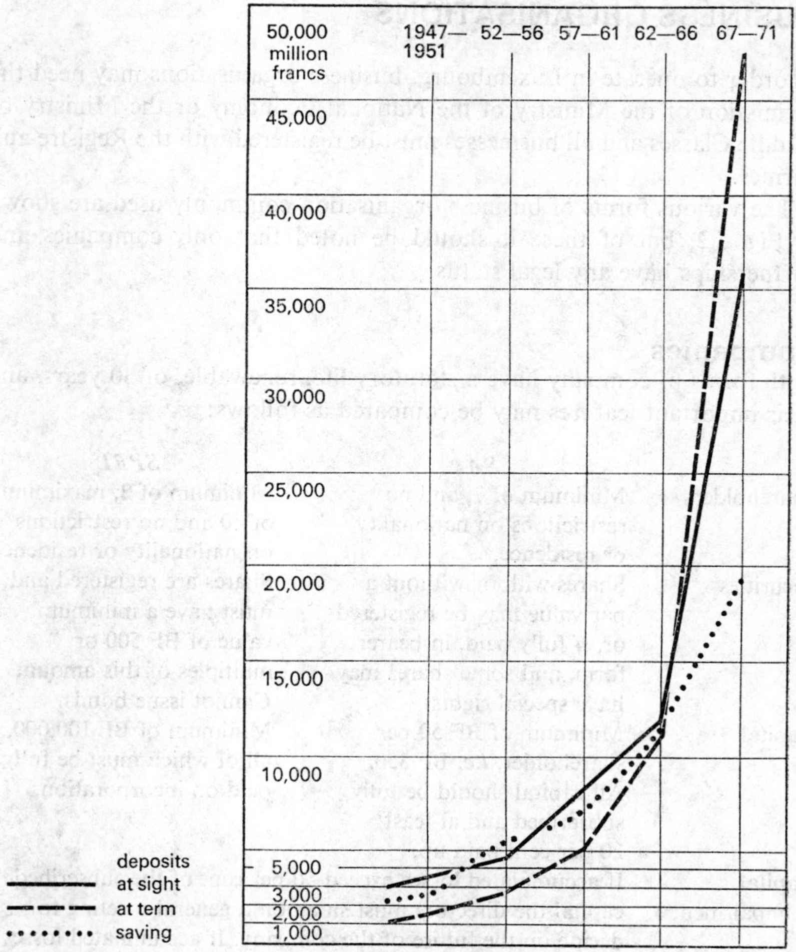

Fig. 5.1 (b) Principal resources of the Luxembourg credit institutions: bank deposits

in 1955 to 70 at the end of 1973; at the same time bank resources have risen astronomically (Fig. 5.1). Surprisingly there is no central bank, but the decision of the EEC to site its most optimistic project of all, the European Monetary Co-operation Fund, in the City of Luxembourg may be taken as an indication of the important role which this very small nation has to play in the new Europe.

BUSINESS ORGANISATIONS

In order to operate in Luxembourg, business organisations may need the permission of the Ministry of the National Economy or the Ministry of Middle Classes and all businesses must be registered with the Registre aux Firmes.

The various forms of business organisation commonly used are shown in Fig. 5.2, but of these it should be noted that only companies and partnerships have any legal status.

Companies

Both forms of company have a statutory life, renewable, of 30 years, and their important features may be compared as follows:

	SA	*SPRL*
Shareholders	Minimum of 7, and no restrictions on nationality or residence.	Minimum of 2, maximum of 40 and no restrictions on nationality or residence.
Securities	Shares with or without a par value may be registered or, if fully paid, in bearer form, and some shares may have special rights.	Shares are registered and must have a minimum value of BF 500 or multiples of this amount. Cannot issue bonds.
Capital	Minimum of BF 50 per shareholder, *i.e.* BF 350. All capital should be fully subscribed and at least 20 per cent paid up.	Minimum of BF 100,000, all of which must be fully paid on incorporation.
Capital impairment	If accumulated losses exceed 50 per cent of the subscribed capital the directors must summon a general meeting to decide on the future of the company. If accumulated losses exceed 75 per cent of the subscribed capital, 25 per cent of the members at the meeting can resolve upon the winding up of the company.	
Annual general meeting	An AGM must be held each year.	

SAs are managed by a minimum of three directors appointed by the shareholders for a period of up to six years. Each director must hold certain qualification shares as determined by the articles.

SPRLs are managed by one or more managers (*gérants*) who need not be members of the company.

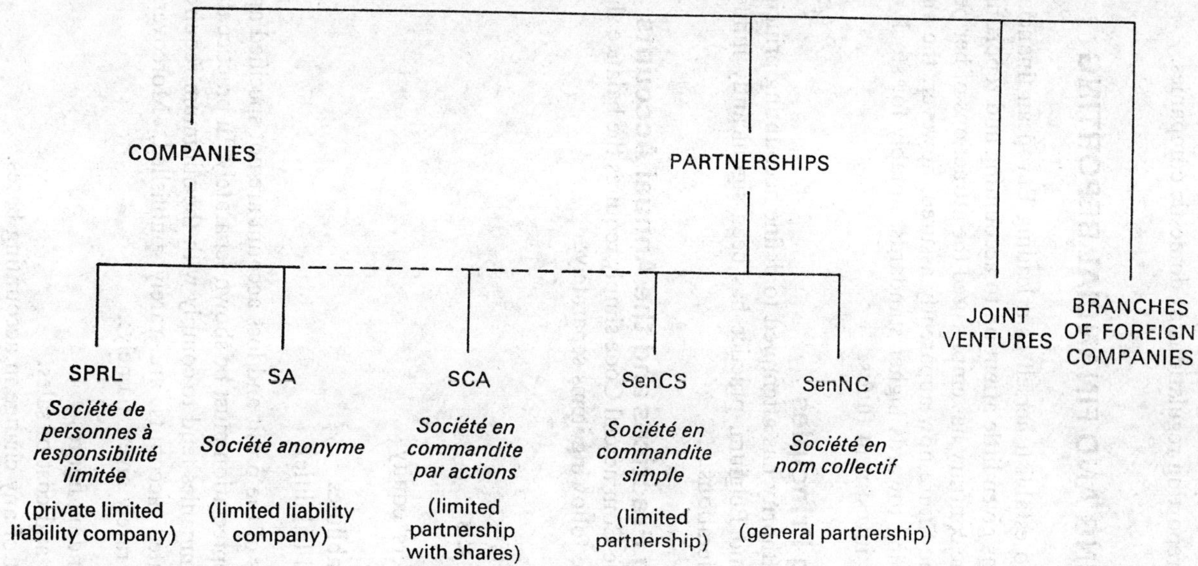

Fig. 5.2 Forms of business organisation in Luxembourg

Branches of Foreign Companies

Foreign companies operating a branch in Luxembourg are subject to the same financial reporting regulations as domestic companies.

ACCOUNTING AND FINANCIAL REPORTING

In her efforts to establish herself as a leading European financial centre, Luxembourg has given little attention to accounting and reporting regulations, but on the contrary has emphasised the attractions of her permissive set-up. With the future now apparently assured, however, the authorities have been moving towards higher standards, notably for stock exchange listings and for investment funds.

Accounting Principles

No separate authority has attempted to define accounting principles and, as in France and Belgium, practice has been significantly influenced by taxation considerations.

Accounting Practices and the Annual Accounts

Article 72 of the Commercial Code simply requires the balance sheet of an SA to show the following items separately:

Assets
- Fixed assets
- Current assets

Liabilities
- Shareholders' equity
- Bonds
- Secured liabilities
- Unsecured liabilities

The contents of the profit and loss account are not specified apart from the fact that depreciation must be shown separately. In practice the annual accounts of companies tend to comply with the minimum required by law and consolidated accounts are rarely published. Moreover, certain information is rarely given, namely:

1. Corresponding figures.
2. Turnover and cost of sales.
3. The effect of any change in accounting bases.
4. Accounting policies.

5. Details of revaluations.
6. Contingent liabilities.
7. Capital commitments.
8. The effect of significant post-balance-sheet events.

It should be mentioned, however, that the Commissaire au Controle des Banques has recently specified a particular format for the financial statements of banks.

The following accounting practices are noteworthy.

The Balance Sheet

Fixed assets. Fixed assets are generally stated at cost but revaluation is permitted. Specifically, any buildings completed prior to 1957 and other fixed assets may be revalued for tax purposes at dates prescribed by tax law. Depreciation rates are agreed with the tax authorities and are usually the same for tax and book purposes since the rates used for tax purposes cannot exceed those used in the commercial accounts. Tax law generally calls for the reducing balance method for all assets except buildings and any fixed assets costing less than BF 15,000 cannot be capitalised. If assets are revalued other than in accordance with tax law, depreciation on the write-up is not an allowable tax deduction.

Inventories. Inventories are valued at the lower of cost or market, and cost may be calculated by any normal method including FIFO if adequate records are maintained.

Liabilities. Normally all liabilities are accounted for, but some, particularly future pension indemnities, are often omitted.

Legal reserve. Companies must create a legal reserve by annual transfers of 5 per cent of net profit until the reserve amounts to 10 per cent of issued share capital. This reserve is not distributable but can be used to absorb losses after all other free reserves have been used.

Publication and Filing of Financial Statements

Fifteen days before the general meeting the company has to supply the shareholders with the statutory auditors' (*commissaires*) report and annual accounts comprising:

1. The balance sheet and profit and loss account.
2. A list of public funds, shares, bonds and other company securities held by the company.
3. A list of shareholders who have shares that are not fully paid up, showing the number of their shares and their addresses.

The above documents are sent to registered shareholders at the same time as the notice of the general meeting and every other shareholder has the right to obtain these documents upon proof of membership.

Having adopted the accounts, the general meeting, as in the case of Belgium, takes a special vote to discharge the directors and *commissaires* from all liability, this discharge being valid only if the "balance sheet" is "correct" and does not conceal the real position.

Within two weeks of being approved, the balance sheet and profit and loss account have to be published in the *Memorial* (Official Gazette). After the balance sheet, the names, forenames, professions and addresses of the directors and auditors in office are published, as well as a table showing the allocation and the disposition of the net profit in accordance with the decisions of the general meeting.

Stock Exchange Listing Requirements

All listing applications need the *Nihil Obstat* of the Commissaire au Controle des Banques who ensures that adequate information is given in the prospectus, which has to be published, by examining numerous documents, including the annual reports and accounts for the last five financial years. Among the items which must be published are the latest published accounts of the company; but if no accounts have yet been published a statement to this effect is sufficient.

Business Records

According to the Code de Commerce companies are obliged to keep:

1. A journal of day-to-day transactions.
2. A record (*livre des inventaires*) of the annual assets and liabilities.

Both books must be presented to the Greffe du Tribunal de Commerce for verification and stamping before use. TVA regulations demand the keeping of invoice registers and the social security laws provide for a personnel register. The registration tax authorities may examine the books of holding companies at any time.

THE ACCOUNTANCY PROFESSION

The Luxembourg accountancy profession is very small, comprising no more than 24 *experts comptables*, of which all but 12 work in three partnerships, the largest of which is Fiduciaire Générale de Luxembourg with eight *experts comptables* and over 100 staff.

The law of 2 June 1962 provided for the regulation of the profession by the Minister of Middle Classes (Ministre des Classes Moyennes). By a Grand Ducal decree issued on 5 March 1970,[1] the profession of accountant is controlled by the State and consists of "organising, controlling, appreciating the value of and adjusting the accounting records and books of whatever kind, and also in analysing by means of the accounting techniques, the situation and the operation of enterprises under their various economic, judicial and financial aspects". All members of the profession belong to a voluntary body, the Ordre des Experts Comptables Luxembourgeois, which was founded in 1951.

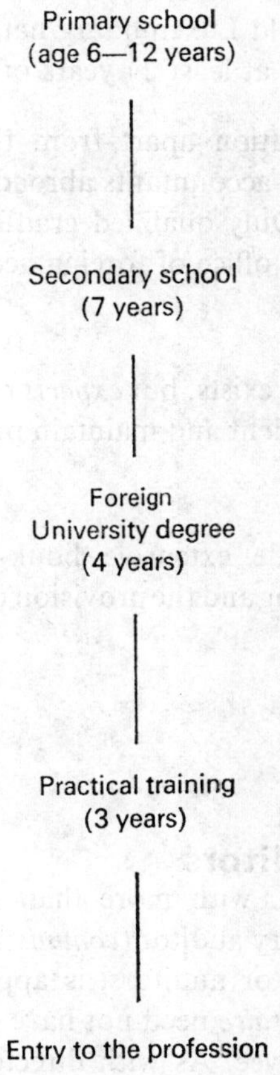

Fig. 5.3 The way to become a Luxembourg accountant

Education and Training

The 1962 law stipulates that all practising accountants hold a written authorisation of the Ministre des Classes Moyennes. The 1970 decree specifies the following conditions which must be met in order to obtain authorisation:

1. Candidates must be graduates of economics or finance and have undergone a three-year period of training, of which two years must be served in the office of a practising Luxembourg *expert comptable*. The rest of the training period may be spent in a bank or other credit institution which the Minister considers will contribute to a proper knowledge of the auditing of accounts and taxation.
2. Candidates should hold Luxembourg nationality.
3. Candidates should be at least 24 years of age.

There is no final examination apart from the above; foreigners duly qualified and recognised as accountants abroad may also be authorised to practise in Luxembourg. Duly qualified graduates can serve one year of their training period in the office of foreign accountants.

Ethics

No established ethical code exists, but *experts comptables* do not advertise, attempt to remain independent and maintain professional secrecy.

Services Provided

Experts comptables provide extensive book-keeping services and are generally involved in auditing and the provision of taxation and management services.

AUDITING

Appointment of Auditors

Each SA and every SPRL with more than 25 members is obliged to appoint at least one statutory auditor (*commissaire*) for any term from one to six years. The auditor, or auditors, is appointed by the members in general meeting. A *commissaire* need not have any qualifications and may even be a company employee. As with directors each *commissaire* must hold a number of qualification shares. These shares need not be held personally but can simply be earmarked as a guarantee by a third party.

Duties and Fieldwork of Auditors

Article 62 of the Commercial Code states that the "auditors have an unlimited right of supervision and control over all company operations. They have access to information from the books, correspondence, minutes and generally all written documents of the company." The law also allows the auditors to appoint an expert to assist them "during the processes leading up to the verification of the books and the accounts of the company". Any such expert must be approved by the company and in the event of any dispute the President of the Commercial Court may choose a suitable expert. In practice, however, such niceties have little relevance: to quote one commentator: "The procedures adopted are mostly either negligible or non-existent."[2]

The Auditors' Report

Each half year the directors render a report to the auditors and at the end of the year the directors have to prepare the annual accounts and submit these, together with a directors' report, to the auditors at least one month before the general meeting. The auditors must submit a report to the general meeting indicating "the results of their efforts, together with any propositions they believe suitable and stating the method by which they have audited inventories". The following is the English text of the report on the 1972 accounts of Arbed:

Arbed

Report of the board of auditors

at the Annual Meeting to be held on 27th April 1973

In accordance with Article 35 of the Company's constitution we have the honour to report to you on the work with which we have been entrusted in respect of the financial year 1972.

On 2nd January 1973 we verified inventories in the Head Office works and mines of the Company. Figures were found to agree with controlled inventories.

The accounts of the divisions and Head Office were verified on 8th and 9th March 1973. The figures are in agreement with those shown in the Balance Sheet presented to you today.

In conformity with Article 32 of the Company's constitution, we would advise you that the following methods of verification have been employed:

for fixed assets, examination of the books
for inventories, sample checks in the divisions
for debtors and creditors, examination of the books
for cash resources, material verification
for the securities portfolio, direct control and sample checks for the number.

On the basis of the verifications mentioned above, we unanimously approve the Balance Sheet and the Profit and Loss Account as proposed to you by the Board of Directors.

Luxembourg, 9th March 1973

The Board of Auditors:
Robert Meyer
Auguste-Charles Laval
Marcel Chautard
Vicomte Gérard le Hardy de Beaulieu
André Ziane
Phillippe Boulin
Vicomte Julien Davignon
Herbert Ensch
Jean du Verdier de Genouillac
Albert Bousson
Pierre-Marie Fourt
Robert Schaffner
Ferdinand Kihn

Remuneration and Removal of Auditors

The general meeting decides upon the auditor's remuneration and may remove him at any time. The fees of the *commissaire* are not tax deductible.

Liability of Auditors

A *commissaire* may be held liable in an action for negligence where damage has been caused to clients or third parties.

Independence of Auditors

As already stated, the Luxembourg *commissaire* is bound by no independence rules and may even be an employee or relation of the directors.

CONCLUSION

The future of the embryonic local profession seems assured. There would also appear to be some opportunity for the international accounting firms which have, so far, taken little interest in Luxembourg, especially when independent statutory audits are made compulsory for the larger companies.

REFERENCES

1. *Memorial*, 24 March 1970, A No. 16.
2. *Reporting, Accounting and Business Practices Abroad*, International Tax and Business Service, Haskins & Sells, 1972.

Chapter 6

Denmark

BACKGROUND

Since the 1950s Denmark has undergone a period of rapid industrialisation which has transformed a primarily agricultural country into a predominantly industrial economy with a large and highly efficient agricultural sector. Manufacturing industries now account for more than 70 per cent of Danish exports; those of machinery and instruments exceed those of agriculture and alone represent more than one-third of the total. This extraordinarily rapid industrial revolution was achieved with the help of foreign direct investment which accounted for one-third of Danish industry's new investment in the 1960s and continues to play a major role (Table 6.1).

Among the EEC countries the Danish "free enterprise plus social welfare" economy has achieved a standard of living second only to that of Germany. Taxation is regarded as the primary instrument in the distribution of wealth and it is estimated that the tax burden will rise from 45 per cent of national income in 1970 to 58 per cent in 1985.

The Stock Exchange is a self-governing institution under the supervision of the Minister of Commerce and its principal feature is the bond market, which is large both in relation to equities and also by international standards. The mortgage credit institutions are the principal sources of bonds (Table 6.2). These credit institutions were established in the latter half of the nineteenth century as associations owned by the borrowers, who were mainly farmers. The system operates on the basis of debentures, secured on a mortgage deed, which are then sold on the market, generally through a bank. Additional mortgages on the basis of increased asset values became a feature of the late 1960s but the Mortgage Credit Act of 10 June 1970 attempted to reform this aspect which not only was considered politically undesirable but also resulted in an imbalance between savings and the supply of bonds. Since 12 October 1971 the special credit institutions have been restricted to two types of credit—"ordinary mortgage credit", the same as the previous first mortgage credit, and "special mortgage credit" which was formerly dealt with by second and third mortgages.

TABLE 6.1. FOREIGN DIRECT INVESTMENT IN DENMARK, 1967–72 (in $ millions)

USA		300
EEC		
UK	126	
Netherlands	55	
Germany	52	
Rest	29	
		262
Sweden		108
Switzerland		54
Other countries		143
		867

Source: The Scandinavian Market, Nordfinanz-Bank Zürich.

A bond market primarily based on property ownership and still biased towards the agricultural sector is not an effective source of finance for industry. Furthermore, the equity market is not developed and of little importance (Table 6.3) since almost all Danish companies are relatively small family firms, typically reluctant to go to the market. So far, therefore, companies have had to rely to a large extent on their own internally generated resources and short- to medium-term finance from the commercial banks.

The absence of an effective capital market for industry may well be one

TABLE 6.2. DISTRIBUTION OF QUOTED BONDS BY TYPE AND OWNER AT THE END OF 1970 (in Kr millions)

	Govt bonds	*Local govt bonds*	*First mortgage bonds*	*Second mort-gage bonds*	*Property bonds*	*Other bonds*	*All bonds*
National Bank	120	99	5,470	815	1,615	2,180	10,299
Commercial banks	101	543	3,469	799	1,076	349	6,337
Savings banks	149	478	1,414	207	578	136	2,962
Insurance companies	1,000	762	11,670	2,098	3,958	120	19,608
Post Office Giro	70	67	468	382	1,071	18	2,076
Others	1,717	1,972	27,257	4,041	7,555	847	43,389
	3,157	**3,921**	**49,748**	**8,342**	**15,853**	**3,650**	**84,671**

Source: Statistical Yearbook, 1973.

of the major problems facing Danish industry if it is to continue to expand: an important factor in this regard is the recent Danish membership of the EEC resulting in unrestricted foreign portfolio investment in Danish bonds and shares from the end of 1974. From January 1978 Danish residents will be free to purchase foreign securities.

Apart from her membership of the EEC, Denmark is also a member of the Nordic Council, which was established in 1952 and includes all the Scandinavian countries. The Nordic Council, founded on the principle of co-operation especially in economic matters, is typified by such joint

TABLE 6.3. THE SUPPLY OF BONDS ON THE STOCK EXCHANGE AND ISSUES OF SHARES (in Kr millions)

	1963	*1966*	*1969*	*1972*
Net supply of mortgage and other bonds excluding Government bonds	3,099	4,199	8,204	13,242
Issues of shares	130	228	318	260
Total	**3,229**	**4,427**	**8,522**	**13,502**
Net supply of Government bonds	191	161	139	230
Net sales by National Bank	130	839	1,648	359
Total	**321**	**1,000**	**1,787**	**589**
Net supply	**2,908**	**3,427**	**6,735**	**12,913**
Increase in the holdings of bonds and shares of major buyers in bonds				
Insurance companies and pension funds	771	847	1,323	2,561
Commercial banks	207	484	141	1,790
Social pension fund and Postal Giro	120	439	664	1,709
Major savings banks	219	35	222	685

Source: Central Bank Monetary Review.

operations as the SAS airline, the Scanservice shipping company and the NAF co-operative purchasing organisation. A common Scandinavian labour market was set up in 1954.

BUSINESS ORGANISATIONS

The principal forms of business organisation in Denmark are shown in Fig. 6.1. Companies and branches of foreign companies must be registered at the Register of Companies (Aktieselskabsregisteret) in Copenhagen.

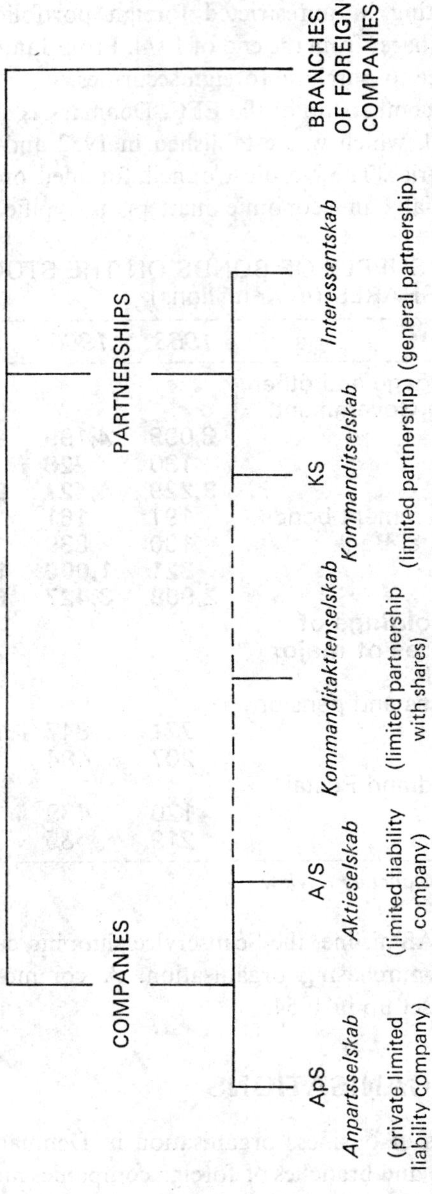

Fig. 6.1 Forms of business organisation in Denmark

Partnerships and limited partnerships with shares are registered separately at the Commercial Register (Handelsregistret), which is maintained in Copenhagen and in principal towns throughout Denmark.

Companies

In accordance with EEC policy the *anpartsselskab* (ApS) company was created by law No. 371 on 13 June 1973 as a separate form of private limited company. The only previous form of company, the *aktieselskab* (A/S—Table 6.4), then became the Danish equivalent of the AG or SA and is regulated by law No. 370 of the same date. The particular features of both forms of company are compared under the following headings:

	A/S	*ApS*
Shareholders	Minimum of 3 promoters but only 1 shareholder required although the minimum number of shares is 3. On formation at least 2 promoters must be domiciled in Denmark subject to exemption from the Minister of Commerce.	Minimum of 1, no maximum. On formation at least 1 promoter must be domiciled in Denmark subject to exemption from the Minister of Commerce.
Securities	Shares may be registered, or bearer if fully paid. Articles may restrict negotiability of registered shares. Shares must have a nominal value and they cannot be issued at a discount. Total convertible debentures may not exceed 50 per cent of paid-up share capital.	Individual holdings (*anparts*) must be registered and may be represented by non-negotiable *anpart* certificates. There are no restrictions on the transfer of *anparts* unless otherwise stated in the articles. *Anparts* have a nominal value and cannot be issued at a discount.
Capital	Minimum Kr 100,000. All share capital must be subscribed on formation. At least 50 per cent of the initial capital to a minimum of Kr 100,000 and 25 per cent of any capital increase must be paid in with the balance	Minimum Kr 30,000. All share capital must be subscribed on formation. At least 50 per cent of the initial capital to a minimum of Kr 30,000 and 25 per cent of any capital increase must be paid in with the balance due within

	A/S	*ApS*
Capital—*contd*	due within one year. Can purchase or receive as security up to 10 per cent of own capital (including subsidiary company holdings in its parent) provided shares are fully paid.	1 year. Cannot normally acquire any part of its own capital.
Capital impairment	The Bankruptcy Act (*Konkursloven*) requires compulsory liquidation when a company has sustained losses for 3 successive years and the deficit resulting after the deduction of share capital, legal reserves and any other reserves exceeds 30 per cent of the total assets.	
Annual general meeting	The ordinary general meeting must be held within 6 months of the end of each accounting year.	

A/S companies are required to have a board of at least three directors (*bestyrelsesmedlemmer*) although those with a capital of less than Kr 400,000 and fewer than 50 employees may have one or two directors and a deputy. In companies with a minimum of 50 employees the employees have the right to appoint two further directors and two deputies from among the employees of the company subject to the proviso that worker-directors cannot constitute a majority of the board. Worker-directors are appointed for two years and other directors for up to four years. The directors of companies with a share capital of Kr 400,000 or more are required to appoint one or more executive managers (*administrerend*

TABLE 6.4. NUMBERS OF A/S COMPANIES (as at 1 January 1972)

Plantations	252
Manufacturing	5,838
Construction	1,422
Electric, gas and water	14
Commerce, etc.	11,102
Transport, storage and communication	878
Others	1,755
Total	*21,261*
In liquidation, etc.	1,097
	20,164

Source: Statistical Yearbook, 1973.

direktører); the executive managers need not be members of the board and the Act states that the majority of directors cannot be executive managers. The new law also provides for the possibility of a supervisory shareholders' committee (*representantskab*) consisting of at least five members but does not make this obligatory. Directors are appointed by the shareholders in general meeting, or, subject to the articles (*vedtaegter*), by any shareholders' committee. The board and the executive managers are responsible for "the administration of the company's affairs", the "suitable organisation of the company's activities" and are obliged to supervise "the book-keeping and administration of the capital in a satisfactory manner". The executive managers are charged with the conduct of the daily business of the company and they must comply with the instructions of the board. Directors and executive managers may be remunerated by a paid salary and a share of net profit (*tantièmes*) but not a share of gross income or gross operating profit. *Tantièmes* can be paid only after deficits from previous years have been covered and legal reserve transfers made. Members of the board and executive managers cannot "undertake or participate in speculative transactions in the shares of the company or shares and *anparts* in companies within the group".

The management regulations for ApS companies follow similar but less stringent lines to those of A/S companies. ApS companies must have one or more executive managers and a board of at least three members; the board of companies with a contributed capital of less than Kr 400,000 and fewer than 50 employees may consist of less than three members and the company need not have any board at all. Directors are appointed by the members while executive managers are appointed by the board or by the members if no board exists.

In companies with a share capital of Kr 400,000 or more, the majority of board members may not be executive managers. If a company has more than 50 employees worker-directors are required as for A/S companies. The duties, periods of appointment and remuneration of directors and executive managers of ApS companies are the same as those for A/S companies. The law on ApS companies contains no reference to a shareholders' committee.

Partnerships

The *interessentskab* (I/S) is an ordinary general partnership. The *kommanditselskab* (KS) is a limited partnership in which any of the general or limited partners may be persons or entities. The firm's name must include the name of at least one general partner.

Limited Partnerships with Shares

The *kommanditaktieselskab* (KA/S) is a partnership limited by shares where the liability of the limited partners is limited to a specified amount of contributed capital evidenced by shares and in which at least one A/S company is a limited partner. The general partners cannot hold shares in the company and the liability of the company is limited to its share capital. Section 173 of the law on A/S companies states that KA/S entities are to be treated as A/S companies.

Branches of Foreign Companies

Branches of foreign companies similar to A/S or ApS companies are authorised to operate in Denmark. Such branches must be registered with the Register of Companies and are obliged to file a certified copy of the company's annual accounts, auditors' statement and management report not later than seven months after the end of the accounting year.

ACCOUNTING AND FINANCIAL REPORTING

The principal users of company accounts in Denmark have been the tax authorities and bank managers, with the result that the development in accounting has been somewhat conservative and tax-oriented. However, beginning in the late 1960s informative accounting has developed and the financial reports of Danish companies are much less conservative than previously.

The provisions of the 1973 companies legislation which came into force on 1 January 1974 represent a major step forward and Denmark can now claim a corporate law which is one of the most modern and up to date in the EEC. The Danish company laws are based largely on the recommendations of a joint committee with representatives from Denmark, Finland, Norway and Sweden which was set up in 1962 in an attempt to harmonise Scandinavian company law. Although the matter was put in abeyance to some extent when Denmark and Norway announced their initial intention to join the EEC it is clear that the other Nordic countries also intend to accept the committee's recommendations.

Accounting Principles

The central theme of the Danish financial reporting regulations is contained in Section 98 of the law on limited liability companies which states that "the annual accounts shall be prepared in accordance with good accounting practice both as regards the valuation of balance sheet items and as regards specifications, arrangement and description in the accounts". The Danish accountancy profession has traditionally adopted an *ad hoc* approach to accounting principles whereby a Committee of Reference could be consulted on specific matters, but in December 1973 the profession established a committee to define what constituted "good accounting practice".

Accounting Practices and the Annual Accounts

The 1973 legislation includes a standard layout indicating the basic disclosures necessary in the balance sheet (Fig. 6.2) and also specifies certain items which must appear in the profit and loss account (Fig. 6.3), but companies are permitted to deviate from these provided this is consistent with "good accounting practice". The disclosures required to amplify any of the items in the balance sheet or profit and loss account may appear in the accounts or by way of notes. Any material change in the basis of accounting from one year to the next must be disclosed and quantified. The law also specifies general valuation rules which must be followed by all companies.

Consolidated Accounts

Danish companies are now obliged for the first time to prepare a consolidated balance sheet or, if special circumstances apply, at least a group report. This statutory duty to consolidate extends not only to conventional subsidiaries but also to other companies which "by reason of shareholding, *anpart* holding or agreement, have a decisive influence over another *aktieselskab* company or *anpartsselskab* company and have a significant share in its results" (*i.e.* associated companies). A subsidiary company is defined as being any company in which another company or group of companies possesses the majority of votes. The law specifies that consolidated accounts consist of a consolidated balance sheet which must also show the group's results for the year and its total "free net capital" (Fig. 6.2) or accumulated deficit after deduction of intra-group items. The consolidated accounts are required to disclose the annual result and "free net capital" or deficit of the parent company, as well as similar information for each subsidiary to the extent that this is not reflected in the valuation at which the investment in the subsidiary in question appears in the parent company's balance sheet. Although companies are not obliged to provide corresponding figures in the annual accounts, consolidated or otherwise, the majority of companies do give this information.

A AKTIVER (ASSETS)

I Omsaetningsativer (Current assets)

1 *Kassebeholdning, banktilgodehavender o. lign.* (Cash, bank balances and similar)
2 *Aktier eller anparter i andre selskaber* (Shares or *anparts* in other companies)
3 *Obligationer og andre vaerdipapirer* (Bonds and other securities)
4 *Veksler* (Notes receivable)
5 *Andre fordringer* (Other receivables)
6 *Igangvaerende arbejder for fremmed regning* (Work in progress for third parties)
7 *Varebeholdninger* (Stock)
8 *Forudbetaling til leverandorer* (Prepayments to suppliers)

II Anlaegsaktiver (Fixed assets)

1 *Aktier eller anparter i datterselskaber* (Shares or *anparts* in subsidiaries)
2 *Aktier eller anparter i andre selskaber* (Shares or *anparts* in other companies)
3 *Obligationer og andre vaerdipapirer* (Bonds and other securities)
4 *Andre fordringer* (Other receivables)
5 *Forudbetaling til leverandorer* (Prepayments to suppliers)
6 *Patent- og lignende rettigheder* (Patent and similar rights)
7 *Goodwill* (Goodwill)
8 *Organisationsomkostninger m.v.* (Deferred charges)
9 *Maskiner, inventar og lignende driftsmidler* (Machinery, equipment and similar stock in trade)
10 *Skibe og luftfartoger* (Ships and aircraft)
11 *Fast ejendam* (Real property)

III 1 *Krav pa aktieindskud* (Shareholders' subscriptions)
2 *Egne aktier* (Own shares)

B GAELD OG EGENKAPITAL (LIABILITIES AND NET CAPITAL)

I Kartfristet gaeld (Short-term liabilities)

1 *Vekselgaeld* (Notes payable)
2 *Skatter, der er eller kan forventes palignet selskabet for tiden for statusdagen* (Taxes payable or accruing at balance sheet date)
3 *Forudbetaling fra kunder* (Prepayments by clients)
4 *Bankgaeld og lignende gaeld* (Bank and similar liabilities)
5 *Anden kortfristet gaeld* (Other short-term liabilities)

II Udbytte til aktionaererne (Dividends to the shareholders)

1 *Ikke haevet udbytte fra tidligere ar* (Previous years, unpaid)
2 *Udbytte for regnskabsaret* (Current year)

III Langfristet gaeld (Long-term liabilities)

1 *Prioritetsgaeld* (Mortgages payable)
2 *Anden gaeld, for hvilken selskabet har stillet sikkerhed* (Other secured debt)
3 *Konvertible gaeldsbreve* (Convertible bonds)
4 *Udbyttegivende gaelsbreve* (Debentures)
5 *Anden langfristet gaeld* (Other liabilities)

IV Investeringsfonds og andre tilsvarende henlaeggelser, hver for sig (Investment funds and other reserves, specified)

Fig. 6.2 Example of Danish balance sheet

V Egenkapital (Net capital)
(a) *Bunden egenkapital* (Frozen net capital)
1 *Aktiekapital* (Share capital)
2 *Lovpligtig reservefond* (Legal reserve)
3 *Opskrivningsfond* (Appreciation account)
(b) *Fri egenkapital* (Free net capital)
1 *Frie reserver, hver for sig* (Free reserves, specified)
2 *Overforsel til naeste ar (underskud for regnskabsaret og tidligere ar optages som fradragsposter)* (Retained earnings (if deficit, deduct))

Status skal—eventuelt inden for linjen—endvidere indeholde oplysning on (The balance sheet shall also show, indented if appropriate):

C PANTSAETNINGER (PLEDGED ASSETS)
1 *Omfanget af pantsaetninger i fast ejendom* (Amount of pledges secured on real property)
2 *Andre pantsaetninger, hver for sig, med angivelse af pantents bogforte vaerdi* (Other pledges, individually, giving the book value of the pledged assets)

D GARANTIFORPLIGTELSER (GUARANTEE OBLIGATIONS)
1 *Diskonterede veksler* (Discounted notes, not yet matured)
2 *Ikke saerligt daekkede kautions- og andre garantiforpligtelser* (Sureties and guarantees that are not specifically secured)

Fig. 6.2—(continued) Example of Danish balance sheet

Indtaegter (Revenue)
1 *Udbytte af aktier i datterselskaber* (Dividends on shares in subsidiaries)
2 *Udbytte af aktier* (Dividends on other shares)
3 *Renteindtaegter* (Interest received)
4 *Fortjeneste ved afhaendelse af anlaegsaktiver, safremt den indgar i resultatopgorelsen* (Profit on disposal of fixed assets if this is included in the profit and loss account)
5 *Andre ekstraordinaere indtaegter* (Other extraordinary items)

Omkéstninger (Expenditure)
1 *Renteomkostninger* (Interest paid)
2 *Afskrivninger og nedskrivninger pa anlaegsaktiver* (Depreciation and write-down on fixed assets)
3 *Tab ved afhaendelse af anlaegsaktiver, safremt det indgar i resultatopgorelsen* (Loss on disposal of fixed assets if this is included in the profit and loss account)
4 *Andre ekstraordinaere omkostninger* (Other extraordinary items)
5 *Det beregnede belob af skatter, som kan forventes palignet arets indkomst, samt eventuelle efterreguleringer vedrorende tidligere ar* (Estimated amount of tax chargeable on the year's income, together with possible adjustments for previous years)
6 *Henlaeggelser til investeringsfonds* (Appropriations to investment fund reserves)

Fig. 6.3 Example of *resultatopsorelse* (profit and loss account disclosures)

The Balance Sheet

Fixed assets. Fixed assets, defined as those "intended for permanent retention or use" by a company, cannot be entered at a value higher than cost including amounts incurred on improvements. However, if fixed assets have appreciated in value and "the increase in value can be assumed to be of a permanent nature" such assets may appear at the higher value. Real property cannot be written up to more than the property value "according to the last official valuation" and the valuation must be given in any case. The surplus on revaluation may be used only for:

1. Depreciation of other fixed assets.
2. The issue of bonus shares.
3. Transfer to an appreciation account which in turn may be used only for (1) or (2). The use to which a revaluation surplus is put must be stated in the accounts.

If fixed assets have an actual value lower than cost as a result of circumstances that cannot be regarded as temporary, they must be written down to the extent considered to be in accordance with good accounting practice. For presentation purposes depreciation is usually netted against the book value at the beginning of the year. After adjustment for sales and purchases during the year, depreciation at least equivalent to actual obsolescence, wear and tear, etc., must be provided each year. The law goes on to state specially that provision for depreciation is necessary "even if the profit and loss account shows or will show a deficit". In practice depreciation rates tend to be the same as those allowed for tax purposes.

The following additional information is necessary for ships, aircraft and real property:

1. The cost according to the balance sheet of the previous year including any revaluation increments.
2. The net amount by which the value of the asset has increased or decreased in the course of the year.
3. Revaluation increments.
4. Aggregate depreciation and write-downs as far as this is possible.

Claims, of a fixed asset nature, can be stated at realisable value even if this exceeds the value at which these appeared in the previous balance sheet.

Goodwill and other intangible assets. Goodwill can be capitalised when purchased; it must be amortised by "a reasonable amount" each year subject to a minimum rate of 10 per cent. Expenditure incurred for technical, commercial or similar purposes, including research and development work which is of significant and permanent value to the company, may be capitalised; such an asset should be amortised by at least 20 per cent per annum unless a lower rate is in special circumstances considered to be consistent with good accounting practice. Commission, direct costs and discount expenses in connection with a long-term loan should either be expensed immediately or be amortised at a reasonable rate before maturity of the loan. Formation expenses cannot be capitalised.

Current assets. Current assets, defined as those assets not intended for permanent retention, may not appear at a value higher than the lower of cost or market value. However, the law goes on to say that they may be stated in excess of cost if, under special circumstances, this is consistent with good accounting practice and the fact is disclosed in the accounts.

Inventories. Until 1970 inventories were a traditional area for the creation of secret reserves and these could be stated anywhere from 0 to 30 per cent less than the lower of cost or realisable value. Furthermore, purchase commitments of up to 25 per cent of normal yearly purchases can result in a write-down of such commitments to the extent of 25 per cent in 1973, 20 per cent in 1974, 10 per cent in 1975, and 0 per cent in 1976.

Best practice requires the disclosure of such provisions and this is by now common. Cost may be calculated on any normal basis apart from LIFO and overheads are not necessarily included in any valuation. The valuation of work in progress for third parties can include an element of profit provided that this fact and the basis of valuation are disclosed.

Shares or anparts in other companies. Equity participation in other companies must be individually stated with details of each company's name, the nominal value of each holding and the amount at which they appear in the balance sheet. This information is not necessary if both the nominal and book value of any holding in a company that is not a subsidiary are less than 5 per cent of the net capital of the company holding the equity.

Bonds and other securities. Quoted securities cannot be stated at a value in excess of the last buying price quoted before the balance sheet date.

Loans to directors and shareholders. The total amount of any loans to shareholders other than a parent company, or to directors or executive managers of the company or its parent, are required to be shown separately on the balance sheet. If the company has afforded a pledge or surety or other guarantee for any of those persons this fact should be stated. Loans or guarantees of this nature may be granted only against adequate security and only to the extent that the company's net capital exceeds "frozen net capital" (Fig. 6.3).

Group companies. Amounts due to or from subsidiary or parent companies included in receivables or payables must be shown separately. Likewise any liens, mortgages and unsecured guarantees on behalf of subsidiary or parent companies have to be similarly specified.

Capital and reserves. The various classes of share capital have to be shown separately and any alterations in the amount or classification of the net capital from that of the previous year must be specified. A/S companies are obliged to establish a legal reserve by annual transfer of at least 10 per cent of the annual surplus, where this has not been used to cover any losses from previous years, until this constitutes at least 10 per cent of the share capital. Thereafter at least 5 per cent must be transferred annually until the reserve represents 25 per cent of the share capital. Except in the case of a capital reduction, the legal reserve can be used for:

1. Covering losses that are not covered by "free net capital".
2. Issuing bonus shares provided that the company does not have an uncovered loss.

Share premiums which have not been used to write off formation expenses have to be transferred to the legal reserve. If a company purchases its own shares these have to be entered, with a statement of their nominal value, as an asset of no value, unless they have been acquired within the last two accounting years when they can be entered in the balance sheet at an amount not in excess of cost. When a company has acquired its own shares during the past year, the nominal value of these shares, the proportion of total share capital that they represent and the acquisition cost should be disclosed. Companies cannot grant loans to finance the purchase of their own shares; nor may they give guarantees in connection with such acquisitions.

Convertible bonds. In respect of each convertible bond issue companies are required to disclose the amount outstanding, the rate of conversion and the expiry date for conversion of the shares. If any debentures or other bonds have been issued in respect of which the interest payable depends wholly or partly on the dividend declared or on the year's profit, the amount of each such issue and the interest terms must be disclosed.

Taxation. In the past, companies have not always accrued taxation consistently on the basis of the profits earned in the current year; the accrual was sometimes made on the basis of the previous year's earnings and in some cases no accrual was made but tax was expensed when paid. Under the new law, however, companies have no choice but to make adequate accruals on the basis of current profits. In addition the total taxes paid in the year should be stated. Although deferred tax accounting was not common practice in the past, companies are now required to set up, or at least disclose, a separate liability in respect of the taxation which could result from a realisation of the assets of the company.

Pension commitments. Companies are required to disclose the full amount on a present value basis of all pension commitments.

The Profit and Loss Account

The profit and loss statement should "be prepared in such a way as to give a satisfactory explanation, consistent with the circumstances of the company, of how the profit or loss for the accounting year has been arrived at" (A/S Companies Act, Section 104). Companies are obliged to disclose their turnover unless, owing to special circumstances, this would be detrimental to them.

Dividends. The directors' recommendations on the allocation of profits should be contained in their report and the general meeting cannot resolve to pay a higher dividend than proposed or agreed by the board of directors. Dividends may be declared only from the surplus for the year according to the certified accounts, plus the surplus retained from previous years and free reserves after deduction of losses, and, in the case of A/S companies, transfer to the legal reserve. Dividends of A/S companies are limited to 6 per cent of paid-in capital until the legal reserve represents 10 per cent of the share capital. No company can declare such high dividends as would be "considered to be at variance with good business practice" (Section 110.2).

Profit or loss on disposal of fixed assets. Any profit or loss on the disposal of fixed assets must be allocated to the relevant balance sheet accounts.

Extraordinary income and expenditure. Each item appearing under these headings should be separately disclosed, as should prior-year adjustments of a material nature.

Publication and Filing of the Financial Statements

A/S Companies

Not later than eight days before the general meeting the annual accounts (and, in the case of parent companies, consolidated accounts) and the auditors' report must be available for inspection by shareholders at the office of the company and also sent to all registered shareholders who have so requested. Under Danish law the annual accounts include the balance sheet, the profit and loss statement and the annual report of the directors. A copy of the annual accounts (and, in the case of parent companies, the consolidated accounts) together with the auditors' report must be filed with the Register of Companies (where they are open for public inspection) within one month of approval and not later than seven months after the year end. If the proposed distributions were altered at the general meeting, a certified copy of the minutes of the meeting, showing the distributions, must also be filed. The directors and executive managers are required to sign the annual and consolidated accounts, while the chairman certifies the accounts filed with the Register of Companies.

Shareholders have the right to ask the directors to provide them with "available information on all affairs of significance for an evaluation of the annual accounts and the standing of the company in general".

If the information is not ready in time for the general meeting it must be made available within 10 days thereafter at the office of the company, provided it is not, in the view of the board, seriously detrimental to the company.

The Annual Report

The annual report must give information, in so far as this is not detrimental to the company, "on matters which need not appear in the balance sheet and profit and loss statement, but which are important to an assessment of the financial position of the company and the results of its operation during the accounting year" (Section 106); the same applies to post-balance-sheet events. In addition, the report has to include information on:

1. The average number of employees during the accounting year.
2. The aggregate salary and emoluments of the directors, executive managers and members of the shareholders' committee.
3. The aggregate salaries and remuneration of other persons employed by the company.
4. The *tantièmes* paid to members of the board.

ApS Companies

All ApS companies are obliged to prepare annual and consolidated accounts as stated above for A/S companies, with the exception of those ApS companies whose assets according to the latest approved annual accounts do not exceed Kr 2 million which need not prepare a directors' report. Companies with assets in excess of Kr 2 million are required to file their annual accounts, consolidated accounts, if any, and an auditors' report, if necessary, with the Register of Companies within one month of their approval and not later than seven months after the close of the accounting year. This provision also applies where the aggregate assets of a group of companies exceed Kr2 million. All other ApS companies need only file copies of their balance sheets with certain notes. If consolidated accounts are necessary, these can be in summarised form denoted by Roman numerals and capitals in Fig. 6.2 (page 166), except for those companies with consolidated assets exceeding Kr 10 million, whose balance sheet must also contain the items denoted by Arabic numerals.

Stock Exchange Listing Requirements

In order to obtain a successful listing of a security the amount offered must be sufficient to permit constant trading and there should already have been considerable trading in the security. Applications which are normally made through a bank are handled by the Committee of the Stock Exchange (Fondsbørsbestyrelsen) and quotations may be refused on grounds of public interest; applications must specify the name of the bank which will service the securities.

For registered or bearer shares to be admitted to quotation and maintain a place in the Official List, the following conditions, among others, must be satisfied:

1. The amount offered for an ordinary quotation should be at least Kr 5 million or in the case of an extraordinary quotation Kr 1 million.
2. Shares must be fully paid.
3. General meetings are public with the admission of the press.
4. Dividends must be published in at least one Copenhagen daily newspaper and in addition, in the case of companies outside Copenhagen, in one local daily newspaper.

If bonds are to be issued a minimum par value of Kr 500,000 is essential. Convertible bonds can be traded only on the unofficial market.

Business Records

The Book-keeping Law of 5 June 1959 does not specify any particular manner in which the accounting records must be maintained, but generally these should be sufficient for their purpose. There is no requirement for legal validation as in France or Italy, but all records must be kept for five years. Companies are specifically obliged to maintain the following books:

1. Minute books of directors' and shareholders' meetings.
2. An auditors' minute book.
3. A share register.
4. A register of share transactions by directors and executive managers.
5. The equivalent of the French *livre d'inventaire* containing the annual accounts duly certified (*cf.* page 24).

THE ACCOUNTANCY PROFESSION

Denmark has a small but competent accountancy profession and Danish accountants enjoy a considerable and rising status in the eyes of the business community. The profession, faced with the necessity of playing a more active role as a result of the recent industrialisation, has entered a new era.

Foreningen af Statsautoriserede Revisorer

The history of the profession dates back to the time when statutory audits were first made obligatory in 1909. The "Foreningen af Statsautoriserede Revisorer" (Association of State-authorised Public Accountants) was formed on 12 January 1912 and the profession is now regulated by a separate law (*Lov om Statsautoriserede Revisorer*) dated 15 March 1967.

The accountancy profession is under the jurisdiction of a Regulatory Board (Revisor-Kommissionen) appointed by the Minister of Commerce, which has the power to grant licences to those satisfying the necessary requirements. Membership of the Foreningen af Statsautoriserede Revisorer is optional but almost all State-authorised public accountants (*statsautoriserede revisorer*) belong (Table 6.5). Any State-authorised public accountant who leaves public practice must deposit his licence with the Ministry until he returns, if at all, to public practice. State-authorised public accountants retain their membership of the Foreningen regardless of their occupation.

State-authorised public accountants are permitted to practise in partnerships, limited liability companies and private limited liability companies and as sole practitioners. The eight largest firms are shown in Table 6.6.

State-authorised public accountants may practise as limited companies only if the executive managers or, if these are not required, the majority of the board of directors are State-authorised public accountants. No other conditions exist and all the shares in such a company can be owned by other persons or companies: in fact one of these firms (Revisions-og Forvaltnings Institutet) is publicly quoted. State-authorised public accountants cannot practise together with non-State-authorised public accountants but they can employ any number of State-authorised public accountants and trainee accountants. Each State-authorised public accountant is also allowed to employ up to three inexperienced assistants for every State-authorised public accountant that he employs with less than three years' experience. In 1972 3040 such assistants were employed, the largest proportion of whom were prospective members of the profession.

TABLE 6.5. MEMBERSHIP OF THE DANISH ACCOUNTANCY PROFESSION (as at 1 January 1973)

1(a)	**Statsautoriserede revisorer**	
	In public practice	**910**
	Members of the Foreningen af Statsautoriserede Revisorer	891
	Others	19
	Not in public practice (*see* 1(b))	**102**
	Members of the Foreningen af Statsautoriserede Revisorer	85
	Others	17
	Total	**1,012**
1(b)	**Statsautoriserede revisorer not in public practice**	
	In public services (mainly taxation and auditing)	24
	In education	4
	Managing (financial) directors	41
	Internal auditing	2
	Retired	31
	Total	**102**
2	**Registerede Revisorer**	
	Members of the Foreningen af Registerede Revisorer	768
	Others	314
	Total	**1,082**

TABLE 6.6. THE EIGHT LARGEST ACCOUNTING FIRMS IN DENMARK, 1973

	Number of statsautoriserede revisorer	*International associate*
1 Revisionsfirmaet C. Jespersen	60	
2 Revisions-og Forvaltnings Institutet A/S	36	Deloitte, Haskins & Sells
3 Revisor-Centret I/S	26	Whinney Murray Ernst & Ernst
4 Die Forenede Revisionsfirmaer	23	Touche Ross
5 Revisorinteressentskabet	22	
6 K. G. Jensen	18	Coopers & Lybrand
7 I/S Revisorgruppen	16	
8 Centralanstalten for Revision	11	Arthur Young

Sources: 1973 *Telephoneregister* and estimates.

Foreningen af Registrerede Revisorer

A 1970 law also provided for registration at the Ministry of Commerce of all other accountants satisfying minimum requirements under the title of *registrerede revisorer* (registered accountants). Registered accountants have their own body, the Foreningen af Registrerede Revisorer, and they are generally concerned only with minor book-keeping and taxation work.

Education and Training

The provisions covering the education of State-authorised public accountants are laid down in an Executive Order of the Ministry of Commerce dated 3 May 1973 following law No. 68 of 15 March 1967 which introduced a new education and training scheme (Fig. 6.4).

In order to obtain a licence under the new scheme a candidate must satisfy the following conditions:

1. Be a Danish subject.
2. Be resident in Denmark.
3. Have completed his twenty-fifth year.
4. Have not been declared incapable of managing his own affairs. Have not been placed under guardianship and against whom proceedings in bankruptcy have not been taken.
5. Have passed the examinations set by the Regulatory Board.
6. Have for at least three years after having completed his eighteenth year been employed in an office of a State-authorised public accountant and performed normal accountancy functions.
7. Have to the extent of at least Kr 100,000 insured against or given security for, any financial liability he may incur during his performance of the duties of a State-authorised public accountant.

Exemption from (1) may be granted by the Minister of Commerce, who also may grant a licence to any person who proves that he has received such training abroad as may be deemed to be an equal to the training referred to in (5) and (6).

The HA degree course is taken over three years of full-time study and includes:

1. Economics, including business economics and social and industrial economics.
2. Statistics.
3. Data processing.

4. Commercial law.
5. History of civilisation.
6. Book-keeping.

Having passed the HA examination, a student then continues with a two-year course of full-time study for the Cand Merc degree. During the first part of the course the student covers general economics, accounting, auditing and tax and company law. The remaining part of the course

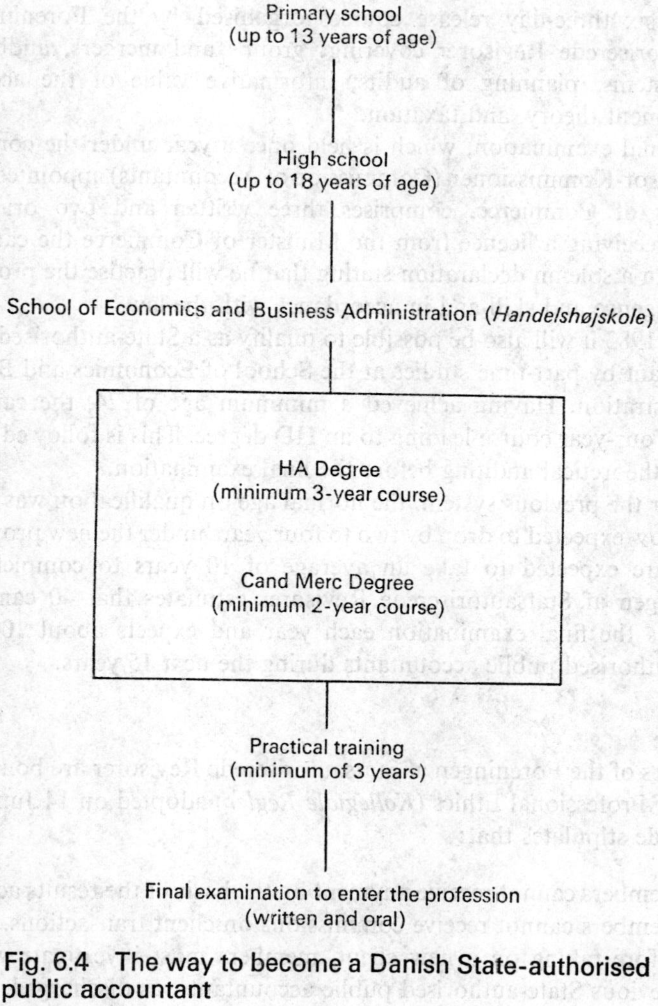

Fig. 6.4 The way to become a Danish State-authorised public accountant

involves the preparation of a thesis on a subject approved by the student's professor. Comparisons of educational standards are always controversial but it is worth noting that the Danes believe that the Cand Merc degree is equivalent to an M.Sc. from the London School of Economics.

After obtaining the Cand Merc degree a student must then spend at least three years with a firm of State-authorised public accountants, taking part in the day-to-day auditing work; he also has the option of spending one of the three years in public practice with a firm before continuing his Cand Merc studies. During the three years of practical training a candidate attends six three-day release courses organised by the Foreningen af Statsautoriserede Revisorer covering: groups and mergers, auditing of EDP-systems, planning of audits, informative value of the accounts, management theory, and taxation.

The final examination, which is held once a year under the control of the Revisor-Kommissionen (Commission of Accountants) appointed by the Minister of Commerce, comprises three written and two oral tests. Before receiving a licence from the Minister of Commerce the candidate must sign a solemn declaration stating that he will practise the profession with diligence and skill and in accordance with the law.

Until 1983 it will also be possible to qualify as a State-authorised public accountant by part-time studies at the School of Economics and Business Administration. Having achieved a minimum age of 24, the candidate takes a four-year course leading to an HD degree. This is followed by one year of theoretical auditing before the final examination.

Under the previous system, the normal age on qualification was 32, but this is now expected to drop by two to four years under the new provisions, which are expected to take an average of 10 years to complete. The Foreningen af Statsautoriserede Revisorer estimates that 40 candidates will pass the final examination each year and expects about 1000 new State-authorised public accountants during the next 15 years.

Ethics

Members of the Foreningen af Statsautoriserede Revisorer are bound by a Code of Professional Ethics (*Kollegiale Regler*) adopted on 14 June 1954. The Code stipulates that:

1. Members cannot receive payment on the basis of the results achieved.
2. Members cannot receive commissions on client transactions.
3. Before taking on a new client, members must investigate why the previous State-authorised public accountant was discharged.

4. Members cannot offer employment to employees of other State-authorised public accountants but this does not apply to unsolicited applications or advertisements.
5. Except in special circumstances, audits cannot be performed free or for unduly low fees.

In addition, the law obliges auditors to observe professional secrecy.

The most notable feature of the rules is that limited advertising of such matters as commencement to practise or change of address is permitted. Advertisements are usually restricted to the name, occupation, address, telephone numbers and office hours of the firm. Figures 6.5(a)–(c) show examples of actual advertisements.

Services Provided

The principal function of members of State-authorised public accountants is the carrying out of statutory audits. They are also authorised to act in bankruptcy matters. The provision of tax advice is common, while individual firms provide data-processing facilities and management services.

AUDITING

Like similar accountancy bodies in other countries the Foreningen af Statsautoriserede Revisorer is very much a profession of auditors. Very few members leave the profession (Table 6.5) and auditing is by far the most important activity of public accounting firms. Indeed, the main reason for not restricting all statutory auditing to State-authorised public accountants was the fact that there are simply not enough to cater for all the registered companies.

Danish auditing standards compare favourably with those of other Continental countries and the Foreningen af Statsautoriserede Revisorer has achieved significant success with the recommendations of its "Auditing Standards Committee" which constitute "good auditing principles" as required by an Order from the Ministry of Commerce dated 28 June 1969. The pronouncements of the "Auditing Standards Committee" are of a high standard.

Appointment of Auditors

All companies are required to select one or more auditors, at least one of whom must be domiciled in Denmark, at the general meeting for a specific

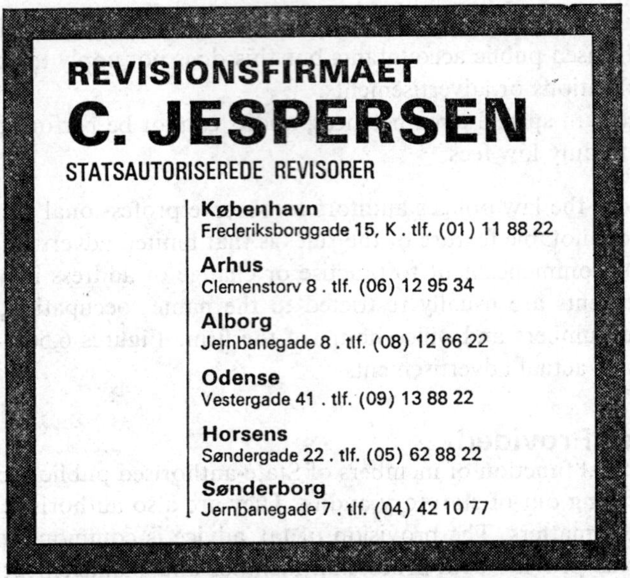

Fig. 6.5 (a) Advertisement of Revionsfirmaet C. Jespersen

Fig. 6.5 (b) Advertisement of Revisions-og Forvaltnings-Institutet

term of years or for an unspecified period. Quoted companies elect two auditors one of whom must be a State-authorised public accountant, and in other A/S companies shareholders representing 10 per cent of the share capital can call for the appointment of a State-authorised public accountant.

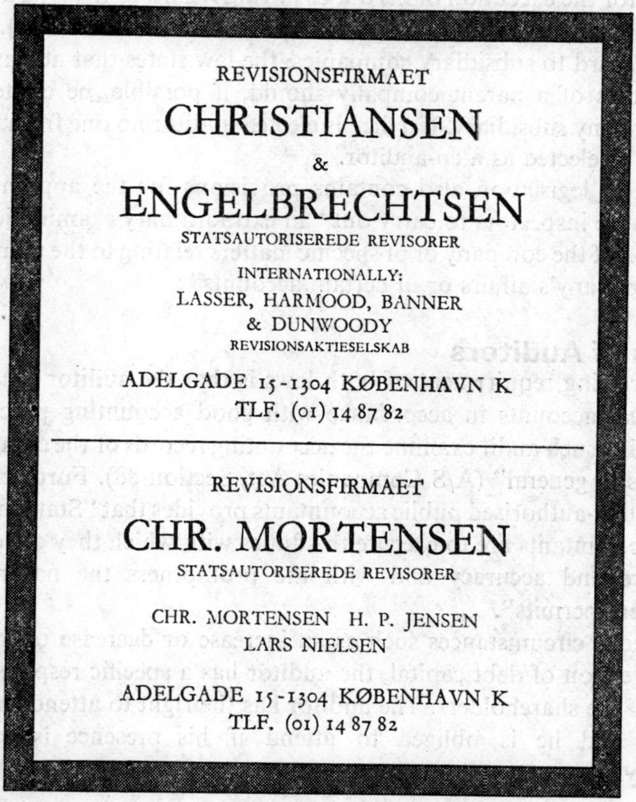

Fig. 6.5 (c) Advertisement of Revisionsfirmaet Christiansen & Engelbrechtsen and Revisionsfirmaet Chr. Mortensen

In the case of all unquoted A/S companies the 1973 law states that at least one auditor should be either a State-authorised or registered public accountant. In addition to the above, members of any company holding 10 per cent of the capital or 25 per cent in the case of ApS companies call upon the board of directors to request the Registrar of Companies to appoint a further auditor to participate with the other auditor or auditors in the audit of the accounts of the company for a period up to and including the next ordinary general meeting.

Generally, therefore, the law contains no qualification requirements for auditors of ApS companies apart from the provision that any auditor must "have the insight and experience in accountancy and financial matters required for the execution of his duties having regard to the type and scope of the company's activities" (ApS Companies Act, Section 64.2).

With regard to subsidiary companies, the law states that at least one of the auditors of a parent company should, if possible, be elected as an auditor of any subsidiary. If a firm is elected auditor no one from the same firm can be elected as a co-auditor.

The 1973 legislation also contains provisions for the appointment of one or more inspectors to carry out "an extraordinary examination of the formation of the company or of specific matters relating to the management of the company's affairs or of certain accounts".

Duties of Auditors

The overriding requirement of both laws is that the auditor must "audit the annual accounts in accordance with good accounting practice, and shall during such audit examine the accounting records of the company and its affairs in general" (A/S Companies Act, Section 88). Furthermore the Act on State-authorised public accountants provides that "State-authorised public accountants are to execute the duties with which they are entrusted with care and accuracy and with the promptness the nature of the assignment permits".

In special circumstances such as an increase or decrease of capital, or the conversion of debt capital, the auditor has a specific responsibility to report to the shareholders. The auditor has the right to attend the general meeting and he is obliged to attend if his presence is considered necessary.

The Auditors' Report

Under Danish law the auditor reports separately to the directors and members of the company. For the purpose of reporting to the Board of Directors the auditor keeps "audit minutes" specifying the audit work carried out and any "defects" found in the book-keeping and accounting of the company. The Foreningen af Statsautoriserede Revisorer proposes that auditors' reports to management should not only point out weaknesses but also make recommendations for improvements on similar lines to the "management letters" common in the United Kingdom. The audit minutes must be presented to a meeting of the directors and signed by all members of the board. The report should contain certain information on:

1. Whether the auditor complies with the statutory requirements as to independence.
2. Whether, in the course of his audit, he has received all the information he has requested to confirm the correctness of the accounts.
3. Whether he considers the accounts to be in accordance with the accounting and auditing provisions of the legislation and the company statutes.

The auditor's approval of the accounts is evidenced by his signature. The 1971 laws stipulate that the auditors' report to the members of the company must specify whether the accounts "are made up as laid down by the law and the articles" and should also indicate "the result of the audit in general". If the accounts do not contain the necessary "information on the results of the company's operations and financial status in general" the auditor must qualify his report and so far as possible provide the necessary supplementary information in his own report. The auditor should complete his audit in sufficient time to have his report in the hands of the directors not later than two weeks before the general meeting.

The following are examples of typical auditors' reports:

De Forenede Bryggerier A/S (The United Breweries Ltd.)
Accounts for the year ended 30 September 1972

We have examined the above Accounts with Notes 1–17 appended and found them to be in conformity with the Company's records. We have obtained the information we have asked for and consider the accounts to have been properly rendered in conformity with the provisions of the Company's Articles of Association and with the book-keeping provisions of the Companies Act and the Book-keeping Act.

In the course of the audit we have ascertained, in accordance with recognised accounting principles, that the assets exist and that valuations have been made in a sound and proper manner. We have further ascertained that the obligations for which the Company to our knowledge is liable have been correctly stated in the accounts.

In our opinion the accounts contain the information required to assess the Company's financial position at 30 September 1972.

F. L. Smidth & Co. A/S
Accounts for the year ended 31 December 1972

The foregoing accounts, which are in accordance with the Company's books, have been audited by us. The existence of the assets listed has been verified. We have been given all information required by us, and in our opinion the accounts are drawn up in accordance with the regulations and as laid down by legislation and the Articles of the Company.

T-T (Thrige-Titan A/S)
Accounts for the year ended 31 December 1972

The accompanying notes 1–8, although not given in English, are an integral part of the accounts.

We find the above accounts, which we have audited, to be in accordance with the Company's books.

Fieldwork

The legislation directs that the board of directors and the executive managers give the auditor "access to undertake such investigations as he finds necessary"; they should also "ensure that he receives such information and assistance as he considers necessary for the execution of his duties". These obligations extend to the management of any subsidiaries.

The importance of an internal control review is emphasised by the Foreningen in an opinion which also points out that an audit consists, "to a large extent, of collecting documentation". Danish auditors tend to attend at stocktaking but do not necessarily rely on direct confirmations of bank balances, debtors and creditors.

Remuneration of Auditors

Audit fees are based on the amount of time and the degree of skill involved.

Removal of Auditors

An auditor may resign or be dismissed by the shareholders or by any other authority appointing him; however, this does not happen very often.

Liability of Auditors

An auditor is liable to shareholders, creditors or third parties if he has wilfully or negligently inflicted loss on the company. It is a condition of obtaining a licence that a State-authorised public accountant give security valued at Kr 100,000 to cover any liability he may incur in the performance of his duties. This is not a liability insurance but an insurance wholly in favour of third parties, and the insurance company has the right of full recourse against the accountant.

Independence of Auditors

The 1971 companies legislation mentions the following as precluded from being elected as auditors of a company and any of its subsidiaries:

1. Members of the board of directors or of the shareholders' committee of the company or its subsidiaries.

2. Persons employed by the company or who are otherwise in a dependent relationship to the company, or to the members of its board of directors, executive managers or staff responsible for the accounts or liquid assets of the company.
3. Persons who are related to members of the board or the executive managers or staff mentioned in (2) above, by marriage, or adoption or by blood or marriage in direct line of ascent or descent or as brothers or sisters.

Moreover, an auditor cannot receive loans from the company or from any other company within the group.

A State-authorised public accountant cannot be a director, manager or employee of any company or organisation apart from a company of accountants. This rule assumes that he cannot act as an independent auditor of a company if he is a member of the board of directors of any other commercial company.

CONCLUSION

Although relatively small, the Danish accountancy profession ranks high in Europe and does not appear unduly reticent about adopting well-tried Anglo-Saxon methods. The latest reform of company law, while sensibly avoiding the temptation to prescribe more than general accounting principles, provides Denmark with a sound basis for negotiation in the EEC.

Chapter 7

Italy

BACKGROUND

The lack of development which characterises the Italian accountancy profession is a direct result of the development structure of Italian industry and the way in which it has evolved.

The economy is dominated by State-owned holding companies whose influence extends to all branches of industry (Table 7.1). The Bourse does not play an important part in company financing, while the number of quoted companies has increased only from 144 in 1950 to 185 today.

TABLE 7.1. COMPOSITION OF INVESTMENT OF PUBLIC CORPORATIONS[1] (1960 and 1971)
(in per cent of total domestic investment)

	1960	*1971*
Industry	**38**	**63**
Basic metals	15	30
Cement	1	1
Transformation of metals and electronics	6	14
Shipbuilding	3	1
Petroleum products[2]	8	6
Chemicals (incl. Petrochemicals)	4	7
Other manufacturing	1	4
Services	**62**	**38**
Telecommunications	26	19
Maritime transport	8	1
Air transport	8	3
Motorways	12	8
Transport and distribution of hydrocarbons	7	6
Cinemas, spas and other services	1	1

1. Excluding electricity.
2. Investment by ENI (State holding oil company) has been equally split between industrial investment and investment in transport and distribution.

Sources: Relazione Programmatica, Ministero Partecipazioni Statali; *Relazione Generale*, 1971.

The bond market is closely regulated, with securities issued by the Treasury and Government-controlled bodies amounting to over 80 per cent of total issues in 1972 (Table 7.2).

The major State holding company, IRI (Instituto per la Ricostruzione Industriale), was set up in 1933 to take over the industrial investments of the commercial banks[1] at a time of severe economic depression. Although it was originally intended that IRI would sell off its investments when conditions improved, this did not prove practical and in 1937 it was given the status of a permanent State holding company. Its investments are split into several industrial divisions under the following subsidiaries:

Finmare	(shipping).
Fincantieri	(shipbuilding).
Finmeccanica	(metal works).
Finsider	(iron and steel).
SME	(other manufacturing services).
STET	(telecommunications).

TABLE 7.2. ANNUAL CAPITAL MARKET NET ISSUES (in L billion)

	1961	*1966*	*1971*	*1972*
1 By issuer and type of security				
Bonds				
Government bonds	150	1,555	2,234	2,660
in per cent of total bonds issues	(21.1)	(55.0)	(44.3)	(36.8)
Special credit Institutions	513	861	2,229	2,446
ENEL, ENI, IRI	115	314	454	822
Business companies	126	3	61	−50
Foreign bonds	15	72	36	106
Total bonds	931	2,805	5,040	5,985
Shares	514	470	939	1,241
Total capital market issues	1,445	2,296	5,980	7,226
2 By subscriber and type of security				
Non-banks				
Bonds	575	1,256	1,829	1,901
(in per cent of total bonds)	(61.8)	(44.4)	(36.3)	(31.8)
Shares	495	449	934	1,233
Banks and other financial institutions				
Bonds	321	1,369	2,289	2,904
(in per cent of total bonds)	(34.5)	(48.4)	(45.4)	(48.5)
Shares	16	15	2	−13
Bank of Italy				
Bonds	35	201	922	1,180
(in per cent of total bonds)	(3.7)	(7.2)	(18.3)	(19.7)
Shares	3	6	3	21

Source: Bank of Italy.

In addition IRI has direct holdings in Alitalia (airline), Radiotelevisione Italiana, and Autostrade (motorways), and almost complete control of the three major commercial banks. Other State holding companies include ENEL (electricity), nationalised in 1962, ENI (oil), formed in 1953, and EFIM, which was created after the war to give temporary aid to engineering firms involved in the war effort. The latest depression has resulted in the establishment of GEPI as a common subsidiary of IRI, IMI, ENI and EFIM, with the object of helping companies with serious financial difficulties.

The holding companies are controlled by the Ministry of State Participations, which ensures that Government investment programmes are carried out. Over the past 20 years productive investment by these public corporations has been rising three times as fast as that of private industry (Fig. 7.1), with the result that their share of industrial investment rose to over 40 per cent in 1971 compared with 15 per cent in the mid 1950s. From being

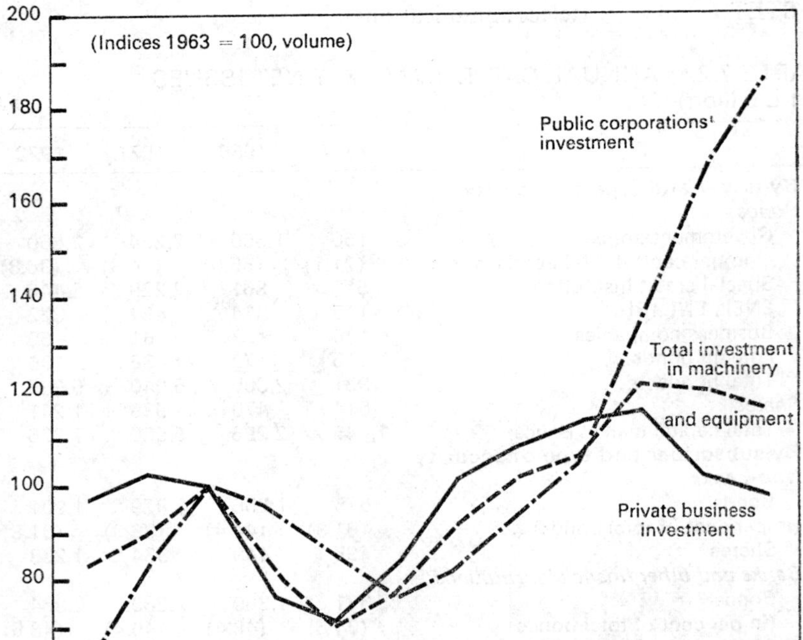

Fig. 7.1 Private and public investment in Italy, 1961–72

Sources: ISTAT *Yearbook of National Accounts*, Relaziore Generale and OECD Economic Surveys

salvage operations originally, the public corporations have now become the Government's major instrument in the effort to correct the regional disequilibrium which divides Italy. Since 1967 they have been compelled to invest at least 40 per cent of total investment, and 60 per cent of investment linked to new industrial incentives, in the Mezzogiorno (South).

Concurrent with this development, the increase from 10·3 per cent in the early 1960s to over 20 per cent today in the share of Government grants in the financing need of the public corporations is noteworthy.

In theory, the banks are not allowed to lend money for more than one year. Instead the so-called "Special Credit Institutions", which obtain the bulk of their funds from bond issues, are the principal providers of medium- and long-term finance. Of particular prominence are IMI (Istituto Mobiliare Italiano), which can grant loans of up to 20 years and take equity participations, and Mediobanca, which is a direct subsidiary of the commercial banks. Subsidised credit is a special feature of the industrialisation of the Mezzogiorno and over 90 per cent of loans by industrial credit institutions are now subsidised.

Italian investors are notorious for their high liquidity preference and lack of confidence in national savings institutions. It is estimated that as much as 10 to 15 per cent of domestic saving is exported each year, mainly to Switzerland. Such a situation is likely to continue until the capital market is substantially improved. More difficult to solve may be the recurrent political crises from which has arisen the traditional lack of confidence; furthermore the impact of the 1963–4 and 1970s depressions with losses, bankruptcies and salvage operations has done little to convince Italians that things have changed.

When considering the extent of foreign investments in Italy it is necessary to tread with some care since Switzerland is seemingly by far the largest investor (Fig. 7.2) because many Italian and foreign shareholders utilise the Swiss holding company device for their Italian investments. Nevertheless there is still a very high foreign participation in Italian industry. A survey of 713 large companies by the Central Institute of Statistics in 1970 disclosed that only 372 (52·2 per cent) were wholly owned by Italians. The foreign participation was over 50 per cent in 152 cases (21·3 per cent) and 99 (13·9 per cent) were wholly owned by non-resident shareholders.

BUSINESS ORGANISATIONS

Unlike other civil jurisdictions Italy has no separate Commercial Code, and the detailed regulations governing the formation and administration

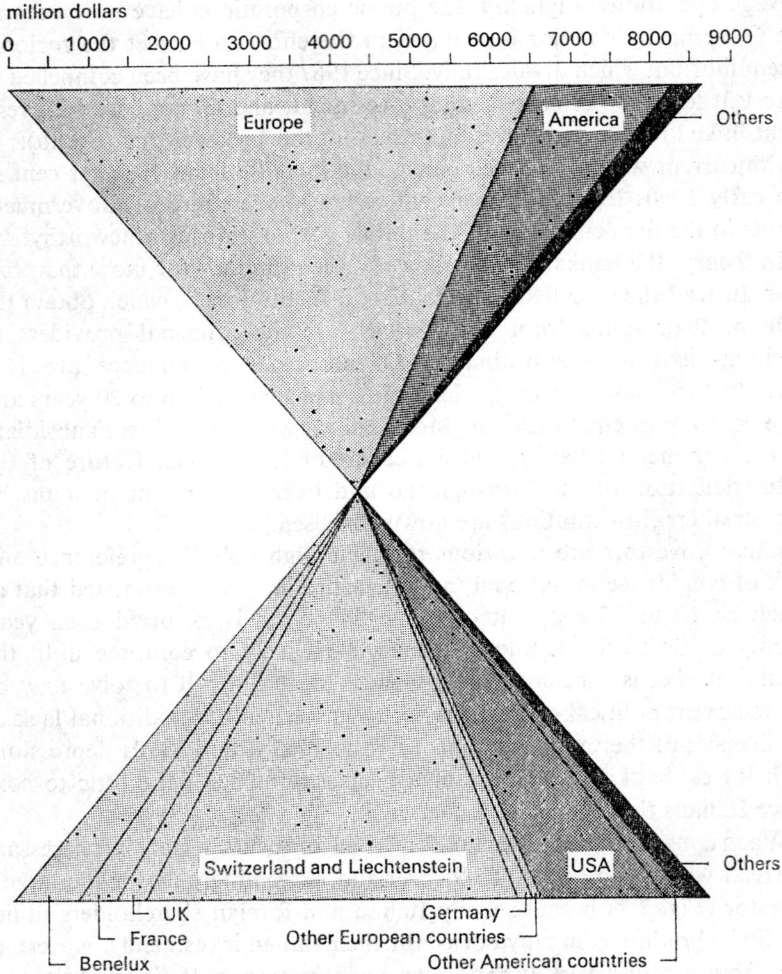

Fig. 7.2 Foreign investment in Italy by countries: amounts as of 31 December 1971

Source: Ufficio Italiano dei Cambi.

of business organisations are contained in the 1942 Civil Code. The 1942 code replaced Italy's first Civil Code of 1865 based on the *Code Napoléon* and it was enacted by royal decree on 16 October 1942.

In Italian law, *società* is the general title for partnerships and companies, the various forms of which are shown in Fig. 7.3. There is a regulation that all business organisations must be registered with the Register of Business

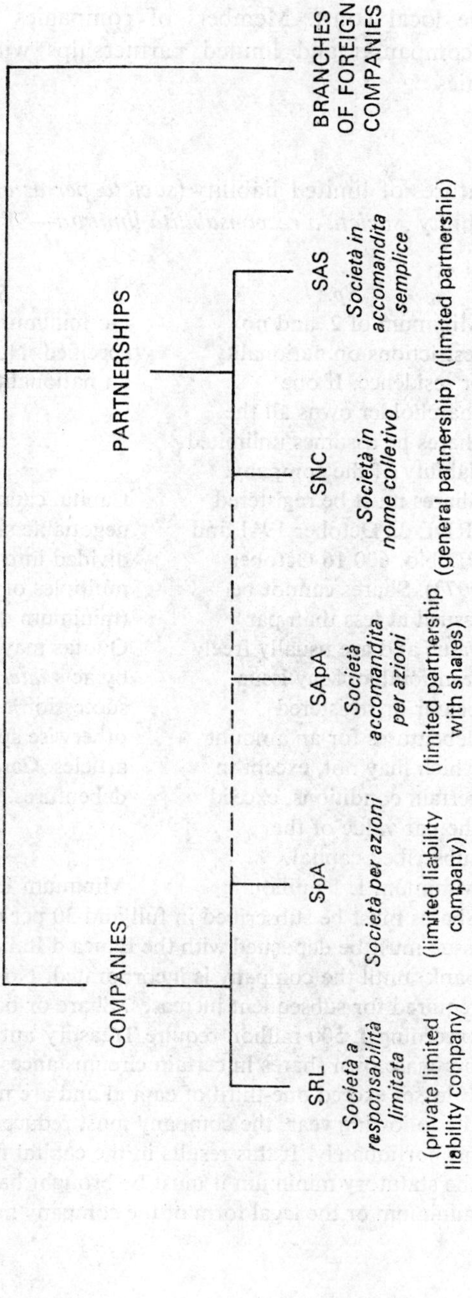

Fig. 7.3 Forms of business organisation in Italy

Enterprises and the local Chamber of Commerce: in fact, however, this former Register has not yet been established and registration therefore takes place at the local court. Members of companies enjoy limited liability and all companies and limited partnerships with shares are separate legal entities.

Companies

The significant features of limited liability (*società per azioni*—SpA) and private limited liability (*società a responsabilità limitata*—SRL) companies are as follows:

<table>
<tr><th></th><th>SpA</th><th>SRL</th></tr>
<tr><td>Shareholders</td><td>Minimum of 2, and no restrictions on nationality or residence. If one shareholder owns all the shares he assumes unlimited liability of the company.</td><td>No minimum or maximum specified. No restrictions on nationality or residence.</td></tr>
<tr><td>Securities</td><td>Shares must be registered (RDL 25 October 1941 and PD No. 600 16 October 1973). Shares cannot be issued at less than par value and are usually freely transferable. May issue bearer or registered debentures for an amount which may not, except in certain conditions, exceed the par value of the subscribed capital.</td><td>Capital cannot consist of negotiable shares but is divided into quotas of multiples of L 1000 (minimum of L 1000). Quotas may be transferred by acts inter vivos or by succession at death unless otherwise specified in the articles. Cannot issue debentures.</td></tr>
<tr><td>Capital</td><td>Minimum L 1 million.</td><td>Minimum L 50,000.</td></tr>
<tr><td></td><td colspan="2">Shares must be subscribed in full and 30 per cent of first issue must be deposited with the Banca d'Italia (central bank) until the company is incorporated. No deposits are required for subsequent increases. Share or bond issues exceeding L 500 million require Treasury authorisation. Can purchase own shares in certain circumstances.</td></tr>
<tr><td>Capital impairment</td><td colspan="2">If losses exceed one-third of capital and are not recovered in the following year, the company must reduce its capital proportionately. If this results in the capital falling below the statutory minimum it must be brought back to the minimum or the legal form of the company must be changed.</td></tr>
</table>

Annual general meeting	The annual general meetings must be held not later than 4 months after the end of the company's fiscal year, although the articles can provide for an extension to 6 months in certain cases.

Both SpAs and SRLs are managed by directors (*amministratori*) who are elected for periods of up to three years by the shareholders. The law does not specify the number of directors to be appointed and in theory any company could have one director. Subject to the articles, the directors may delegate their functions to an executive committee, composed of some of their members, or to one or more executive managers. Corporate bodies cannot be directors. Directors are required to deposit a guarantee in registered shares (*Azioni di Garanzia*) of the company or in registered securities issued or guaranteed by the State to the extent of at least 2 per cent of the share capital subject to any stipulation in the memorandum of association that the guarantee shall not exceed L 200,000 at the par value of the shares or securities. The remuneration and share of profits attributable to the directors may be specified in the company statutes or fixed by the shareholders. Remuneration for special appointments is fixed by the other members of the board in consultation with the board of auditors.

TABLE 7.3. STATISTICS OF ITALIAN BUSINESS ORGANISATIONS

SpA and SApA (December 1971)	43,536
Società—all forms (October 1961)	175,995

Partnerships

The *società in nome colletivo* is the usual form of partnership where all the partners have unlimited liability for the obligations of the partnership.

In the case of the *società in accomandita semplice* the limited partners are liable only to the extent of their contribution which cannot be in the form of shares. The liability of a limited partner becomes unlimited if his name is included in the firm's name (unless he was a former general partner) or if he participates in the management of the partnership.

Limited Partnerships with Shares

The *società in accomandita per azioni* is the Italian equivalent of the French *société en commandite par actions*. The liability of the limited partners is limited to the extent of their subscribed capital, which is in the form of transferable shares. The general partners, whose liability is unlimited, manage the SApA.

Branches of Foreign Companies

The establishment of a foreign branch without resort to incorporation has many disadvantages in Italy where foreign branches are subject to the same regulations as Italian companies. Most foreign businesses setting up in Italy prefer to adopt the *società per anzioni* (SpA) form.

ACCOUNTING AND FINANCIAL REPORTING

The accounts of Italian companies are prepared primarily for tax purposes and are consequently of little value to investors. This unfortunate state of affairs arises from the mutual distrust between taxpayers and the authorities. The tax authorities have compiled data on expected net profit percentages and these they apply to declared turnover to measure whether declared profits meet their criteria. On the other hand, companies frequently underdeclare their profits in order that in the ensuing negotiation process they are able to concede a certain amount without incurring a disproportionate tax liability. Although the law has long provided that companies are subject to taxation on the basis of their financial statements, these are largely ignored in practice. The annual tax return has traditionally contained three columns: one for the company's figures, another for the tax authorities' estimates and the third for the negotiated figures upon which the company is assessed to tax—but it is hoped that the 1973 tax reform will change all this. In such a situation of compromise, there is obviously little incentive for companies to disclose their true results.

The lack of sophistication in Italian accounting cannot, however, be attributed entirely to the tax authorities. The absence of any sizeable and demanding body of shareholders has resulted in companies regarding the annual accounts as primarily fiscal documents and this attitude is enforced by the many accounting rules in tax law which are now standard accounting practice in Italy.

Italian accounting anomalies are many and varied and include the omission of sales, understatement of assets (especially inventories) and the introduction of fictitious liabilities. Secret bank accounts are not unusual. While opinion differs as to whether many Italian companies keep more than two sets of books, an additional set could merely comprise a series of adjustments to the official accounts to eliminate fictitious entries or to incorporate sales or other income not entered therein.

Accounting Principles

Article 2423 of the Civil Code demands that the directors draw up a balance sheet and profit and loss account each year which shows "with clarity and precision the financial position of the company and the profits gained or the losses sustained".

Accounting Practices and the Annual Accounts

Article 2424 specifies the contents of the balance sheet (Fig. 7.4) and lists 14 asset and 11 liability items as well as certain memorandum accounts to be entered on both sides of the balance sheet. Various broad valuation criteria, to be adhered to unless special circumstances make departures necessary, are outlined in subsequent articles of the Civil Code.

Corresponding figures for the previous year are not required; nor need financial statements be consistent from year to year.

Consolidated Accounts

No reference is made to consolidated accounts in the law and very few companies consolidate.

The Balance Sheet

Fixed assets. The Civil Code states that fixed assets cannot be carried at a value higher than cost price and this valuation must be reduced by an "amount (appearing among the liabilities) proportionate to depreciation and consumption during each year". In practice, depreciation is usually provided in accordance with rates laid down in tax law[2] and depreciation is allowable for tax purposes only if it is recorded in the accounts. Accelerated depreciation within specific limits is permitted and it is unusual for depreciation charges to be deferred to profitable years in order to minimise the tax liability. In cases where the tax authorities disallow depreciation or repairs it is normal for these items to be capitalised and credited to a special "taxed reserve" account which will fluctuate from year to year.

Revaluations of fixed assets were permitted by special laws in 1946, 1948 and 1952. Any unofficial revaluation could result in taxation of the surplus.

Intangible assets. The Civil Code states that patents, copyrights, concessions and trademarks cannot be carried at a value higher than cost price.

Attivo (Assets)
Azionisti per Sottoscrizione azioni (Subscriptions owing by the shareholders)
Terreni e Fabricati (Land and buildings)
Macchinari e impianti (Machinery and equipment)
Brevetti e diritti di licenza (Patents and copyrights)
Marche di fabrica e avviamento (Trademarks and goodwill)
Mobili d'ufficio (Furniture and fixtures)
Merci scorte e materiali in lavorazione (Inventories of raw materials and merchandise)
Cassa (Cash on hand)
Titooli a reddito fisso (Fixed-interest securities)
Investimenti (Investments)
Clienti (Accounts receivable customers)
Disponibilità presso banche (Cash at banks)
Crediti verso società collegate (Accounts receivable from affiliated companies)
Azioni proprie (Treasury stock)
Altri crediti (Other receivables)
Per contra Conti d'ordine (Memorandum accounts)
Passivo (Liabilities)
Capitale sociale (Share capital)
Riserva legale (Statutory [legal] reserve)
Riserva diverse (Other reserves)
Fondo ammortamento (Reserve for amortisation and depreciation of fixed assets)
Fondo indeminità fino servizio (Reserve for termination indemnities)
Passivita conti con garanzia (Liabilities for which collateral security is given)
Fornitori (Trade accounts payable)
Banche—saldi passivi (Amounts owing to bankers and other lenders)
Creditori verso società collegate (Amounts owing to affiliated companies)
Obligazioni emesse (Debentures issued)
Altri creditori (Other liabilities)
Per contra Conti d'ordine (Memorandum accounts)

Fig. 7.4 Italian balance sheet format based on Civil Code requirements

Amortisation must be provided each year in proportion to the life of the assets, or to the loss or diminution of their utilisation.

Goodwill may be capitalised only if purchased and must be written off according to the prudent judgement of the directors and auditors "over its useful life".

Inventories. The Civil Code provides that inventories cannot be carried at a value higher than the lower of the cost or market price. Tax law defines cost as including raw materials, direct labour and manufacturing overheads, and specifies that the LIFO method must be used where quantities have decreased during the year. However, the moving average and FIFO methods are more commonly employed. It is normal to take a very conservative view of market value, with the result that inventories are frequently undervalued. The basis of valuation is rarely disclosed in the annual accounts.

Investments. It is stated in the Civil Code that the directors shall use prudent judgement in the valuation of investments taking into account the level of market prices for securities listed on a stock exchange. Securities are normally valued at the lower of cost or a conservative estimation of market value and, if written down below cost as a result, they may be carried at that amount in subsequent years.

Treasury stock. Article 2357 of the Civil Code permits companies to purchase their own shares (Treasury stock) with the approval of the members in general meeting provided that the shares are fully paid and purchased "with sums taken from duly verified net profits". Such shares lose voting rights and can be sold only with the approval of shareholders. They must appear as a separate item on the balance sheet.

Receivables. The Civil Code states that "receivables shall be valued in accordance with their presumed collection value". The fiscal reform which came into effect on 1 January 1974 permits the setting up of doubtful debt provisions, by annual instalments, up to a maximum of 5 per cent of the gross receivables.

Prepaid and deferred expenses may include unamortised debenture discount, formation expenses and other deferred charges. Debenture discount should be written off over the life of the issue and formation expenses expensed within five years.

Memorandum accounts. There is no requirement in the Civil Code to amplify the accounts by way of notes, but certain items which would normally appear as notes in other countries must be shown on both sides of the balance sheet. The Civil Code states that directors' and employees' bonds, other clearing entries, and contra accounts and liabilities as guarantor shall be so listed.

Few companies take the opportunity to disclose contingent liabilities and capital commitments in this or any other way. Offsetting of balance sheet items is strictly forbidden.

Share capital. Share capital must appear at par value and the various categories of shares separately disclosed.

Legal reserves. A legal reserve fund, equal to one-fifth of the company's capital, and set up by annual transfers of at least 5 per cent of profit, is prescribed by the Civil Code. This reserve may be used to write off losses, but must then be reinstated by further transfers at the minimum required from future profits.

Other reserves. Apart from the legal reserve already mentioned, companies may also have monetary revaluation reserves and other reserves as specified in their articles. Monetary revaluation reserves arise from various revaluations of fixed assets, investments and inventories which were permitted by special laws between 1946 and 1952 to allow for the declining purchasing power of the lira. A reserve for termination indemnities must be "gradually and adequately established" by the directors and included under liabilities. It is not necessary to disclose movements on reserve accounts and very few companies give this information.

Apart from those secret reserves which result from the undervaluation of assets it is not unusual for specific secret reserves to be set up, particularly in times of difficulty.

An amnesty was offered in 1954 whereby companies are allowed to disclose such reserves free of taxation liability provided that the reserves were not transferred to capital or distributed; any secret reserves disclosed were exempt from tax provided that they were not capitalised or distributed.

Share premiums. Share premiums can be distributed when the legal reserve requirements are satisfied.

Taxation and other current liabilities. Because of the old taxation system Italian companies have not been encouraged to accrue taxation on current profits since this might result in serious pecuniary disadvantages in the negotiation with the tax authorities. Generally in smaller companies tax is accounted for on a cash basis, although some larger companies and most financial institutions do make adequate provisions. In contrast the overstatement of other liabilities should be seen as normal strategy for the tax negotiations.

Debentures. Only SpA companies are able to issue debentures and the amount issued can only exceed the paid-in capital of the company according to its last approved balance sheet only when:

1. The debentures are secured up to the extent of two-thirds of the value by a mortgage on land and buildings owned by the company.
2. The amount by which the debentures exceed the paid-in capital is secured by registered securities issued or guaranteed by the State, having a maturity date earlier than that of the debentures or by equivalent claims to annuities or subsidies payable by the State or other public bodies.
3. Special reasons affecting the national economy exist and special government authority is given.

There is no requirement to disclose interest rates, maturity dates or security provisions for debentures, and few companies supply these details in the annual accounts.

The Profit and Loss Account

There are no specific statutory requirements with regard to the profit and loss statement apart from the provision mentioned above that the statement should set forth "with clarity and precision . . . the profits gained or the losses sustained". There is no standard layout for the income statement but that shown in Fig. 7.5 may be considered typical. However, recent judicial decisions provide a valuable indication as to what the income statement should reasonably include.[3] It is also worth noting that the long overdue, but limited, reform proposals, discussed at the end of this chapter, will oblige quoted companies to disclose considerable detail in their income statement.

Ricavi (Income)
1 *Utile lordo* (Gross profit)
2 *Redditi immobiliari* (Income from real property)
3 *Proventi finanziari* (Investment income)
4 *Proventi diversi* (Other income)
Spese e perdite (Costs and expenses)
1 *Spese generali e amministrative* (General and administrative expenses)
2 *Spese di vendita* (Selling expenses)
3 *Oneri tributari* (Taxes)
4 *Oneri finanziari* (Interest expense and bank charges)
5 *Ammortamenti* (Provision for depreciation)
6 *Utile netto* (Net income)

Fig. 7.5 Typical Italian profit and loss account format

Turnover is rarely disclosed except in the case of leading companies while extraordinary and prior-year items are not separated and reserve accounting is sometimes practised. The Civil Code states that the distribution of profits must be decided on by the shareholders in general meeting. Accordingly the annual accounts do not take account of appropriations, but the directors' report will include the proposed allocations. Appropriations include directors' bonuses and it is normal to allocate all profits so that the caption "retained earnings" rarely appears in Italian accounts.

Dividends. Dividends can be distributed only out of actual profits and, if a loss in a company's capital occurs, no distribution of profits can be made until the capital is reinstated or reduced proportionately. Dividends paid in violation of these provisions cannot be recovered if the shareholders received them in good faith on the basis of a regularly approved balance sheet showing corresponding net profits.

Dividends are normally paid once a year, but some companies make interim payments. When declared, dividends must be notified to the Schedario Generale delle Azioni e delle Obbligazioni in Rome.

Publication and Filing of Financial Statements

The balance sheet, profit and loss account, and directors' and auditors' reports of all SpA and SRL companies must be submitted to the shareholders' meeting for approval, usually within four months of the year end. Although no obligation exists to supply shareholders with the accounts before the general meeting, a company must keep copies of the financial statements and auditors' and directors' reports on deposit at its legal address during the 15 days preceding the meeting and until the accounts are approved. Within 30 days of the members' approval, the balance sheet and profit and loss account, together with the reports of the directors and of the board of auditors and the minutes of the meeting's approval, have to be filed (in theory with the non-existent Registrar of Business Enterprises) at the local court, where they may be inspected by the public, and published in the *Foglio Annunci Legali* (Legal Bulletin) and *BUSA* (Companies Bulletin).

Directors' Report

Article 2423 of the Civil Code simply states that "the balance sheet shall be accompanied by a report of the directors on the company's operations". Article 2621 lays down penal provisions against directors, managers and others who "in reports, balance sheets, or other information concerning the affairs of the company, fraudulently represent facts which do not correspond to the truth about the formation or the financial condition of the company or who conceal, wholly or partly, such condition".

In practice the quality of directors' reports varies enormously, but a few, for example the political-speech-type reports of the Fiat directors, make interesting reading.

Stock Exchange Listing Requirements

An offer of bonds or shares to the public must be approved by the shareholders' meeting and a summary of the resolutions published in the *Legal Bulletin* and *BUSA*. The Civil Code provides for the formation of SpA companies by public subscription on the basis of a prospectus. The Chamber of Commerce and the Bank of Italy sanction the listing of all securities, which in the case of bonds are usually subscribed in advance by a syndicate consisting of the special credit institutions (such as Mediobanca) and the principal banks, which later resell them to investors through their branches.

Although the Italian stock exchanges, of which the major one is the Milan Bourse, have, in the past, been little more than a speculator's pastime, there seems to be a growing realisation that the equity market must be expanded into a worthwhile activity.

Business Records

Paradoxically, the rules governing the keeping of business records are very strict and it is a serious offence not to comply with them. All businesses are required to keep a journal (*libro giornale*) showing day-to-day transactions and a balance book (*libro inventari*) containing each year's closing trial balance and accounts. Before being used, both books must be progressively numbered and stamped on each sheet by a notary. In addition Article 2214 provides that businesses shall "keep other accounting records required by the nature and size of the enterprise and preserve in an orderly manner for each transaction the originals of the letters, telegrams and invoices received as well as copies of the letters, telegrams and invoices sent out".

It is obligatory for companies to maintain registers of members and debenture holders and minute books for meetings of shareholders, directors, statutory auditors (*sindaci*) and the executive committee, if one exists. Labour and social insurance laws lay down that payroll and personnel registers be maintained. Finally tax regulations stipulate the following:

1. A chart of amounts in which the content of each amount is specified.
2. A record of the principles of evaluation for each item in the balance sheet.
3. A record of depreciable assets and annual and accumulated depreciation (plant register).
4. A detailed inventory of all movements of goods.
5. A chronological record of all commissions, fees, interest and bonuses paid.

Article 2219 states that "All records shall be kept in accordance with the rules of proper accounting, without leaving blank spaces, interlineations, or marginal notations; no erasures can be made and if it is necessary to make any cancellation it must be done in such a manner as to leave legible the cancelled words." All records must be retained for at least 10 years.

THE ACCOUNTANCY PROFESSION

Italian accountants have not managed to achieve the status of a profession capable of playing a leading role in public affairs. The Italian profession remains very much a regional set-up with accountants generally working as sole practitioners and primarily concerned with individual financial affairs and tax matters. The Government dominates the activities of the profession and the Ministry of Justice regulates the two accountancy bodies. The members of these bodies (Table 7.4) enjoy a virtual monopoly in certain specific areas. The older body, the Collegio dei Ragionieri e Periti Commerciali (College of Accountants and Commercial Experts), was officially recognised in 1906 but does not possess the same status as the Ordine dei Dottori Commercialisti (Order of Doctors of Commerce), which was formed in 1924 and recognised in 1929. Although both bodies merged before the Ordine was recognised, the Collegio continued as a separate organisation. However, since members of either body carry out more or less the same functions, it may be said that any difference is academic, relating primarily to the higher education and social status of the *dottori commercialisti*.

TABLE 7.4. MEMBERSHIP OF THE ITALIAN ACCOUNTANCY PROFESSION

Dottori commercialisti (31 December 1973)	14,203
of whom: Not entitled to practise	2,745
Entitled to practise	11,458
Ragionieri (31 December 1970)	6,321

Both professional bodies are regulated by separate laws under a decree promulgated on 27 October 1953 which charged the Ministry of Justice with responsibility for establishing the purposes, status, fees and rules of conduct of the profession. Accordingly the activities to which both *dottori commercialisti* and *ragionieri* can devote themselves are specified as follows:

1. Administration and liquidation of business enterprises, personal estates and specific assets.
2. Accounting assistance and technical advice.
3. Auditing or any other reviews pertaining to the truthfulness of balance sheets, accounts, records and any other accounting documents of business enterprises.
4. Administrative inspections and audits.
5. Adjustment and settlement of average, except for maritime average.
6. Settlement and liquidation of damages.
7. Receivers for business enterprises.
8. Statutory auditors (*sindaci*).

9. Consultation assistance and representation in taxation affairs; in Italy this activity is restricted to professional persons on certain registers among which are the registers of *dottori commercialisti* and *ragionieri*.

Members of the Collegio dei Ragionieri e Periti Commerciali are allowed to undertake the following additional activities:

10. Organisation of the accounting systems of public and private enterprises and the accounting aspects of reorganisation within the framework of administration and management.
11. Establishment of cost accounting systems and rectification of any other general accounting and administrative matters.
12. Adjustment and settlement of maritime average.

Although it is normal for *dottori commercialisti* and *ragionieri* to be *sindaci* (members of boards of auditors), this is only a very small part of the profession's activities which has developed more as providing business and fiscal advice; however, the Civil Code's regulation that individuals alone may act as *sindaci* is probably one of the major reasons for the present state of development of the profession. In keeping with the individual approach both bodies are organised on a local basis and every zone (*circondario*) with at least 15 *dottori commercialisti* or *ragionieri* has its own association and keeps a list of members in that zone. It is not possible to be listed on more than one list, but members may practise their profession anywhere in Italy. The official membership lists (*albi professionali*) of both bodies contain two separate sections, covering members in practice and members who do not exercise their profession.

Neither of the Italian accountancy bodies has issued any guidance to its members on accounting or auditing matters and therefore many prominent Italians feel that they must be held equally responsible with the tax authorities for the lack of credibility which characterises Italian accounting today.

On the other hand Italian accountants have never considered themselves responsible for the establishment of independent national standards. The national council (*consinglio nazionale*) of each body has not yet attained anything like the status that the Italian profession now needs so much.

Education and Training

The normal routes to either branch of the Italian accountancy profession are outlined in Fig. 7.6. Membership of either professional body is available only to Italian citizens or citizens of other countries granting reciprocal arrangements.

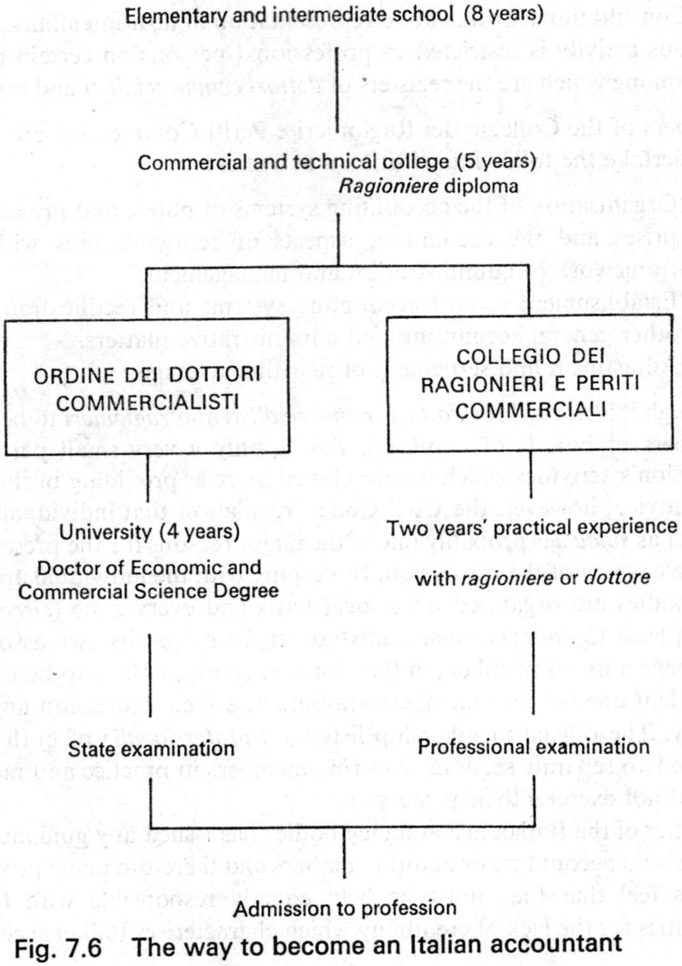

Fig. 7.6 The way to become an Italian accountant

Ordine dei Dottori Commercialisti

In order to become members of the Ordine candidates must:

1. Hold the university degree of Dottore in Scienze Economicle e Commerciale (Doctor of Economic and Commercial Science) or a corresponding equivalent qualification resulting from a course of study extending over four years. The university course includes:
   (a) Examinations in Economics, Accounting, Banking, Public, Civil and Commercial Law, Mathematics and Statistics, and two foreign languages.

(b) A thesis.
(c) An oral examination by a board of professors appointed by the State.

2. Pass a State examination for *dottore commercialista* covering accounting, banking, taxation and commercial law.

It is usual for prospective members of the Ordine to obtain the *ragioniere* diploma before commencing university studies. Although there is no requirement for practical experience, the nature of the State examination, which, however, is not identical from province to province, is such that candidates cannot pass without having had several years' experience in public practice, and most qualify between the ages of 28 and 35. It is notable that auditing does not figure in any of the examinations.

Collegio dei Ragionieri e Periti Commerciali

The training of the *ragioniere* is much more practical than that of the *dottore commercialista*. The *ragioniere* diploma from technical college is not particular to future members of the Collegio and is available to all successful students as part of the conventional education system. The five-year technical college course covers accounting, mathematics and commercial law and the professional examination, taken after at least two years' professional experience with a *dottore commercialista* or *ragioniere*, includes accounting, company law and taxation. As with the *dottori commercialisti*, there is no course or examination in auditing.

Ethics

Apart from the Civil Code requirements, the Italian accountancy bodies do not have any formal ethical codes, although for instance the Milan Order of *dottori commercialisti* has on occasion issued further notifications on various matters. The law requires accountants to keep the professional secret and states that a *dottore commercialista* or *ragioniere* cannot exercise any trade in his own name or for a third party and cannot be a notary public, minister of religion, professional journalist, broker, tax collector, director of public funds or employee of the State or other public body.

Fiduciary and Auditing Companies

International accounting firms operating in Italy are regulated by law No. 1966 of 23 November 1939, and are subject to the authorisation and control of the Ministry of Industry and Trade. Under Italian law they are referred to by the general title of *società fiduciare e di revisione* (fiduciary and auditing companies) whose activities are specified as being:

1. The administration of property on behalf of third parties.
2. Auditing, accounting and the provision of management services.
3. The representation of shareholders and bondholders.

An auditing company cannot act as a statutory auditor (*sindaco*), administrator of bankruptcies, judicial expert in civil or penal matters and in general cannot act in all those cases exclusively reserved for individual members of the "professional and special orders".

Società fiduciari e di revisione may be organised as partnerships or limited liability companies (SpAs); in the latter event they must have a minimum paid-up share capital of L 1 million of which 50 per cent, up to a maximum of L 500,000, must be invested in State bonds, guaranteed by the State, for the duration of the company.

The following regulations apply to the membership and management of the auditing companies:

1. At least two-thirds of the directors must be Italian citizens.
2. The president and executive managers must be Italian citizens.
3. All members of the board of auditors (*sindaci*) must be chosen from professional lists and at least two must be *dottori commercialisti* or *ragionieri* or members of the *Ruolo dei Revisori Ufficiali dei Conti.*
4. At least one director, in the case of companies with more than one director and two in the case of companies with five or more directors, must be chosen from the above professional lists.
5. All personnel employed by such companies, apart from clerical personnel, must have the same education and meet the same requirements as those listed on the professional lists mentioned above.

The auditing companies must file an "annual balance sheet" with the Ministry of Industry and Trade supplying "all information and presenting all documents requested by the Government inspector or directly by the Ministry of Industry and Trade".

Apart from the usual international accounting firms, there are also a few branches of Swiss accounting firms in Italy. The most important of these are Fides, which audits the Pirelli companies, and Fidital, a subsidiary of Schweizierische Treuhand Gesellschaft, which operates a joint firm with Coopers & Lybrand under the title "Fidital-Coopers & Lybrand". The international accounting firms, which are reckoned to have fewer than 1500 qualified staff in Italy, still confine their work almost exclusively to UK and US subsidiaries. Some top Italian companies have recently decided to carry out conventional audits, but the process of transferring to UK and US "generally accepted accounting standards" is usually accomplished over several years and is aptly referred to in one accounting firm as "tunnelling up". This trend will continue as increasing numbers of companies realise that conventional independent audits will eventually become obligatory. The mini-reform of company law, promulgated in March 1975 provides for the audit of all quoted companies by auditing firms registered with a National (SEC-type) Commission for Companies and the Stock Exchange. The initial register will be composed of those accounting firms registered as *società fiduciare e di revisione* under the provisions of the 1939 law. Not surprisingly, the local accountancy bodies do not relish the prospect of all the leading Italian companies being audited by foreigners, and opposition to the activities of the international firms is strong and well organised. Despite this, their future seems assured, and there is clearly an awareness in top financial circles in Rome that they have a big part to play in the future.

AUDITING

Italian companies are not subject to conventional audits as known in Anglo-Saxon countries and audit reports on the accounts of the few companies who opt for UK-style audits have no legal significance. Although the *sindaci* are supposed to carry out the audit function the truth is that their work is a mere formality.

Appointment of the Board of Auditors

The Civil Code prescribes that the following appoint a *collegio sindacale* (board of auditors):

1. SpA (limited liability) companies.
2. SRL (private limited liability) companies with a share capital of not less than L 1 million.
3. SApA (limited partnership with shares) companies.

Members of the board of auditors (*sindaci*) are first appointed in the articles and subsequently by the shareholders in general meeting for terms of three years, which are renewable. The board is composed of three or five regular members, who may or may not be shareholders, and two alternate members. Companies with a capital of not less than L 50 million must select at least one of the regular *sindaci*, where the board consists of three auditors, and at least two where it consists of five members: and in both cases one of the alternate *sindaci* from the Roll of Official Examiners of Accounts (*Ruolo dei Revisori Ufficiali dei Conti*).

Other companies select at least one regular *sindaco* and one other from the professional lists of the Ordine dei Dottori Commercialisti or the Collegio dei Ragionieri e Periti Commerciali. In companies with no board of auditors members have the right to obtain information concerning the progress of the company's affairs from the directors and to inspect the company's books. Members representing no less than one-third of the capital may have audits carried out annually at their own expense. The chairman of the *sindaci* of any company whose board of auditors includes an official examiner of accounts must himself be an official examiner of accounts.

Ruolo dei Revisori Ufficiali dei Conti

The Roll of Official Examiners of Accounts (*Ruolo dei Revisori Ufficiali dei Conti*) is maintained by the Ministry of Justice, copies of the list being kept by the provincial chambers of commerce, industry and agriculture. Enrolment is in the hands of a central committee composed of:

1. One president designated by the Ministry of Justice.
2. The General Director of Civil Affairs of the Ministry of Justice or one of his representatives.
3. One officer from the Ministry of Finance.
4. Two officers from the Ministry of Industry and Commerce.
5. One officer from the Bank of Italy.
6. One representative of the Association of the Italian Corporations (Associazione Italiana tra le Società per Azioni).

In order to be enrolled it is necessary for candidates to be Italians of the highest integrity and to have served for at least five years as an active statutory auditor or as a director, administrative or accounting officer (*dirigente*) of a company having a share capital of not less than L 50 million or to have satisfactorily performed other similar duties. The term may be reduced to three years for *dottori commercialisti* who have been members of the Ordine dei Dottori Commercialisti for at least five years and to four years for *ragionieri* who have been members of the Collegio dei Ragonieri e Perite Commerciali for at least six years. It is notable that only in exceptional cases are non-professional applicants admitted; on the other hand, there is no requirement for applicants to be competent in accounting. Those whose names appear on the roll are deemed to be acting as public officials when carrying out their duties.

Duties of the Board of Auditors

The duties of the Collegio Sindacale, contained for the most part in the Civil Code, are many and varied. It is pointless, however, to talk about auditing standards: the list of standard audit practices which are not performed by the *sindaci* is as long as their list of duties. The specific duties of the Collegio Sindacale indicate that this body was conceived as serving the dual role of supervisory board and statutory auditor.

General duties.

1. To fulfil their duties with care.
2. To be truthful in their report and certificates.
3. To keep the professional secret.

Specific duties.

Accounting and auditing:

4. To verify the regular keeping of the accounts.
5. To verify the consistency of the balance sheet and profit and loss account with the company's books and accounting records.
6. To ensure that the valuation rules (Article 2425) have been complied with; any departures must be reported and justified by the *sindaci* and directors.
7. To approve the calculation of prepayments and accruals and to report on this to the general meeting.
8. To verify the amount of cash on hand and the existence of valuables and securities owned by the company, or received by way of pledge, security or custody, at least every three months.
9. To meet at least once in every three months and to record all proceedings in a minute book, to be signed by all present.
10. To report to the general meeting on the results of the company and the keeping of its accounts and to make remarks and recommendations relating to the balance sheet and its approval.

The duties of the Collegio Sindacale also extend to the following special circumstances:

11. Within six months, together with the directors, to examine and if necessary revise the valuation attributed to any property in kind contributed as part of the capital of the company.

12. To report losses resulting in a capital reduction to the general meeting.
13. To report any increase in capital as a result of monetary revaluations to the general meeting.
14. To report on the final balance sheet in the case of the liquidation of the company.

Management and supervision:

15. To supervise the management of the company.
16. To ensure that the company complies with the law and the articles of association; the *sindaci* may be held jointly liable with the directors when acts and omissions of the latter might have been avoided if the Collegio Sindacale had carried out its duties.
17. To attend all meetings of the directors and shareholders; the *sindaci* may also attend meetings of the executive committee if such exists.
18. To call shareholders' meetings and deal with the publications prescribed by law if the directors fail to do so.
19. To receive the resignation of the directors, notify the local court of this fact, and resolve upon their substitution.
20. Together with the directors to determine the fees of those directors who have carried out particular functions.
21. To investigate complaints from shareholders; if members representing 5 per cent of the capital complain, the *sindaci* must carry out an immediate investigation and report their findings and any recommendations to the shareholders calling a special meeting where this appears necessary.
22. The chairman of the board of auditors must certify the annual income-tax return; the *sindaci* are obliged to amend the income-tax return where this is necessary as a result of omissions, fictitious entries and alterations.

Clearly the Collegio Sindacale is much more suited to the supervisory function and it is this which the proposed reform intends that it should carry out in the future, at least so far as quoted companies are concerned.

Report of the Board of Auditors

The annual report of the *sindaci* is usually a lengthy document. A typical report has the following sections:

1. Summaries of the balance sheet and profit and loss account.
2. Report of the *sindaci* on the accounts and their work during the year.

3. Explanations of the valuation criteria.
4. Recommendation that the meeting should approve the accounts.

The following are the reports of the boards of auditors on the 1973 accounts of Fiat and Pirelli SpA:

Fiat

Auditors' report

To Fiat Stockholders:

The Board of Directors has outlined the sound basis on which the various aspects of the financial statement and of the balance sheet have been developed for the period ending 31/12/73 which may be summarized as follows:

Balance Sheet		
Assets		L 3,497,047,813,783
Liabilities	L 1,505,693,157,178	
Depreciation fund	» 1,567,864,860,584	
		» 3,073,558,017,762
		L 423,489,796,021
Share capital	L 150,000,000,000	
Reserves and provisions	» 273,228,250,506	
		» 423,228,250,506
Net profit		L 261,545,515
Contra accounts: assets and liabilities		L 395,573,774,934
Profit and Loss Account		
Revenues		L 2,453,037,676,336
Costs		» 2,452,776,130,821
Net profit (as above)		L 261,545,515

Having carried out a careful examination of the balance sheet submitted for your approval, we declare that the books and accounts correspond with the requirements of the law.

In the financial year in question we have attended meetings of the Board of Directors and of the Executive Committee and carried out periodic verifications of the financial accounts, cash in hand, Securities held or receivable by the Company by way of guarantee or pledge.

We have thus satisfied ourselves of the sound overall administration applied particularly in respect of the requirements of the law.

Valuation of individual items of the balance sheet is based on conservative valuations communicated to us at the proper time by the Board of Directors with which we have agreed and on the basis of the principals pertaining we detail the following:

property, plant, machinery and equipment, furniture and fittings and patents have been entered in the balance sheet at actual cost value.

We agree with the principles laid down by the Board which have resulted in the inclusion among these items of the balances resulting from the agreed fiscal treatment of the balance sheet to 31/12/71 and of the automatic fiscal definition of the balance sheet at 31/12/72 and of the balance sheets of associated companies resulting from the application of law no. 823 of 19/12/73.

raw materials, withdrawals, and stocks have been valued either at cost or at probable market value whichever was the lower;

debtors have been entered at the anticipated realization value;

accruals and prepayments, whether assets or liabilities, represent the appropriate charges for the period, accruals being in accordance with assumed liabilities and receipts estimated on a conservative basis;

fixed interest credits have been entered at the lowest of three valuations: book value, latest Stock Exchange quotation and average disposal price over the last quarter;

shareholdings have been valued as follows:

for companies listed on the Stock Exchange the Board with our approval has proceeded to align book values with the lower of the latest prices quoted on the Stock Exchange and the average disposal price in the last quarter.

Upward variations have been made on a conservative basis taking advantage of the requirements of law no. 823 of 19/12/73. In the case of non-quoted companies where they have been operating at a loss, the book value has been adjusted to that of the latest approved balance sheet valuation of the company concerned.

normal and accelerated depreciation of fixed capital have been increased on the basis of the rates specified by the Board;

personnel indemnity fund covers the entire liability concerned, having been duly increased to provide for the indemnity accrued for personnel employed at 31/12/73;

The balance sheet submitted has our approval as does the proposal to distribute 3 SAI (Società Assicuratrice Industriale) shares for every 1000 ordinary and preference Fiat shares held with a corresponding reduction of the taxed reserves equal to 30 lire for each preference and ordinary share amounting to 9,000,000,000 lire from the dividend fluctuation and retained profits fund.

We accordingly invite you to approve the balance sheet presented by the Board of Directors.

The Auditors' Committee would wish to be associated with the condolences expressed by the Board of Directors to the families of Fiat employees who died during the past year, and in particular to record the productive contribution made in the development of the Company's iron and steel interests by Ing. Domenico Taccone, former Member of the Board and General Manager.

Turin, 28 March 1974

Federico Gamna
Carlo Dal Verme
Lamberto Jona Celesia

Pirelli SpA
Auditors' report

Ladies and Gentlemen,

The accounts at 30th April, 1973 which are submitted for approval show the following results, net of guarantees and per contra accounts amounting to lire 97,811,872,675.

Assets		L 250,890,042,898
Share capital	L 69,926,214,000	
Reserves	L 58,150,233,067	
Reserve from Transfers	L 46,160,459,029	
Tax assessments	L 446,301,275	
Liabilities	L 76,206,835,527	
		L 250,890,042,898

This balance is confirmed by the profit and loss account which is as follows:

Income	L 8,014,302,451
Withdrawal from Reserve from Transfers	L 26,363,262,005
	L 34,377,564,456
Expenditure & Losses	L 7,137,199,323
Amounts written off to Investments	L 27,240,365,133
	L 34,377,564,456

The Board of Directors have explained the reason for the nil balance, achieved by withdrawing from the Reserve from Transfers the amount needed to cover the difference between income and expenditure. Amounts written off to Investments formed a large proportion in the value of the investment in Industrie Pirelli SpA.

During the year the Board of Auditors has made all appropriate tests and checks and has attended all meetings of the Board of Directors, paying particular attention to developments in the Union with Dunlop, as reported by the Board of Directors.

The accounts which are submitted for approval have been drawn up under the careful scrutiny of the Board of Auditors. These accounts are accompanied by the schedule required by Law for registered holding companies.

The Board of Auditors confirms that the items appearing in the accounts are consistent with the accounting records, which have been properly kept, and that the accounts have been prepared in accordance with legal requirements. We further confirm that:

1. with regard to investments and fixed interest securities the Board of Auditors has been notified of the methods of valuation adopted which it fully approves in that:
   (a) investments in subsidiary and associate companies have been valued at cost at the beginning of the year—naturally taking into account the *Fund for Fluctuations in Value of Holdings in Subsidiary and Associate Companies*—with variations resulting from: subscriptions during the year to increases in the share capital of subsidiaries; resolutions passed by subsidiaries during the year to cover accounting losses; the allocation of further lire 737 million to the *Fund for Fluctuations in Value of Holdings in Subsidiary and Associate Companies* to cover losses recorded by subsidiaries during the year and brought forward;
   (b) shares quoted on the stock market have been valued at cost which in every case was below quoted selling prices for the month of April 1973 in the case of Italian shares, and the quotations at the end of April 1973 in the case of foreign shares. Unquoted shares, other than those mentioned under (a), have been valued at cost which in total corresponds to the values arrived at from their accounts;
   (c) shares in your own company have been shown at cost under assets, although the *Fund for Fluctuations in Value of Own Shares* appearing under liabilities has been increased to adjust this value to the April 1973 market quotation; a corresponding reduction has been made to the *Reserve for Purchase of Own Shares* leaving the total of the two items unchanged;
   (d) fixed interest securities have been valued—in the case of quoted shares—at cost or stock market value at the end of April 1973, whichever was the lower; unquoted debentures have been included at par value.

2. accrued income and charges have, with our approval, been calculated and allocated to the period according to time apportionments;
3. amounts written off issue expenses incurred at the time of issue of the debenture loans have been correctly calculated in relation to the duration of the loans in question;
4. the *Staff Severance and Providential Fund* has been eliminated as the Company has no staff.

The Board of Auditors accordingly recommends approval of the accounts.

Luigi Chiaraviglio
Enrico Biamonti
Angelo Corridori

The directors should submit the annual accounts and their annual report to the *sindaci* at least 30 days before the general meeting. The situation is such that, since shareholders have a right to inspect the accounts and the reports of the board of directors and auditors during the 15 days before the general meeting, the year-end work of the *sindaci* may be limited to a maximum of 15 days; moreover, the members of the Collegio Sindacale are not allowed to delegate any work to assistants.

Remuneration of the Board of Auditors

The annual remuneration of the *sindaci*, if not specified in the articles of association, must be fixed for their entire term of office by the general meeting at the time of their appointment. The professional bodies have laid down a fee scale based on the capital and assets of the company without taking into consideration the time involved.

Removal of the Board of Auditors

The Civil Code provides that the *sindaci* cannot be removed except for just cause. However, if members representing 10 per cent of the company's capital "have a basis for suspicion of serious irregularities in the discharge of the duties of the directors and auditors they may report the facts to the court which may order an investigation of the management at the expense of the petitioning members". In the most serious cases, the court can discharge the directors and auditors, and actions may be brought against them. The directors are required to notify all changes in the appointment of *sindaci* to the court within 15 days of their occurrence.

Independence of the Board of Auditors

Article 2399 bars "those who are related by blood or marriage within the fourth degree and those who are connected with the company or companies controlled by it by a continuous relationship of remunerated services" from becoming *sindaci*. *Sindaci* may have financial interests in client companies.

THE MINI-REFORM OF ITALIAN COMPANY LAW

Following the report of a special Commission presented in October 1973, Italian company law took a decisive step forward in March 1975 when a decree was issued relating to the audit and certification of financial statements of quoted companies. The reform is limited to quoted companies (of which there are less than 200) and essentially it provides for the establishment of a National Commission for Companies and the Stock Exchange and the audit of quoted companies' accounts by auditing firms registered with and approved by the National Commission.

The Audit of the Accounts of Quoted Companies by Auditing Firms

Appointment and Removal of Auditing Firms

The auditing firm is appointed by the company in general meeting. Initially the appointment is for three years; it may be renewed not more than twice and may be given again to the same firm only after an interval of five years.

All appointments must be submitted for the approval of the National Commission for Companies and the Stock Exchange within fifteen days, and within ten days of such notification the Commission may deny approval if it finds that the firm does not satisfy the independence rules, or does not have the technical competence to undertake the audit either with respect to its own organisation or to the number of appointments already undertaken.

The shareholders' meeting may resolve to terminate the appointment for just cause even before the period of appointment elapses. However, the Commission has the right to reject the resolution within ten days after receiving notice thereof. The Commission may also revoke an existing appointment where it finds that any of the independence rules have been infringed.

Remuneration

In making an appointment the shareholders' meeting determines the fee due to the auditing firms in accordance with general criteria to be fixed by the Commission.

Duties of the Auditing Firm

Article 1 of the decree implies that the auditor is required to determine whether proper books of accounts have been kept, whether the balance sheet and profit and loss account conform to the underlying records and whether the valuation rules laid down in the Civil Code have been observed.

The auditing firm has the right to obtain from the directors all documents and information useful for audit purpose and no limitations are placed upon its work.

Independence

An auditing firm may not be appointed if it finds itself "in a situation of incompatibility" deriving from contractual relationships or capital participation, or if its partners, directors, statutory auditors or general managers satisfy any of the exclusions laid down in the decree.

Report

The accounts and the directors' report must be submitted to the auditing firm at least forty-five days prior to the date of the AGM. The decree states that if the balance sheet and profit and loss account are in conformity with the accounting records confirmed by the examination made and are in conformity with the rules concerning the preparation and contents of the balance sheet and profit and loss account and if the results of operations are correctly shown in the accounts in accordance with correct accounting principles (*corretti principi contabili*) "the auditing firm must issue an audit certificate together with an appropriate report". This report must be made available to the shareholders and published in the same way as the accounts and other documents.

Registration and Regulation of Auditing Firms

The roll of auditing firms, which is under the jurisdiction of the National Commission for Companies and the Stock Exchange, will consist initially of those firms already regulated by Law No. 1966 of 23 November 1939 (*see* "Fiduciary and Auditing Companies" above). However, it is expected that all of the initial members of the roll as well as any new firm seeking registration will eventually have to satisfy the following requirements:

1. The activities of the firm must be limited to the auditing of the accounts of enterprises.
2. A majority of the directors/partners must consist of:

(a) *dottori commercialisti* or *ragionieri* listed in their respective professional rolls or on the rolls of official examiners of accounts (*revisoriufficiali dei conti*) and who have either been engaged in auditing activities for at least five years, or who have passed the annual qualifying examination of the Commission;
(b) persons who have a diploma which is not inferior to the diploma of an institute of secondary education of the second degree and who have engaged for at least five years in appropriate activities.

3. In the case of limited companies the share capital may not be less than 500 million lire and the shareholders may be only:
   (a) credit institutions under public law;
   (b) banks of national interest;
   (c) institutions which engage in medium- and long-term credit transactions throughout Italy.

Enrolment and Supervision

The Commission will grant enrolment only to an auditing firm "on the basis of a valuation of the independence, organisation and technical competence of the firm".

The Commission will supervise auditing firms on the roll and may carry out inspections and "recommend the adoption of principles and criteria for the audit and certification of corporate financial statements".

Transitional Provisions

Companies whose shares were already listed on a stock exchange on the date of entry into effect of the decree and those whose shares are admitted to listing prior to the publication of the roll must provide for the appointment of an auditing firm within the following terms:

1. One year for holding companies and for companies having, at 31 December 1974, a corporate capital in excess of 50 billion lire;
2. Two years for companies having, on 31 December 1974, corporate capital in excess of 10 but less than 50 billion lire;
3. Three years for the remaining companies;
4. Four years for credit companies and institutions whatever the amount of their corporate capital.

REFERENCES

1. The three commercial banks, known as banks of "national interest", are as follows (the proportion of the share capital of each bank held by IRI is shown in brackets):

Banca Commerciale Italiana (95·4 per cent).
Banco di Roma (81·4 per cent).
Credito Italiano (96 per cent).

2. For example the 1972 accounts of Fiat contained the following note: "The depreciation charge is made up as follows:
ordinary depreciation at rates allowed under regulations currently in force (Revenue Department Order No. 105 dated 1 December 1965):
3·5 per cent on property; 10 per cent on plant and machinery; 17·5 per cent on automatic equipment; 12·5 per cent on furnaces and ancillary equipment; 17·5 per cent on electrolytic cells and other equipment using chemical reagents; 10 per cent on equipment; 17·5 per cent on automatic devices; 12 per cent on furniture and fixtures; 20 per cent on motor vehicles.
accelerated depreciation (Article 98 of Direct Taxation Law No. 645 dated 29 January 1958). For this year a rate of 10 per cent has been used instead of 15 per cent for investments made during the last year, while the maximum rates allowed for investments in the previous three years have been left unchanged."
Unfortunately, very few Italian companies provide this information.
3. Tribunal of Milan, 27 April 1970. *Cova Minotti* v. *Italenka* in *Giurisprudenza Italiana* 1970 I,2,724: Accounts held void on grounds that profit and loss account did not analytically set forth items of income and costs expenses.
Tribunal of Milan, 24 September 1970, No. 4752. *Marefin S.A., Previdenza del Lavero SpA* v. *SARF* in *Giurisprudenza Italiana* 1971, I,2,410: Profit and loss statement void since it did not analytically set forth items of revenue and expenditures.

Chapter 8

The United Kingdom

BACKGROUND

Foremost among the financial centres of the world, with apparent disregard for the winds of change, stands the City of London, undoubtedly the United Kingdom's most impressive bequest to the new Europe.

From its early development during the eighteenth century as a source of bill finance the City assumed the role of the world's main financial centre after the Napoleonic Wars, remaining supreme throughout the great days of the Empire when sterling was the basis of the world's monetary system and the Bank of England was the guardian of the gold standard. Today, more foreign securities are quoted on the London Exchange than on any other; London is the insurance capital of the world; it houses more foreign banks than any other city; it dominates the Eurodollar market and is also the primary centre for international medium-term finance. The City's vast overseas earnings, particularly in the insurance market, make a major contribution to the United Kingdom's balance of payments (Table 8.1).

As a securities market, the London Stock Exchange overshadows all other European exchanges. On the other hand, it is evident that the Stock Exchange is declining in its primary role as a source of capital. Indeed it is calculated that, since 1968, the Stock Exchange has provided less than 7 per cent of industrial finance alongside a threefold increase in bank loans which now represent some 30 per cent of industry's capital needs.

Of particular importance to the City is the extensive secondary market provided by the institutions—the insurance companies, pension funds, investment trusts and unit trusts which channel the greater part of personal savings on to the Stock Exchange. Although the United Kingdom's $2\frac{1}{2}$ million private investors still have a powerful influence, the institutional involvement has increased enormously and in 1970 accounted for 37 per cent of the turnover in equities and 58 per cent of the turnover in fixed-interest securities.[1]

The UK banking system is dominated by the "Big Four" clearing banks[2] (Barclays, Lloyds, Midland and National Westminster) which have

TABLE 8.1. THE CONTRIBUTION OF THE CITY OF LONDON TO THE UNITED KINGDOM'S BALANCE OF PAYMENTS

1 The Balance of Payments (in £ millions)	*1968*	*1969*	*1970*	*1971*	*1972*
Deficit before invisibles	−1,125	−610	−495	−241	−1,233
Net private invisibles	+841	+1,055	+1,187	+1,302	+1,316
of which:					
Investment income	*+571*	*+833*	*+777*	*+715*	*+603*
Tourism	*+11*	*+35*	*+50*	*+52*	*+22*
Air and shipping	*+40*	*+76*	*+87*	*+97*	*+86*
City of London	*+392*	*+516*	*+608*	*+622*	*+679*
Balance of payments on current account	−284	+445	+692	+1,061	+83

2 What the City of London Earns (in £ millions)	*1968*	*1969*	*1970*	*1971*	*1972*
Insurance					
Companies	90	111	111	137	160
Lloyd's	74	105	156	189	206
Brokers	34	42	50	55	58
Total insurance	198	258	317	380	424
Banking					
Credits	178	235	262	252	316
Debits	111	119	134	101	208
Net bank earnings	67	116	128	101	108
Investment trusts	31	31	31	31	31
Unit trusts	2	3	4	5	6
Pension funds	5	5	6	7	8
Merchanting[1]	35–40	40–45	40–45	45–50	40–45
Brokerage, etc.	51	60	7	50	59
of which:					
Baltic Exchange	*n.a.*	*33*	*47*	*25*	*n.a.*
Stock Exchange	*9*	*9*	*9*	*10*	*16*
Lloyd's Register of Shipping[2]	*3*	*4*	*5*	*6*	*n.a.*
The City of London	392	516	608	622	679

1. Profits on third country trade and on re-exports; this category includes the earnings of the commodity markets.

2. Figures are from mid-year to mid-year and are therefore not strictly comparable with annual figures elsewhere.

Source: Derived from sources in the *City of London and UK Balance of Payments 1972* (The Pink Book), HMSO.

branch offices all over the country as well as extensive overseas operations.

As well as some wholesale banking, the merchant banks offer a whole spectrum of financial services ranging from acceptance and issuance business to takeovers and mergers.

The foreign banks, many of which are subsidiaries of US and, to a much lesser extent, Japanese banks, are principally concerned with international banking business, in the main to finance US subsidiaries in Europe, and general finance of international trade. Some offices are nevertheless little more than information centres.

The British tradition of self-regulation is nowhere more apparent than in the City. Here the Bank of England, nationalised in 1946, is on the one hand the Government's representative in the City, having particular responsibility for the banking system as well as a somewhat vaguer obligation to maintain overall good order, and is on the other hand the City's voice and most persuasive advocate, in all quarters and not least with the Government. In 1959, when the City found itself faced with the possibility of statutory controls over takeovers and mergers, the Bank of England saved the day by setting up a committee to work out a voluntary policing system. The result, the City Code on Takeovers and Mergers, remained in force until its revision in 1969 when the present Panel on Takeovers and Mergers, equipped with sanctions, was established.

But, however flexible and unique the self-regulatory system may be, it seems inevitable, if only for political reasons, that it must give way eventually to some system of statutory controls.

In May 1974 the Labour Party published a Green Paper, *The Community and the Company*, which concluded that:

> at present the control and regulation of company affairs is confused and fragmented. It also relies far too much on the system of self-regulation—itself confused, overlapping and sometimes contradictory—which has manifestly failed to work effectively even on its own terms.[3]

The Green Paper recommended that a new public supervisory body, the Companies Commission (similar to the Stock Exchange Commission in the United States), should be appointed. The Companies Commission would have "a continuing role in the control and regulation of company activities, particularly with reference to the form and frequency of disclosure of information", it would be principally concerned with the regulation and control of limited liability companies, and it would "oversee the work of the self-regulatory bodies and professional associations involved in the field of company activity and, in areas to be defined, have

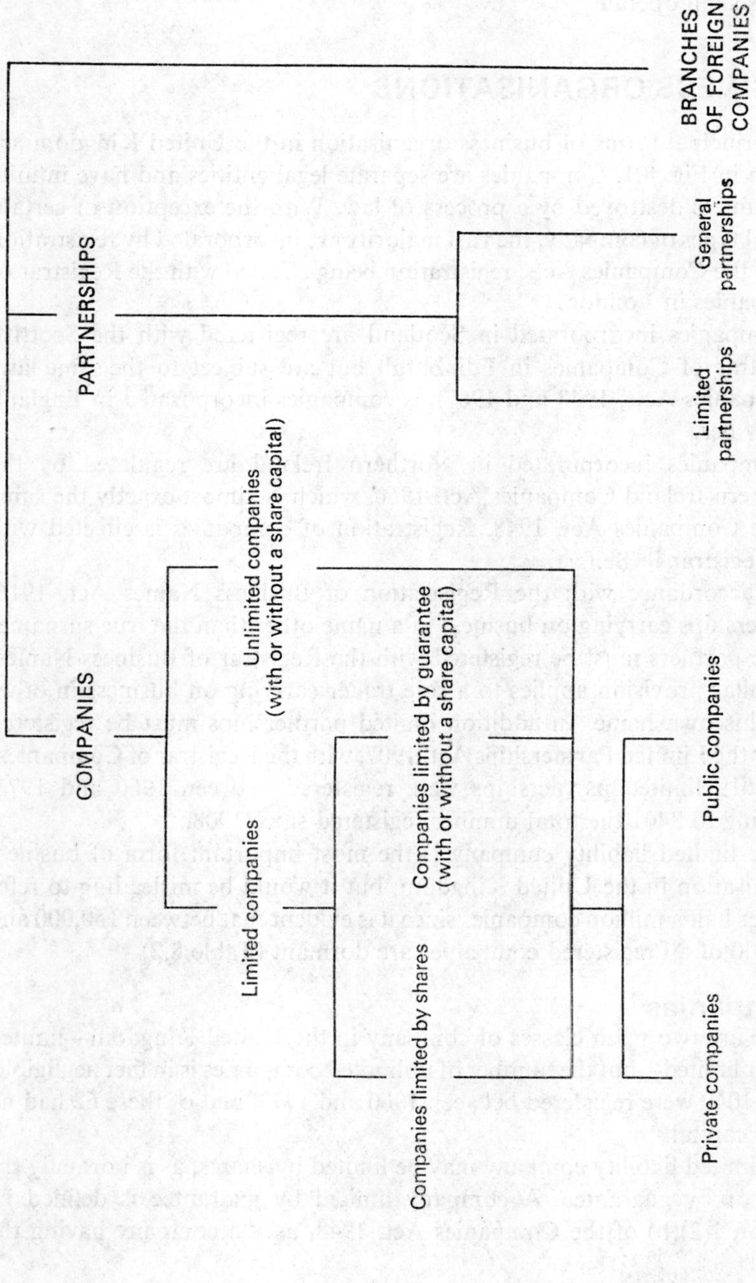

Fig. 8.1 Forms of business organisation in the United Kingdom

the ultimate authority . . . for deciding the rules under which these various bodies shall operate".[4]

BUSINESS ORGANISATIONS

The principal forms of business organisation in the United Kingdom are shown in Fig. 8.1. Companies are separate legal entities and have infinite lives unless destroyed by a process of law. With the exception of certain special types of company, the vast majority are incorporated by registration under the Companies Acts, registration being effected with the Registrar of Companies in London.

Companies incorporated in Scotland are registered with the Scottish Registrar of Companies in Edinburgh but are subject to the same laws (Companies Acts, 1948 and 1967) as companies incorporated in England and Wales.

Companies incorporated in Northern Ireland are regulated by the Northern Ireland Companies Act, 1960, which is almost exactly the same as the Companies Act, 1948. Registration of companies is effected with the Registrar in Belfast.

In accordance with the Registration of Business Names Act, 1916, partnerships carrying on business in a name other than the true surnames of the partners must be registered with the Registrar of Business Names. A similar provision applies to a sole trader carrying on business in other than his own name. In addition limited partnerships must be registered under the Limited Partnerships Act, 1907, with the Registrar of Companies; only 619 limited partnerships were registered between 1960 and 1973, bringing to 2401 the total number registered since 1908.

The limited liability company is the most important form of business organisation in the United Kingdom, but it would be misleading to refer to over half a million companies since it is evident that between 150,000 and 175,000 of all registered companies are dormant (Table 8.2).

Companies

There are two main classes of company in the United Kingdom—limited and unlimited—but the number of unlimited companies is in fact negligible. Only 1049 were registered between 1960 and 1973, and of these 62 had no share capital.

A limited liability company may be limited by shares, as is normally the case, or by guarantee. A company limited by guarantee is defined by Section 1(2)(b) of the Companies Act, 1948, as: "a company having the

TABLE 8.2. STATISTICS OF BUSINESS ORGANISATIONS IN THE UNITED KINGDOM (excluding Northern Ireland)

Inland Revenue Statistics, 1969	
Companies	345,600
Partnerships	326,700
Companies Registration Statistics, 1972	
Private companies	527,048
Public companies	15,530
Effective number on Registers	542,578
Stock Exchange Statistics, 1972	
Public quoted companies	3,132

liability of its members limited by the memorandum to such amount as the members may respectively thereby undertake to contribute to the assets of the company in the event of its being wound up". Apart from its guarantee capital a company limited by guarantee may also have a share capital, in which case a member is liable not only for the amount of the guarantee but also, as is the case with a company limited by shares, for the amount unpaid on the shares held. Such companies are generally used for educational or charitable purposes.

The Companies Acts make a further differentiation between "private" and "public" companies, but, as Professor Schmittoff makes clear, there is a conceptual difference between the Continental type of private company exemplified by the German GmbH and the French SàRL, and the UK private company limited by shares. As Professor Schmittoff explains:

> The Continental company of private type originated in the German GmbH, introduced by an enactment of 1892. . . . The French, Belgian and Italian company of private type follows the German model. According to this Continental conception, the company of private type is a form of business organisation *sui generis*, a legal person in form and a partnership in essence, economically a hybrid between a company and a partnership. In the British view . . . there is only one concept of company, which is subdivided into the public and the private company, and all provisions of our Companies Acts, 1948 and 1967, apply to both types of company unless the Acts state otherwise.[5]

The outmoded and confusing distinctions between the various forms of UK company have long been criticised. In a memorandum submitted to the President of the Board of Trade (now Department of Trade) in March 1969, the Allied Accountancy Bodies[6] stated that "the present basis of distinction between private and public companies is inappropriate and should be abolished". Instead, it was recommended that companies should be classified as "proprietary" or "stewardship" companies.[7]

Confronted with the possibility that a UK private company might be treated in the same way as a public company by the EEC directives (*see* Chapter 10), the 1973 Companies Bill, which lapsed as a result of the change of Government early in 1974, proposed that the name of any limited company should include the appropriate designation of its status, *viz.*

1. In the case of a public company, the words "public limited company" or the letters "p.l.c."
2. In the case of a private company, the word "limited" or the abbreviation "ltd."
3. In the case of a company limited by guarantee (not being a public company or a private company), the words "company limited by guarantee" or the letters "c.l.g."

The Bill further proposed to restrict the classification of private and public companies to:

1. Companies limited by shares.
2. Companies limited by guarantee having a share capital. (No company limited by guarantee would thereafter have a share capital unless it had one when the proposed law came into operation.)

Meanwhile, and for the foreseeable future, the existing distinction between private and public companies remains. The following comparison highlights the essential differences between these two types of company:

	Public	*Private*
Shareholders	Minimum of 7, and no restrictions on nationality or residence.	Minimum of 2, maximum of 50 (excluding present and past employees) and no restrictions on nationality or residence.
Securities	Shares are almost invariably registered. Bearer warrants can be issued only if shares are fully paid, Treasury consent has been obtained (Exchange Control Act, 1947) and the securities are kept in an authorised depository, *e.g.* a bank.	Shares can only be registered. The articles must restrict the right to transfer the shares and prohibit any invitation to the public to subscribe for any shares or debentures in the company.

	Public	*Private*
Securities *contd*	Shares in existence include: (1) preference shares; (2) redeemable preference shares; (3) ordinary shares; (4) deferred shares. All shares have a nominal value and cannot be issued at a discount unless authorised by the general meeting and sanctioned by the court.	
Capital	No minimum. However, the 1973 Companies Bill (which lapsed) proposed to oblige companies to have a minimum paid-up capital before starting business and to empower the Secretary of State to prescribe different amounts for public and private companies.	
Capital impairment	Section 66 of the Companies Act, 1948, states *inter alia* that a company "may cancel any paid-up share capital not represented by available assets". Such action, which must be authorised by the articles, needs a special resolution of the members and must be confirmed by the court. Apart from this, Section 222 provides that the court may wind up a company "if it is unable to pay its debts" or "if the court is of the opinion that it is just and equitable that the company should be wound up".	
Annual general meeting	An annual general meeting must be held each year, not later than 15 months after the last annual general meeting.	

Companies are managed by a board of directors, every public company having at least two directors and every private company at least one. The directors normally appoint one of their number "managing director" with responsibility for the day-to-day affairs of the company. As well as the directors, every company must have a secretary, who may also be a director, unless there is only one director. The secretary is concerned with the administration of the company; his obligations usually entail maintaining the statutory books, filing the necessary returns and keeping the minutes of general and board meetings. The directors are appointed in accordance with the articles and may be removed by ordinary resolution (simple majority) of the members. If the articles impose share qualifications these must be acquired within a maximum of two months after appointment. A director of a public company (or a private company which is a subsidiary of a public company) who has attained the age of 70 must vacate office at the next annual general meeting. However, the articles can alter or remove this age limit: thus a director may, in effect, be appointed at any age, provided the appointment is approved in general meeting and special notice (28 days' notice to the company and 21 days' notice by the company to the members) of the resolution is given stating the director's age.

As far as directors' remuneration is concerned, this may be fixed by the company in general meeting, but more commonly directors have service contracts with the company. Directors may not normally receive loans from the company; nor may they on any account receive tax-free remuneration.

Partnerships

Partnerships are regulated by the Partnership Act, 1890, and the Limited Partnership Act, 1907. The former statute defines a partnership as "the relation which subsists between persons carrying on a business in common with a view of profit".

A limited partnership arises when there is at least one general partner with unlimited liability and at least one limited partner whose liability is limited to his capital contribution. Various restrictions apply to the limited partner: he cannot take part in the management of the partnership business (if he does, his liability becomes unlimited); he cannot dissolve the partnership by notice; nor does his death, bankruptcy or lunacy dissolve the partnership.

With certain exceptions, the maximum number of partners allowed in a partnership (Part IV, Companies Act, 1967) is 20. In the case of the partnership business being banking, each of the partners must be authorised by the Department of Trade. The exceptions, where the number of partners can exceed 20, include partnerships of solicitors, accountants, members of the Stock Exchange and several other professions.

Branches of Foreign Companies

Within one month of setting up a branch operation in the United Kingdom, foreign companies are obliged to file certain documents with the Registrar of Companies. Section 410(1) of the 1948 Act states that:

> every overseas company shall, in every calendar year, make out a balance sheet and profit and loss account and, if the company is a holding company, group accounts, in such form, and containing such particulars and including such documents, as under the provisions of this Act (subject, however, to any prescribed exceptions) it would, if it had been a company within the meaning of this Act, have been required to make out and lay before the company in general meeting, and deliver copies of those documents to the Registrar of Companies.

The number of overseas companies registered as having a place of business in the United Kingdom was 4037 at December 1972 and, of these, 1061 were US companies.

ACCOUNTING AND FINANCIAL REPORTING

The relative sophistication and superiority of accounting in the United Kingdom may be ascribed to various complex and interrelated factors, the most obvious of which must be connected with the Empire, the City, the rapid establishment of the limited company in the United Kingdom and the parallel development of the accountancy profession.

The registration of companies as corporate entities was first permitted in 1844; the principle of limited liability was recognised in 1855, but it was the Companies Act, 1862, containing the first comprehensive code of company law, which gave the greatest impetus to the formation of companies as the main form of business organisation. Today there are approximately as many companies in the United Kingdom as in the rest of the EEC countries together.

The establishment of the UK accountancy profession took place between 1850 and 1880, and, although at first the profession concerned itself mainly with bankruptcies and liquidations, the scope of accountants' work rapidly expanded and they were increasingly called upon to carry out audits before these became compulsory in 1900. The determination of acceptable rules for the preparation of accounts also fell to them, as Peter Bird explains:

> The Companies Acts say little more than that the capital of a company shall not be returned to the shareholders. . . . It was left to the accounting profession to produce rules of practice for profit calculation with a view to determining the maximum permitted dividend. From this creditor-oriented viewpoint accountants could see that much less harm was done if profits were understated than if they were overstated. . . . They developed conventions that are with us today—under which profits are not recognised until realised, but anticipated losses are taken into account.[8]

From such beginnings accounting has gradually evolved in the United Kingdom in response to the various needs of the time and, so far at least, without any substantial intervention by Government.

The importance of disclosure in financial reporting was first recognised by law in 1908 when public companies were obliged to file their accounts for public inspection. Since then the disclosures required by law have tended to follow in the wake of what was considered to be best practice by the more progressive companies. Current company law is contained in the Companies Act, 1948, as amended and extended by the Companies Act, 1967.

Perhaps the single most significant feature of financial reporting in the

United Kingdom is that it is accepted practice for companies to make voluntary as well as mandatory disclosures in their annual accounts. The Stock Exchange has always placed great emphasis on the regular supply of adequate information both to shareholders and to the investing public. The provisions of the Stock Exchange Listing Agreement, which is signed by every quoted company, go far beyond the requirements of the Companies Acts. The Statements of Standard Accounting Practice issued by the accountancy bodies must be followed in the preparation of the annual accounts if a company is to avoid a qualified auditors' report. (Note that some accounting standards apply only to quoted companies.) Finally, the influence of the UK financial press has, beyond doubt, played a major role in the development of accounting and financial reporting standards. In the latter half of the 1960s, for instance, it was the massive publicity given by the financial press to the apparent proliferation of alternative accounting methods which eventually forced the accountancy profession to set up an Accounting Standards Steering Committee.

Accounting Principles

The obligation to give a true and fair view is the central and overriding requirement of all UK accounting rules. Section 149 of the Companies Act, 1948, states that:

> every balance sheet of a company shall give a true and fair view of the state of affairs of the company as at the end of its financial year, and every profit and loss of a company shall give a true and fair view of the profit or loss of the company for the financial year.

What exactly is meant by "true and fair view" is not always clear. The term was first introduced by the Companies Act, 1948, superseding the previous reference to a "true and correct view". The concept has never been defined but has always been regarded as a matter of individual judgement. One explanation of what it means is that a company must provide such information in its accounts as will give the reader the same view as the company knows its true position to be.

The UK accountancy profession first became formally involved with defining generally accepted accounting principles as far back as 1942 when the Institute of Chartered Accountants in England and Wales began to issue Recommendations on Accounting Principles. These statements, which were based on what was considered to be best practice, depended for their recognition on being generally accepted by the business community and were not binding on members of the Institute. This system continued until the end of the 1960s, when a series of public cases (AEI, Rolls Razor,

Pergamon Press) focused the attention of the public and indeed that of the Government on the situation. The accountancy profession had no option but to take a more definitive approach to accounting principles.

In a "Statement of Intent on Accounting Standards in the 1970s", issued in December 1969, the Institute of Chartered Accountants in England and Wales proclaimed its intention to advance accounting standards along the following lines:

1. Narrowing the areas of difference and variety in accounting practice.
2. Disclosure of accounting bases.
3. Disclosure of departures from established definitive accounting standards.
4. Wider exposure for major new proposals on accounting standards.
5. Continuing programme for encouraging improved accounting standards in legal and regulatory measures.

Shortly afterwards, the Institute (in association with other professional bodies) established an Accounting Standards Steering Committee (ASSC) to implement the Statement of Intent. The ASSC is charged with the task of defining accounting standards and these, when approved by the Council of the Institute, are to be applied "to all financial accounts intended to give a true and fair view of financial position and profit or loss".[10]

The Councils of the professional bodies represented on the ASSC require their members to observe accounting standards in the preparation or auditing of accounts. The Council of the Stock Exchange actively supports the accounting standards programme and requires the inclusion in the directors' report of a statement of the reasons for adopting an alternative basis of accounting in any case where the auditors have stated that the accounts are not drawn up in accordance with defined standards. This indeed is a big step from the tame Recommendations, the introduction to each of which generally included a statement such as:

> Whilst it is recognised that the form in which the accounts are submitted to shareholders is (subject to compliance with the Companies Act) a matter within the discretion of directors, it is hoped that these recommendations will be helpful to members in advising, in appropriate cases, as to what is regarded as the best practice.

The ASSC publishes its proposals for accounting standards in the form of Exposure Drafts (EDs) "for comment by persons interested in financial reporting". In some cases, for example that of inflation accounting, Discussion Papers are issued to stimulate public discussion in advance of the more definitive proposals of Exposure Drafts. Having considered all comments on a particular proposal, the ASSC then proceeds to issue a Statement of Standard Accounting Practice (SSAP). The following extracts from the Explanatory Foreword set out the main implications of SSAPs:

DISCLOSURE OF SIGNIFICANT DEPARTURES

Significant departures in financial accounts from applicable accounting standards should be disclosed and explained. The financial effects should be estimated and disclosed unless this would be impracticable or misleading in the context of giving a true and fair view. If the financial effects of departures from standard are not disclosed, the reasons should be stated.

EXCEPTIONAL AND BORDERLINE CASES

Accounting standards are not intended to be a comprehensive code of rigid rules. It would be impracticable to establish a code sufficiently elaborate to cater for all business situations and circumstances and every exceptional or marginal case. Nor could any code of rules provide in advance for innovations in business and financial practice.

Moreover, it must be recognised that there may be situations in which for justifiable reasons accounting standards are not strictly applicable because they are impracticable or, exceptionally, having regard to the circumstances, would be inappropriate or give a misleading view.

STATUS OF RECOMMENDATIONS ON ACCOUNTING PRINCIPLES

In so far as they are not replaced by Statements of Standard Accounting Practice, the Council's "Recommendations on Accounting Principles" will continue in effect as guidance statements and indicators of best practice. They are persuasive in intent and departures from them do not necessarily require disclosure as do departures from accounting standards.

APPLICATION OF ACCOUNTING STANDARDS OVERSEAS

Statements of Standard Accounting Practice are not intended to apply to accounts prepared and audited in overseas territories for local purposes where different requirements of law or generally accepted practice prevail, but are intended to be applied where accounts of overseas subsidiaries and associated companies are incorporated in UK group accounts.

FUTURE DEVELOPMENTS

Methods of financial accounting evolve and alter in response to changing business and economic needs. From time to time new accounting standards will be drawn at progressive levels, and established standards will be reviewed with the object of improvement in the light of new needs and developments.

Inflation Accounting

The problem of whether and how best to account for inflation, and more generally for rising price levels, has occupied the attention of UK accountants for over 25 years. In the post-war period when the governments of

Continental countries such as France and Italy were permitting the revaluation of assets by the use of specific price indices, opinion within the UK profession was split. In recommendation N 12 ("Rising Price Levels in Relation to Accounts"), issued in January 1949, the Institute of Chartered Accountants in England and Wales concluded that "any amount set aside to finance replacement (whether of fixed or current assets) at enhanced costs should not be treated as a provision which must be made before profit for the year can be ascertained, but as a transfer to reserve", *i.e.* a specific capital reserve. For balance sheet purposes it was recommended that "fixed assets should not, in general, be written up on the basis of estimated replacement costs, especially in the absence of a measure of stability in the price level". The Association of Certified (and Corporate, at that time) Accountants thought otherwise, maintaining that the best remedy would be to divide the depreciation charge in two parts:[11]

(a) the basic charge calculated on recorded cost and designed to recover it over the useful life of the asset; and
(b) a supplementary charge for the difference by which the basic charge falls short of the amount which would appear as an expense if it were calculated on a basis homogeneous with maintenance repair and other current expenses

The basic depreciation would continue to be deducted from the book value of the assets in the balance sheet and the supplementary depreciation brought to a special replacement provision account.

However, the opinion stated that the choice of a suitable coefficient for measuring the trend in the purchasing power of money presented some difficulty and reported that no "comprehensive or official index appears to exist".

On 30 May 1952, just over three years after N 12, the Institute of Chartered Accountants in England and Wales issued recommendation N 15 ("Accounting in Relation to Changes in the Purchasing Power of Money") in which it sought to give "a brief description of the limitations on the significance of accounts prepared on the generally accepted basis known as historical cost . . . and to make recommendations as to the procedure which should be followed in preparing annual accounts unless and until a generally accepted alternative to the historical cost basis is available". N 15 repeated the recommendations of N 12 but in addition urged that accountants should draw the attention of directors or officers of companies to the desirability of:

(a) setting amounts aside from profits to reserve in recognition of the effects which changes in the purchasing power of money have had upon the affairs of the business . . .;

(b) showing in the directors' report or otherwise the effects which changes in the purchasing power of money have had on the affairs of the business . . .; and
(c) experimenting with methods of measuring the effects of changes in the purchasing power of money on profits and on financial statements. . . .

At the same time as N 15 was issued, the Institute of Chartered Accountants in England and Wales declared its intention to invite other professional bodies to join with it in a further study of the subject. Nevertheless, after only two meetings, a brief statement—issued on 16 January 1954—announced that since none of the representatives of the other bodies "felt there was any likelihood of agreement being reached . . . it was decided that the discussion should be regarded as closed".[12] Thus, no progress was made.

The situation remained unchanged until August 1968, which saw the publication by the Research Foundation of the Institute of Chartered Accountants of a paper entitled "Accounting for Stewardship in a Period of Inflation". This paper proposed the restatement of the principal figures in the accounts in terms of pounds of current purchasing power by the application of the Consumer Price Index. Indeed, current purchasing power (CPP) accounting had been one of the four alternatives considered in N 15. The conclusion reached in that recommendation was that all the alternatives raised issues affecting "not merely every business but also every individual and they involve major considerations of general monetary and social policy which go far beyond the question whether one accounting method of computing business profits is more free from limitations than another".[13]

The inflation accounting debate actually began in earnest in August 1971 with the ASSC's publication of a discussion paper and fact sheet entitled "Inflation and Accounts" following confidential discussions with representatives of the Government, industry and the City institutions. "Inflation and Accounts" took the same line as the proposals contained in the Research Foundation's paper. It was followed up in January 1973 by an exposure draft, ED 8 ("Accounting for Changes in the Purchasing Power of Money"), and later by "A Working Guide to the Accounting Procedures" to be used. The ASSC aimed to limit the application of ED 8 to quoted companies which would be obliged to account for the effects of inflation by preparing a supplementary statement to the annual accounts, showing, in terms of purchasing power at the end of the year to which the accounts relate, the financial position at that date and the results for the year. In converting from basic historical-cost accounts to supplementary purchasing power statements, monetary items (fundamentally cash, debtors and creditors) in the balance sheet at the end of the period remain the same, while non-monetary items are increased (or reduced) in proportion to the inflation (or deflation) that has accrued since their acquisition or revaluation. The index originally suggested for use in the conversion process, the Consumer Price Index, was subsequently replaced on the advice of the Central Statistical Office by an index of prices of consumer goods and services.[14]

In essence the CPP method is very simple; it has the advantage of retaining the historical-cost convention and, to quote the ASSC, produces figures which are reasonably comparable between companies and over the course of time. On the other hand it is materially different from replacement value accounting as practised by a number of Dutch companies, and in particular it does not reflect changes due to other factors such as technology or market pressures.

The inflation accounting controversy reached a new peak when, in July 1973, the Government declared that it was appointing a committee of inquiry with the following terms of reference:

> To consider whether, and if so how, company accounts should allow for changes (including relative changes) in costs and prices, having regard to established accounting conventions based on historic costs, the proposal for current general purchasing power accounting put forward by the Accounting Standards Steering Committee, and other possible methods of allowing for price changes, and to make recommendations. In considering the question, the following matters, *inter alia*, should be taken into account:
> (i) the effects upon investment and other management decisions, and upon the efficiency of companies generally;
> (ii) the effect on the efficient allocation of resources through the capital market;
> (iii) the need to restrain inflation in the United Kingdom;
> (iv) the requirements of investors, creditors, employees, Government and the public for information;
> (v) any implications for the taxation of the profits and capital gains of companies, the assumption being that the share of the total direct tax burden borne by the company sector remains unchanged;
> (vi) the repercussions on the accounts of other corporate bodies;
> (vii) procedures in other countries, particularly EEC.

This unique intervention into what had hitherto been regarded as the exclusive realm of the accountancy profession was justified on the grounds that "the subject ranged well beyond accounting technicalities and into spheres of economic policy which must necessarily be the affairs of Government".[15]

Pending the report of the official "Inflation Accounting Committee", the ASSC announced in September 1973 that, since it considered the subject too important to be held in abeyance, a "provisional standard" would be issued.

Accordingly, in May 1974, ED 8 became SSAP 7, but, unlike other standards, departures from its recommended procedures need not be disclosed in annual accounts; nor are auditors obliged to refer in their reports to any such departures.

Accounting Practices and the Annual Accounts

Unlike France or Germany, there are no standardised forms of accounts in the United Kingdom and there is indeed considerable variety in the formats which individual companies adopt. A special feature of the accounts of most UK companies is that much of the detail found on the face of the French or German balance sheet or profit and loss account is generally relegated to notes, which, of course, also form part of the accounts.

Figures 8.2 and 8.3, which show the 1972 consolidated profit and loss account and consolidated balance sheet of the Burmah Oil Company Limited, are good examples of the forms of presentation used by UK companies in their annual accounts.[16]

Since 1968–9, the Institute of Chartered Accountants in England and Wales has carried out a comprehensive annual survey of the accounting practices followed by major UK companies. The 1972–3 survey[17] disclosed that, out of 300 industrial companies surveyed, all companies presented a vertical or "statement" form of profit and loss account and some 90 per cent presented a vertical balance sheet.

The accounting practices generally followed in the preparation of annual accounts are discussed in the following sections.

Consolidated Accounts

Consolidated accounts have been required in the United Kingdom since the Companies Act, 1948, came into force. Section 150 of this Act states that where at the end of its financial year a company has subsidiaries it must, in addition to its own accounts, lay before its members accounts or statements, referred to as group accounts, which show the combined state of affairs and profit and loss of the group. A company is a subsidiary of another company if that other company is one of its members and controls the composition of its board of directors, or holds more than half of the equity share capital. Section 151 of the same Act provides that the

The Burmah Oil Company Limited
Consolidated profit and loss account for the year 1972

	1972 £ thousands	1971 £ thousands
Turnover net of duties	**348,507**	272,851
Profit on trading	**37,987**	28,787
Depreciation, depletion and amortisation	**11,722**	9,724
Net operating profit	**26,265**	19,063
Share of profits of associates	**5,970**	7,671
Income from trade investments	**3,442**	3,942
Income from trading and trade investments	**35,677**	30,676
Dividends from The British Petroleum Co Ltd	**16,554**	17,111
	52,231	47,787
Interest	**9,771**	7,744
Profit before taxation	**42,460**	40,043
Taxation	**9,411**	9,434
Profit after taxation	**33,049**	30,609
Minority interests and pre-acquisition profit	**1,499**	1,081
Profit available to the group	**31,550**	29,528
Preference stock dividends	**1,387**	1,387
Earnings attributable to ordinary stockholders	**30,163**	28,141
Ordinary stock dividends	**24,428**	22,182
Retained earnings	**5,735**	5,959
Extraordinary items	**1,751**	(2,357)
Retentions	**7,486**	3,602
Earnings per ordinary stock unit	**21·36p**	20·93p

Fig. 8.2 Example of consolidated profit and loss account

form of group accounts laid before a holding company must be consolidated accounts comprising a consolidated balance sheet and a consolidated profit and loss account unless the directors consider that equivalent information can be better appreciated in an alternative form. A holding company need not publish a profit and loss account in addition to the consolidated profit and loss account, provided that this states how much of the consolidated profit and loss for the financial year is dealt with in

The Burmah Oil Company Limited Consolidated balance sheet at 31st December 1972

Funds employed		**1972** £ thousands		**1971** £ thousands
Share capital and reserves				
Issued capital				
Preference		**19,000**		19,000
Ordinary		**142,685**		134,434
		161,685		153,434
Reserves				
Share premium	**26,295**		2,396	
Capital surplus	**21,660**		18,040	
Investment revaluation	**453,352**		387,403	
General retentions	**67,599**		63,983	
	568,906		471,822	
Less				
Goodwill including that arising on consolidation	**63,900**	**505,006**	18,840	452,982
		666,691		606,416
Minority interests		**31,999**		27,888
Loan capital		**118,744**		105,920
Deferred liabilities		**23,804**		8,466
		841,238		748,690

J A Lumsden
N J D Williams — Directors

Fig. 8.3 Example of consolidated balance sheet

Employment of funds		**1972** £ thousands		**1971** £ thousands
Fixed assets				
Properties and operating assets		**218,191**		161,202
Investments				
Associated companies	**34,398**		37,090	
Trade	**76,530**		77,400	
The British Petroleum Co Ltd	**494,324**		424,739	
Long-term interests in tankers	**8,438**		1,282	
Deposits with bank	**3,803**		4,389	
		617,493		544,900
Net current assets				
Stores and materials	**4,603**		3,900	
Crude oil, products and other stocks	**68,413**		43,434	
Debtors and prepayments	**100,996**		76,127	
Short-term investments	**20,092**		23,307	
Bank balances and cash	**7,690**		7,721	
	201,794		154,489	
Less				
Creditors, accrued liabilities, and provisions	**102,579**		57,122	
Bank and other advances	**63,485**		35,613	
Taxation	**5,417**		5,055	
Dividends	**24,759**		14,111	
	196,240		111,901	
		5,554		42,588
		841,238		748,690

the accounts of the holding company. Consolidated accounts must comprise the information shown in the separate accounts of the individual companies, subject to "such adjustments, if any, as the directors of the holding company think necessary". Apart from this provision, the consolidated accounts must comply with the Companies Acts as if they were the accounts of an actual company.

The obligation to prepare consolidated accounts does not apply to a company having subsidiaries which is itself the wholly owned subsidiary of another company incorporated in the United Kingdom. Moreover, group accounts need not deal with a subsidiary if the directors of the holding company consider that:

1. It is impracticable or would be of no real value to members of the company, in view of the insignificant amounts involved, or would involve expense or delay out of proportion to the value to the members of the company; or
2. The result would be misleading or harmful to the business of the company or any of its subsidiaries; or
3. The business of the holding company and that of the subsidiary are so different that they cannot reasonably be treated as one undertaking.

In the latter two cases, any omission of a subsidiary from consolidated accounts requires the approval of the Department of Trade.

Where a holding company does not prepare group accounts or if any subsidiaries are omitted from consolidated accounts, the following information must be given in a statement annexed to the balance sheet:

1. The reasons for the omission.
2. The net aggregate amounts attributable to the holding company of profits less losses of such subsidiaries:
   (a) dealt with in the company's accounts;
   (b) not so dealt with for:
      (i) the respective financial years of the subsidiaries ending with or during the financial year of the company;
      (ii) their previous financial years since acquisition.
3. Any qualifications in audit reports on accounts of subsidiaries or notes on accounts which, if not made, would properly have been the subject of qualification, so far as they are not covered by the holding company's accounts and are material from the point of view of its members.
4. If any of the above information is unobtainable, a statement to that effect.

The requirements of (2) above do not apply to a wholly owned subsidiary of a company incorporated in the United Kingdom if a statement is annexed to the balance sheet that in the opinion of the directors the aggregate value of its interests in subsidiaries is not less than the aggregate amount shown in the balance sheet (Companies (Accounts) Regulations, 1973).

Holding companies. Holding companies are obliged to disclose the following information:

1. The aggregate amount respectively of shares in subsidiaries, and amounts owing to and by subsidiaries.
2. Details of any shares and debentures in the holding company held by subsidiaries; such holdings are effectively banned by Section 27 of the 1948 Act.
3. In respect of all subsidiaries:
   (a) their names;
   (b) the country of incorporation if outside the United Kingdom, or, if their domicile is different from the reporting company, whether registered in England or Scotland;
   (c) a description and the proportion of the nominal value of the issued shares of each class held, distinguishing between shares held by parent and shares held through subsidiaries.

Subsidiary companies. Subsidiary companies are required to disclose the name and country of incorporation of the company (if any) which the directors regard as the ultimate holding company.

Group companies generally. The following must be shown:

1. The aggregate of amounts owing to, and by, the holding company and fellow subsidiaries, distinguishing in each case between debentures and other indebtedness.
2. (a) The aggregate amount of shares in fellow subsidiaries.
   (b) The directors' valuation or information on share of profits and reserves of fellow subsidiaries (*cf.* page 243, item 3).
   (c) Particulars of investments in excess of 10 per cent (*cf.* page 243, item 4).

The Balance Sheet

Fixed assets. Fixed assets are generally stated at cost less depreciation, but revaluations are frequently carried out, particularly in the case of property. Depreciation bases vary from company to company, but the straight-line basis is by far the most common, followed by the reducing balance basis. It is common practice not to provide depreciation for various categories of property assets, mainly freehold land and long leaseholds (leases of more than 50 years to run at the balance sheet date); however, ASSC Exposure Draft ED 15 states that it is necessary "to regard freehold land and buildings as separate assets and to depreciate buildings over their useful life". The treatment of Government grants, such as investment grants, varies between those companies which treat the grant as a deduction from the cost of the asset, and depreciate the net cost, and others, which treat such grants either as reserves or as deferred credits. In SSAP 4 ("The Accounting Investment of Government Grants") it is stated that grants of this nature should be deducted from the cost of the asset or treated as deferred credits pending transfer to profit and loss account on a basis which fairly reflects the benefit over the expected life of the asset.

The Companies Acts require that the various classes of fixed assets must be stated in the accounts, showing separately the aggregate cost, or valuation, and the aggregate depreciation. With regard to any fixed assets valued on the replacement basis, these must be shown with the means by which their replacement is provided for and the aggregate amount of the provision (if any) made for renewals and not used. For any asset shown at a valuation made during the current year the names or qualifications of the valuers and the basis of the valuation must be stated; if a revaluation was made in previous years, the year and the amount of the valuation. The aggregate amounts of all movements on fixed assets during the year with the aggregate of additions and disposals (it is not necessary to show separately those affecting the depreciation provision but it is normal to do so) must be stated. Any items of land and building should be separated between freeholds, long leaseholds and short leaseholds.

Intangible assets. In accordance with the Acts, the aggregate amount of goodwill, patents and trade-marks, in so far as not written off, must be disclosed. The following should also be stated separately in so far as they are not written off:

1. Preliminary expenses.
2. Share or debenture issue expenses.
3. Commission paid in respect of shares or debentures.
4. Discount on debentures.
5. Discount on share issued. (Shares cannot normally be issued at a discount; where they are, the issue must be authorised by the general meeting and sanctioned by the court.)

All of the above items are generally written off at, or as soon as possible after, the time of the expenditure is incurred. Section 56 of the Companies

Act, 1948, provides that all such expenses may be written off against a premium received on shares issued.

Goodwill appears in the accounts on acquisition and may be retained at that value or written off arbitrarily over a number of years. Patents and trademarks are usually written off over their useful lives, which in the case of a patent may be its statutory life of (normally) 16 years. Research and development expenditure is commonly written off in the year that the expenditure is incurred, as requested in ASSC Exposure Draft ED 14.

Investments. The information necessitated by the Companies Act, 1967, in relation to investments, other than investments in subsidiaries, is as follows:

1. The aggregate amounts of quoted and unquoted investments respectively must be shown separately.
2. In respect of quoted investments:
   (a) The aggregate market value, where this differs from the book amount, and the stock exchange value of any investments of which the market value is taken to be higher than the stock exchange value.
   (b) A subdivision of the aggregate amount between investments quoted on The Stock Exchange (of Great Britain and Ireland) and those quoted on a stock exchange of repute outside the British Isles.
3. In respect of unquoted investments:
   (a) If the investments are shown as fixed assets, either the directors' valuation or the cost of revaluation as shown in the company's books, the aggregate provision for depreciation and the net figure.
   (b) If the investments are in equity share capital, the accounts must either show the directors' valuation or give particulars of:
      (i) the aggregate income for the year from such investments;
      (ii) the investing company's share of aggregate profits less losses before and after tax shown in accounts during its financial year by the companies in which investments are held;
      (iii) the investing company's share of post-acquisition undistributed profits less losses;
      (iv) the manner in which losses of such companies have been dealt with in the investing company's accounts.
4. Where a company holds more than one-tenth of any class of equity share capital of another company, or holds shares which are stated

in its accounts at an amount which represents more than one-tenth of its total assets, the following particulars for all companies:

(a) Their name.

(b) The country of incorporation if outside the United Kingdom or, if their domicile is different from the reporting company, whether registered in England or Scotland.

(c) A description and the proportion of the nominal value of the issued shares of each class held.

If these particulars would be of excessive length the information provided may be confined to companies principally affecting the profit and loss account or the assets of the investing company, in which case this fact must be disclosed.

SSAP 1 ("Accounting for the Results of Associated Companies") lays down a standard practice for the treatment of associated companies whereby the investing company's share of the post-acquisition retained profits or surplus is reflected in its consolidated balance sheet (as an addition to the cost of the investment, less any amount written off) although not in its own balance sheet as a legal entity. An investment falls within the definition of an associated company when the investing company's interest is effectively that of a partner in a joint venture or consortium, or when the interest is long term and a substantial proportion (20 per cent or more) of the equity voting rights, and the investing company is in a position to exercise a significant influence. The investing company should give particulars of the names of and its interest in companies treated as associated companies, and of any other companies in which it holds not less than 20 per cent of the equity voting rights which are not treated as associated companies (*see also* page 251).

Other assets. Trade debtors are commonly reduced by specific and general provisions for bad or doubtful debts, but, unless material, these are not disclosed.

Companies are obliged by the Companies Acts to disclose the aggregate amount of loans to employees for the purchase of shares in the company or its holding company. Similarly, the amount of any loans to officers (directors, secretary or managers) of the company made during the year and outstanding from previous years must be given. Directors are not normally allowed to receive loans from a company.

Stocks and work in progress. Stocks are generally stated at the lower of cost and net realisable value. Bases of calculating cost vary but the FIFO method is frequently used, while LIFO is seldom encountered, primarily because it is not acceptable for tax purposes. The Companies Act, 1967, requires companies to disclose the manner in which stock has been computed, where this is material for the appreciation by the members of the state of affairs or the profit or loss. The Exposure Draft, ED 6 ("Stocks and Work in Progress"), proposes that stocks and work in progress should be stated at:

1. The total of the lower of cost and net realisable value of the separate items of stock or of groups of similar stock items.
2. In the case of long-term contract work in progress, cost plus attributable profit, less anticipated losses. If anticipated losses on individual contracts exceed cost incurred to date, such expenses should be separately shown as provisions.

The Exposure Draft rejects as unacceptable the valuation of stocks at replacement cost on the grounds that "the effect is to take account of a loss greater than that which is expected to be incurred". The LIFO and base-stock methods of determining cost are both considered unacceptable for the reason that they do not "bear a reasonable relationship to actual costs obtaining during the period".

The Exposure Draft goes on to propose that companies should disclose the accounting policies followed in arriving at the amount at which stocks and work in progress are stated. In addition, the methods used to calculate cost (including overheads) and to arrive at net realisable value should be given "if they are material for an understanding of the accounts". A complete analysis of the separate amounts included and deducted in respect of long-term contracts as shown in the balance sheet, as well as an analysis of the profit or loss arising from long-term contracts, should be disclosed in the accounts.

Capital. Companies are bound by the Companies Acts to provide a summary of shares authorised and issued. The amount of redeemable preference shares must be separately disclosed, stating: (1) the earliest and latest dates of redemption; (2) whether redemption is mandatory or at the company's option; (3) the premium (if any) payable on redemption. Preference shares generally accumulate dividends if for some reason these are not paid. Accordingly, the gross arrears of all such dividends and the period of arrears for each class of share must be stated.

The issue of redeemable preference shares is governed by Section 58 of the Companies Act, 1948, which provides that:

1. Such shares can be redeemed only out of profits of the company which would otherwise be available for dividend, or out of the

proceeds of a fresh issue of shares made for the purposes of the redemption.

2. The shares can be redeemed only if they are fully paid.
3. The premium, if any, payable on redemption must have been provided for out of the profits or out of the company's share premium account before the shares are issued.
4. Where such shares are redeemed otherwise than out of the proceeds of a fresh issue, a sum equal to the nominal amount of the shares must be transferred out of profits, which would otherwise be available for dividend, to a reserve fund, called the "Capital Redemption Reserve Fund". This fund, therefore, has the same status as paid-up share capital of the company. It is normally transferred to share capital by the issue of bonus shares.

Reserves and provisions. Both of these terms are defined in the Companies Acts:

1. A *provision* means "any amount written off or retained by way of providing for depreciation renewals or diminution in value of assets or retained by way of providing for any known liability of which the amount cannot be determined with substantial accuracy".
2. A *reserve* cannot be any amount which falls within the above definition of provision.

There are no legal reserve requirements in UK company law similar to those found in many Continental countries set up by annual transfers from profits. There exist, however, two other statutory reserves—the capital redemption reserve fund, mentioned above under "Capital", and the share premium account. The purposes to which the share premium account can be applied are strictly regulated by Section 56 of the Companies Act, 1948: it may be used for paying up unissued shares of the company to be issued to members as fully paid bonus shares, or in writing off (1) the preliminary expenses of the company, or (2) the expenses of or the commission paid or the discount allowed on any issue of shares or debentures of the company, or in providing for the premium payable on redemption of any redeemable preference shares or of any debentures of the company.

Companies are obliged to disclose the amount of any share premium account, any capital redemption reserve fund and the aggregate amounts respectively of other reserves and provisions if material. If not otherwise shown in the profit and loss account, the source and application of all material movements in reserves must be stated; similarly in the case of provisions (excluding those for depreciation, renewals or diminution in the values of assets) there must be shown the source of all increases and the application of all decreases, unless these are applied for their original purpose. Since the 1967 Act there is no longer any necessity to classify reserves as "capital" or "revenue".

Taxation. The Companies Act, 1967, demands disclosure of the basis upon which the amount set aside for UK corporation tax is shown in the accounts. As far as deferred taxation is concerned, the same Act specifies that "if an amount is set aside for the purpose of its being used to prevent undue fluctuations in charges for taxation, it shall be stated"; in the case of such a sum being used for other purposes the facts must be disclosed.

The extensive recommendation N 27 ("Treatment of Taxation in Accounts of Companies") urges the point that "the liability for corporation tax on the profits of the period covered by the accounts should be disclosed either as an item of current liabilities or as a separate liability with the due date for payment shown. Corporation tax for earlier periods not yet paid should normally be shown as such under current liabilities."

Deferred tax accounting is normal in the United Kingdom, such accounts arising primarily from the disparity between capital allowances for taxation purposes and the depreciation charged against profits in respect of the same assets. N 27 recommends that such accounts should be set up according to the "liability method", but ED 11 opts for the alternative "deferral" method. Under the former, the balances remaining from earlier years are adjusted for any subsequent change in the rate of tax; under the "deferral" method the balances are not adjusted for changes in the rate of taxation. It is expected, however, that the SSAP will revert to the liability method.

N 27 further advances the idea that, when a capital surplus on the scale of fixed assets, which results in a chargeable gain, is realised, the corporation tax on the chargeable gain should be charged against the surplus. Where a revaluation of assets gives rise to a market value in excess of cost, N 27 states that the corporation tax on any chargeable gain should either be charged against the surplus or credited to a deferred taxation account, or, alternatively, be stated in a note to the accounts.

Another stipulation found in the lengthy N 27 is that the taxation status (*i.e.* whether "close" or otherwise) of a company should be disclosed by way of note. A "close" company is defined, broadly, as one which is controlled by its directors, or by five or fewer shareholders, and in which the public do not hold an interest of at least 35 per cent.

Liabilities. In accordance with the Companies Acts, the following liabilities have to be stated separately:

1. The aggregate of bank loans and overdrafts; balances in hand cannot be netted unless there is a right of set-off.
2. The aggregate amount of loans (other than bank loans) not wholly repayable within five years from the balance sheet date, giving also the terms of repayment and rates of interest.
3. The aggregate amount (before deduction of income tax) of any proposed dividend.
4. Particulars of any redeemed debentures capable of reissue.
5. Debentures issued by the company and held for the company by a nominee or a trustee, disclosing the nominal amount and book value.
6. Any liability secured on the assets otherwise than by law.

In SSAP 8 ("The Treatment of Taxation under the Imputation System in the Accounts of Companies, including the effect on earnings per share") it is stated that "proposed dividends should be included in current liabilities in the balance sheet without the addition of the related advance corporation tax (ACT): the ACT on proposed dividends, whether or not recoverable, should be included as a current tax liability. If the ACT on proposed dividends is regarded as recoverable, it should be deducted from the deferred tax account, if such an account is available for this purpose—otherwise it should be shown as a deferred asset.

Contingent liabilities. Particulars of any charge on the assets of a company to secure the liabilities of any other person must be disclosed, stating, where practicable, the amount secured.

The general nature of any other material contingencies not provided for should be stated, giving, where practicable, the aggregate or estimated accounts.

The above provisions apply equally to a holding company's contingent liability in respect of guarantees given on behalf of subsidiaries.

Capital commitments. Where practicable and material, the estimated amounts of future capital expenditure must be stated as follows:

1. The aggregate amount contracted.
2. The aggregate amount authorised by the directors but not yet contracted for.

General.

1. If any current assets have a market value which, in the directors' opinion, is less than book value, that fact must be stated.

2. The basis of conversion of all foreign currencies must be disclosed where the assets or liabilities affected are material. Two main methods are used for the conversion of foreign currencies: the "closing rate" method whereby all items in the overseas accounts are translated into sterling at the rate ruling on the balance sheet date, and the "historic rate" method, whereby assets and liabilities are translated into sterling at the rate ruling at the time when they were acquired or incurred. In 1970 the Research and Publications Committee of the Institute of Chartered Accountants of Scotland recommended the use of the closing rate method for all items: this is now used by the majority of companies.

3. Corresponding amounts at the end of the immediately preceding financial year must be given for all items shown in the balance sheet except movements of fixed assets and reserves.

The Profit and Loss Account

The amount of information disclosed in the profit and loss accounts of UK companies is not generally as high as that of French or German companies. Any breakdown of the difference between turnover and profit before taxation seldom exists; moreover, the items actually disclosed in accordance with the Companies Acts tend to be shown separately and without any apparent direct connection with each other, or the other figures in the profit and loss account.

Dividends. The articles of most companies empower the directors to pay interim dividends on ordinary shares but a resolution of the members in general meeting is necessary to sanction the payment of final dividends. However, certain court decisions[18] have established that the directors do in fact have the power to make whatever appropriations they consider necessary and that dividends cannot be declared unless previously recommended by the directors. Accordingly, the annual accounts of UK companies are drawn up after appropriations.

Disclosures required under the Companies Acts. The following must be shown in the accounts or by way of notes thereto.

TURNOVER

1. The amount of turnover and the method by which it is stated. SSAP 5 ("Accounting for Value Added Tax") states that turnover shown in the profit and loss account should exclude VAT on taxable outputs. Exemption from disclosure is available for:

(a) a company (not being a group company) with a total turnover of not over £250,000;

(b) turnover attributable to banking, discounting, etc. (if omitted, that fact and the reason therefor must be stated).

INCOME

2. The net income from rents of land and buildings if it forms a substantial part of the company's income.

3. There must be shown separately:
(a) income from quoted investments;
(b) income from unquoted investments.

DIRECTORS' EMOLUMENTS

4. In respect of those persons who, during the accounting period, were directors of the reporting company, there must be stated the emoluments for services to the reporting company or its subsidiaries while they were directors, distinguishing between:
(a) fees as directors;
(b) other emoluments;
(c) pensions (paid other than from schemes maintained by contributions);
(d) compensation for loss of office.

5. Unless the duties are mainly discharged outside the United Kingdom there must be disclosed:
(a) the emoluments of the chairman (or, if more than one chairman, their separate emoluments);
(b) the emoluments of the highest-paid director if these are in excess of the aggregate emoluments of the chairmen;
(c) the number of directors in each ascending £2500 band of emoluments (from and including Nil).

Emoluments cover items in 4(a) and 4(b) above, excluding pension contributions.

Non-group companies with emoluments under £15,000 are exempt from this disclosure.

6. The number of directors who have waived rights to emoluments and the aggregate amount thereof.

OTHER EXPENDITURE

7. Interest payable, showing separately:
(a) interest on bank loans, bank overdrafts and loans wholly repayable within five years of balance sheet date;
(b) all other loans.

8. The amount (if material) charged to revenue for hire of plant and machinery.

9. Auditors' remuneration (including expenses).

DEPRECIATION:

10. The provision for depreciation, renewals or diminution in value of fixed assets charged to revenue.

11. Any provision made for renewals of assets which are also depreciated.

12. If the depreciation is not calculated on balance sheet values the fact should be stated.

13. The method of providing for depreciation or replacement of fixed assets other than by a depreciation charge or provision for renewals.

14. If no provision for depreciation or replacement of fixed assets has been made the fact should be stated.

RESERVES AND PROVISIONS

15. Amounts provided respectively for the redemption of:
(a) share capital;
(b) loans.

16. If material, the transfers made or proposed:
(a) to or from reserves;
(b) to provisions (other than depreciation, etc.) and from provisions unless applied for the original purpose.

TAXATION

17. There must be disclosed the amount of the charge for:
(a) UK corporation tax (stating the basis);
(b) UK income tax (stating the basis);
(c) overseas taxation.

18. The amount of UK corporation tax before relief for double taxation.

19. Any special circumstances affecting liability in respect of taxation on profits, income or capital gains for the current financial year or for succeeding financial years.

DIVIDENDS

20. Aggregate amount (before deduction of income tax) of dividends paid and proposed.

GENERAL

21. The number of employees (excluding directors and persons working mainly outside the United Kingdom) in rising bands of £2500 each with emoluments over £10,000 a year.

22. The corresponding amounts for the immediately preceding financial year for all items shown in the profit and loss account.

23. Any material effect of a change in the basis of accounting.

24. Any material effect of unusual transactions or other circumstances of an exceptional or non-recurrent nature.

25. Charges or credits arising in consequence of occurrences in preceding years (unless included in a heading relating to other matters).

Associated companies. SSAP 1 ("Accounting for the Results of Associated Companies") lays down a standard basis of accounting for income of associated companies. The group's share of profits less losses of associated companies should be brought into account unless this would involve excessive expense or delay or would be misleading.

A company (not being a subsidiary of the investing group or company) is an associated company of the investing group or company if:

1. The investing group or company's interest in the associated company is effectively that of a partner in a joint venture or consortium; or
2. The investing group or company's interest in the associated company is for the long term and is substantial (*i.e.* not less than 20 per cent of the voting rights), and, having regard to the disposition of the other shareholdings, the investing group or company is in a position to exercise a significant influence over the associated company.

In both cases it is essential that the investing group or company participates (usually through representation on the board) in commercial and financial policy decisions on the associated company, including the distribution of profits.

Income from investments by a company or its subsidiaries in associated companies should be brought into account on the following bases:

1. In the investing company's own accounts:
   (a) dividends received up to the accounting date of the investing company; and
   (b) dividends receivable in respect of accounting periods ending on or before that date and declared before the accounts of the investing company are approved by the directors.
2. In the investing group's consolidated accounts: the investing group's share of profits less losses of associated companies.

Where the investing company has no subsidiaries, or otherwise does not prepare consolidated accounts, it must adapt its profit and loss account, suitably titled, to incorporate the additional information required by the Statement.

The investing company's or group's share of the following items should be taken into account:

1. Profits before tax of associated companies.
2. Taxation.
3. Extraordinary items where material.
4. Net profit retained by associated companies.

The share of extraordinary items should be included with the group's own extraordinary items, unless the amount is material in the context of the group's results, when it should be separately disclosed.

Where the associated company prepares group accounts, the share of minority interests, if any, should be included in the investing group's minority interests. (*See also* page 244.)

Extraordinary items. SSAP 6 ("Extraordinary Items and Prior-year Adjustments") sets out to eliminate the practice of reserve accounting, except in the case of unrealised surpluses on the revaluation of fixed assets. Extraordinary items are defined in Part 2 of the Statement as:

> those material items which derive from events or transactions outside the ordinary activities of the business and which are not expected to recur frequently or regularly. They do not include items which, though exceptional on account of size and incidence (and which therefore may require separate disclosure), derive from the ordinary activities of the business. Neither do they include prior-year items merely because they relate to a prior year.

The following are the relevant extracts from the Statement of Standard Accounting Practice:

> *Profit after extraordinary items.* The profit and loss account for the year should show a profit or loss after extraordinary items, reflecting all profits and losses recognised in the accounts of the year other than prior year adjustments as defined in Part 2 and unrealised surpluses on revaluation of fixed assets, which should be credited direct to reserves.
>
> Items of an abnormal size and incidence which are derived from the ordinary activities of the business should be included in arriving at the profit for the year before taxation and extraordinary items, and their nature and size disclosed.
>
> *Extraordinary items* as defined in Part 2 (less attributable taxation) should be shown separately in the profit and loss account for the year after the results derived from ordinary activities and their nature and size disclosed.
>
> *Prior year adjustments* as defined in Part 2 (less attributable taxation) should be accounted for by restating prior years, with the result that the opening balance of retained profits will be adjusted accordingly. The effect of the change should be disclosed where practicable by showing separately in the restatement of the previous year the amount involved. Items which represent the normal recurring corrections and adjustments of accounting estimates made in prior years should be included in the profit and loss account for the year and, if material, their nature and size should be disclosed.
>
> *Profit and loss account presentation.* As a result of the foregoing, the profit and loss account for the year should, if there are extraordinary items, include the following elements:
>
> Profit before extraordinary items
> Extraordinary items (less taxation attributable thereto)
> Profit after extraordinary items.
>
> A statement of retained profits/reserves showing any prior year adjustments should immediately follow the profit and loss account for the year.

Earnings per share. SSAP 3 requires that quoted companies disclose their earnings per share on the face of the profit and loss account on the net basis, both for the period under review, and for the corresponding previous period. Under the *net basis* the charge for taxation used in determining earnings includes:

1. Any irrecoverable advance corporation tax (ACT).
2. Any unrelieved overseas tax arising from the payment or proposed payment of dividends.

The basis of calculating earnings per share must be disclosed either in the profit and loss account or in a note thereto, and in particular the amount of the earnings and the number of equity shares used in the calculation must be stated.

"Earnings per share" are defined by the Statement as:

> the profit in pence attributable to each equity share based on the consolidated profit of the period after tax and after deducting minority interests and preference dividends, but before taking into account extraordinary items, divided by the number of equity shares in issue and ranking for dividend in respect of the period.

Disclosure of Accounting Policies

The second Statement of Standard Accounting Practice defines four generally accepted *fundamental accounting concepts* and states that, if accounts are prepared on the basis of assumptions which differ in material respects from any of these concepts, the facts should be explained. In the absence of a clear statement to the contrary, there is a presumption that the four fundamental accounting concepts have been observed. SSAP 2 demands the disclosure by way of note of "the *accounting policies* followed for dealing with items which are judged material or critical in determining profit or loss for the year and in stating the financial position". The explanation should be "clear, fair and as brief as possible".

The Statement includes the following definitions of terms:

> *Fundamental accounting concepts* are the broad basic assumptions which underlie the periodic financial accounts of business enterprises. At the present time the four following fundamental concepts (the relative importance of which will vary according to the circumstances of the particular case) are regarded as having general acceptability:
>
> (a) the "going concern" concept: the enterprise will continue in operational existence for the foreseeable future. This means in particular that the

profit and loss account and balance sheet assume no intention or necessity to liquidate or curtail significantly the scale of operation;

(b) the "accruals" concept: revenue and costs are accrued (that is, recognised as they are earned or incurred, not as money is received or paid), matched with one another so far as their relationship can be established or justifiably assumed, and dealt with in the profit and loss account of the period to which they relate; provided that where the accruals concept is inconsistent with the "prudence" concept (paragraph (d) below), the latter prevails. The accruals concept implies that the profit and loss account reflects changes in the amount of net assets that arise out of the transactions of the relevant period (other than distributions or subscriptions of capital and unrealised surpluses arising on revaluation of fixed assets). Revenue and profits dealt with in the profit and loss account are matched with associated costs and expenses by including in the same account the costs incurred in earning them (so far as these are material and identifiable);

(c) the "consistency" concept: there is consistency of accounting treatment of like items within each accounting period and from one period to the next;

(d) the concept of "prudence": revenue and profits are not anticipated, but are recognised by inclusion in the profit and loss account only when realised in the form either of cash or of other assets the ultimate cash realisation of which can be assessed with reasonable certainty; provision is made for all known liabilities (expenses and losses) whether the amount of these is known with certainty or is a best estimate in the light of the information available.

Accounting bases are the methods developed for applying fundamental accounting concepts to financial transactions and items, for the purpose of financial accounts, and in particular (a) for determining the accounting periods in which revenue and costs should be recognised in the profit and loss account and (b) for determining the amounts at which material items should be stated in the balance sheet.

Accounting policies are the specific accounting bases selected and consistently followed by a business enterprise as being, in the opinion of the management, appropriate to its circumstances and best suited to present fairly its results and financial position.

SSAP 2 lists the following as examples of matters for which different accounting bases are recognised:

1. Depreciation of fixed assets.
2. Treatment and amortisation of intangibles such as research and development expenditure, patents and trademarks.

3. Stocks and work in progress.
4. Long-term contracts.
5. Deferred taxation.
6. Hire-purchase or instalment transactions.
7. Leasing and rental transactions.
8. Conversion of foreign currencies.
9. Repairs and renewals.
10. Consolidation policies.
11. Property development transactions.
12. Warranties for products or services.

This list is not exhaustive, and may vary according to the nature of the operations conducted.

The 1972–73 *Survey of Published Accounts*[19] records that an increasing number of companies present information on their accounting policies in summarised statements. The following serves as an example of one such statement as reproduced in the above-mentioned Survey:

Associated Engineering Ltd 30th September, 1972
Statement of accounting policies:
The following notes describe the main accounting policies followed by the Group.

CONSOLIDATION
The consolidated profit and loss account and balance sheet include the accounts of the parent company and its UK subsidiaries made up to the Saturday nearest to 30th September and the overseas subsidiaries to 30th September.

Those subsidiaries which, in the opinion of the Directors, principally affect the profit or assets of the Group are listed on pages . . .

Internal sales and profits are eliminated on consolidation and all sales and profit figures relate to external transactions only.

ACQUISITIONS
When subsidiary companies are acquired any excess of the consideration over the net tangible assets at the date of acquisition is deducted from capital reserves on consolidation.

OVERSEAS TRADE INVESTMENTS
Details of the Group's overseas trade investments are shown on page. . . . In view of the size and geographical spread of these investments, the Group only exercises a limited influence on their affairs and their results have not been consolidated in the Group figures.

FOREIGN CURRENCY CONVERSIONS
It is the policy of the Group to ignore minor fluctuations in rates of exchange. The rates used in respect of the principal overseas subsidiaries for the current year are set out on page. . . .

RESEARCH AND DEVELOPMENT
Research and development expenditure is charged to profits in the year in which it is incurred, except for small amounts which have been capitalised as the cost of new plant.

FIXED ASSETS
It is the policy of the Group to revalue freehold land and buildings from time to time on a going concern basis as determined by independent valuers to reflect major changes in the values of such assets.

Plant and machinery is capitalised at cost, including carriage and installation charges, less investment grants.

Repairs and renewal costs are written off to revenue. Exceptional reconditioning that will extend the life of an asset is capitalised.

DEPRECIATION OF FIXED ASSETS
The book value of fixed assets is written off evenly over the estimated remaining life of the asset. Investment grants are deducted from the cost of plant and machinery acquired and depreciation is calculated on the net sum on a straight line basis, mainly at the following rates:

Buildings (excluding land)	1½% pa
Plant (including fixed plant in buildings)	10% pa
Tooling	33⅓% pa
Vehicles	25% pa

PATENTS
Expenditure by the Group on the development of patents is written off to revenue as incurred.

LEASING, HIRE PURCHASE AND RENTAL TRANSACTIONS
Plant and machinery is leased for 10 years from various dates commencing in the year ended 30 September, 1970, with a five year primary rental and a five year or unlimited secondary period at a nominal rental.

Computers and ancillary equipment are leased on annual rentals.

All rentals are charged to revenue in respect of the year in which they become due.

STOCKS AND WORK IN PROGRESS
Stocks including work in progress are valued at works cost less certain provisions. Works cost represents materials, direct labour and factory overheads including depreciation.

The provisions cover three main factors:

(i) In the case of stocks intended for the manufacturers of original equipment the provisions where applicable reduce the valuation to estimated net realisable value.

(ii) In the case of stocks held for the replacement trade the provisions reduce the valuation of stocks that are likely to prove obsolete to scrap value.

(iii) In the case of raw materials the provisions reduce to replacement cost the valuation of those materials whose price has fallen since they were acquired.

PENSION SCHEMES

It is the policy of the Group to fund pension liabilities by payments to trusts and insurance companies independent from the finances of the Group.

Statements of Source and Application of Funds

ED 13 ("Statements of Source and Application of Funds") proposes that it should be standard practice for the audited financial accounts of a company to "include a statement of source and application of funds both for the period under review and for the corresponding previous period". Where the accounts are those of a group, the statement of source and application of funds should be so framed as to reflect the operations of the group.

The Interpretation of Material

The concept of materiality bears particular reference to the accounts of UK companies. The word is used several times in the Companies Acts, but nowhere is there any definition of what is meant by "material". In 1968 the Institute of Chartered Accountants in England and Wales issued a guidance statement (V 10), entitled "The Interpretation of Material in Relation to Accounts", containing the following points:

> A matter is material if its non-disclosure, misstatement or omission would be likely to distort the view given by the accounts or other statement under consideration .... The interpretation of what is "material" is a matter for the exercise of professional judgement based on experience and the requirement to give a true and fair view.... Materiality can only be considered in relative terms. In a small business £100 may be material, whereas £1 million may not be material in classifying the expenditure of a large undertaking, especially as too much elaboration could obscure the true and fair view.... An item may be material in either a general or a particular context. The general context refers to the true and fair view given by the statement as a whole. The particular context relates to the total of which an item forms or should

form a part and any directly associated items. If an item is not material in the general context, the degree of latitude acceptable in the particular context may depend upon its nature. There is an important distinction between cases where the amount at issue is arrived at on the basis of assumption, and exercise of judgement, and those where it it capable of precise and objective determination. . . .

Post balance sheet events

Recommendation N 17 ("Events Occurring after the Balance Sheet Date"), issued by the English Institute, declares that:

> events which, at the time of preparing annual accounts, are known to have occurred after the balance sheet date should not normally be taken into account when preparing accounts unless:
>
> (a) they assist in forming an opinion as to the amount properly attributable, in the conditions existing at the balance sheet date, to any item the amount of which was subject to uncertainty at that date; or
>
> (b) they arise from legislation affecting items in the accounts, for example, appropriations and proposed appropriations of profit.

Events properly excluded from the accounts "may nevertheless be of such importance that they need to be disclosed to shareholders through some other medium".

Publication and Filing of Financial Statements

The balance sheet of every company has to be signed on behalf of the board by two directors (except where there is only one director). The profit and loss account and, in so far as not incorporated in the balance sheet or profit and loss account, any group accounts laid before the company must be annexed to the balance sheet, together with the auditors' report and the directors' report. Copies of all the above documents are sent to every member of the company and to every debenture holder not less than 21 days before the annual general meeting. These provisions do not apply to members and debenture holders of companies not having a share capital; nor are the members and debenture holders of such companies entitled to receive notice of general meetings.

The auditors' report is read before the members in general meeting and remains open to inspection by any member.

Within 42 days of the annual general meeting, the accounts and reports specified above must be filed with the Registrar of Companies annexed to a detailed annual return, the contents of which are laid down in the Sixth

Schedule to the 1948 Act. All documents filed with the Registrar of Companies are open to public inspection.

Directors' Report

In accordance with the Companies Acts, 1948 and 1967, the following matters must be dealt with in the directors' report:

FINANCIAL

1. The state of the company's affairs.
2. The amount, if any, recommended for dividend.
3. The amount, if any, proposed to be carried to reserves.
4. Principal activities of the reporting company and its subsidiaries during the year, including any significant changes.
5. Significant changes in fixed assets of the company or of its subsidiaries during the year.
6. The amount (as precisely as practicable) of any substantial difference between book and market values of interests in land and buildings (if the directors think it is of significance to the members).
7. In respect of each class of shares or debentures issued during the year:
   (a) the number or amount issued (stating the class);
   (b) the consideration received;
   (c) the reasons for the issue.
8. If substantially differing classes of business are carried on:
   (a) the proportion of turnover attributable to each class of business;
   (b) the approximate extent (in the directors' opinion) to which each class of business has contributed (in amount) to the pre-tax revenue results.

Consolidated accounts must show the group figures. Non-group companies are exempt from disclosure if total turnover is not over £250,000.

9. The value of goods exported as a principal or otherwise a statement that there were no exports. Consolidated accounts must show the group figures. Exemption from disclosure is given if turnover of the company (or group) is not over £250,000.
10. If political and charitable contributions together total more than £50, separate totals for each must be shown as well as each political contribution over £50, stating the political party or recipient.

Wholly owned subsidiaries of companies incorporated in the United Kingdom are exempt from this requirement, but the holding company must disclose the groups' contributions.

11. Particulars of any matters required by members for an appreciation of the company's affairs, unless disclosure would be harmful to the company or its subsidiaries.
12. Comparative figures where any items are included in the directors' report instead of in the accounts.

EMPLOYEES

13. The average number of persons employed in each week of the year, excluding persons working mainly outside the United Kingdom:

(a) by the company; or

(b) by the company and its subsidiaries (if it had subsidiaries at the year end).

Exemption from this disclosure is granted in the case of a wholly owned subsidiary of a UK incorporated company or where the average number employed by the company (and its subsidiaries) is less than 100.

14. The aggregate gross remuneration (including bonuses) payable for the year to employees.

DIRECTORS

15. The names of persons who were directors of the reporting company at any time during the year.

16. The interests of any director in contracts with the company held at any time in the year, naming the director or other parties thereto, and stating the nature of the contract and interests; this applies only to material interests or contracts significant to the company's business.

17. Rights given to directors to acquire shares or debentures in the company or any other company under an arrangement to which the reporting company is a party. The arrangements must be explained and the names of the directors concerned disclosed.

18. For those persons who were directors of the reporting company at the year end, the interest of each (including interests of spouse or infant children) in shares or debentures of the reporting company and other group companies:

(a) at the beginning of the year or date of later appointment;

(b) at the year end.

If a director has no such interest, that fact must be stated.

Exemption from this disclosure is given in respect of:

(a) Interests in shares or debentures in any group company held by directors of a wholly owned subsidiary of a UK incorporated company, who are also directors of the holding company.

(b) Interests in shares or debentures in any overseas group company held by directors of a wholly owned subsidiary of an overseas incorporated company.

Stock Exchange Listing Agreement. In accordance with The Stock Exchange Listing Agreement,[20] the directors' report of a quoted company must contain the following additional information:

STATEMENTS OF STANDARD ACCOUNTING PRACTICE

1. A statement by the directors as to the reasons for adopting an alternative basis of accounting in any case where the auditors have stated that the accounts are not drawn up in accordance with standard accounting practices.

GEOGRAPHICAL ANALYSIS

2. A geographical analysis of turnover and of the contribution to trading results of trading operations carried on outside the United Kingdom. In the case of Irish companies, this means Ireland.

SUBSIDIARIES

3. The name of the principal country in which each subsidiary operates.

INVESTMENTS

4. In respect of investments in companies where the group interest in the equity capital is 20 per cent or more:

(a) the principal country of operation must be stated; as well as
(b) particulars of interests in share and loan capital, and, except where the company is treated as an associated company, the total amount of its reserves; and
(c) the percentage of each class of loan capital attributable to the company's interest.

Where the number of companies is large, only those that principally affect the profit or assets need be given.

DIRECTORS' INTERESTS

5. A statement of directors' interests in share and loan capital:

(a) distinguishing between beneficial and non-beneficial interests; and
(b) including by way of note any change in those interests occurring between the end of the financial year and a date not more than one month prior to the date of the notice of the AGM. If there has been no such change, that fact must be stated.

SUBSTANTIAL SHAREHOLDERS

6. A statement, as at a date not more than one month prior to the date of the notice of the AGM, of an interest of any person (other than a director) in any substantial part of the share capital of the company and the amount of the interest. If there is no such holding, a negative statement is required. A substantial holding amounts to 10 per cent or more in the nominal value of any class of share capital having full voting rights.

TAX STATUS

7. A statement showing:

(a) whether or not the company is a close company; and
(b) where applicable, whether the company is a recognised investment trust under the provisions of the Taxes Act 1970. A close company is, broadly, one which is controlled by its directors or by five or fewer shareholders and in which the public do not hold an interest of at least 35 per cent.

The statement should include details of any changes since the financial year end.

DIRECTORS' INTERESTS IN CONTRACTS

8. Particulars of any contract subsisting during or at the end of the year in which a director is or was materially interested or was significant in relation to the company's business.

DIRECTORS' WAIVER OF EMOLUMENTS

9. Particulars of any arrangements under which a director has waived or agreed to waive any emoluments.

WAIVER OF DIVIDENDS

10. Particulars of any arrangement under which a shareholder has waived or agreed to waive any dividends.

Interim Reports. Apart from the annual accounts, quoted companies are bound by Paragraph 8 of The Stock Exchange Listing Agreement "to prepare a half-yearly or interim report which must be sent to the holders of securities or inserted as paid advertisements in two leading daily newspapers not later than six months from the date of the notice convening the annual general meeting".

The minimum information to be included in a half-yearly or interim report is laid down as follows—group figures apply in all cases unless the company is not a holding company:

1. Turnover.
2. Profit (or loss) after all charges including taxation.
3. UK and, where material, overseas taxation charged in arriving at (2).
4. The amount of (2) attributable to members of the holding company (if applicable), *i.e.* after deduction of outside interests.
5. If material, the extent to which (2) has been affected by special credits (including transfers and reserves) and/or debits.
6. Rates of dividends paid and proposed and the amount absorbed thereby.
7. In respect of any year or other full accounting period, earnings per share expressed as pence per share.
8. Comparative figures in all cases for the corresponding previous period.
9. Any supplementary information, which, in the opinion of the directors, is necessary for a reasonable appreciation of the results or of other material changes in the aggregate of the balance, of the profit and loss account and other reserves of the group.

Stock Exchange Listing Requirements

The London, provincial and Irish stock exchanges merged in March 1973 to form "The Stock Exchange".

All applications for listing are made by a sponsoring broker who must be a member of The Stock Exchange. Applications are considered from companies whose listed securities are expected to have an initial aggregate market value of at least £500,000. An application will not be considered in respect of any security whose initial market capitalisation is expected to be below £200,000. Generally, in the case of equity issues at least 35 per cent of any class of issued share capital, or securities convertible into equity capital, is required to be in the hands of the public excluding major shareholders or persons who are associated with the directors. A listing may be obtained by:

1. *A prospectus issue*, which is an offer by a company of its own securities to the public.
2. *An offer for sale*, which is an offer to the public by an issuing house (generally a merchant bank), or broker, of securities already in issue or for which they have agreed to subscribe.
3. *A placing*, whereby an issuing house or broker places an issue with its own clients; generally this is allowed only where there is not likely to be a significant public demand for the securities.
4. *An introduction*, which describes an application where no marketing arrangements are required because the securities to be listed are already of such an amount and so widely held that their adequate marketability can be assured.

In the case of prospectus issues and offers for sale, a prospectus, duly approved by The Stock Exchange, must then be issued and advertised. Great emphasis is placed on the adequacy of the information contained in the prospectus; on admission to listing every company is obliged to sign the Listing Agreement requiring them, *inter alia*, to maintain a regular supply of information to its shareholders and to the investing public (*see* page 261). Each prospectus has to contain a report by the auditors of the company, dealing with:

1. The profits or losses of the company (and, in the case of a holding company, the profits or losses of the company and of its subsidiaries) for each of the previous five years.
2. The rate of dividend on each class of shares for each of the previous five years.
3. The balance sheet of the company and in the case of an issue by a holding company the consolidated balance sheet of the company and its subsidiaries at the end of each accounting period reported upon and at the beginning of the first such period.

4. Any other matters which appear to the auditors to be relevant having regard to the purpose of the report.

A prospectus must also include a statement as to the financial and trading prospects of the company or of the group. Where a profit forecast appears in any prospectus, the principal assumption, including commercial assumptions, upon which the directors have based their profit forecast must be stated. The accounting bases and calculations for the forecast must be examined and reported on by the auditors to the company.

If after the date of the last audited accounts the company or any of its subsidiaries has acquired, or is proposing to acquire, the shares of another unquoted company, the prospectus must additionally contain an accountants' report, along similar lines to the auditors' report, on the company being acquired. In making such reports both auditors and reporting accountants are expected to make any adjustments which they consider appropriate.

Business Records

Section 147 of the Companies Act, 1948, demands that every company should keep "proper books of account" with regard to:

1. All sums of money received and expended by the company and the matters in respect of which the receipt and expenditure took place.
2. All sales and purchases of goods by the company.
3. The assets and liabilities of the company.

"Proper books of account" are defined as "such books as are necessary to give a true and fair view of the state of the company's affairs, and to explain its transactions". Besides the commercial books of account, companies must keep certain other statutory books, including registers of members, directors and secretaries, and a register of charges. All businesses have to maintain specific records for taxation and payroll purposes.

No time limit has yet been set for the retention of business records, but one of the proposals contained in the 1973 Companies Bill was a minimum retention period of five years for all accounting records.

THE ACCOUNTANCY PROFESSION

Paradoxically, the UK accountancy profession is one of the most developed in the world and yet bears the distinction of being one of the most disorganised in Europe. No national accountancy body exists similar to the

German Wirtschaftsprüfkammer or the French Ordre des Experts Comptables et des Comptables Agréés. Indeed, in the past the profession has strenuously resisted any attempt to have accountants registered with the State. The individual professional bodies are private organisations laying down their own conditions for membership. Thus, anyone is able to practise as a public accountant in the United Kingdom, the one restriction being that audits of limited companies can be carried out only by members of the accountancy bodies recognised by the Department of Trade, under Section 161 of the Companies Act, 1948, or by a person authorised by that Department as having obtained, outside the United Kingdom, a qualification similar to that of one of the recognised UK bodies.

There are five principal accountancy bodies in the United Kingdom (Table 8.3):

1. The Institute of Chartered Accountants in England and Wales.
2. The Association of Certified Accountants.
3. The Institute of Chartered Accountants of Scotland.
4. The Institute of Cost and Management Accountants.
5. The Chartered Institute of Public Finance and Accountancy.

It should be appreciated that, as well as these bodies, the Institute of Chartered Accountants in Ireland is at the same time both a UK and an Irish accountancy body.

The accountancy bodies were involved in an historic attempt at integration in 1970 under the Institutes of Chartered Accountants which failed at the eleventh hour in the absence of an adequate majority for the scheme from the largest body. There is nevertheless still considerable co-operation at many levels, but the individual bodies insist on pursuing, for the most part, separate and apparently unco-ordinated development schemes.

Existing consultative links between the six accountancy bodies of the British Isles (*i.e.* the above five plus the Institute of Chartered Accountants in Ireland) were strengthened by the formation in May 1974 of the Consultative Committee of Accountancy Bodies (CCAB).

To many people, both in the United Kingdom and on the Continent, a UK accountant means a chartered accountant. There are distinctive historical reasons for this. Chartered accountants obtained Royal Charters in Scotland in 1854, in England and Wales in 1880, and in Ireland in 1888. Thus established, these bodies began to attract men of the highest standing to their ranks. Prospective members had to meet stiff entry requirements and pass professional examinations; besides this, they were compelled to

TABLE 8.3. MEMBERSHIP OF THE UNITED KINGDOM PUBLIC ACCOUNTANCY PROFESSION

	The Institute of Chartered Accountants in England and Wales (31 Dec. 1973)	*The Association of Certified Accountants* (19 Oct. 1973)	*The Institute of Chartered Accountants in Scotland* (31 Dec. 1973)	*Total*
Principals in public practice				
in the UK	13,432	2,432	1,386	17,250
outside the UK	1,326	409	203	1,938
	14,758	2,841	1,589	19,188
Members working in public practice	10,000(E)	2,040	1,100(E)	13,140
Total in public practice	24,758	4,881	2,689	32,328
Other members	31,667	9,613	6,039	47,319
Total members	**56,425**	**14,494**	**8,728**	**79,647**
Practising firms				
Partnerships	4,453	Not known	400(E)	
Sole practitioners	4,364		300(E)	

(E) indicates estimated figures.

Source: The individual professional bodies.

serve a period of articled clerkship with a chartered accountant in public practice. Articles could not be served otherwise than with a practising chartered accountant, and this system has remained largely unchanged, the rule still being that every prospective member of the Institutes must undergo an obligatory period of training with a chartered accountant in public practice. It is this fact which continues to distinguish the chartered accountant today.

Until the Second World War it was common, as indeed in the case of the legal profession, for articled clerks to pay substantial premiums to their principals which effectively restricted the possibility of becoming a chartered accountant to all but the fortunate few. Such a situation prompted the founding in 1891 of the Association of Certified Accountants, providing the "common man's" alternative to the Institute of Chartered Accountants. In order to obtain the qualification of certified accountant it was not necessary to serve articles; experience could be gained in public practice, industry or commerce. Consequently the certified accountant's background and experience are sometimes less highly regarded and considered less exclusive than those of the chartered accountant.[21] At present the vast majority of certified accountants work in industry and commerce, with relatively few engaging in public practice, although they are recognised, together with the English, Scottish and Irish chartered accountants, as competent to carry out statutory audits in the United Kingdom.

The Institute of Cost and Management Accountants was formed in 1919 to foster what was then a new branch of accountancy, following the success of costing systems in controlling the soaring prices of war materials during the First World War. This body has gained much status in recent years and many distinguished UK accountants foresee an eventual division of the profession between chartered accountants in public practice and cost and management accountants in industry and commerce. At 31 December 1973 there were 13,363 cost and management accountants.

The Chartered Institute of Public Finance and Accountancy (formerly the Institute of Municipal Treasurers and Accountants) was founded in 1885 as a body specialising in public finance and accountancy. At 31 December 1973 there were 6855 members, almost all of whom were employed by local and public authorities.

The public practice side of the profession is dominated by chartered accountants and, more particularly, by a handful of very large firms having extensive international connections. Chartered accountants can practise only alone, or in partnership; members of the English, Scottish and Irish Institutes may practise together, but, apart from this, no other persons can practise together with a chartered accountant and retain the designation "chartered accountant".

The Top 20 Firms

Table 8.4 ranks the top 20 UK accounting firms according to their audits of companies in two separate listings of the United Kingdom's 1000 largest companies. Significantly, although the placings are different, the top 10 are the same in both cases and, with one exception in each case, so are the top 20. It must be stressed, however, that neither ranking can be regarded as an absolute criterion of the sizes of the individual firms. In particular, they do not reflect fees from management consulting, taxation services, liquidations and receiverships, investigations or any of the other specialist services provided by these firms.

TABLE 8.4. THE TOP 20 UK ACCOUNTING FIRMS

1 Ranked according to their number of audits of the top 1,000 companies (ranked by market capitalisation of equity shares) **listed on the London Stock Exchange at 31 March 1972**

	First 500	*Next 500*	*Total*
1 Peat, Marwick, Mitchell	39	52	91
2 Deloitte (including Harmood Banner)	55	34	89
3 Price Waterhouse	44	28	72
4 Coopers & Lybrand	33	22	55
5 Thomson McLintock	10	16	26
6 Spicer & Pegler	8	18	26
7 Arthur Young McClelland Moores	14	8	22
8 Turquands Barton Mayhew	12	9	21
9 Whinney Murray	13	5	18
10 Touche Ross	10	7	17
11 Josolyne Layton-Bennett	8	6	14
12 Mann Judd	3	11	14
13 Thornton Baker	8	5	13
14 Binder Hamlyn (now Binder Hamlyn Singleton Fabian)	7	5	12
15 Robson Rhodes	3	6	9
16 Fuller Jenks Beecroft	5	3	8
17 Pannell Fitzpatrick	4	4	8
18 Tansley Witt	5	2	7
19 Armitage & Norton	2	5	7
20 Chalmers Impey	4	1	5
Attributable to top 20	287	247	534
Rest	213	253	466
	500	500	1,000

TABLE 8.4—(continued) THE TOP 20 UK ACCOUNTING FIRMS

2 Ranked according to their number of audits in the 1972 Times list of top 1,000 companies

	First 100	*Next 900*	*Total*
1 Peat, Marwick, Mitchell	9	89	98
2 Price Waterhouse	11	61	72
3 Deloitte (including Harmood Banner)	11	54	65
4 Coopers & Lybrand	9	50	59
5 Thomson McLintock	4	26	30
6 Turquands Barton Mayhew	7	20	27
7 Whinney Murray	8	11	19
8 Arthur Young McClelland Moores	1	17	18
9 Touche Ross	4	12	16
10 Spicer & Pegler	2	12	14
11 Mann Judd	–	14	14
12 Binder Hamlyn (now Binder Hamlyn Singleton Fabian)	–	13	13
13 Armitage & Norton	2	10	12
14 Thornton Baker	–	12	12
15 Robson Rhodes	–	10	10
16 Fuller Jenks Beecroft	1	7	8
17 Chalmers Impey	2	5	7
18 Tansley Witt	1	6	7
19 Josolyne Layton-Bennett	–	7	7
20 Hodgson Harris	2	4	6
Attributable to top 20	74	440	514
Rest	26	460	486
	100	900	1,000

The best yardstick, of course, would be the turnover of the firms, but, since this is not public knowledge, even the best "guesstimates" must be treated with considerable caution. With this in mind, Table 8.5 presents one well-informed City accountant's estimate of the top 12 UK firms, in order of their estimated 1972 turnover. Since then, however, the Deloitte–Harmood Banner merger has, almost certainly, put the new firm into second place.

TABLE 8.5. THE TOP 12 UK ACCOUNTING FIRMS IN 1972: SUBJECTIVE BASIS

1	Peat, Marwick, Mitchell	The "Big Four"
2	Price Waterhouse	
3	Coopers & Lybrand	
4	Deloitte	
5	Touche Ross	All reasonably close
6	Arthur Young McClelland Moores	
7	Whinney Murray	
8	Thomson McLintock	
9	Arthur Andersen	
10	Turquands Barton Mayhew	
11	Harmood Banner	
12	Spicer & Pegler	

Another leading City accountant estimates that the 1973 turnover of the "Big Four" ranged from £25 million for Peat, Marwick, Mitchell to £15 million for Coopers & Lybrand. He reckons that the total fees of the other firms listed in Table 8.5 ranged from £10 million to £4 million, but in his opinion Whinney Murray and Thomson McLintock should have been in fifth and sixth places respectively. Some day, perhaps there will be no need to guess!

Education and Training

Since the failure of the integration scheme, all the UK accountancy bodies have devoted considerable attention to their education and training arrangements. The most impressive are those of the Institute of Chartered Accountants of Scotland (Fig. 8.4). The prospective Scottish chartered accountant must hold either an appropriate approved university degree or a Higher National Diploma (HND) in Accounting following two years' full-time study at a College of Further Education. The student then undertakes a training contract with a practising chartered accountant, which in the case of a graduate lasts three years and for the HND student

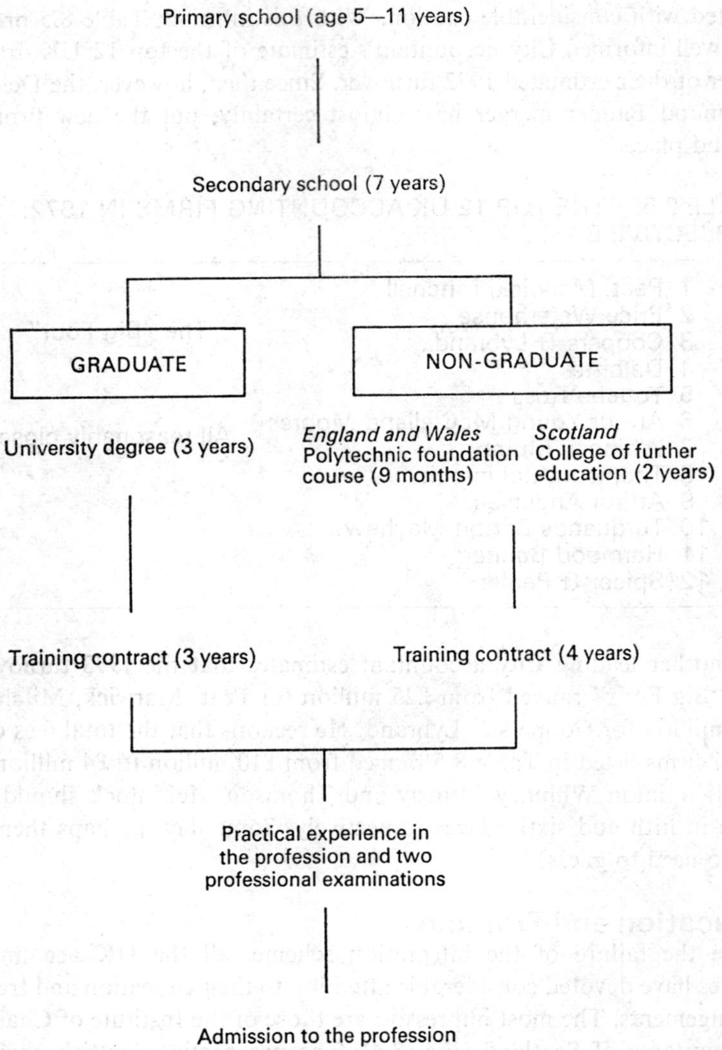

Fig. 8.4 The way to become a British chartered accountant

four years. During his training contract the candidate must prepare for his examinations by attending Institute courses as follows:

Part I Examination:	Three courses each of four, three and two weeks' duration.
Part II Examination:	Three courses each of two weeks' duration. In certain circumstances candidates may also be called for an oral examination.[22]

The prospective English chartered accountant, having attained a satisfactory level of secondary education, has two options: he can go to a university and obtain either an approved degree or any other degree, or alternatively he can attend a nine-months foundation course at a polytechnic or technical college. Students holding an approved university degree are exempt from the Institute foundation examination, whereas other graduates are not. All graduates are then required to undertake a three-year training contract (*i.e.* articles) with a practising chartered accountant authorised to accept students by the Institute. Each principal cannot have more than four students. Non-graduates successfully completing a polytechnic foundation course are also exempt from the Institute's foundation examination but they must sign a four-year training contract. During the term of their training contract all students are bound to sit two professional examinations, for which they are allowed periods of study leave to undertake courses organised both by the polytechnics and by the technical colleges, or by certain private sector institutions. The minimum age for entry to the Institute of Chartered Accountants in England and Wales is 21, but the average age of entry is approximately 24.

The Chartered Institute of Public Finance and Accountancy has also adopted the foundation course scheme, as has, to a lesser extent, the Association of Certified Accountants, and the Institute of Cost and Management Accountants so far as their UK students are concerned. It is significant that all four of the bodies in England and Wales have made considerable efforts to approve similar foundation courses.

At the end of 1973 over 90,000 students were registered with the five main UK accountancy bodies (Table 8.6). However, these figures are misleading in one sense, since students registering their intent to become members of the Association of Certified Accountants or of the Institute of Cost and Management Accountants are not under the same obligation as prospective chartered accountants to commence, let alone complete, their training. Some 19,000 and 9000 respectively of the students registered with the Association of Certified Accountants and the Institute of Cost and Management Accountants are domiciled outside the United Kingdom; accordingly examinations are held throughout the world, but more particularly in the Commonwealth countries. It is also noteworthy that large numbers of overseas students, predominantly from the Commonwealth regions, come to the United Kingdom to qualify as chartered accountants or as members of the Chartered Institute of Public Finance and Accountancy.

TABLE 8.6. STUDENTS UNDER TRAINING IN THE BRITISH ACCOUNTANCY PROFESSION (as at 31 December 1973)

The Institute of Chartered Accountants in England and Wales	19,000[1]
The Institute of Chartered Accountants in Scotland	1,683
The Association of Certified Accountants	35,428
The Institute of Cost and Management Accountants	30,415
The Chartered Institute of Public Finance and Accountancy	3,878
	90,404

1. Including an estimated 1,500 non-registered students on foundation courses.

In view of the large number of overseas students studying for the examinations of all the UK accountancy bodies, drawing a satisfactory comparison of their mutual educational standards presents some difficulty. During 1973, 45 per cent of students registering with the Institute of Chartered Accountants in England and Wales held UK or Irish degrees, another 30 per cent were also UK students, and these, together with the 25 per cent from overseas, were of pre-foundation course standard. However, besides those students registering with the Institute, it is estimated that a further 1500 commenced foundation courses, so that the overall percentage of British Isles graduates is nearer to 30 per cent. Of the 35,428 students registered with the Association of Certified Accountants at the end of 1973 a mere 926 (less than 3 per cent) were graduates of the British Isles. Some 8 per cent of students registered with the Institute of Cost and Management Accountants were UK or Irish graduates.

The examinations of each of British accountancy bodies include the following examination papers.

The Institute of Chartered Accountants in England and Wales.

Foundation Examination

Accounting
Law
Economics
Statistics

Professional Examination I

Financial Accounting I
Taxation I
Law
Auditing, Systems and Data Processing

Professional Examination II

Financial Accounting II
Auditing
Taxation II
Management Accounting
Elements of Financial Decisions

The Institute of Chartered Accountants of Scotland.

Part I

Mathematics and Management
Financial Accounting
Taxation

Part II

Auditing
Interpretation of Accounts
Management Accounting

The Association of Certified Accountants.

Foundation Examination

Part A

Accounting I
Law I—Principles of Law
Economics and the Business Environment

Part B

Data Processing and Systems Design
Statistics
Accounting II—Costing

Professional Examination

Section 1

Taxation I
Accounting III
Auditing
Law II—Company Law

Section 2
- Law III—Insolvency Executorship and Trusteeship
- Management Mathematics
- Accounting IV
- Accounting V—Management Accounting

Section 3
- Auditing and Investigations
- Taxation II
- Business Management
- Accounting VI—Financial Management

The Institute of Cost and Management Accountants.

Foundation Stage

Section A
- Financial Accounting
- Cost Accounting
- Economics

Section B
- Mathematics and Statistics
- Business Law
- Organisation of Production

Professional Stage

Part I
- Financial Accounting
- Cost Accounting
- Economic Analysis
- Quantitative Techniques

Part II
- Financial Accounting
- Company Law and Taxation
- Management Information Systems and Data Processing
- Organisation and Marketing Management

Part III
- Management Accounting (Two Papers)
- Financial Management
- Corporate Planning and Control

The Chartered Institute of Public Finance and Accountancy.

Professional Examination 1

Accountancy and Audit
Management Accountancy
Analytical Techniques and Data Processing

Professional Examination 2

Public Finance
Management in the Public Sector
Accountancy and Audit in the Public Sector

Professional Examination 3

Application of Analytical Techniques
Organisation of the Finance and Accountancy Function
Application of the Finance and Accountancy Function to Management

In May 1974, *Prospectus for a Profession*, the report of a long-range enquiry into education and training for the accountancy profession in the British Isles was published. The principal recommendations of the report (the "Solomons Report") are as follows:

1. Subject to certain exceptions for mature candidates and other special cases, candidates for the profession should be required to complete a minimum of two years' full-time study at a university or polytechnic, leading to a "Diploma in Higher Education".
2. Basic education should be followed by a shorter period of practical instruction, not necessarily continuous, simulating work experience in a concentrated form and in a controlled environment.
3. A minimum period of three years' approved experience (including the period of practical instruction) should be required of all prospective accountants, with no distinction in this regard between graduates and non-graduates. Not less than one of these three years should be spent in public practice, and not less than one in commerce, industry or the public service. Approved experience would be gained only with businesses and practices designated as "recognised training establishments".
4. Admission to membership of the professional body should be by a test of practical competence on completion of the approved experience.
5. Two years' post-qualification experience, desirably to be monitored for its nature and quality as well as its duration, should be the minimum safeguard for the award of a practising certificate.

Ethics

Members of all the main UK accountancy bodies are expected to observe the highest ethical standards. The Institutes of Chartered Accountants do not have specific ethical codes, but various rules are laid down in their Royal Charters and in Council Statements of Professional Conduct. The fundamental core of ethical rules is contained in the English Institute's Statement of Professional Conduct E 1, which specifies the following:

1. A member must not allow a non-member to practise in his name unless he is in partnership with that non-member.
2. A member in practice cannot share his fee with anyone other than another public accountant or a person in his own employment.
3. A member in practice cannot accept any share of the fees of any other person apart from a public accountant or a person in his own regular employment.
4. A member in employment cannot carry on the work of a public accountant on behalf of an employer who is not a practising chartered accountant but whose business is such as would normally be performed by a member of the Institute in practice.
5. A member in practice cannot carry on any business incompatible with the practice of accountancy.

Statement of Professional Conduct E 7 lists certain activities as being, or possibly being, objectionable, among which rates the carrying on the business of an auctioneer or a stockbroker.

Other Statements of Professional Conduct deal with:

1. Changes in a Professional Appointment: a member must consult the existing accountant before acting for a client as auditor or otherwise.
2. Publicity: publicity, advertising and all forms of solicitation for clients are strictly prohibited.
3. Remuneration: a member in practice should not accept a charge for his services on a percentage basis.
4. Consultancy: members offering management consultancy services are subject to less demanding publicity rules.

At the time of going to press the ethical rules of the English, Scottish and Irish Institutes of Chartered Accountants are subject to review. It is to be hoped that the new rules will contain much more stringent requirements for the independence of auditors. All shareholdings in clients should be banned and firms should be told that no more than a certain percentage of their fees should come from any one client.

Services Provided

Chartered accountants in public practice are prevalently engaged in auditing, but most of the larger firms have specialist taxation, management consultancy, investigation, insolvency, company secretarial and other departments. Smaller firms are also involved in the provision of accounting, taxation and other general financial advice. The importance of the accountant as the prime source of business advice in the United Kingdom is well demonstrated by a survey carried out in 1969 by the Association of British Chambers of Commerce (Table 8.7) which pointed out that 37 per cent of businessmen would turn to their accountant if they needed assistance in preference to their lawyer or bank manager (15 per cent respectively).

TABLE 8.7. "IF YOU NEED HELP, TO WHICH OF THE FOLLOWING WOULD YOU BE MOST LIKELY TO TURN?" Replies to a Survey carried out by the Association of British Chambers of Commerce

		%
Accountant	1,383	37
Solicitor (lawyer)	561	15
Bank manager	543	15
Chamber of commerce	496	13
Trade association	485	13
Business consultant	143	4
Confederation of British Industry	129	3
	3,740	**100**

AUDITING

Like that of the accountancy profession, the development of auditing in the United Kingdom went hand in hand with the development of companies. While accountants were already being appointed as auditors to companies before statutory audits were made obligatory in 1900, the following extract from the Royal Charter of the Institute of Chartered Accountants in England and Wales makes it clear that, in 1888, this was by no means their predominant activity:

> the profession of Public Accountants in England and Wales is a numerous one and their functions are of great and increasing importance in respect of their employment in the capacities of Liquidators acting in the winding up of

companies and of Receivers under decrees and of Trustees in bankruptcies or arrangements with creditors and in various positions of trust under Courts of Justice as also in the auditing of the accounts of public companies and of partnerships and otherwise.

During the early years, indeed right up to the Second World War, auditing was generally a rather mundane "tick and bash" affair with far more attention being paid to book-keeping accuracy than to internal control and systems. It was not until after 1945 that the first comprehensive audit manual was brought into use by Coopers & Lybrand (then Cooper Brothers).[23] The Institute of Chartered Accountants in England and Wales started to issue Statements on Auditing in 1961, but the actual turning-point came in the subsequent decade as auditors found themselves faced with the increasing complexities of business and the rapid growth in the use of the computer. During those years audit programmes became much more sophisticated, the whole range of audit techniques underwent a major transformation, systems flow-charts and statistical sampling became commonplace and the auditor himself emerged as a more competent and capable figure than he had hitherto been.

Appointment of Auditors

At each annual general meeting, every company is required to appoint an auditor or auditors to hold office until the conclusion of the next annual general meeting. However, apart from the exceptional case, a retiring auditor is automatically reappointed at any general meeting with no resolution being passed to this effect. The first auditors of a company may be appointed by the directors, but, again, these may be removed by the company in general meeting. If the general meeting fails to appoint auditors, the Department of Trade may assume the duty of appointing a person to fill the vacancy. Such a person is described by Section 161 of the Companies Act, 1948, which states that

a person shall not be qualified for appointment as auditor of a company unless either

(a) he is a member of a body of accountants established in the United Kingdom and for the time being recognised for the purposes of this provision by the Board of Trade [now the Department of Trade]; or

(b) he is for the time being authorised by the Board of Trade to be so appointed either as having similar qualifications obtained outside the United Kingdom or as having obtained similar adequate knowledge and experience in the course of his employment by a member of a body of accountants recognised for the purposes of the foregoing paragraph or as having before the sixth day of August, nineteen hundred and forty-seven, practised in Great Britain as an accountant.

The following bodies of accountants established in the United Kingdom have been recognised by the Department for the purposes of Section 161 of the Companies Act, 1948:

1. The Institute of Chartered Accountants in England and Wales.
2. The Institute of Chartered Accountants of Scotland.
3. The Association of Certified Accountants.
4. The Institute of Chartered Accountants in Ireland.

Between July 1948 and December 1972 the following persons have also been authorised under Section 161 of the Act:[24]

1. Having similar qualifications obtained outside the United Kingdom	1516
2. Having obtained adequate knowledge and experience in the course of employment by a member of a recognised body of accountants	928
3. Having before 6 August 1947 practised in Great Britain as an accountant	962
	3406

It is understood that members of the following accountancy bodies in the other EEC countries are included in the total for (1) above:

1. *Belgium:* Institut des Réviseurs d'Entreprises.
2. *Denmark:* Foreningen af Statsautoriserede Revisorer.
3. *France: Experts comptables* from the Ordre des Experts Comptables et des Comptables Agréés.
4. *Germany:* Wirtschaftsprüferkammer.
5. *The Netherlands:* Nederlands Instituut van Registeraccountants.

The Companies Acts also contain extensive provisions for the appointment of inspectors to carry out investigations into companies.

Duties of Auditors

Section 14 of the Companies Act, 1967, lays down that the auditors of a company must report to the members on the accounts examined by them, and on all balance sheets, profit and loss accounts and group accounts laid before the company in general meeting during their tenure of office, stating:

1. Whether, in their opinion, the said accounts have been properly prepared in accordance with the Acts and give a true and fair view:
   (a) in the case of the balance sheet, of the state of the company's affairs at the end of the financial year; and
   (b) in the case of the profit and loss account, of the profit or loss for its financial year.
2. Whether, in the case of a holding company submitting group accounts, in their opinion the group accounts have been properly prepared in accordance with the provisions of the Acts so as to give a true and fair view of the state of affairs and profit or loss of the company and its subsidiaries dealt with thereby, so far as concerns members of the company.

In preparing their report the Act provides that it is the auditors' duty to carry out such investigations as will enable them to form an opinion as to the following matters, that is to say:

1. Whether proper books of account have been kept by the company and proper returns adequate for their audit have been received from branches not visited by them.
2. Whether the company's balance sheet and (unless it is framed as a consolidated profit and loss account) profit and loss account are in agreement with the books of account and returns.

The auditors are entitled to attend any general meeting and to receive all notices of, and other communications relating to, any general meeting which any member of the company is entitled to receive, and to be heard at any general meeting which they attend on any part of the business of the meeting which concerns them as auditors.

The Auditors' Report

As well as the matters described above, Section 14 of the Companies Act, 1967, states that:

> if the auditors are of the opinion that proper books of account have not been kept by the company or that proper returns adequate for their audit have not been received from branches not visited by them, or if the balance sheet and

> (unless it is framed as a consolidated profit and loss account) profit and loss account are not in agreement with the books of account and returns, the auditors shall state that fact in their report.

Moreover, the Act goes on to say:

> if the auditors fail to obtain all the information and explanations which, to the best of their knowledge and belief, are necessary for the purposes of their audit, they shall state that fact in their report.

If not otherwise stated in the accounts, the following matters must be stated by way of note to the auditors' report:

1. Any material respects in which any items shown in the profit and loss account are affected:
   (a) by transactions of a sort not usually undertaken by the company or otherwise by circumstances of an exceptional or non-recurrent nature; or
   (b) by any change in the basis of accounting.
2. Particulars of loans to officers of the company.
3. Particulars of directors' emoluments.
4. Particulars of directors' emoluments waived.

In Statement on Auditing U 10, the Institute of Chartered Accountants in England and Wales recommended the following forms of unqualified audit reports, and these are virtually in universal use:

Companies not submitting group accounts

Auditors' report to the members of. . . .

In our opinion, the accounts set out on pages . . . to . . . give a true and fair view of the state of the company's affairs at . . . and of its profit (or loss) for the year ended on that date and comply with the Companies Acts, 1948 and 1967.

Companies submitting group accounts

Auditors' report to the members of. . . .

In our opinion, the accounts set out on pages . . . to . . . together give, so far as concerns members of the holding company, a true and fair view of the state of affairs at . . . and of the profit (or loss) for the year ended on that date and comply with the Companies Acts, 1948 and 1967.

The Institute further recommended that when consolidated accounts incorporated the accounts of material subsidiaries which the auditors of the holding company have not themselves audited, this fact should be stated at the end of the audit report: hence it is common to read: "The accounts of certain subsidiaries have been audited by other firms."

After the establishment of the ASSC, the Institute of Chartered Accountants in England and Wales issued a statement on "The Effect of Statements of Standard Accounting Practice on Auditors" (U 17). Similar statements appeared from the other bodies recognised under Section 161 of the Companies Act, 1948. U 17 makes it clear that all significant departures from accounting standards should be referred to in the auditors' report, and that, if the auditors consider that the true and fair view required to be shown by the accounts is impaired by a departure, they should express a qualified opinion and quantify the financial effect of the departure, unless this is impracticable. The statement recognises that there may be exceptional circumstances, when the auditors consider that the directors, in preparing the accounts, have necessarily departed from an accounting standard in order to show a true and fair view. Even in such circumstances the auditors must nevertheless refer to the departure in their report, stating that they concur, but they should not express a qualified opinion or quantify the financial effect of the departure on the accounts. Finally, the statement deals with the rare case in which adherence to an accounting standard does not, in the auditors' view, produce a true and fair view. Under such circumstances the auditor should express a qualified opinion and quantify the financial effect on the accounts, unless this is impracticable.

The following two examples of UK auditors' reports are taken from a selection reproduced by the 1972–73 Survey of Published Accounts:[25]

The Rank Organisation Ltd. 31st October 1972

Report of the Auditors to the Members of The Rank Organisation Limited

We have examined the balance sheet and consolidated accounts and the statement of source and application of funds set out on pages. . . .

In our opinion the balance sheet and consolidated accounts comply with the Companies Acts, 1948 and 1967, and give respectively a true and fair view of the state of the Company's affairs at 31 October, 1972 and so far as concerns members of the Company, a true and fair view of the state of affairs and of the profit of the Group.

In our opinion the statement on page . . . gives a true and fair view of the source and application of the Group's funds for the year ended 31 October 1972.

PEAT, MARWICK, MITCHELL & CO.
Chartered Accountants

London
5th March, 1973

George Wimpey & Co. Ltd. 31st December 1972
Report of the Auditors to the Members

Note 15(c) on the accounts indicates the extent to which the group's share of the results and reserves of associated companies have not been incoporated in the consolidated accounts. We concur with this departure from standard accounting practice and in our opinion, the accounts and notes set out on pages . . . give, so far as concerns members of the holding company, a true and fair view of the state of affairs at 31 December 1972 and of the profit for the year ended on that date and comply with the Companies Acts 1948 and 1967. The accounts of certain subsidiaries have been audited by other firms.

HARMOOD BANNER & CO.
Chartered Accountants

London
6th April, 1973

Extract from notes (part of Note 15(c)):

(i) The directors do not consider it appropriate to include the results of associated companies in the consolidated accounts because the wide divergence of accounting dates would have a misleading effect and the cost of providing unaudited accounts would not be justified. However, provision has been made for losses by two trading companies. In relation to the operations of De Long–Wimpey (Overseas) Limited a provision of £1,589,248 (1971 £1,062,000) has been made covering all losses to the completion of current contracts. The provision for Marinex Gravel Limited losses amounts to £197,000 (1971 £120,000). These provisions are not included in the statement on page. . . .

Fieldwork

Section 14(5) of the Companies Act, 1967, states that:

> Every auditor of a company shall have a right of access at all times to the books and accounts and vouchers of the company, and shall be entitled to require from the officers of the company such information and explanation as he thinks necessary for the performance of his duties.

Thus there is no limitation on the extent of the auditor's work.

The Institute of Chartered Accountants in England and Wales has been issuing "Statements on Auditing" since 1961, indicating what is best audit practice. At the time of going to press, an Audit Practices Committee of the Institute has been asked to determine the extent to which auditing standards, along the same lines as accounting standards, are necessary.

Standards of fieldwork vary according to the amount of time and money devoted by individual firms to staff training and audit reviews. In this regard, perhaps the larger firms are better placed. Indeed, some reckon to spend about 5 per cent of gross fees solely on training and review costs. In comparative terms, however, the general standard of auditing in the United Kingdom must be very high. Paramount reliance is placed on the system of internal control; direct confirmations of bank balances are essential. Debtors' circularisations are recommended by the Institute in Statement U 7 and are regarded as normal audit practice. Creditors' circularisations are also common. In Statement U 9 ("Attendance at Stocktaking") it is recommended that, wherever practicable, auditors should attend physical stocktakes and indeed this has come to be considered as standard practice. For several years also, statistical sampling techniques have been in use.

At the end of each audit, it is standard practice for the auditor to submit a "Letter of Recommendation" or "Management Letter" to the client, containing recommendations for improvements and possibly dealing in some detail with the audit work carried out. To some extent, this is comparable to the long-form audit report to management which is compulsory in Germany.

It is also recommended practice for the UK auditor to obtain a "Letter of Representation" from his client at the end of each audit.[26] In this letter, the directors normally acknowledge their responsibilities for the preparation of the accounts, and, in particular, the valuation and accounting rules applied in the accounts, which are detailed.

Where not included in a letter of representation, Auditing Statement U 11 ("Stock in Trade and Work in Progress") states that "it is usual and desirable practice to obtain from a director or other responsible official of the company a written statement [*i.e.* "an inventory letter"] outlining in detail the method of ascertaining stock quantities and bases of valuation".

The following is a copy of a standard long-form "Clients' Representation Letter" reproduced here by kind permission of Arthur Young McClelland Moores & Co.:

Client's Representation Letter (long form)

NOTES

(*i*) *The letter should be typed on the client's stationery and be signed by the chief executive or, if the chief executive signs the short form letter, the financial director or controller should be asked to sign this letter.*

(*ii*) *The letter should be modified to cover the specific representations* (e.g., *representations concerning events subsequent to the balance sheet date in the case of US financial statements*).

(Date)

Dear Sirs,

In connection with your examination of the accounts of (company, branch, division, etc.) for the (year, period) ended (balance sheet date) I confirm the following information:

1. *Accounts receivable*

(1) The amounts shown as due by debtors represent valid claims as at (balance sheet date) and do not include amounts in respect of goods on consignment to others.

(2) Adequate provision has been made for uncollectable accounts and for costs or expenses which may be incurred with respect to sales made or services rendered prior to (balance sheet date) including rebates due and expenses under service or repair warranties or contracts.

(3) There has not been any abnormally high return of goods by customers since (balance sheet date) in respect of goods delivered prior to the close of business on that date, nor is any abnormally high rate of return expected.

2. *Current assets*

The directors are of the opinion that the current assets have a value, on realisation in the ordinary course of the company's business, at least equal to the amount at which they are stated in the company's accounts.

3. *Investments*

Unquoted investments have been valued by the directors at £.............. on the following basis:

(Describe basis)

4. *Fixed assets*

The net book amount at which property, plant and equipment is shown in the balance sheet is reached:

(1) After taking into account as additions all expenditure during the year which represents capital outlay on those assets but no expenditure of a revenue nature.

(2) After writing off all amounts relating to items which had been sold or scrapped by (balance sheet date).

(3) After providing for depreciation at a rate sufficient to reduce the net book amounts of the assets to their residual value by the time they become no longer economically useful to the company.

5. *Liabilities*

(1) Adequate provision has been made in the accounts for all liabilities incurred by the company to (balance sheet date) other than contingent liabilities in respect of which no actual liability is expected to arise.

(2) Except as indicated in the accounts none of the liabilities were at balance sheet date secured (otherwise than by operation of law) on any assets of the company and the assets shown in the balance sheet at that date were then owned by the company free of any charge in favour of third parties other than by charges created by:

(3) At the balance sheet date there were no material contingent liabilities other than:

(4) There were no material commitments under contracts placed for capital expenditure at (balance sheet date) except:

6. *Profit and loss account*

(1) Provision has been made in the accounts for all losses expected to arise from events which had occurred by the balance sheet date.

(2) All income up to the balance sheet date has been brought into account.

(3) Except as disclosed in the accounts, the results for the year as shown in the profit and loss account were not materially affected by transactions of a nature not usually undertaken by the company, circumstances of a non-recurring nature, or by charges or credits relating to prior years.

Yours faithfully

(Title)

Auditing Statement U 12 covers "Auditors' Working Papers"; as well as this, the Institute has published model audit programmes and working paper files.

Remuneration of Auditors

Section 159(7) of the Companies Act, 1948, specifies that, if the directors appoint an auditor, they must fix his remuneration; besides this, the company itself must fix it in general meeting or determine how otherwise it is to be fixed.

In practice the audit fee, which is often fixed in advance, is based on the estimated time to be spent and the seniority of the staff involved. The auditors' remuneration, including expenses, must be disclosed as a separate heading in the profit and loss account.

Removal of Auditors

Although the directors have power to appoint auditors, such auditors and any other duly appointed auditors can be removed only by the members in general meeting. As already mentioned, a retiring auditor is considered to be reappointed at any annual general meeting unless:

1. He is not qualified.
2. A resolution has been passed at that meeting appointing someone instead of him, or providing that he shall not be reappointed.
3. He has given written notice to the company of his unwillingness.

Where it is proposed to appoint a person other than the retiring auditor, special notice of the intention to move such a resolution must be given to the company by a shareholder not less than 28 days before the AGM; the company must then give the members not less than 21 days' notice of the motion. On receipt of such a notice the company must immediately send a copy to the retiring auditor. He has the right to make representations to the members, both in writing and orally at the AGM.

Liability of Auditors

There are no limitations to the UK auditor's liability: he may be held liable under common law, civil law (the Companies Acts) and criminal law. Until the case of *Hedley Byrne & Co. Ltd* v. *Heller & Partners Ltd* (1963) it was generally considered that auditors could not be held liable in actions for professional negligence to third parties who had suffered financial loss through their reliance on the professional skill and judgement of those auditors and with whom they were not in contractual or fiduciary relationship. As a result of the decision in *Hedley Byrne*, the Institute of Chartered Accountants in England and Wales concluded in a statement that:

> accountants may now be held in law to owe a duty of care to persons other than those with whom they are in a contractual or fiduciary relationship and may be held liable for neglect of that duty if, but only if, they know or ought to know that a financial report, account or statement prepared by them has been prepared for a specific purpose or transaction will be shown to a particular class of person or class of persons, and may be relied on by that person or class of persons in that particular connection.[27]

The position may become further clarified when the ASSC issues an accounting standard on the "Fundamental Objects and Principles of Periodic Financial Statements"—one of the items listed on its future programme.

In comparison with the situation in the United States, actions for negligence against UK auditors are still rare although there has been a substantial increase in recent years. Generally accountants hold professional indemnity insurance. The Institute of Chartered Accountants in England and Wales has arranged a special "Chartered Accountants' Indemnity Insurance Scheme" which is primarily designed for small and medium-sized firms.

Most of the large firms are probably "covered", as one partner explained, "for $100 million which is the maximum obtainable". Of course, the top $80 million is very inexpensive compared with the first $20 million.

Independence of Auditors

Section 161 of the Companies Act, 1948, states that none of the following can act as auditor to a company:

1. An officer (director, secretary or manager) of the company.
2. A partner or employee of an officer or servant of the company.
3. An officer or servant, or partner or employee of an officer or servant of any company within the same group.

There is, however, no restriction on an employee of the auditor acting as an officer or servant of the company being audited. (*See also* "Ethics", page 278.)

CONCLUSION

However impolitic may have been Sir Henry Benson's assertion that "taken as a whole [in relation to the state of accountancy in the other EEC countries] the UK is in the lead by a large margin",[28] there can be no doubt that this is the view held by UK accountants. While it may be difficult to dispute this, UK accountants are by no means beyond reproach. The disunity of the UK accountancy profession is the cause of considerable confusion at home and of bewilderment overseas. The Continentals must be forgiven for questioning the UK auditor's ability so long as such public disasters as Rolls-Royce, Pergamon Press, Rolls Razor, Vehicle & General, etc., continue to take place. European financial analysts may also be forgiven their cynicism at the ease with which, they say, many UK quoted companies are confidently able to predict their next year's results. The shady areas of stock valuation, depreciation provisions and income recognition still leave far too much room for manoeuvre. Of course the answer is not simply a matter of auditing, but if audits are to mean anything in the future they must consist of more than a mere historical survey of past events. The following extract from a paper by Graham Corbett of Peat, Marwick, Mitchell might appear to overstate the problem, but the future may not be so rosy:

> If out of a hundred-page report packed with useful and relevant information the auditor reports on only certain financial information contained in the last dozen or so pages, shareholders and others may well feel that a watchdog that cannot climb the stairs is really not worth his keep.[29]

REFERENCES

1. *Bank of England Quarterly Bulletin*, June 1971.
2. In addition to the "Big Four", two other banks – Williams & Glyns and Coutts (a subsidiary of National Westminster) – are also termed "clearing banks". The clearing banks are so called because of their membership of the London Clearing House, which settles all cheques drawn on these and other banks.
3. *The Community and the Company*, Report of a Working Party of the Labour Party Industrial Policy Sub-committee, page 22.
4. *Ibid.*, page 22.
5. Clive M. Schmittoff in *The Journal of Business Law*, October 1973, pages 312–321.
6. The Allied Accountancy Bodies comprise:
   The Institute of Chartered Accountants in England and Wales.
   The Institute of Chartered Accountants of Scotland.
   The Institute of Chartered Accountants in Ireland.
   The Association of Certified Accountants.
7. A proprietary company is defined in the Memorandum as one which has consistently satisfied, over three successive accounting year-ends (or since incorporation if shorter), all the following conditions:
   (a) It is managed and controlled by substantially the same persons.
   (b) It is not under the control of another company which is not itself a proprietary company.
   (c) It limits the right to transfer its shares.
   (d) It prohibits any offer of its shares to the public.
   (e) It limits the number of its members to 25.
   (f) Its average number of employees per week does not exceed 200.
   (g) It has an annual turnover not exceeding £500,000.
8. Peter Bird, "Accountability: Standards in Financial Reporting", *Accountancy Age*, 1973, pages 27–28.
9. Reproduced in *Accountancy*, January 1970, page 2.

10. "Explanatory Foreword" to the "Statements of Standard Accounting Practice": reproduced in *Accountancy*, February 1971, page 61.
11. Association of Certified and Corporate Accountants, *Accounting for Inflation: A Study of Techniques under Conditions of Changing Price Levels* (Gee & Co., 1952).
12. Institute of Chartered Accountants in England and Wales, *Members' Handbook*, Statement appended to N 15.
13. *Ibid.*, N 15, para. 27.
14. The Index of Prices of Consumer Goods and Services includes the following indices for the relevant periods:

    (a) For periods up to 1938, the Ministry of Labour cost-of-living index.
    (b) For periods between 1938 and 1962, the consumers' expenditure deflator.
    (c) For periods from 1962 onwards, the general index of retail prices.

    This recommendation is in essence similar to that contained in the final report of the CBI Committee on Inflation and Accounts under the chairmanship of Sir David Barran.
15. Lord Limerick – then Parliamentary Under-Secretary of State for Trade – quoted in *The Times*.
16. The Burmah Oil annual report and accounts for 1972 were selected for *The Accountant* Annual Award for a large company in 1974. These awards were established in 1954 by *The Accountant* magazine to encourage the preparation by public companies of well-presented and informative annual reports and accounts. Two awards are made each year – one for large companies, the other for smaller companies requiring less complex accounts than those of a large group. The only condition of entry for the award is that companies should be quoted on The Stock Exchange (*i.e.* the United Stock Exchanges of Great Britain and Ireland). Some day, perhaps, a non-UK company will obtain an award.
17. Institute of Chartered Accountants in England and Wales, *Survey of Published Accounts*, 1972–73.
18. In *Bond* v. *Barrow Haematite Steel Co.* (1902), 1 Ch. 353, and in *Burland* v. *Earle* (1902), AC 93.
19. As 17 above.
20. Reproduced in *Admission of Securities to Listing* issued by authority of The Stock Exchange.
21. See for instance Touche Ross International, *Executive Digest – United Kingdom*, October 1969.
22. Institute of Chartered Accountants of Scotland, *The CA Student Guide*, February 1973.
23. This manual is still used by the firm's offices all over the world and it has been published under the title of *A Manual of Auditing* by V. R. V. Cooper (Gee & Co., 1966).

24. *Companies in* 1972 (HMSO), page 31.
25. Institute of Chartered Accountants in England and Wales, *Survey of Published Accounts*, 1972–73, pages 192–195.
26. Institute of Chartered Accountants in England and Wales, *Members' Handbook*, U 11, para. 15.
27. As 26 above, V 8.
28. *The Accountant*, 14 December 1972, page 758.
29. *Accountancy Age*, 5 April 1974.

Chapter 9

Ireland

BACKGROUND

When the British finally surrendered most of Ireland to the Irish they left behind a terrible legacy of economic neglect from which Ireland took a long time to recover. The turning-point came in the early 1960s, since when Ireland has had an average growth rate of 4 per cent in real terms which may well increase if the 1973 performance, when the economy is estimated to have grown by a new-record 7 per cent, is repeated. This high growth rate has been achieved with the aid of considerable foreign investment (Table 9.1) attracted by an incentive package second to none in Europe. (The main incentive for the encouragement of new manufacturing industries is the "tax holiday"—15 years' complete exemption from taxes on profits from exports.) The extent of the overseas contribution is such that during the 1960s foreign enterprises accounted for 70 per cent of industrial investment and more than 75 per cent of estimated new employment.

The Industrial Development Authority (IDA), originally formed in 1949, is the State body with national responsibility for industrial development which administers the system of State grants and incentives, and generally co-ordinates the planning and finance of almost all new and existing enterprises. The success of the IDA in transforming a predominantly agricultural country into a more industrialised economy providing a much higher level of employment is evident from Table 9.2. Although Ireland still has a higher dependency ratio than any other OECD country, except Turkey, the emigration rate has now dropped to a mere trickle of what is was during the 1950s and is now comprised almost entirely of voluntary rather than forced emigration. The 1971 population census showed an increase in population in Ireland for the first time in 50 years and is indicative of a growing trend among Irish people in the United Kingdom and elsewhere to return to IDA-created jobs in their native towns.

At the same time, the Irish financial system has been changing. The associated (*i.e.* commercial) banks have been rationalised and their

TABLE 9.1. NEW IDA INDUSTRIES/MAJOR EXPANSIONS: COUNTRY OF ORIGIN (as at 31 March 1973)

Country of origin	*No. of projects*	*Total investment*	*Total projected employment*	*% of total employment*
Ireland	212[1]	£52.9 m	14,467	25.2
UK	182	£41.0 m	11,490	20.0
USA	113	£69.0 m	13,342	23.2
Germany	85	£14.0 m	8,200	14.0
Other countries	76	£45.0 m	10,161	17.6
Total	**668**	**£221.9 m**	**57,660**	**100.0**

1. Irish projects include Irish/overseas joint ventures.

Source: Annual Report, IDA, Dublin 1973.

number has dropped from eight in 1960 to four today.[1] On the other hand the number of non-associated banks has leapt from 14 in 1960 to 39 at the end of 1973 and their total assets amount to 50 per cent of those of the associated banks. The most important of the non-associated banks are the seven merchant banks, providers of wholesale finance, and the five North American banks, which are largely concerned with servicing American subsidiaries.

TABLE 9.2. GRANT-AIDED NEW INDUSTRY

	Jan. '52 to 31 Mar. '67	*1 Apr. '67 to 31 Mar. '71*	*1 Apr. '71 to 31 Mar. '72*	*1 Apr. '72 to 31 Mar. '73*	*Total Jan. '52 to 31 Mar. '73*
New industry[1]					
Number of firms	177	207	71	63	518
Total grants paid (£ million)	14.8	27.7	18.5	14.2	75.2
Employment ('000)	16.1	22.0	6.7	7.0	51.8
Grant per job (£)	915	1,260	2,761	2,029	1,452

1. Excluding firms at Shannon Industrial Estate, 3,900 persons in the beginning of 1971. Grants paid at the 25 per cent level applicable to adaptation grants (£1.8 million) have been excluded. For existing Irish firms in receipt of new industry grants for major expansions a correction has been made for that part of their labour force not involved in the expansion projects.

Source: Annual Reports, IDA, Dublin, 1971, 1972 and 1973.

Bank overdrafts are the main source of external finance while long-term funds are available from the merchant banks, the Industrial Credit Company Ltd (a State-owned company) and the insurance companies. The level of capital market activity is low (Table 9.3), but any comparison is distorted by the fact that Irish investors are free to buy and sell UK securities. This was emphasised by the decision of the Irish Stock Exchange to join with its UK counterparts to form The United Stock Exchange in March 1973.

TABLE 9.3. NEW CAPITAL RAISED BY MARKETABLE SECURITIES (in £ million)[1]

	Fixed Interest		**Equity**	
	The Minister of Finance	*State-owned companies*	*Industrial and commercial companies*	*Total*
1968	53.5	6.9	5.1	65.5
1969	48.2	—	4.8	53.0
1970	25.0	15.2	0.4	40.6
1971	55.2	—	5.9	61.1
1972	40.2	11.9	17.1	69.2

1. Differences due to rounding.

Source: Annual Report, Central Bank of Ireland, 1972–73.

BUSINESS ORGANISATIONS*

The various forms of Irish business organisation are the same as those found in the United Kingdom. Only companies (Fig. 9.1) have legal personalities separate from their members and are regulated by the Companies Act, 1963, which is a virtual copy of the UK Companies Act, 1948. All companies are registered with the Registrar of Companies in Dublin.

* It should be noted that companies incorporated in Northern Ireland are governed by the provisions of the Northern Ireland Companies Act, 1960, which is almost an exact copy of the UK Companies Act, 1948. Conveniently, the company laws of both Irish jurisdictions are, therefore, for the most part, identical. Northern Ireland companies are registered with the Registrar of Companies in Belfast.

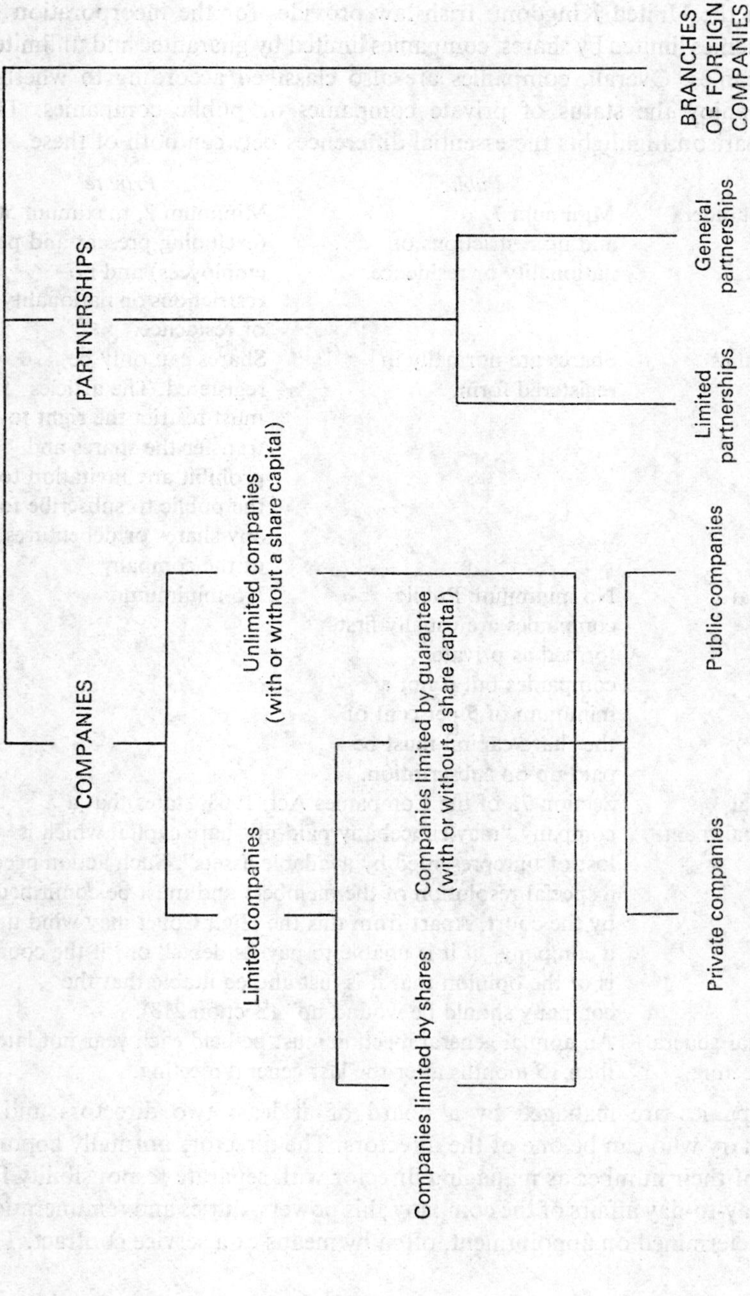

Fig. 9.1 Forms of business organisation in Ireland

Companies

As in the United Kingdom, Irish law provides for the incorporation of companies limited by shares, companies limited by guarantee and unlimited companies. Overall, companies are also classified according to whether they enjoy the status of private companies or public companies. The comparison highlights the essential differences between both of these.

	Public	*Private*
Shareholders	Minimum 7, and no restrictions on nationality or residence.	Minimum 2, maximum 50 (excluding present and past employees) and no restrictions on nationality or residence.
Securities	Shares are normally in registered form.	Shares can only be registered. The articles must restrict the right to transfer the shares and prohibit any invitation to the public to subscribe for any shares or debentures of the company.
Capital	No minimum. Public companies are usually first formed as private companies but if not a minimum of 5 per cent of the share capital must be paid up on subscription.	No minimum.
Capital impairment	Section 72 of the Companies Act, 1963, states that a company "may cancel any paid-up share capital which is lost or unrepresented by available assets". Such action needs a special resolution of the members and must be confirmed by the court. Apart from this the High Court may wind up a company "if it is unable to pay its debts" or "if the court is of the opinion that it is just and equitable that the company should be wound up" (Section 213).	
Annual general meeting	An annual general meeting must be held each year not later than 15 months after the last general meeting.	

Companies are managed by a board of at least two directors and a secretary who can be one of the directors. The directors normally appoint one of their number as managing director with separate responsibility for the day-to-day affairs of the company; his powers, duties and remuneration are determined on appointment, often by means of a service contract. The

TABLE 9.4. STATISTICS OF IRISH COMPANIES
(as at 31 December 1972)

Private companies	26,733	Companies with a share capital	27,100
Public companies	890	Companies without a share capital	523
Number of companies on Register	**27,623**		**27,623**

Source: Companies, Fifty-first Annual Report by the Department of Industry and Commerce, 1972, Stationery Office, Dublin.

directors are appointed by the shareholders in general meeting and may be removed at any time, except in the case of a director of a private company holding office for life. If the articles impose any share qualifications these must be taken up on appointment. The directors are responsible for the preparation of the annual accounts, for giving a report thereon, and for having them audited.

A company limited by guarantee is defined by Section 5(2)(b) of the Companies Act, 1963, as "a company having the liability of its members limited by the memorandum to such amount as the members may respectively thereby undertake to contribute to the assets of the company in the event of its being wound up". This form of company is rarely used commercially, being virtually restricted to charitable and non profit-making associations.

An unlimited company is a company which does not limit the liability of its members and differs only from a general partnership to the extent that it enjoys a legal personality separate from that of its members.

Partnerships

Individuals can carry on business in Ireland in the form of partnerships. Limited partnerships, whereby some but not all of the partners have limited liability, may be formed under the Limited Partnerships Act, 1907. Only five such partnerships have been registered between 1967 and 1972. The limited partners may not take part in the management of the partnership. Section 376 of the Companies Act limits the number of partners in any partnership to 20 except in the case of a bank, when the limit is 10.

Branches of Foreign Companies

Few formalities are necessary to establish an unincorporated branch operation in Ireland. Within one month of setting up business the branch must register and file certain documents with the Registrar of Companies. If the company carrying on an Irish branch operation is of the same form as an Irish public company it must file annual reports and accounts, similar to those required from an Irish public company, with the Registrar of Companies. The number of foreign companies so registered amounted to 1655 at the end of 1972.

ACCOUNTING AND FINANCIAL REPORTING

Largely influenced by the United Kingdom, accounting and financial reporting standards are relatively sophisticated in Ireland.

Accounting Principles

In common with UK company law, the Irish Companies Act generally avoids any attempt to define accounting principles beyond the overall stipulation of Section 149 that "every balance sheet of a company shall give a true and fair view of the state of affairs of the company as at the end of the financial year, and any profit and loss account of a company shall give a true and fair view of the profit or loss of the company for the financial year".

The Irish accountancy profession has generally observed all the "Recommendations on Accounting Principles" of the Institute of Chartered Accountants in England and Wales. The Institute of Chartered Accountants in Ireland has also issued a few statements on specific matters of local interest.

The Irish Institute is a member of the Accounting Standards Steering Committee (ASSC) set up in 1970 by the Institute of Chartered Accountants in England and Wales to define the accounting standards to be applied "to all financial accounts intended to give a true and fair view of financial position and profit or loss".[2] Statements of Standard Accounting Practice (SSAPs) are effectively binding on all companies for which they are intended and it is only when the directors are of the opinion that the application of any particular SSAP would not give a true and fair view that departures are permitted. In such exceptional circumstances the auditors' report must refer to the departure and quantify its financial effect.

Accounting Practices and the Annual Accounts

In general it may be said that Irish accounting and reporting practices differ from those of the United Kingdom only to the extent that the disclosure rules principally contained in the Sixth Schedule of the 1963 Companies Act (virtually identical to the Eighth Schedule of the UK Companies

Act, 1948) are not as demanding as those of the UK 1967 Act. Accordingly, the discussion of the various items in this section is restricted to the specific requirements of the Irish Companies Act and the Statements of Standard Accounting Practice. What follows should therefore be read in the context of the corresponding section of the chapter on the United Kingdom.

Consolidated Accounts

Under the Companies Act every quoted company having one or more subsidiaries (*i.e.* when it holds more than 50 per cent of the equity or voting rights) is required to prepare consolidated accounts unless the company is itself the wholly owned subsidiary of another Irish company or the directors are of the opinion that (1) it is impracticable, or would be of no real value, or (2) the result would be misleading; and if the directors are of such an opinion about each of the company's subsidiaries, group accounts are not required.

If group accounts are not submitted or a subsidiary is omitted from consolidated accounts, it is necessary to state:

1. The directors' reasons therefor.
2. The net aggregate amount attributable to the holding company of profits less losses of such subsidiaries for the financial years ending with or during the financial year of the holding company (i) dealt with and (ii) not dealt with in its accounts, in each case further subdivided between:
   (a) Financial years of subsidiaries.
   (b) Their previous financial years since acquisition.
3. Any qualifications in audit reports on accounts of subsidiaries or notes on accounts which, if not made, would have been subject of qualification, so far as not covered by holding company's accounts.
4. That information is not obtainable, where this is the case.

In addition, in respect of any subsidiaries omitted from consolidated accounts, the consolidated balance sheet must show:

1. The shares in and amount due from such subsidiaries.
2. The number, description and amount of shares or debentures of the company beneficially held by subsidiaries.

If the financial years of any subsidiaries do not coincide with that of the holding company, the directors' reasons therefor must be given and the subsidiaries' last accounting dates before that of the company (or earliest and latest of those dates) must be disclosed.

Consolidated accounts include a consolidated balance sheet and a consolidated profit and loss account. A holding company need not present a profit and loss account in addition to a consolidated profit and loss account provided that the latter shows how much of the consolidated profit and loss for the financial year is dealt with in the accounts of the holding company.

In a supplement to SSAP 1 ("Accounting for the Results of Associated Companies") the Institute of Chartered Accountants in Ireland has pointed out that in order to comply with the Statements' minimum requirements private companies incorporated in the Republic of Ireland which have interests in subsidiaries that are material but do not present consolidated accounts should deal with the profits and losses of their subsidiaries and give information about their assets and liabilities in a manner similar to that required in the Statement in respect of associated companies. (The particular requirements of SSAP 1 are dealt with below under "Investments".) The Act also contains a provision that, if a private company does not consolidate, any member of the company, within 14 days of so requesting, is entitled to be furnished with copies of the annual accounts of all subsidiaries for the last 10 years and copies of their latest directors' and auditors' reports.

The Balance Sheet

Fixed assets. The methods used to arrive at the amount of each main heading of fixed assets must be disclosed. In respect of each heading there should be stated the aggregate of cost or valuation, accumulated depreciation and net book value, except in the case of assets the replacement of which is provided for wholly or partly

1. By making provision for renewals and charging the cost of replacement against the provision so made; or
2. By charging the cost of replacement direct to revenue, in which event the means of replacement and any outstanding provision must be given.

Intangible assets. The aggregate of goodwill, patents and trademarks so far as they are not written off must be stated as must any expenditure not written off in respect of:

1. Preliminary expenses.
2. Expenses of issue of shares or debentures.

3. Commission paid on shares or debentures.
4. Discounts allowed on debentures.
5. Discounts allowed on shares.

Investments. The Act requires the disclosure of:

1. The aggregate amounts of quoted and unquoted investments.
2. The market value of quoted investments and the Stock Exchange value where the market value is taken to be high.

SSAP 1 ("Accounting for the Results of Associated Companies") requires that the investing company's (or group's) share of the post-acquisition retained profits or surplus of associated companies be reflected in its consolidated balance sheet (as an addition to the cost of the investment, less any amounts written off) but not in its own balance sheet. If a company does not have subsidiaries its share of profits or losses in associated companies should be shown as a note to the balance sheet. An investment falls within the definition of an associated company when the investing company's interest:

1. Is effectively that of a partner in a joint venture, or
2. Is for the long term, carries not less than 20 per cent of the equity voting rights and puts the investor in a position to exercise a significant influence over the company.

(*See also* under "Associated Companies" below.)

Other assets. The Act requires the disclosure of the following:

1. The amount of shares in subsidiaries, and the amounts due from subsidiaries.
2. Amounts due from holding and fellow subsidiaries; amounts due in respect of debentures must be separately stated.
3. Loans (other than loans made in the ordinary course of the company's business where this includes the lending of money and, under certain conditions, loans not exceeding £2000 made during the period to directors of the company and to bodies corporate in which the directors of the company have more than a 20 per cent interest (whether or not repaid) and the amounts outstanding).
4. Loans to their employees or their trustees to purchase shares in the company or its holding company (if any).
5. The nominal and book values of any debentures of the company held by nominees or trustees for the company.
6. The number, description and amount of debentures of the company beneficially held by subsidiaries.

Capital. A summary of authorised and issued share capital is required. In respect of any redeemable preference shares, there must be specified:

1. The earliest and latest dates of redemption.
2. Whether redemption is at the company's option or obligatory.
3. Whether any (and if so what) premium is payable on redemption.

The gross arrears of fixed cumulative dividends and the periods of the arrears should be stated by way of note.

Reserves. The only area where the Act contains any accounting rules is in respect of reserves. Pre-acquisition profits may not be distributed unless the directors and auditors agree and certify "that it would be fair and reasonable and would not prejudice the rights and interests of any person" (Section 149).

The Act rules that a capital surplus arising on the revaluation of unrealised fixed assets cannot be distributed. However, an unrealised net capital surplus (established by a *bona fide* revaluation of all the fixed assets of the company) in excess of the previous book value of the assets may be used in paying up unissued shares of the company, other than redeemable preference shares, to be issued to members as fully paid bonus shares. In the Irish Act there is still a distinction between capital and revenue reserves (this distinction was dropped in the UK 1967 Act). The Act states that a reserve cannot "include any amount written off or retained by way of providing for depreciation, renewals or diminution in value of assets or retained by way of providing for any known liability". A capital reserve cannot include "any amount regarded as free for distribution through the profit and loss account, and 'revenue reserve' shall mean any reserve other than a capital reserve".

The Act requires the disclosure of the aggregate amount of reserves classified under sub-headings appropriate to the company's business. The source of any increase or application of any reserves under each sub-heading must be given when this information is given in the profit and loss account. The amounts of any share premium account and any capital redemption reserve fund are required to be separately stated.

Provisions. A provision is defined in the Sixth Schedule of the Act as "any amount written off or retained by way of providing for depreciation, renewals or diminution in value of assets or retained by way of providing for any known liability of which the amount cannot be determined with substantial accuracy". The balance sheet must show the aggregate amount of provisions other than provisions for depreciation, renewals or diminution in value of assets, under a separate heading, but classified under sub-headings appropriate to the company's business.

There must also be shown the source of any increase or application of any decrease (other than for the purpose for which provision was set up) in such provisions under each sub-heading, unless this is shown in the profit and loss account.

Amounts set aside to meet future liabilities or for tax equalisation purposes should be separately indicated.

Taxation. The Act requires that the basis of computing the amount, if any, set aside for taxation be disclosed.

Liabilities. The Act requires that liabilities should be summarised with such particulars as are necessary to disclose the general nature, classified under headings appropriate to the company's business. The following must also be disclosed:

1. Particulars of redeemed debentures which the company has power to reissue.
2. Any liabilities secured on assets (not necessarily specifying which assets) otherwise than by operation of law.
3. Particulars of any charge on assets to secure liabilities of another person and (where practicable) the amount secured.
4. Amounts due to subsidiaries, separately from all other liabilities.
5. Amounts due to holding and fellow subsidiary companies, distinguishing debentures.
6. Recommended dividends (net).
7. The aggregate amount of bank loans and overdrafts.

General.

1. If in the opinion of the directors any current assets are not realisable at least at balance sheet value, that fact should be stated.
2. Where the amount of the assets or liabilities affected is material, the basis of converting foreign currencies must be disclosed.
3. The amounts of capital commitments and capital expenditure authorised but not provided for must be given.
4. The general nature of any contingent liabilities not provided for and, where practicable, the aggregate amount must be stated.
5. The corresponding amounts at the end of the immediately preceding financial year are required to be disclosed in respect of all items shown in the balance sheet.

The Profit and Loss Account

Disclosures under the Companies Act. The following must be shown in the accounts or by way of note thereto:

1. Income from investments.
2. Directors' emoluments distinguishing between all amounts paid by or receivable from:
   (a) The company.
   (b) The company's subsidiaries.
   (c) Any other person.
   showing the aggregate amount of emoluments, pensions and compensation for loss of office.
3. Auditors' remuneration, including expenses.
4. Interest payable on debentures and other fixed loans.
5. The amount provided for depreciation, renewals or diminution in value of fixed assets.
6. (a) the method of providing for depreciation or replacement of any fixed assets otherwise than by a depreciation charge;
   (b) the fact that depreciation or replacement is not provided for on any fixed asset (this does not apply to freehold land).
7. The tax change divided between:
   (a) Income tax.
   (b) Other taxation on profits.
   (c) Taxation payable outside the State, distinguishing if possible between income tax and other taxation.
8. Basis of computation of all taxes payable.
9. Amounts provided for the redemption of shares and of loans.
10. Transfers to and from reserves, excluding amounts which would not normally pass through the profit and loss account.
11. Transfers to provisions (other than provision for depreciation, etc.) and withdrawals therefrom for other purposes, excluding amounts which would not normally pass through the profit and loss account.
12. Aggregate dividends paid or proposed and, in the case of dividends proposed, whether these are subject to deduction for income tax.
13. Unusual, exceptional or non-recurrent transactions or any material change in the basis of accounting affecting the profit and loss account.
14. The corresponding amounts at the end of the immediately preceding financial year for all items required to be shown in the profit and loss account.

Associated companies. SSAP 1 ("Accounting for the Results of Associated Companies") lays down a standard basis of accounting for income from associated companies. A company (not being a subsidiary of the investing group or company) is an associated company of the investing group or company if:

1. The investing group or company's interest in the associated company is effectively that of a partner in a joint venture or consortium, or
2. The investing group or company's interest in the associated company is for the long term and is substantial (*i.e.* not less than 20 per cent of the equity voting rights), and, having regard to the disposition of the other shareholdings, the investing group or company is in a position to exercise a significant influence over the associated company.

In both cases it is essential that the investing group or company participates (usually through representation on the board) in commercial and financial policy decisions of the associated company, including the distribution of profits.

Income from investments by a company or its subsidiaries in associated companies should be brought into account on the following bases unless this would involve excessive expense or delay or would be misleading:

1. In the investing company's own accounts:
   (a) dividends received up to the accounting date of the investing company and
   (b) dividends receivable in respect of accounting periods ending on or before that date and declared before the accounts of the investing company are approved by the directors.
2. In the investing group's consolidated accounts: the investing group's share of profits less losses of associated companies.

Where the investing company has no subsidiaries, or otherwise does not prepare consolidated accounts, it must adapt its profit and loss account, suitably titled, to incorporate the additional information required by the Statement.

The investing company's or group's share of the following items should be taken into account:

1. Profits before tax of associated companies.
2. Taxation.
3. Extraordinary items where material.
4. Net profit retained by associated companies.

The share of extraordinary items should be included with the group's own extraordinary items, unless the amount is material in the context of the group's results, when it should be separately disclosed.

Where the associated company prepares group accounts, the share of minority interests, if any, should be included in the investing group's minority interests.

(*See also* under "Consolidated Accounts" above.)

Earnings per share. In accordance with SSAP 3, quoted companies must disclose their earnings per share on the face of the profit and loss account both for the period under review and for the corresponding period. The basis of calculating earnings per share should be disclosed in detail, and in particular the amount of the earnings and the number of equity shares used in the calculation must be stated.

Disclosure of Accounting Policies

SSAP 2 defines four generally accepted fundamental accounting concepts and requires that, if accounts are prepared on the basis of assumptions which differ in material respects from any of these concepts, the facts should be explained. In the absence of a clear statement to the contrary it is presumed that the four concepts have been applied. The Statement also requires the disclosure by way of note of "the accounting policies followed for dealing with items which are judged material or critical in determining profit or loss for the year and in stating the financial position".

Publication and Filing of Financial Statements

Copies of the annual accounts, and the directors' and auditors' reports must be sent, not later than 21 days before the annual general meeting, to every shareholder and debenture holder. The annual accounts comprise the balance sheet and profit and loss account, signed by two directors, together with all notes thereon, and, in so far as not incorporated in the balance sheet or profit and loss account, any group accounts to be laid before the general meeting. Within 60 days of the annual general meeting every quoted company must file the following documents annexed to a detailed annual return, the contents of which are set out in the Fifth Schedule to the Act:

1. A written copy, certified both by a director and by the secretary to be a true copy, of every set of accounts laid before the annual general meeting of the company held during the period to which the return relates.

2. A copy of the report of the auditors on, and the report of the directors accompanying, each set of accounts duly certified.

All annual returns and other documents filed with the Registrar of Companies are open for public inspection.

Directors' Report

In accordance with Section 158 of the Act the directors' report must deal with the following matters:

1. The state of the company's affairs.
2. Proposed dividends.
3. Proposed transfers to reserves.
4. Any significant changes in the nature of the business of the company and of its subsidiaries.

The report should include a list of bodies corporate which are either subsidiaries or other companies of whose equity voting share capital the company holds more than 20 per cent in nominal value, stating in each case:

1. The name of the company.
2. Where it is incorporated.
3. The nature of the business carried on.

The directors' report should be signed by two directors.

Stock Exchange Listing Agreement

In accordance with the Stock Exchange Listing Agreement, the directors' report of quoted companies must contain a considerable amount of additional disclosures. Following the unification of the British and Irish Stock Exchanges, Irish companies are subject to the same requirements as UK companies. These requirements are detailed in Chapter 8, page 261.

Stock Exchange Listing Requirements

Irish companies seeking public quotations on the Stock Exchange are subject to the same requirements as UK companies. These are summarised in Chapter 8, page 263.

Business Records

Section 147 of the Companies Act demands that every company keep "proper books of account" relating to:

1. All sums of money received and expended by the company and the matters in respect of which the receipt and expenditure take place.

2. All sales and purchases of goods by the company.
3. The assets and liabilities of the company.

"Proper books of account" are defined as such books as are "necessary to give a true and fair view of the state of the company's affairs and to explain its transactions". Every record must be retained for a minimum of six years after the date to which it relates. Companies are also required to keep certain other statutory books, including registers of members, directors and secretaries, and a register of charges.

THE ACCOUNTANCY PROFESSION

The Institute of Chartered Accountants in Ireland

In 1761 a certain Thomas Hogan, who carried on business in Dublin, was the only known accountant in Ireland.[3] The profession numbered 41 in 1888 when the Institute of Chartered Accountants in Ireland received a Royal Charter from Queen Victoria. The Institute of Chartered Accountants in Ireland has always retained close links with Britain and particularly with the British accountancy profession with which it took part in the abortive attempt at integration in 1970. Since then the Chartered Institutes of England and Wales, Scotland and Ireland have continued to move closer together not only through joint action on accounting standards but also by making provision for reciprocal membership of each Institute. The Institute of Chartered Accountants in Ireland is in the somewhat peculiar position of being both a Republic of Ireland and a UK accountancy body. This arises from the fact that it is a body for the whole (32 counties) of Ireland.

As in the United Kingdom, Irish chartered accountants enjoy a high status in the business community. Although the profession is small (Table 9.5) members of the Irish Institute are in the forefront of the development which is rapidly changing the face of Ireland.

TABLE 9.5. MEMBERSHIP OF THE INSTITUTE OF CHARTERED ACCOUNTANTS IN IRELAND (as at 31 July 1973)

	Ireland	*Great Britain*	*Elsewhere*	*Total*
In practice	663	20	23	706
Not in practice				
In professional office	321	22	60	403
Others	1,281	135	172	1,588
Total	**2,265**	**177**	**255**	**2,697**

Members of the Institute in public practice operate through some 450 firms either in the form of partnerships or as sole practitioners; as in the United Kingdom they cannot form limited companies. As in other countries, the larger firms (Table 9.6) are expanding rapidly, frequently taking over smaller firms. Craig Gardner has long-standing connections with Price Waterhouse and, through Price Waterhouse & Co. Republic of Ireland firm, is represented on the General Council of Price Waterhouse International. Stokes, Kennedy, Crowley is one of the most strikingly dynamic and aggressive of the Irish firms. It has connections with Peat, Marwick, Mitchell and also looks after the Irish clients of Arthur Young. Coopers & Lybrand (now merged with Purtill & Co.) originated from three Irish firms which came together some years ago to become the Irish arm of what was then Cooper Brothers.

The Institute of Certified Public Accountants in Ireland

The Companies Act, 1963, also recognises the members of a small body of accountants, the Institute of Certified and Public Accountants in Ireland, as being competent to carry out statutory audits.

Education and Training

Prospective members of the Institute of Chartered Accountants in Ireland may qualify for entry to the profession in any of the three ways shown in Fig. 9.2. All candidates must enter into a training contract with a member of the Institute in practice; in the case of graduates the period of the contract is three years, while non-graduates must serve five years, nine months of which may be spent on a full-time commencement course.

The following is an outline of the syllabus for the various parts of the Institute examination.

Part I Business Administration
Accounts I
Statistics

Part II Economics
Accounts II
Law I (General Principles and Mercantile Law)
Law II (Company and Partnership Law)

Part III Auditing I
Accounts III
Taxation I
Management

Part IV Taxation II
Accounts IV
Management Accounting I
Data Processing and Quantitative Methods

Part V Auditing II
Accounts IV
Management Accounting II
Financial Management

Business studies graduates are granted extensive exemptions from Parts I to III of the professional examinations, while other graduates are exempted from Part I.

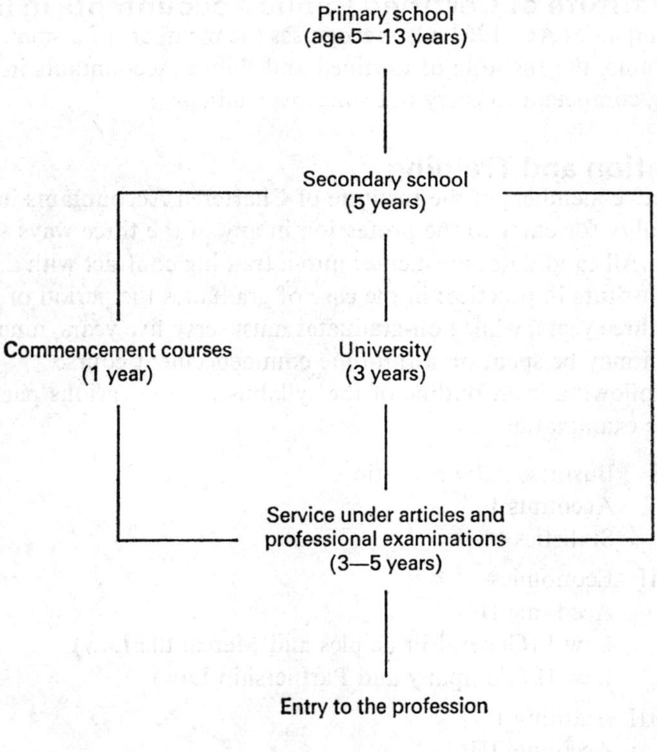

Fig. 9.2 The way to become an Irish chartered accountant

TABLE 9.6. LEADING FIVE ACCOUNTING FIRMS IN IRELAND

1 Ranked by audit clients[1]

	Top 75			Semi-state		Overall	
	Number of clients	*Net assets (£ millions)*	*Ranking*	*Number of clients*	*Net assets (£ millions)*	*Combined net assets (£ millions)*	*Ranking*
Craig Gardner/Atkins Cairnside	30	150	1	1	37	187	2
Stokes, Kennedy, Crowley	8	35	2	3	422	457	1
Reynolds, McCarron	6	33	3	1	57	90	3
Coopers & Lybrand } now merged	4	29	4	2	38	68	4
Purtill & Co. } now merged	3	29	5	–	–	–	–

2 Ranked by number of partners

	Partners	*Employees*
Craig Gardner/Atkins Cairnside	21	400
Stokes, Kennedy, Crowley	20	410
Coopers & Lybrand	17	200
Reynolds, McCarron	16	200
Cooper, Kenny, Magennis	14	112

1. The figures are based on a survey of the accounts of the top 75 Irish companies and semi-state concerns published during the year ended 31 December 1973.

Source: The Irish Independent.

Ethics

The ethical rules of the Institute of Chartered Accountants in Ireland are mainly contained in the Royal Charter, as amended, and to all intents and purposes are the same as those for the English Institute. In broadest terms the professional ethic of the Irish chartered accountant requires an unswerving commitment to honourable behaviour, even at the sacrifice of personal advantage.

At the time of going to press the ethical rules of the English, Scottish and Irish Institutes of Chartered Accountants are subject to review.

Services Provided

Essentially engaged in auditing, practising chartered accountants also enjoy a virtual monopoly in the field of taxation services. The larger firms have parallel management consultancy firms and the smaller firms are often engaged in book-keeping services.

AUDITING

The history of statutory auditing in Ireland dates back to the time when statutory audits were first made compulsory in the United Kingdom in 1900.

Appointment of Auditors

Every company is required to appoint an auditor or auditors at each annual general meeting to hold office until the next annual general meeting. In order to qualify for appointment as a statutory auditor of a company a person must be:

1. A member of one of the bodies of accountants for the time being recognised by the Minister of Industry and Commerce, or
2. Authorised by the Minister to be so appointed either as having obtained similar qualification otherwise than from such a body or as having obtained adequate knowledge and experience prior to 23 December 1963 in the course of his employment by a member of a recognised body of accountants or as having before 23 December 1963 practised in the State as an accountant.

Members of the following accountancy bodies are authorised to act as statutory auditors:

The Institute of Chartered Accountants in Ireland.
The Institute of Certified Public Accountants in Ireland.

The Institute of Chartered Accountants in England and Wales.
The Association of Certified Accountants.
The Institute of Chartered Accountants of Scotland.

The Companies Act also provides that the Minister of Industry and Commerce may appoint one or more competent inspectors to investigate the affairs of a company.

Duties of Auditors and the Auditors' Report

Section 163(1) of the Companies Act states that "the auditors shall make a report to the members on the accounts examined by them and on every balance sheet, every profit and loss account and all group accounts laid before the company in general meeting during their tenure of office". The auditors' report is read at the AGM and is open for inspection by any member. The Seventh Schedule to the Act states that the auditors' report must specify:

1. Whether they have obtained all the information and explanations which to the best of their knowledge and belief were necessary for the purposes of their audit.

2. Whether, in their opinion, proper books of account have been kept by the company, so far as appears from their examination of those books, and proper returns adequate for the purpose of their audit have been received from branches not visited by them.

3. (1) Whether the company's balance sheet and (unless it is framed as a consolidated profit and loss account) profit and loss account dealt with by the report are in agreement with the books of account and returns.

(2) Whether, in their opinion and to the best of their information and according to the explanations given to them, the said accounts give the information required by this Act in the manner so required and give a true and fair view:

(a) in the case of the balance sheet, of the state of the company's affairs as at the end of its financial year; and
(b) in the case of the profit and loss account, of the profit or loss for its financial year;

or, as the case may be, give a true and fair view thereof subject to the non-disclosure of any matters (to be indicated in the report) which by virtue of Part III of the Sixth Schedule[4] are not required to be disclosed.

4. In the case of a company which is a holding company and which submits group accounts whether, in their opinion, the group accounts have been properly prepared in accordance with the provisions of this Act so as to give a true and fair view of the state of affairs and profit and loss of the company and its subsidiaries dealt with thereby, so far as concerns members of the company,

or, as the case may be, so as to give a true and fair view thereof subject to the non-disclosure of any matters (to be indicated in the report) which by virtue of Part III of the Sixth Schedule are not required to be disclosed.

If not otherwise shown in the accounts the auditors' report must also include particulars of directors' salaries and payments, and particulars of loans to directors.

Any significant departures from the Statements of Standard Accounting Practice should be referred to in the auditors' report. If the auditors consider that the true and fair view required to be shown by the accounts is impaired by a departure they must express a qualified opinion and quantify the financial effect of a departure, unless this is impracticable.

The following "typical" auditors' reports are taken from the annual reports of Waterford Glass Ltd and Allied British Banks Ltd:

Auditors' Report to the Members of Waterford Glass Limited

In our opinion the foregoing Accounts give a true and fair view of the state of affairs as at 31st December 1972, and of the profit for the year ended on that date of the Company and of the Group consisting of the Company and its Subsidiaries.

The Accounts of certain Subsidiaries have been audited by other firms.

We have obtained all the information and explanations which we considered necessary. The Company has kept proper books and the Balance Sheet of the Company, which is in agreement therewith, gives with the Group Accounts and Notes in the prescribed manner the information required by the Companies Act, 1963.

Craig Gardner & Co.
Chartered Accountants

Gardner House
Ballsbridge
Dublin 4
28th February 1973

Auditors' Report to the Members of Allied Irish Banks Limited

The balance sheet of the Company set out on pages 10 and 11 is in agreement with the books which, in our opinion, have been properly kept. We obtained the information and explanations we required.

In our opinion, based on our examination and the reports of the auditors of certain Subsidiaries not audited by us, the accounts set out on pages 7 to 17 together give a true and fair view of the state of affairs at 31st March, 1973 and of the profit for the year ended on that date and comply with the Companies Act, 1963.

Coopers and Lybrand
Purtill & Company
Chartered Accountants
Dublin, 21st May, 1973

Fieldwork

The act states that "every auditor of a company shall have a right of access at all reasonable times to the books and accounts and vouchers of the company, and shall be entitled to require from the affairs in the company such information and explanations as he thinks necessary for the performance of the duties of the auditors".

Standards of fieldwork are high and the Irish auditor examines and places a great deal of reliance on internal control. Statistical sampling techniques are used mainly by the larger firms with bigger clients. It is normal to attend physical stocktakes and independent confirmation of such items as title deeds, receivables and bank balances is usual audit practice.

Remuneration of Auditors

The remuneration of the auditor is fixed by the company except where, in exceptional circumstances, the Minister of Industry and Commerce is obliged to appoint an auditor, when the Minister fixes the remuneration. The auditor's remuneration, including expenses, must be disclosed in the annual accounts.

Removal of Auditors

An auditor may be removed at any time by the members in general meeting. In the normal course of events, however, the auditor is considered re-elected unless a resolution for the appointment of another auditor in his place is passed. Such a resolution needs "extended notice", whereby the company must be informed of the intention to move the resolution not less than 28 days before the meeting and the company has to give the members not less than 21 days' notice. In this event the auditor must be informed immediately by the company. He has the right to make representations to the shareholders, both in writing and orally at the general meeting.

Liability of Auditors

The Irish auditor is liable for negligence to the company. It was not thought that he could be held liable to third parties, but the decision of the English courts in *Hedley Byrne & Co. Ltd* v. *Heller & Partners Ltd* (1963) might be influential in the event of any action arising.

Independence of Auditors

A person cannot act as the statutory auditor of a company if he

1. Is an officer or servant of the company.

2. Except where the company is a private company, is a person who is a partner of or in the employment of an officer or servant of the company.

The reason for the exemption for private companies in (2) above is the fact that there were simply insufficient auditors to meet the demand that would otherwise arise; apart from this, the Irish business community is still small and closely knit. An auditor is not prohibited from having a material financial interest in his clients and nor is he precluded from providing any other services.

CONCLUSION

Thanks to the UK influence Ireland enjoys the services of a competent and highly qualified accountancy profession.

A major reform of company law, now being planned, is essential if the needs of a wider investing public and more aware employers are to be met.

REFERENCES

1. The associated banks comprise:
   Allied Irish Banks Ltd.
   Bank of Ireland Ltd.
   The Ulster Bank Ltd (subsidiary of the British National Westminster Bank Ltd).
   The Northern Bank Ltd (subsidiary of the British Midland Bank Ltd).
2. "Explanatory Foreword" to Statements of Standard Accounting Practice ("accounting standards") approved by the Council of the Institute of Chartered Accountants in England and Wales in association with the Institute of Chartered Accountants in Scotland, the Institute of Chartered Accountants in Ireland, the Association of Certified Accountants, and the Institute of Cost and Management Accountants.
3. Refer to Howard W. Robinson, *A History of Accountants in Ireland* published by the Institute of Chartered Accountants in Ireland, 1964.
4. Part III of the Sixth Schedule exempts banking and discount companies from certain of the disclosure requirements.

Chapter 10

Harmonisation of EEC Company Law

BACKGROUND

The European Economic Community (EEC) was established by the Treaty of Rome on 25 March 1957 with the following objectives:

(*a*) the elimination, as between Member States, of customs duties and of quantitative restrictions in regard to the import and export of goods, as well as of all other measures having equivalent effect;
(*b*) the establishment of a common customs tariff and of a common commercial policy towards third countries;
(*c*) the abolition, as between Member States, of obstacles to the free movement of persons, services and capital;
(*d*) the inauguration of a common policy in the field of agriculture;
(*e*) the inauguration of a common policy in the field of transport;
(*f*) the establishment of a system ensuring that competition in the Common Market is not distorted;
(*g*) the adoption of procedures permitting the co-ordination of the economic policies of Member States and the correction of instability in their balances of payments;
(*h*) the approximation of their respective national laws to the extent required for the Common Market to function in an orderly manner;
(*i*) the creation of a European Social Fund in order to improve the possibilities of employment for workers and to contribute to the raising of their standard of living;
(*j*) the establishment of a European Investment Bank to facilitate the economic expansion of the Community by opening up fresh resources; and
(*k*) the association of overseas countries and territories with a view to increasing trade and to pursuing jointly the task of economic and social development.

Thus the EEC is intended to be far more than just a customs union; it is rather the basis of a much greater ideal "determined to establish the foundations of an ever closer union among the European peoples".[1] That ideal envisages the gradual achievement of political unity in Europe on the logical basis of closer economic co-operation between the Member States. It is this eventual economic union or Common Market which the common industrial policy of the EEC is designed to achieve.

The main themes of the EEC's common industrial policy as put forward in a memorandum submitted by the Commission (Fig. 10.1) to the Council of Ministers in March 1970 are:

1. The removal of the remaining barriers to the establishment of a single market embracing the whole Community;
2. The creation of a unified business environment, involving the harmonisation of company law and taxation, and the creation of a Community capital market;
3. The reorganisation of industry to take account of the dimensions of the Common Market;
4. The promotion of technological progress in the Community;
5. The need to recognise the social and regional aspects of industrial development.[2]

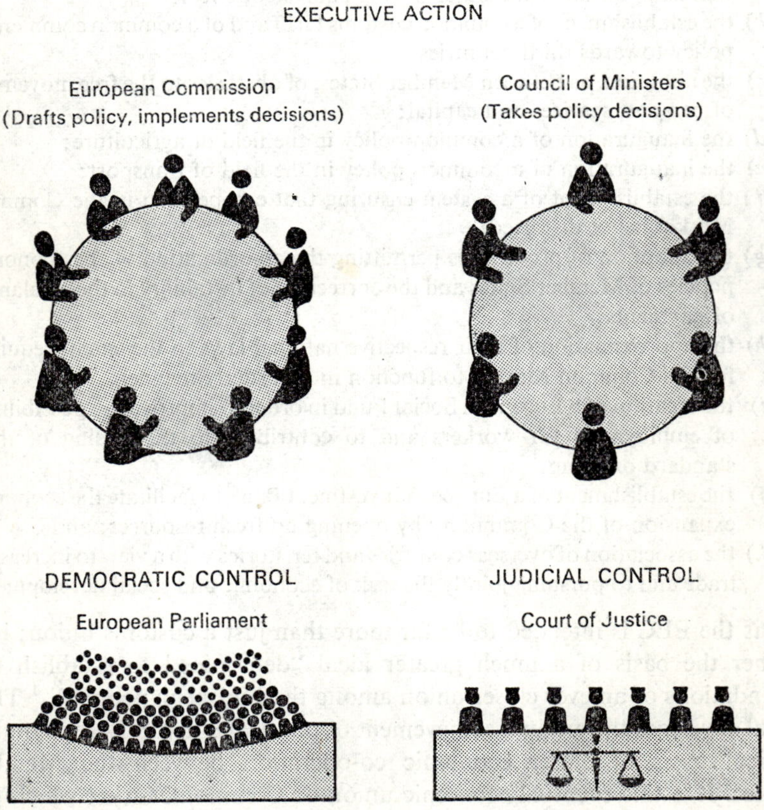

Fig. 10.1 The European Community institutions

All of these aims are of profound importance, but it is the second which is of particular significance in the context of this book.

Towards the achievement of this policy the Commission has embarked upon a major programme of company law harmonisation designed to implement Article 54(3)(g) of the Treaty of Rome, which calls for "the co-ordination of the safeguards required from companies in the Member States, to protect the interests both of members and of third parties". One Directive[3] has already been adopted by the Member States and in addition the Commission has published five further proposed Directives.

The First Directive. The First Directive of 9 March 1968 included simple provisions dealing with the validity of contracts entered into by a company (in particular the application of the *ultra vires* doctrine to contracts entered into by a third party in good faith is prohibited), the public disclosure of certain basic information, the establishment of company registries and the liquidation and winding up of companies. This Directive, which was contained in Section 9 of the European Communities Act, 1972, had comparatively little effect on UK company law apart from the substantial modification of the *ultra vires* doctrine.

The amended proposal for a Second Directive.[4] This proposal deals with the formation of SA/AG-type companies and the maintenance and alteration of their capital. As amended, the Directive prescribes a minimum capital of 25,000 units of account[5] (£10,000) which may be reduced in the case of UK or Irish companies to 4000 units of account (£2000) satisfying the following conditions:

1. They cannot issue bearer shares, certificates relating to registered shares or debentures.
2. Their shares cannot be quoted on a stock exchange.
3. The statutes restrict the right to transfer the shares.
4. The name of the company must include the word "private".

There are also strenuous provisions covering the payment of dividends.

The proposal for a Third Directive.[6] The proposed Third Directive governs particular forms of mergers between SA/AG-type companies. The nearest UK comparison is a reconstruction or amalgamation under Section 208 of the Companies Act, 1948.

The proposal for a Fourth Directive.[7] The amended proposal for a Fourth Directive (originally published in November 1971), which was reissued in February 1974, contains detailed requirements concerning the form and context of the annual accounts of limited companies. The provisions of this proposal are of the utmost importance and they are considered in detail in the section of this chapter on Accounting and Financial Reporting.

The proposal for a Fifth Directive.[8] The Fifth Directive proposal deals with the structure, management and audit of SA/AG-type companies. The proposal rejects the classical management structure prevalent in the United Kingdom and provides instead that every SA-type company must have a two-tier board on the German or Dutch models. In the case of companies which employ 500 staff or more, the proposed Directive provides that not less than a third of the members of the supervisory board must be appointed by the employees or their representatives. Otherwise the members of the supervisory board are appointed by the general meeting and the members of the board of management are appointed, and may be dismissed at any time, by the supervisory board. Appointments in either case must be for a specified period not exceeding six years and members may be reappointed. No person may be a member of both boards at the same time; members of the board of management cannot, without the authorisation of the supervisory board, carry on within another undertaking any activity whether remunerated or not, and no one can be a member of the supervisory board of more than 10 companies. The management organ is responsible for the everyday management of the company's affairs upon whose progress it must report quarterly to the supervisory organ. The authorisation of the supervisory board must be obtained for decisions relating to:

1. The closure or transfer of the undertaking or of substantial parts thereof.
2. Substantial curtailment or extension of the activities of the undertaking.
3. Substantial organisation changes within the undertaking.
4. Establishment of long-term co-operation with other undertakings or the termination thereof.

The proposed Directive states that "the management organ and the supervisory organ shall not fix the remuneration of their own members" (Article 8).

The proposed Directive on Prospectuses.[9] This unnumbered Directive contains provisions concerning the content, checking and distribution of the prospectuses to be published when securities issued by companies are admitted to official stock exchange quotation.

The European Company Statute. Apart from the harmonisation Directives, the Commission has also published a draft regulation[10] embodying a statute for a European Company (Societas Europea—"SE").[11] This is undoubtedly the most ambitious and prestigious of the Commission's proposals and the Council of Ministers agreed in June 1970 that priority should be given to the completion of the project. It envisages the SE as a truly European company registered with the European Court in Luxembourg and subject to specific laws as laid down by the EEC.

The draft statute covers all aspects of the SE's formation, administration, accounts, audit, merger and liquidation, and includes elaborate provisions for worker representation and two-tier boards. The object of the proposed SE is to enable at least two companies of different nationality in the Community to merge wholly or partly without one company being absorbed by the other. It would thus enable multi-national companies to assume the character of a national company in each EEC country and should facilitate mergers across frontiers, such as those of Dunlop–Pirelli, Agfa–Gevaert, Shell/Royal Dutch and the Unilever companies.

ACCOUNTING AND FINANCIAL REPORTING

In February 1974, just over a year after the enlargement of the EEC, the Commission of the European Communities issued an amended proposal for a Fourth Directive on the annual accounts of limited liability companies which was revised to "take into account the laws of the new Member States".[12] The original proposal was submitted to the Council of Ministers on 10 November 1971, having been drafted over a period of nearly five years by a working party of representatives from the then Member States under the chairmanship of the German accountant Dr Wilhelm Elmendorff.

The Commission's approach, like that of most Continental countries, is prescriptive. In particular the proposal is "quite noticeably permeated by concepts that seem to have been borrowed from the German stock corporation law",[13] *i.e.* the 1965 AG Law. Thus as in German law the proposed Fourth Directive includes model layouts of accounts and prescribes certain valuation rules which companies will be obliged to follow in the preparation of their annual accounts. This is in fundamental contrast to the situation in the United Kingdom and Ireland where companies are free to choose any form of presentation, provided the "true and fair" view requirement is satisfied, and the accountancy profession is generally left to work out and develop suitable accounting rules. Furthermore, in a section (later amended) taken directly from the 1965 German AG Law the original draft of the Directive made any over-riding provision, such as the true and fair view, subservient to the valuation rules and the prescribed forms of accounts.

Such was the daunting problem facing the UK and Irish accountancy professions when the EEC became a Community of Nine on 1 January 1973. Before this, however, the Institute of Chartered Accountants in England and Wales had submitted a memorandum in 1970 to the President of the Commission, M Jean Rey, commenting on the Elmendorff proposals and urging the establishment of a European committee on company law "whose task would be to review European company law and prepare for the Commission's consideration a uniform code available for adoption by any European country".[14] The danger of harmonisation on the basis of the laws of the existing Member States was only too obvious, but it was probably too late to expect the Commission to change, let alone to accept, such an ambitious suggestion. The United Kingdom's first opportunity to influence the final outcome of the Fourth Directive came when at the end of 1971 the Groupe d'Etudes (EEC Accountants' Study Group—an informal body with representatives from the main accountancy bodies in the EEC) invited representatives from those countries which had manifested their interest in entering the EEC to join it in discussing the proposal. The Groupe d'Etudes submitted two memoranda to the Commission, both reflecting a strong UK influence and calling for substantial amendments to the original proposal. The amended proposal is designed to take account of these and other recommendations from the Economic and Social Committee[15] and the European Parliament.

But, although the revised proposal of the Commission is regarded—in official UK professional circles at least—as a major improvement on the original document, it is not too difficult to appreciate that it still represents the greatest potential threat to development that UK accounting has ever faced. The French and German philosophy of a codification of accounting policy making remains as the cornerstone of the proposal. As such it is alien to the Anglo-Saxon tradition.

The bulk of French and German accounting theory has long centred on the basic double-entry book-keeping model. This emphasis in turn has led to a great deal of attention being paid to matters such as national charts of accounts—*Kontenrahmen* in Germany and *plans comptables* in France. Coupled with the code law system prevailing in both countries the result has been the codification of rules and regulations for accounting and financial reporting. In other words, the law determines where, when and how accounting is applied and accountants are left to interpret what the legal draughtsmen have decided.

There are three fundamentally different financial accounting situations to be found in the original six Member States of the EEC. Nevertheless, in the proposed Fourth Directive the French and German approach has triumphed almost entirely.

The Netherlands, as in the case of the United Kingdom and Ireland, represents the professional and private sector approach to accounting policy making. France, Germany and Belgium depend on codification and thus public sector organisation of accounting policy—while Italy and Luxembourg, which are also code law jurisdictions, really have no body of broadly usable accounting and financial reporting standards. Therefore the departure point was policy making directly by the profession as in the Netherlands or by politicians as in France, Germany and Belgium.

Incredible though it may seem, there is every reason to believe that the very freedom from Government interference which UK and Anglo-Saxon accountants generally have so long cherished is now being lost—and, it would seem, lost unwittingly—at best for the sake of harmonisation and the Common Industrial Policy, at worst for the sake of at least some achievement in the Internal Market Department (the department responsible for the harmonisation of EEC company law) in Brussels.

The ideal solution would have been to start all over again when the United Kingdom, Ireland and Denmark joined the Community, but this, it appears, was out of the question. It is, however, indicative of the importance attached by the UK Government to the whole company law harmonisation programme that when the Commission staff was being reorganised in 1973 no one demanded, or even publicly called for, the appointment of a UK or Irish official to a senior post in the Internal Market Department. As it is, this department continues to be dominated by French and German lawyers whose frame of reference, quite naturally, is the approach to accounting found in their own countries. It is noteworthy, too, that there are no accountants on the Commission staff.

Having said all this, it would be wrong to assume that everything is lost as far as Anglo-Saxon/Dutch accounting is concerned. First of all the proposed Directive must be discussed in the Council of Ministers where it can be amended, delayed or even sent back to the Commission for further revision. It is only when the Council has given its approval—and precedent requires that the approval be unanimous—that the Directive becomes binding on the Member States. Secondly, having reluctantly accepted much more prescription than it would have wished for, the UK accounting profession is now committed to the establishment of some form of flexible machinery for the development of accounting standards for the

Community. It would be pointless to limit this to the present EEC countries or to dwell on the pious hope that any other European body would be capable of any real progress. Perhaps the best hope lies with the International Accounting Standards Committee (IASC)—a body which was undoubtedly intended by its original founders to play a major part in the preservation of the Anglo-Saxon approach to accounting.

The reasons for harmonisation

The preamble to the proposal for a Fourth Directive lists the following reasons for harmonisation in this field:

> Whereas co-ordination of the national provisions concerning the presentation and contents of the annual accounts and report methods of valuation and publication of these documents in respect of [the various forms of company] . . . is of special importance for the protection of members and third parties.
>
> Whereas simultaneous co-ordination is requisite in these fields for those forms of company because on the one hand the activities of those companies frequently extend beyond the frontiers of their national territory and, on the other hand, they offer no safeguards to third parties beyond the amount of their assets. . . .
>
> Whereas it is also necessary to establish in the Community equivalent legal requirements as regards the extent of the financial information that should be made available to the public by companies that are in competition with one another and have the same legal form.
>
> Whereas the annual accounts must give a true and fair view of the company's assets and liabilities, financial position and results, whereas to this end a layout comprising items that in principle are obligatory must be prescribed for drawing up the balance sheet and profit and loss account, and whereas on the other hand the different methods permitted in the Member States for valuation of assets and liabilities must be co-ordinated to ensure that annual accounts present equivalent information.
>
> Whereas the annual accounts of SAs, AGs . . . [including the equivalent UK public companies] . . . must be available in the fullest possible measure to shareholders and third parties, and whereas to this end it is essential that they be published in full in a national gazette.
>
> Whereas as far as regards SàRLs, GmbHs, etc. . . . [including the equivalent form of UK private company] . . . a distinction may be made between the information to be given to the members and that to be given to third parties, whereas the members thereof should be given the same information as the shareholders in an SA, AG, etc. . . ., whereas for the information of third parties the same particulars should as a general rule be disclosed as in the case of these latter types of company by reason of the fact that the liability of the members is limited, but some relief can nevertheless be allowed in the case of the smaller companies.

Whereas when a company belongs to a group only the presentation of consolidated accounts of the group can give a true and fair, as well as a complete, view of the situation of the companies concerned, whereas in anticipation of the co-ordination of national rules in the field and in view of the fact that the Commission has committed itself to submit a proposal as soon as possible, Member States will take care that consolidated accounts provided for by their legislation are established in conformity with the principle of this Directive.

Principal sections of proposed Fourth Directive

These are as follows:

General requirements (Articles 1–2).
Layout of the annual accounts (Articles 3–6).
Balance sheet layout (Articles 7–18).
Profit and loss account layout (Articles 19–27).
Valuation rules (Articles 28–38).
Contents of the notes on the accounts (Articles 40–42).
Contents of the annual report (Article 43).
Publication (Articles 44–47).
Special provisions relating to certain private companies (Articles 14–50).

UK criticisms

The main UK criticisms levelled against the original draft Fourth Directive were:

1. That there was no over-riding requirement that the accounts should give a true and fair view.
2. That the prescribed layouts of the annual accounts were too rigid.
3. That the establishment of valuation or accounting rules was not a matter for legal prescription but for the accountancy profession.
4. That there was no provision for requiring group accounts.

The True and Fair View

The amended proposal requires that "the annual accounts [defined as the balance sheet, profit and loss account and the notes on the accounts] shall give a true and fair view of the company's assets, liabilities, financial position and results". They must be drawn up clearly and in conformity with the provisions of the Directive (Article 2). This contrasts with the previous stipulation that "the annual accounts shall conform to the principles of regular and proper accounting". The original version also went on to state that the accounts "shall be drawn up clearly and, in the context of the provisions regarding the valuation of assets and liabilities and the layout of accounts, shall reflect as accurately as possible the company's assets, liabilities, financial position and results". The Groupe d'Etudes commented that the expression "as accurately as possible" was too restrictive "as it allows businessmen a freedom of interpretation which could diminish the value of the information being provided". For this reason the Groupe felt that it was necessary to introduce the notion of *fidelité* which corresponds to the UK expression "true and fair view".[16]

Speaking at a *Financial Times* conference in London, in September 1973, Fernand Braun had this to say about what he termed UK "misunderstandings as to the real import of the proposal".

> It is certainly not true that the fundamental issue of the true and fair view has been disregarded. . . . As has been clearly said in the explanatory notes, the proposal requires additional information to be given if the application of the stringent provisions of the Directive is not sufficient to reflect as accurately as possible, etc. . . . In this respect, the adoption of the proposal in its present form will have no consequences for the British concept of a true and fair view.[17]

Explaining the Commission's decision to adopt the UK formula in the amended proposal, it is stated in the Explanatory Memorandum that:

> It [the true and fair view] brings out more clearly [than the previous wording] the essential principle that the annual accounts should be drawn up in such a way as to give a true and fair view of the position of the company. This principle implies that, should the specific provisions of the Directive be of themselves insufficient to ensure that this objective is attained, the company will be legally obliged to provide further information.

Layout of the Annual Accounts

The draft proposal prescribes alternative "statement" and "account" layouts for the balance sheet as well as for two forms of profit and loss account, depending upon whether expenses are shown by type of expense or by operational centres. All of these are reproduced in Appendixes 1 and 2 at the end of this chapter. Article 3 stipulates that "the layout of the balance sheet and of the profit and loss account, particularly as regards the form adopted for their presentation, may not be changed from one year to the next", except in exceptional circumstances when an indication thereof must be given in the notes on the accounts together with an explanation of the reasons therefor. Article 4 provides some flexibility by allowing for a more detailed sub-division of the items preceded by Arabic numerals, Furthermore, the amended proposal specifies that items preceded by Arabic numerals may be regrouped where (1) they are of secondary interest only in relation to the overall requirement to give a true and fair view, or (2) such regrouping makes for greater clarity, provided that the regrouped items are dealt with in the notes on the accounts.

It may be argued that this latter amendment offers sufficient flexibility to any company, but, if it were interpreted as UK accountants would wish, it would be bound to conflict with the principal requirements of Article 3 mentioned above. It may be presumed, however, that the Directive will incorporate other alternative layouts more in line with best UK and Irish practice before it receives the approval of the Council. Appendix 3 to this chapter reproduces the draft proposals in this regard of the UK and Irish accountancy bodies.

Special provisions relating to certain items in the balance sheet.

1. *Fixed assets.* Fixed assets are defined as comprising "those elements which are intended to be used on a continuing basis to enable the undertaking to operate" (Article 12.2). The movements in the items of fixed assets must be shown in the balance sheet or in the notes on the accounts. To this end, there must be shown, starting with the purchase price or production cost, separately for each of the items of fixed assets, on the one hand the additions, disposals, transfers and upward corrections during the year, and on the other hand the cumulative value adjustments (depreciation) as at the date of the balance sheet. Where fixed assets are accounted for at replacement value or according to some other method which takes into account current values the statement of movements must include a separate mention of the cumulative amounts at the date of the balance sheet, (1) on the one hand, of differences between valuation on the replacement or other method and valuation according to the general rule of purchase price or production cost, and, (2) on the other hand, of the additional value adjustments.

Value adjustments may be shown either in the balance sheet as a clear deduction from the relevant item or in the notes on the accounts. Where the purchase price or production cost of any fixed asset cannot be determined without untoward expense or delay, the residual value at the beginning of the year may be taken instead provided that the fact is mentioned in the notes. The above provisions, except for those relating to valuation by any method other than purchase price or production costs, also apply to formation expenses. Under the item "Land and buildings" there must be shown "land not built on as well as the land built on and the buildings thereon, together with fixtures and fittings" (Article 13).

2. *Current assets.* The proposed Directive also calls for disclosure of any value adjustments (*i.e.* depreciation) to individual items of current assets. Article 12.4(a) provides that:

> Movements in the various items of current assets shall be presented in the balance sheet or the notes on the accounts. To this end there shall be shown, separately for each of the items of current assets, on the one hand the purchase price or production cost of the elements shown in the balance sheet, and on the other hand the value adjustments.

Value adjustments should be shown either in the balance sheet, as a clear deduction from the relevant item, or in the notes on the accounts. The provisions concerning the disclosure of movements as a result of the valuation of assets at replacement values or by other methods designed to take into account current values, discussed under "Fixed assets" above, apply equally to stocks.

3. *Participating interests.* The term "participating interests" is used in the Directive to mean:

> rights in the capital of other undertakings, whether or not represented by certificates which by creating a desirable link with them are intended to contribute to the activities of the company. A holding of 10 per cent of the subscribed capital of another undertaking shall be presumed to constitute a participating interest (Article 14).

4. *Associated undertakings.* Although the Fourth Directive contains numerous references to associated undertakings, these are nowhere defined. The commentary on Article 51 of the proposal explains that a definition will be given in a subsequent Directive on consolidated accounts, and for this reason it has been provided that the obligation to give the particulars required in respect of associated undertakings will enter into force at the same time as this later Directive. It seems clear, however, that the draughtsman is primarily thinking of what are commonly referred to as subsidiary companies.

5. *Pre-payments.* This item includes "expenditure incurred during the year but relating to a subsequent year, together with the earnings relating to the year, to the extent that they will not be received until after the close of the year" (Article 15). The latter, however, may also be shown under "Debtors". Where the amount involved is considerable, an explanation must be given in the notes.

6. *Provisions for contingencies and charges.* Provision for contingencies and charges under the Directive are intended:

> to cover either the certain cost of major maintenance work or of major repairs which will be incurred in the course of subsequent years, or losses or charges the nature of which is clearly defined but which at the date of the balance sheet are either likely to be incurred or are certain to be incurred but are indeterminate as to amount or as to the date on which they will arise (Article 17).

Such provisions may not be used to adjust the value of assets.
7. *Accruals.* Under accruals there must be shown "income received before the date of the balance sheet but attributable to a subsequent year, together with charges which, though relating to the year in question, will only be paid in the course of a subsequent year" (Article 18). The latter may also be shown under "Creditors". Where the amount involved is considerable, an explanation must be given in the notes.

Special provisions relating to certain items in the profit and loss account.
1. *Turnover.* Article 25 states that "turnover includes receipts from sales of products, goods and services falling within the usual operation of the company, after allowing for any price deduction in respect of those sales and for value added tax and other taxes directly tied to turnover".
2. *Exceptional earnings and exceptional charges.* Under this item there must be shown "earnings and charges that are attributable to another year together with any earnings and charges that do not arise out of the usual operations of the undertaking" (Article 26). Unless such items are immaterial, explanations of their amount and nature must be given in the notes.
3. *Taxes on the result.* There must be shown separately the actual amount of taxes payable for the year, and the amount of the future liability to tax.

Valuation Rules

Dr Elmendorff reports that the members of his committee found it "relatively easy to agree on generally accepted valuation rules".[18] Here again the Continental tradition differs from that of the United Kingdom; indeed, of all those countries it is only the Netherlands and Denmark which are approaching the problem of accounting standards in the same way as the UK and Irish professions, although Danish law also prescribes some broad valuation rules. The Groupe d'Etudes did not press for the removal of these rules but merely commented in the first memorandum that "the valuation rules proposed in the draft Directive only cover certain of the generally accepted accounting principles".

General principles. In the second memorandum the Groupe d'Etudes recommended the inclusion of the four fundamental accounting concepts defined in the UK SSAP 2 and these the Commission has accepted as follows:

1. The company shall be presumed to continue its business as a going concern.
2. The methods of valuation may not be changed from one year to another.
3. Valuation must be made on a conservative basis, and in particular:
   (a) Only the profits earned at the date of the balance sheet may be included in it; account shall nevertheless be taken of all contingencies foreseeable at that date.
   (b) Account shall be taken of any deficiencies that do not become apparent until after the date of the balance sheet, but which do become apparent before it is drawn up, if they arise in the course of the year to which the annual accounts relate.
   (c) Account shall be taken of any depreciation, whether the year closes with a loss or with a profit.
4. Account shall be taken of earnings and charges arising during the year to which the accounts relate, irrespective of the date of receipt of payment of such earnings or charges.
5. The components of the asset and liability items shall be valued separately.
6. The opening balance sheet for each year shall correspond to the closing balance sheet for the preceding year.

Departures from the above general principles are permitted only in exceptional circumstances, in which case each departure must be stated and justified in the notes on the accounts.

Historic cost and replacement value. Article 29 of the proposed Directive states that, in general, valuation must be based on purchase price or production cost. Notwithstanding this provision it is also stated that the Member States may authorise:

1. For tangible fixed assets with a limited useful life, and for stocks, valuation by the replacement value method.
2. For tangible fixed assets, for participating interests and other financial assets, and for stocks, valuation by methods other than that mentioned in (1), and which take into account current values.

Where these provisions are applied, the amount of the difference between valuation by the replacement value method, or other methods as above, and valuation in accordance with the general rule of purchase price or production cost, must be shown under liabilities as a "revaluation reserve" with any future taxation being shown clearly as a deduction. This item should be subdivided into:

1. Reserve for tangible fixed assets.
2. Reserve for participating interests and other financial assets.
3. Reserve for stocks.

The revaluation reserve must be reduced "to the extent that the amounts transferred thereto are no longer necessary to maintain the potential of the undertaking" (Article 30.4). The amounts in question have to be added to the result for the year and shown separately in the profit and loss account. Value adjustments are to be calculated each year on the basis of the value shown for the year in question.

Apart from this, the Member States have the power to authorise revaluation of the tangible fixed assets, participating interests and other financial assets, in which case provisions similar to those stated above apply (the revaluation reserve must be reduced to the extent that the increases in value concerned have been actually realised). Where such authorisation is availed of by a company, full particulars of the method, and the balance sheet and profit and loss account items concerned, must be given in the notes.

Formation expenses, goodwill and research and development expenses. Where capitalised, all of the above items must be written off over a maximum period of five years. No distribution of profits may take place until formation expenses and research and development expenses have been written off, or are fully covered by reserves. It is not clear whether goodwill arising on consolidation falls within these provisions. All of the items must be explained in the notes.

Here the Commission has ignored the Groupe d'Etudes' recommendation that R & D and goodwill acquired for valuable consideration should be amortised over a prudent estimate of their useful lives.

Fixed assets. Fixed assets should be valued at purchase price or production cost and those having a limited useful life should "be reduced by value adjustments calculated according to a method that satisfies the requirements of good management" (Article 33.1(b)). Value adjustments must be made in respect of all fixed assets, whether or not their useful life is limited, so that they are valued at the lowest figure to be attributed to them at the balance sheet date if it is expected that the depreciation in value will be permanent.

Participating interests, and other financial interests, are to be valued at the lowest figure to be attributed to them at the date of the balance sheet. Unlike the situation in Germany, valuation at the lowest figure must be discontinued if the reasons for which the value adjustments were made have ceased to apply. Any exceptional value adjustments to fixed assets, solely for the purpose of fiscal law, must be disclosed together with the relevant future taxation. All value adjustments must be shown separately in the profit and loss account.

The production costs of fixed assets are stated to include the manufacturing costs directly attributable to the product as well as a reasonable proportion of the indirect manufacturing costs attributable to the product to the extent that they relate to the period of manufacture. Interest on capital borrowed to finance the manufacture of fixed assets may also be included in production cost to the extent that it relates to the period of manufacture. This must be disclosed in the notes. The possibility of including interest in the company's own capital has been excluded on the recommendation of the Groupe d'Etudes. Tangible fixed assets, and raw and auxiliary materials, which are constantly being replaced and of which the overall value is of secondary importance to the undertaking, may be shown under assets at a fixed quantity and value, if the quantity, value and composition thereof do not vary appreciably.

Current assets. Article 36 provides that current assets must be valued at the lowest figure attributable to them at the date of the balance sheet. The Member States may authorise exceptional value adjustments "if, on the basis of reasonable commercial assessment, these are necessary so that the valuation of these items does not have to be modified in the near future because of fluctuations in value" (Article 36.1(c)). Valuation at the lowest figure must be discontinued if the reasons for the adjustments have ceased to apply. Such value adjustments must be shown separately in the profit and loss account. As with fixed assets, when current assets are subject to exceptional value adjustments solely for the purpose of fiscal law these and all other exceptional value adjustments must be disclosed.

Stocks. Article 37 provides that, apart from actual cost, the purchase price or production cost of stocks of goods in the same category may be calculated either on the basis of weighted average prices or by the FIFO, LIFO or some similar method. If the amount shown differs considerably from the actual cost the difference must be disclosed in the notes.

Discount on debentures. Where the amount of any debt repayable is greater than the amount received, the difference may be shown as an asset. It must be shown separately on the balance sheet or the notes on the accounts and written off not later than the time when repayment of the debt is due.

Provisions for contingencies and charges. Provisions for contingencies and charges shall not exceed in amount the sums which a reasonable businessman would consider necessary.

Group Accounts

The greatest weakness of the proposal for a Fourth Directive is the absence of any simultaneous provisions governing the preparation of group accounts. If only for this reason it is difficult to see what relevance it can have to UK companies who have been preparing consolidated accounts since 1948.

Preparation of the *avant-projet* for the proposed Directive on consolidated accounts began early in 1974 when the Commission appointed a working party consisting of Dr Elmendorff and Stanley Wilkins, one of his partners in the London office of Deloitte, Haskins & Sells, which was expected to report back before the end of the year. It would be most regrettable if the Commission is not prepared to delay implementation of the Fourth Directive until the consolidations Directive is also ready.

Contents of the Notes on the Accounts

In general, Article 40 of the amended proposal provides that "the notes on the accounts shall contain commentary on the balance sheet and profit and loss account in such manner as to give a true and fair view of the company's assets, liabilities, financial position and results". In addition to the information required under other provisions of the Directive the notes on the accounts must set out information in respect of the following matters in any event.

1. The valuation methods applied to the various items in the annual accounts, and the methods employed in calculating the value adjustments. For foreign currency debtors and creditors, the method used for calculating the rate of exchange must be shown.

2. The name and head office address of each of the undertakings in which the company holds at least 10 per cent of the capital, showing the proportion of the capital held and the amount of the subscribed capital, the

amount of the reserves and the results for the latest business year of the undertaking concerned.

3. The way in which the authorised capital has been employed, if any such capital has been created[19].

4. Whether there are any entitlements carrying the right to a share of profits, and whether there are any convertible debentures or similar securities or rights, specifying the number thereof and what rights they confer.

5. The overall amount of the financial commitments that are not shown in the balance sheet, in so far as this information is of assistance in assessing the financial position. Commitments existing with regard to associated undertakings have to be shown separately.

6. The net amount of turnover within the meaning of Article 25 of the Directive, broken down by categories of products and activities and by geographical markets. The amount contributed by each category and market to the result for the year must be indicated.

7. The number of persons employed during the year, broken down by categories, and, if they are not shown separately in the profit and loss account, the whole of the personnel costs relating to the accounting period, broken down as provided by item 20.1.6 of the first alternative profit and loss account layout (Appendix 2 to this chapter).

8. The taxes included in the operating result, the financial result or exceptional result.

9. The amount of the changes in the result for the year due to the application of fiscal laws.

10. The amount of the emoluments granted during the year to the members of the administrative, managerial and supervisory bodies by reason of their responsibilities, and any commitments arising or entered into in respect of retirement pensions for ex-members of those bodies, showing the total for each category.

11. The amount of advances and credits granted to the members of administrative, managerial and supervisory bodies, and commitments entered into on their account by way of guarantees of any kind, showing the total for each category.

The Member States are given authority to allow the items mentioned in Note 2 to be either (1) deposited for inspection in accordance with the provision of the First Directive, in order to avoid overloading the notes, or (2) omitted where in the opinion of a reasonable businessman they would be seriously prejudicial to any of the undertakings concerned. In that case the omission must be mentioned in the notes.

Contents of the Annual Report

Apart from the annual accounts the proposed Fourth Directive also contains a few simple provisions concerning the contents of the annual report, *i.e.* the management or directors' report: Article 43 states that "the annual report shall contain a detailed review of the development of the company's business and of its position". The report must give particulars of:

1. Any important events that have occurred since the close of the business year.
2. The company's likely future development.
3. The activities in the field of research and development and the costs thereof.

The Preparation, Adoption and Publication of the Annual Financial Statements

Article 11.2 of the proposal for a Fifth Directive provides that the board of management must, within three months following the end of each financial year, present to the supervisory board the draft annual accounts and draft annual report in accordance with the proposed Fourth Directive. Article 48 of the same Directive states that the annual accounts shall be adopted by the general meeting, but it is left to the Member States to choose between giving exclusive or subsidiary competence thereto. Under the latter system, as is the case in Germany, the supervisory and management boards adopt the accounts and the general meeting does no more than act as arbitrator between them.

The Groupe d'Etudes has recommended that the Directive should specify a period of months within which the annual accounts should be presented to the general meeting.

In accordance with Article 49 of the Fifth Directive proposal, 5 per cent of the result of each year, reduced where appropriate by losses brought forward from previous years, must be appropriated to a legal reserve until that reserve amounts to not less than 10 per cent of the capital subscribed. So long as the legal reserve does not exceed this amount it cannot be used except to set off losses and then only if other reserves are inadequate for that purpose. The general meeting has the power to decide on the appropriation of the results, reduced where permissible by losses from previous years, but the company statutes may provide that the board of management is to appropriate up to 50 per cent of the result.

Section II of the amended proposal for a Second Directive contains detailed and stringent provisions concerning the "maintenance of the integrity of the company's capital" and lays down precise rules as to when it is permissible to pay dividends. In general, except as specified in the Directive, no distribution may be made to the shareholders "when the net assets of a company fall below the amount of the subscribed capital plus the unavailable reserves".

The proposed Fourth Directive provides that the annual accounts duly approved and the annual report, together with the auditors' report (*see* below), must be filed without delay for public inspection in accordance with the First Directive. Furthermore, the annual accounts and the auditors' report must be published in full in a national gazette designated by the Member State. This latter provision, which is specifically designed to cater for the bearer share system prevailing throughout the Continental EEC countries, apart from Italy, is both unnecessary and impractical as far as the United Kingdom is concerned. Article 45 of the proposed Fourth Directive also provides that:

> on any other occasion when publication is made in full, the annual accounts and report shall be reproduced in like form and text on the basis of which the person responsible for auditing the accounts drew up his report. They shall be accompanied by the full text of the certificate. If the person responsible for auditing the accounts made any qualifications or refused to certify the accounts, the fact shall be stated, and reasons given.

In any cases where the accounts are not published in full (*e.g.* for publicity purposes) it must be stated that the version published is abridged and reference made to the national gazette in which they were published. It must also be stated whether the auditors' certificate was with or without qualification or was refused. Finally, Article 47 requires that there should be published along with the annual accounts, and in like manner, (1) the proposed allocation of the result and (2) the allocation of the results in cases where these items do not appear in the annual accounts.

Application of the Fourth Directive to Private Companies of the SàRL/GmbH Type

The Fourth Directive is not intended to apply uniformly to all companies regardless of size. The extent of the disclosure required is linked to the size of the company in accordance with the First Directive. So-called public companies of the SA/AG type are, with one exception, subject to the full provisions. Private companies of the SàRL/GmbH type are divided into three categories, depending upon their importance to the national economy and the EEC. Those in the first category are subject to the same publicity requirements as the SA/AG form of company. So far as the second category is concerned, Member States have the same powers of exemption as are provided in Article 24 in respect of the SA/AG of comparable size. Thus the profit and loss account need not show the net turnover separately. Companies in the third category may be exempted by the Member States from the publication of the profit and loss account and need only publish an abridged form of balance sheet. The solutions adopted are summarised in Table 10.1.

TABLE 10.1. APPLICATION OF THE FOURTH DIRECTIVE TO PRIVATE COMPANIES OF THE SàRL/GmbH TYPE

Categories	*Balance sheet total in units of account*	*Net turnover in units of account*	*Average no. of employees over the year*	*Disclosure required*
I. See Art. 50.1	Exceeding 1 million	Exceeding 2 million	Exceeding 100	Annual accounts, annual report, auditors' report
II. See Art. 50.2(a)	From 100,000 to 1 million	From 200,001 to 2 million	From 21 to 100	As for I; the national law may provide that the profit and loss account need not compulsorily show the net turnover separately
III. See Art. 50.2(b)	Up to 100,000	Up to 200,000	Up to 20	As for I; the national law may provide that publication of an abridged balance sheet and abridged notes on the accounts is sufficient

Transfer to the second or to the first category takes place when any one of the conditions applicable to these categories is satisfied.
The above table first appeared in the notes to the original proposal for a Fourth Directive.

An abridged balance sheet must at least show those items preceded by letters and Roman numerals with separate particulars of

1. The information required by the provisions in brackets under items D.II of the assets and E of the liabilities in Article 8 (Appendix 1) and under items D.II, E and I in Article 9, but showing the total for the items concerned.
2. Claims on debts to members.
3. Notes on the accounts but not necessarily including the explanation required in the case of Notes 4 to 11.

Full publication of the balance sheet and notes in a national gazette is not required in the case of companies in the second and third categories. It is sufficient to file the necessary information in accordance with the First Directive. Once approved, the Directive allows the Member States a period of 18 months in which to make the necessary amendments to their laws, and in addition a further period of 12 months is allowed for bringing these amendments into force.

AUDITING

The Commission's proposals for the harmonisation of the laws relating to the audit of the annual accounts of companies are primarily contained in the draft Fifth Directive. In common with the other proposals, the Directive was drafted and published before the enlargement of the Community. However, since it seems probable that the provisions relating to two-tier boards and worker participation will require some amendment to be acceptable to the United Kingdom, it is also possible that those dealing with the audit of the accounts will be subject to some revision. Furthermore, although proposed Directives on professional law dealing with freedom of establishment and freedom to supply services have been published and the working draft of a Directive concerning the minimum educational qualifications of auditors has been released, these are still far from complete. For all these reasons this section is restricted to the essential requirements as laid down in the proposal for a Fifth Directive.

Appointment of auditors

Article 51.1 states that one or more persons shall be made responsible for auditing the accounts. The auditors must be appointed by the general meeting, but where such appointment is not made in due time or where any of the persons appointed is unable to carry out his duties, the board of management, the supervisory board or any shareholder has the right to apply to the court for appointment of one or more persons to audit the accounts. Only persons who are nominated or approved by a judicial or administrative authority may be charged with responsibility for auditing the accounts. The auditors are to be appointed for a certain period of not less than three years or more than six years; they may be reappointed.

Article 49 of the proposal for a Fourth Directive provides that the Member States may exempt from the requirements to undergo a statutory audit those SàRL-type companies falling into category III mentioned above (page 339), namely:

1. Their balance sheet does not exceed 100,000 units of account.
2. Their net turnover does not exceed 200,000 units of account.
3. Their average number of employees during the year did not exceed 20.

Duties of auditors

The auditor must examine whether the annual accounts and the annual report are "in conformity with the law and the statutes" (Article 58.1). On the basis of the amended proposal for a Fourth Directive this provision should therefore be amended to require an examination as to whether the annual accounts give a true and fair view of the company's assets, liabilities, financial position and results.

The auditors' report

Article 58 of the proposed Directive states that "if they have no reservation to make, the persons responsible for the audit shall so certify on the annual accounts; otherwise they shall issue their certificate subject to reservations or shall refuse their certificate". As is the case in Germany and Denmark, the Fifth Directive envisages two separate audit reports—one the attestation as above and in addition a detailed report relating to the results of the auditor's work. Article 60 provides that the detailed report shall contain the following at least:

1. An indication of whether the provisions concerning their appointment as laid down by Article 51(1) have been observed.
2. Observations concerning any infringements of law or of the statutes which have been found in the company's accounts, in its annual accounts or in the management report.
3. Observations concerning any facts noted which constitute a serious danger to the financial situation of the company.
4. The complete text of the certificate given pursuant to Article 58, as above. Where reservations have been made or where the certificate has been withheld, the reasons therefore must be specified.

From a reading of Article 44 of the amended Fourth Directive proposal, which requires the publication of the annual accounts, together with the auditors' report "as referred to in Article 60" of the Fifth Directive, it appears, but is surely inconceivable, that the Commission wishes to have the long-form report, and not the attestation, published with the accounts.

Fieldwork

Article 59 of the proposed Directive provides that "the persons responsible for auditing the accounts shall be entitled to obtain from the company all information and relevant documents, and to undertake all such investigations, as may be necessary". The question of whether this right applies to other group companies is to be dealt with in the Directive on consolidated accounts.

Remuneration of auditors

The remuneration of the auditors "shall be fixed for the whole of their period of office before it commences" (Article 57.1) and no other remuneration may be paid in respect of their auditing of the accounts. It is made clear that the total amount need not be fixed exactly in advance but reference may be made to a scale.

Removal of auditors

The proposed Directive provides in Article 61 that the auditors shall not be dismissed by the general meeting before the end of their period of office, "save where proper grounds exist". Apart from this, Article 55.3 states that the court must have power to dismiss, where there are proper grounds, any person appointed by the general meeting to audit the accounts, and must also have power to appoint some other person for that purpose if application is made by the management organ, supervisory organ or one or more shareholders constituting an adequate minority.

Liability of auditors

Similar provisions in respect of civil liability as those applicable to members of the management and supervisory boards apply to auditors "so as to ensure that compensation is made for any damage sustained by the company, any shareholder or third party as a result of wrongful acts committed by those persons . . . in carrying out their dutes" (Article 62).

In a memorandum submitted to the Commission in July 1974 the Groupe d'Etudes pointed out that these proposals are likely to have unforeseen consequences on the existing law of Member States, since alien elements will be grafted on to the existing national legal structures with their own highly developed system of checks and balances.

The memorandum points out that it is contrary to natural justice to reverse the burden of proof (Article 14.2), so that an auditor accused of negligence must prove that no fault is attributable to him; and that it is misleading and dangerous to encourage shareholders and others to believe that auditors have unlimited means to make good any loss of any amount to any number of plaintiffs.

The Groupe d'Etude's main conclusions are summarised as follows:

1. Member States should clarify the legal liability of auditors where loss has been suffered through reliance on an auditors' report along the lines suggested below.
2. Proceedings should be brought against auditors only after all proper rights of recourse against the company's officers have been exhausted.
3. Where there has been deliberate misfeasance by the auditors, they should be liable to make restitution in full.
4. Where loss has been caused by the auditors' unintentional negligence their liability should be limited to 10 times the audit fee concerned; but this limit should not apply if the loss is under 100,000 units of account (£40,000), and there should be an absolute ceiling to auditors' liability of 1,000,000 units of account (£400,000).
5. Auditors shall be jointly and severally liable for negligence, but individuals may be exonerated from joint liability if they can show that no blame is attributable to them.
6. The court may reduce the amount of damages payable if the auditors can show mitigating circumstances (*i.e.* contributory negligence only).
7. The time limit for bringing a negligence action against auditors should be three years from the date of publication of the audit report concerned, or, if the fault has been concealed, three years from its discovery.
8. Auditors must take out professional liability insurance up to the potential amount of damages for each audit and must prove that they have the relevant cover to their professional accountancy body.

Independence of auditors

Above all, the provisions of the Fifth Directive are designed to ensure the independence of the auditor. Articles 53 and 54 contain the following provisions:

> The audit of the accounts shall in no case be undertaken by persons who are members, or who during the last three years have been members, of the management organ, supervisory organ or staff of the company whose accounts are to be audited.
>
> Further, the audit of the accounts shall in no case be undertaken by companies or firms whose members or partners, members of the management organ or supervisory organ, or of which the persons who have power of

representation are members, or during the last three years have been members, of the management organ, supervisory organ or staff of the company whose accounts are to be audited.

The persons who have audited the accounts shall in no case be, or for a period of three years following the cessation of their duties become, members of the management organ, supervisory organ or staff of the company whose accounts have been audited.

Further, the members or partners, members of the management organ or supervisory organ, or the persons who have power of representation of the companies or firms who have audited the accounts, shall in no case become members of the management organ, supervisory organ or staff of the company whose accounts have been audited, less than three years after cessation of their duties.

Nullity or voidability of the annual accounts

Without prejudice to rights required in good faith by third parties, all resolutions adopting the annual accounts are void or voidable where:

1. The annual accounts have not been audited in conformity with the Directive.
2. The certificate relating to the annual accounts has been refused.
3. The annual accounts have not been audited by a person nominated or approved in accordance with the Directive.
4. The annual accounts have been audited by a person who should not have been made responsible for the audit, or who has been dismissed by the court or by the general meeting where proper grounds exist.
5. The annual accounts have been audited by a person who was not appointed by the general meeting or was not appointed by the court.

Proceedings for nullity or voidability may be brought "at least by any shareholder" (Article 63).

REFERENCES

1. Common Market Treaty, Rome, 25 March 1957.
2. *Industrial Policy and the European Community* (Commission of the European Communities, November 1972), page 5.
3. In the implementation of the Rome Treaty the Council and Commission issue regulations, directives, decisions, recommendations and opinions. Regulations are of general application, they are binding in every respect and they have direct force of law in every Member State. Directives are binding on the Member States to which they are addressed as regards the result to be achieved, but leave the mode and means to the discretion of the national

authorities. Decisions may be addressed either to a Government or to an enterprise or private individual; they are binding in every respect on the party or parties named. Recommendations and opinions are not binding.

4. *Official Journal*, 24 April 1970.
5. One unit of account is equivalent to one US dollar at the pre-devaluation rate of exchange, *i.e.* prior to 1972.
6. *Official Journal*, 14 July 1970.
7. *Official Journal*, 28 January 1972.
8. *Official Journal*, 13 December 1972.
9. *Ibid.*
10. *Cf.* reference 3 above.
11. *Official Journal*, 10 October 1970. The Commission at its meeting in Luxembourg on 30 April 1975 approved a revised proposal for the European company statute.
12. "Explanatory Memorandum to the Amended Proposal for a Fourth Council Directive", page I.
13. Rudolph Niehus, "Harmonised EEC Accounting: A German View of the Draft Directive for Uniform Accounting Rules", *The International Journal of Accounting Education and Research*, Vol. 2, pages 91–125.
14. "Uniform Code of European Company Law" (Institute of Chartered Accountants in England and Wales, 16 January 1970), Ref. 16-5-1.
15. The Council of Ministers and the Commission are assisted by the Economic and Social Committee, a consultative body (of 144 members) representing a cross-section of economic interests in the Community. Although it has no powers of decision, the Committee exercises a strong influence on policy making.
16. "Groupe d'Etudes' Observations on the Proposed Fourth Directive: 26.6.72", (Institute of Chartered Accountants in England and Wales), page 1, Ref. 16-5-1.
17. Reproduced in *The Accountant*, 20 September 1973, pages 363–366.
18. "Co-ordination of the legal accountancy requirements of the various countries of the European Economic Community", *Journal UEC*, October 1967, page 217 *et seq.*
19. Despite extensive enquiries it has not been possible for the author to determine what this provision is intended to mean.

Appendix 1

THE TWO ALTERNATIVE FORMS OF BALANCE SHEET LAID DOWN IN THE PROPOSED FOURTH DIRECTIVE

ARTICLE 8

Assets

A. *Subscribed capital UNPAID*
—of which there has been called.

B. *Formation expenses in so far as the national law permits them to be recorded as assets.*

C. *Fixed assets:*

I. Intangible assets:
1 Cost of research and development in so far as the national law permits them to be recorded as assets.
2 Concessions, patents, licences, trade marks, and similar rights and values, if they were:
(a) acquired for valuable consideration and are not to be shown under C(I)(3).
(b) created by the undertaking itself, in so far as the national law permits them to be recorded as assets.
3 Goodwill, to the extent that it was acquired for valuable consideration.
4 Payments on account.

II. Tangible assets:
1 Land and buildings.
2 Plant and machinery.
3 Other fixtures, tools and equipment.
4 Payments on account and tangible assets in process of construction.

III. Participating interests and other financial assets:
1 Holdings in associated undertakings.
2 Claims on associated undertakings.
3 Participating interests.
4 Claims on undertakings with which the company is associated by virtue of a participating interest.
5 Securities ranking as fixed assets.
6 Other claims.
7 Own shares (indicating their nominal value or proportionate value) to the extent that the national law permits them to be included in the balance sheet.

D. *Current assets:*

I. Stocks
1 Raw and auxiliary materials.
2 Goods in course of production and waste products.
3 Finished products and stock in hand.
4 Payments on account.

II. Debtors:
(Amounts becoming due and payable within one year shall be shown separately for each item.)
1 Claims in respect of sales and services rendered.
2 Claims on associated undertakings.
3 Claims on undertakings in which the company has a participating interest.
4 Other claims.

III. Securities forming part of the current assets, and liquid assets:
1 Holdings in associated undertakings.
2 Bills of exchange.

Appendix 1—*continued*

3 Bank balances, postal cheque account balances, cheques and cash in hand.
4 Own shares (indicating their nominal value or proportionate value) to the extent that the national law permits them to be included in the balance sheet.
5 Other securities.

E. Pre-payments.

F. Loss:
(in so far as the losses are not shown under liabilities)

I. For the year.
II. Brought forward.

Liabilities

A. Subscribed capital
(The shares must be shown by classes, indicating their nominal value or proportionate value.)

B. Reserves:
1 Legal reserve.
2 Share premium account.
3 Revaluation reserve.
4 Reserve for own shares.
5 Statutory reserves.
6 Optional reserves.

C. Total of subscribed capital and reserves, less losses, in so far as these are not shown under assets
(the result for the year and results brought forward must be shown as separate items).

D. Provisions for contingencies and charges:
1 Provisions for pensions and similar obligations.
2 Provisions for taxation including future taxation.
3 Other provisions.

E. Creditors:
(Amounts becoming due and payable within one year, amounts becoming due and payable after more than five years, and amounts covered by valuable security furnished by the company, must be shown separately for each item.)
1 Debenture loans, showing convertible loans separately.
2 Debts to credit institutions.
3 Payments received on account of orders.
4 Debts in respect of purchases and services received.
5 Debts represented by bills of exchange.
6 Debts to associated undertakings.
7 Debts to undertakings with which the company is associated by virtue of a participating interest.
8 Other creditors.

F. Accruals.

G. Profit:

I. For the year.
II. Brought forward.

ARTICLE 9

A. Subscribed capital UNPAID
—of which there has been called.

B. Formation expenses in so far as the national law permits them to be recorded as assets.

Appendix 1—*continued*

C. Fixed assets:

I. Intangible assets:
1 Cost of research and development, in so far as the national law permits them to be recorded as assets.
2 Concessions, patents, licences, trade marks, and similar rights and values, if they were:
(a) acquired for valuable consideration and are not to be shown under C(I)(3).
(b) created by the undertaking itself, in so far as the national law permits them to be recorded as assets.
3 Goodwill, to the extent that it was acquired for valuable consideration.
4 Payments on account.

II. Tangible assets:
1 Land and buildings.
2 Plant and machinery.
3 Other fixtures, tools and equipment.
4 Payments on account and tangible assets in process of construction.

III. Participating interests and other financial assets:
1 Holdings in associated undertakings.
2 Claims on associated undertakings.
3 Participating interests.
4 Claims on undertakings with which the company is associated by virtue of a participating interest.
5 Securities ranking as fixed assets.
6 Other claims.
7 Own shares (indicating their nominal value or proportionate value) to the extent that the national law permits them to be included in the balance sheet.

D. Current assets.

I. Stocks:
1 Raw and auxiliary materials.
2 Goods in course of production and waste products.
3 Finished products and stock in hand.
4 Payments on account.

II. Debtors:
(Amounts becoming due and payable within one year must be shown separately in each case.)
1 Claims in respect of sales and services rendered.
2 Claims on associated undertakings.

Appendix 1—*continued*

3 Claims on undertakings with which the company is associated by virtue of a participating interest.
4 Other claims.

III. Securities forming part of the current assets, and liquid assets:
1 Holdings in associated undertakings.
2 Bills of exchange.
3 Bank balances, postal cheque account balances, cheques and cash in hand.
4 Own shares (indicating their nominal value or proportionate value) to the extent that the national law permits them to be included in the balance sheet.
5 Other securities.

E. Pre-payments.

F. Debts becoming due and payable within one year:
(Amounts covered by valuable security furnished by the company must be shown separately for each item.)
1 Debenture loans, showing convertible loans separately.
2 Debts to credit institutions.
3 Payments received on account of orders.
4 Debts in respect of purchases and services received.
5 Debts represented by bills of exchange.
6 Debts to associated undertakings.
7 Debts to undertakings with which the company is associated by virtue of a participating interest.
8 Other debts.

G. Current assets in excess of the debts becoming due and payable within one year.

H. Total amount of asset items after deduction of the debts becoming due and payable within one year.

I. Creditors for amounts becoming due and payable after more than one year:
(Amounts becoming due and payable after more than five years and amounts covered by valuable security furnished by the company must be shown separately for each item.)
1 Debenture loans, showing convertible loans separately.
2 Debts to credit institutions.
3 Payments received on account of orders.
4 Debts in respect of purchases and services received.
5 Debts represented by bills of exchange.
6 Debts to associated undertakings.
7 Debts to undertakings with which the company is associated by virtue of a participating interest.
8 Other creditors.

Appendix 1—*continued*

J. Provisions for contingencies and charges:

1 Provisions for pensions and similar obligations.

2 Provisions for taxation, including future taxation.

3 Other provisions.

K. Accruals.

L. Subscribed capital.

(The shares must be shown by classes, indicating their nominal value or proportionate value.)

M. Reserves:

1 Legal reserve.

2 Share premium account.

3 Revaluation reserve.

4 Reserve for own shares.

5 Statutory reserves.

6 Optional reserves.

N. Result for the year.

O. Results brought forward.

Appendix 2

THE FOUR ALTERNATIVE FORMS OF PROFIT AND LOSS ACCOUNT LAID DOWN IN THE PROPOSED FOURTH DIRECTIVE

ARTICLE 20

I. Operating result (excluding any earnings and charges shown under II):

1 Net turnover.
2 Changes in stocks of finished and semi-finished products.
3 Work effected by the undertaking for its own account and shown under assets.
4 Other operating receipts.
5 Cost of raw and auxiliary materials.
6 Staff costs.
(a) Wages and salaries.
(b) Compulsory social security costs.
(c) Other social security costs, showing as a separate item those relating to old age pensions.
7 (a) Value adjustments in respect of formation expenses and of tangible and intangible fixed assets.
(b) Value adjustments in respect of elements of current assets.
8 Other operating expenses.
9 Operating result.

II. Financial result:

10 Earnings from participating interests, showing separately those derived from associated undertakings.
11 Earnings from other securities and from claims forming part of the fixed assets, showing separately those derived from associated undertakings.
12 Other interest and similar earnings, showing separately those derived from associated undertakings.
13 Value adjustments in respect of participating interests and other financial assets and of securities forming part of the current assets.
14 Interest and similar charges, showing separately those concerning associated undertakings.
15 Financial result.

III. Exceptional result:

16 Exceptional earnings.
17 Exceptional charges.
18 Exceptional result.

IV. Sub-total.

Appendix 2—*continued*

V. Taxes:
- 19 Taxes on the result:
  - —actual.
  - —future.
- 20 Other taxes not shown under I, II or III above.

VI. Result for the year.

ARTICLE 21

A. Charges:

I. Operating expenses (excluding any shown under II):
- 1 Reduction in the stock of finished and semi-finished products.
- 2 Cost of raw and auxiliary materials.
- 3 Staff costs:
  - (a) Wages and salaries.
  - (b) Compulsory social security costs.
  - (c) Other social security costs, showing as a separate item those relating to old age pensions.
- 4 (a) Value adjustments in respect of formation expenses and of tangible and intangible fixed assets.
  - (b) Value adjustments in respect of elements of current assets.
- 5 Other operating expenses.

II. Financial charges:
- 1 Value adjustments in respect of participating interests and other financial assets and of securities forming part of the current assets.
- 2 Interest and similar charges, showing separately those concerning associated undertakings.

III. Exceptional charges.

IV. Taxes:
- 1 Taxes on the result: —actual.
  - —future.
- 2 Other taxes not shown under I, II and III above.

V. Result for the year.

B. Receipts:

I. Operating receipts (excluding any shown under II):
- 1 Net turnover.
- 2 Increase in stocks of finished and semi-finished products.
- 3 Work effected by the undertaking for its own account and shown under assets.
- 4 Other operating receipts.

II. Financial earnings:
- 1 Earnings from participating interests, showing separately those derived from associated undertakings.
- 2 Earnings from other securities and from claims forming part of the fixed assets, showing separately those derived from associated undertakings.
- 3 Other interest and similar earnings, showing separately those derived from associated undertakings.

III. Exceptional earnings.

IV. Result for the year.

Appendix 2—*continued*

ARTICLE 22

I. Operating result (excluding any earnings and charges shown under II):

1 Net turnover.
2 Production costs of output supplied and making-up the turnover (including value adjustments).
3. Gross result achieved from turnover.
4. Distribution expenses (including value adjustments).
5 Administrative expenses (including value adjustments).
6 Other operating receipts.
7 Operating result.

II. Financial result:

8 Earnings from participating interests, showing separately those derived from associated undertakings.
9 Earnings from other securities and from claims forming part of the fixed assets, showing separately those derived from associated undertakings.
10 Other interest and similar earnings, showing separately those derived from associated undertakings.
11 Value adjustments in respect of participating interests and other financial fixed assets and of securities forming part of the current assets.
12 Interest and similar charges, showing separately those concerning undertakings.
13 Financial result.

III. Exceptional result:

14 Exceptional earnings.
15 Exceptional charges.
16 Exceptional result.

IV. Sub-Total.

V. Taxes:

17 Taxes on the result:
—actual.
—future.
18 Other taxes not shown under I, II or III above.

VI. Result for the year.

Appendix 2—*continued*

ARTICLE 23

A. Charges:

I. Operating expenses (excluding any shown under II):
  1 Production costs of output supplied and making-up the turnover (including value adjustments).
  2 Distribution expenses (including value adjustments).
  3 Administrative expenses (including value adjustments).

II. Financial charges:
  1 Value adjustments in respect of participating interests and other financial fixed assets and of securities forming part of the current assets.
  2 Interest and similar charges, showing separately those concerning associated undertakings.

III. Exceptional charges.

IV. Taxes:
  1 Taxes on the result:
    —actual.
    —future.
  2 Other taxes not shown under I, II or III above.

V. Result for the year.

B. Receipts:

I. Operating receipts (excluding any shown under II):
  1 Net turnover.
  2 Other operating receipts.

II. Financial earnings:
  1 Earnings from participating interests, showing separately those derived from associated undertakings.
  2 Earnings from other securities and from claims forming part of the fixed assets, showing separately those derived from associated undertakings.
  3 Other interest and similar earnings, showing separately those derived from associated undertakings.

III. Exceptional earnings.

IV. Result for the year.

Appendix 3

PROPOSED STANDARD LAYOUT OF COMPANY ACCOUNTS FOR EEC COMPANY LAW

Alternative layout of annual accounts for incorporation in the proposed Fourth Directive prepared for discussion by a working party of:

Institute of Chartered Accountants in England and Wales
Institute of Chartered Accountants of Scotland
Institute of Chartered Accountants in Ireland
Association of Certified Accountants
Institute of Cost and Management Accountants

BALANCE SHEET

	1975			1974		
	Cost or valuation	*accumulated depreciation*		*Cost or valuation*	*accumulated depreciation*	
	£	£	£	£	£	£
A. Fixed assets						
I. Property, plant and equipment						
1 Land and buildings	—	—	—	—	—	—
2 Plant and machinery	—	—	—	—	—	—
3 Other fixtures, tools and equipment	—	—	—	—	—	—
4 Capital work in progress	—	—	—	—	—	—
	—	—	—	—	—	—

Appendix 3—*continued*

	1975			1974		
	Cost or valuation	*accumulated depreciation*		*Cost or valuation*	*accumulated depreciation*	
	£	£	£	£	£	£
II. Investments (provisions, if any, to be disclosed)						
1 Investments in group companies		—			—	
2 Loans to group companies		—			—	
3 Investments in associated companies		—			—	
4 Loans to associated companies		—			—	
5 Other investments held as fixed assets		—			—	
6 Other loans		—			—	
7 Own shares		—			—	
		—			—	
			—			—
			—			—
			—			—
B. Current assets						
I. Stocks and work in progress						
1 Raw materials		—			—	
2 Work in progress		—			—	
3 Finished goods		—			—	
		—			—	

II. Debtors				
1 Trade debtors	—		—	
2 Amounts due from group companies on current account	—		—	
3 Amount due from associated companies on current account	—		—	
4 Other debtors	—		—	
5 Prepayments	—		—	
	—		—	
III. Liquid assets, including investments held as such				
1 Investments in group companies	—		—	
2 Own shares	—		—	
3 Other securities	—		—	
4 Bills of exchange	—		—	
5 Bank and postal cheque account balances and cheques and cash in hand	—		—	
	—		—	
	—	—	—	—
LESS: Forward	—	—	—	—
	—	—	—	—
C. Current liabilities (due and payable within one year)				
1 Debenture loans	—		—	
2 Debts to banks and other credit institutions	—		—	

Appendix 3—*continued*

	1975			1974		
	Cost or valuation	*accumulated depreciation*		*Cost or valuation*	*accumulated depreciation*	
	£	£	£	£	£	£
3 Customers' deposits		—			—	
4 Trade creditors and accruals		—			—	
5 Bills of exchange		—			—	
6 Current accounts with group companies		—			—	
7 Current accounts with associated companies		—			—	
8 Taxation		—			—	
9 Provisions		—			—	
10 Other current liabilities		—			—	
		—			—	
D. Net current assets			—			—
			—			—
E. Liabilities due after more than one year						
1 Debenture loans		—			—	
2 Debts to banks and other credit institutions		—			—	
3 Customers' deposits		—			—	
4 Trade creditors		—			—	
5 Bills of exchange		—			—	
6 Amounts due to group companies		—			—	

7 Amounts due to associated companies	—		—	
8 Taxation	—		—	
9 Pensions and similar obligations	—		—	
10 Provisions	—		—	
11 Other non-current liabilities	—		—	
		—		—
		—		—
F. Deferred credits				
1 Deferred taxation	—		—	
2 Deferred income	—		—	
3 Other	—		—	
		—		—
		—		—
G. Intangible assets (so far as not written off)				
1 Research and development	—		—	
2 Concessions, patents, licences and trade marks and similar rights and values	—		—	
3 Goodwill	—		—	
		—		—
H. Formation expenses (so far as not written off)		—		—
		—		—
		—		—

Appendix 3—*continued*

	£	£	£	£	£	£
		1975			1974	
	Cost or valuation	*accumulated depreciation*		*Cost or valuation*	*accumulated depreciation*	
I. Share capital						
1 (Analysed by classes and show nominal values)		—			—	
2 *Less:* Uncalled share capital		—			—	
			—			—
J. Reserves						
1 Legal reserve		—			—	
2 Share premium account		—			—	
3 Revaluation reserve		—			—	
4 Reserve for own shares		—			—	
5 Statutory reserves		—			—	
6 Optional reserves		—			—	
			—			—
K. Profit and loss account						
1 Results for the year		—			—	
2 Results brought forward		—			—	
			—			—
			—			—

PROFIT AND LOSS ACCOUNT

A. Sales			—	—
B. ***Less*****: Cost of sales**			—	—
C. Gross profit			—	—
D. Distribution expenses and administrative expenses			—	—
E. Other operating receipts			—	—
F. Operating result			—	—
G. Net income from investments				
Earnings from shareholdings in group and association companies				
1 Group companies	—	—		
2 Associated companies	—	—		
Income from other securities and loans				
3 Group companies	—	—		
4 Others	—	—		
Other interest receivable				
5 Group companies	—	—		
6 Others	—	—		

	1975			1974		
	Cost or valuation	accumulated depreciation		Cost or valuation	accumulated depreciation	
	£	£	£	£	£	£
		—			—	
7 *Less:* Provisions against investments		—			—	
Interest payable						
8 Group companies		—			—	
9 Others		—			—	
			—			—
			—			—
H. *Less:* **Taxation** (on operating and investment income)			—			—
			—			—
I. Extraordinary items						
1 Extraordinary earnings		—			—	
2 *Less:* Extraordinary charges		—			—	
		—			—	
3 Taxation on extraordinary items		—			—	
			—			—
J. Profit (loss) after extraordinary items			—			—

Chapter 11

The European Method*

Faced with the complexity and variety of different European accounting practices and commercial habits, financial analysts have developed a method which goes some way towards solving the problem of comparability by means of a rational and systematic re-presentation of financial statements in accordance with a European standard. The "European method" of investment analysis is the result of a study carried out by a Permanent Commission on Standardisation set up by the European Federation of Financial Analysts' Societies (EFFAS) in 1963 "to establish a form of presentation of the information given in company accounts suitable for investment analysis and standard on the European level".

This ambitious aim might at first sight appear to be "such stuff as dreams are made on"; what point could there be in attempting to achieve a uniform presentation of European accounts when the underlying bases of calculation differ so greatly from country to country? It is in the answer to this question that in fact both the significance and the limits of the Standardisation Committee's work are highlighted. Either the analyst, after a detailed examination of a company's annual accounts, chairman's statements and other reports and, usually, via direct contact with the company, is in a position to know what underlies a given figure in the accounts, or else the information required is simply lacking or the reality behind it is so nebulous that, whatever is done to juggle with its presentation, it will never be capable of meaningful interpretation. In the former case all the basic data are available to attain the objective of the Committee: in the second, little further can be done. At least the analyst's work is probably not in vain, since in arriving at this negative conclusion his

* This chapter is substantially based on an article by David Gibson-Moore, MA, ACA, a member of the Permanent Commission on Standardisation of the European Federation of Financial Analysts' Societies, which appeared in the January 1973 issue of *Accountancy* (the official journal of the Institute of Chartered Accountants in England and Wales).

researches have almost inevitably given him a greater understanding of the company and consequently he is often in a position to reconstitute the missing information by suitable hypothesis.

The Standardisation Committee's approach in establishing the European form of presentation was first to define, in quite general terms, a method of presentation which would be as widely acceptable as possible. The different account headings and the relationships between them having been defined, the Committee members were then asked to examine how, in the context of their own countries' accounting methods, this scheme could best be accommodated. Thus, armed with a clear understanding of each of the concepts in the proposed overall presentation, the members' task was to extract those elements in the accounts of their own countries which compared most closely with the defined concepts.

The end-product of the Committee's work was presented to the EFFAS congress in Noordwijk in September 1966 in the form of a project, and the project text, with a few later modifications, now constitutes the reference document[1] for the European method of financial analysis. Essentially the method involves the preparation of three "presentation tables" in vertical form highlighting various totals and sub-totals of interest to the analyst, *viz.*

1. Profit and loss account (Fig. 11.1).
2. Financing table (source and application of funds statement) (Fig. 11.2).
3. Balance sheet (Fig. 11.3).

Although the layout of the European method's presentation tables is, to a certain extent, influenced by UK practice, there are, nevertheless, instances where UK companies do not provide enough information for a complete analysis. For example, it is rarely possible to calculate for UK companies the "total product", defined broadly as the sales, net of sales taxes, adjusted by the increase or decrease in stocks of finished goods and work in progress. This figure is an excellent measure of overall activity in any accounting period. The cost of raw materials and other external expenses are, moreover, not generally known. The Committee also elaborated a "working sheet" the purpose of which is to provide a means of transferring the relevant data from company reports to the presentation tables by analysing and rearranging the published information. The working sheet, which is adapted for use in the United Kingdom, France and Germany, provides a matrix in which the analyst can carry out his calculations and adjustments in order to arrive at the figures on the presentation

	197–	197–	197–	197–
Turnover (including taxes)				
Net turnover				
± Change in stocks				
+ Work on own account				
+ Royalties received				
= **Total product**				
− Cost of raw materials used				
− Royalties paid				
− Other external expenses				
= **Added value**				
− Wages, salaries, etc.				
− Other internal expenses				
= **Trading profit before depreciation**				
− Depreciation				
= **Trading profit after depreciation**				
+ Income from trade investments, etc.				
− Financial charges				
= **Profit before tax**				
− Current taxation				
− Minority interests				
= **Earnings for ordinary**				
Ordinary dividend				
Retained income (attributable to ordinary)				
Balance of exceptional items (after tax)				
Exceptional dividend				
Profit declared by the company				
Earnings plus depreciation (EPD)				

Fig. 11.1 "European method" profit and loss account

	197–	197–	197–	197–
Retained income (attributable to ordinary) + Retained income (attributable to minorities) + Depreciation + Change in provisions for liabilities deferred for more than a year				
= **Income finance**				
Exceptional income retained (except on sale of assets) + Sale of assets + Indemnities and subsidies				
= **Miscellaneous finance**				
Ordinary capital + Minority interests + Non-participating preference capital + Convertible loans + Other loan capital				
= **Issue finance**				
= **TOTAL FINANCE**				
Change in: Gross fixed assets + Trade investments and other fixed assets				
= **Acquisition of fixed assets**				
Change in: Stocks + Debtors and equivalents – Creditors and equivalents + Net cash balance				
= **Change in net current assets**				
TOTAL INVESTMENT				

Fig 11.2 "European method" financing table (source and application of funds statement).

	197–	197–	197–	197–
Ordinary capital + Reserves				
= Ordinary shareholders' funds + Minority interests + Non-participating preference capital				
= Group funds + Provisions for liabilities deferred for more than a year + Convertible loans + Other loan capital				
= Long-term funds				
Gross fixed assets − Depreciation				
= Net fixed assets + Trade investments, etc.				
= Total fixed assets				
Stocks + Debtors and equivalents + Cash and equivalents				
= Current assets − Provisions and other short term debts − Bank overdrafts and other short term borrowings				
= Net current assets				

Fig. 11.3. "European method" balance sheet.

tables with a minimum error risk. The analyst will normally start by entering the balance sheet figures for the current and previous year on the working sheet. The current figures form the basis for the balance sheet in the final presentation table and the mathematical difference between the two, after appropriate and sometimes complex adjustment, is used to compile the financing table. Another part of the working sheet is reserved for the preparation of, and the necessary calculations on, the profit and loss account.

At the centre of the Committee's work was the pivotal concept of earnings and the elaboration of a definition of "current earnings". This orientation was imposed by the fact that the analyst, as often as not, was examining a set of accounts the principal aim of whose author was to reduce the profits as much as possible, in certain cases right down to the level of the year's distribution. Thus an analysis of the historic growth of earnings and estimates for future potential earnings and per-share ratios was *a priori* impossible.

Most of the important decisions regarding the definition of current earnings require little adjustment in the case of UK or US companies. However, in the jungle of Continental provisions and reserves the unwary investor is very likely to get lost. Many appropriations of profits are allowable for tax purposes, and hence, in the fiscally oriented Continental presentations, charged to earnings for the year. By a careful analysis of the various types of provisions encountered, the European method has evolved definite rules to eliminate such arbitrary accounting practices which mask a company's true operating result.

The absence of reliable consolidated accounts has long been a thorn in the flesh of European investment analysts and the different techniques encountered represent a veritable kaleidoscope of ingenuity. The technique of creeping consolidation, whereby a subsidiary is accounted for as an investment one year and consolidated the next, crops up frequently, especially with Dutch groups. In this way, for instance, the fixed assets acquisitions of Hoogovens (now merged with Hoesch), the Dutch steel giant, have often proved difficult to separate from movements caused by changes in consolidation policy. Two other examples—Michelin, which produces virtually meaningless unconsolidated holding company accounts, documented down to the last centime, and the Compagnie Générale d'Electricité, which does not consolidate several of its operating subsidiaries —spring to mind.

The initial task that the analyst is frequently compelled to perform consists, as often as not, of a scrutiny of the consolidation status, if any, of the published group accounts. If this is deemed inadequate, he must then, marshalling all the supplementary information available, attempt to compose his own consolidation before he can proceed to the analysis proper of the group as a whole. This is clearly a tedious, sometimes discouraging process and important information is often simply not available. Nevertheless, to date, the published accounts of many European holding companies have been greatly improved by analysts' work on consolidation, undertaken principally by the Société de Documentation et d'Analyses Financières (DAFSA)[2] in Paris. By 1974 the principles embodied in the European method had been applied by DAFSA to the accounts of more than 1000 European companies, half of them French, and a considerable body of practical experience built up. It is thus possible, always taking into account the inherent and inevitable limitations of any such subject, to compare quickly such figures as turnover and current earnings, in the knowledge that they are, so far as possible, homogeneous.

The European method is still mainly used on the Continent but it is probable that now, with increased UK interest in Continental investment, its use will become more widespread in the United Kingdom.[3] This method of analysis is not simply a static framework of rules but, in essence, a whole approach to comparability. It has in the past altered to meet changing company practice and regulation and will continue to be modified in the future so as to keep abreast of changing conditions. The European method, by insisting on the calculation of, and analysing and emphasising the most suitable method of presentation of, the financing table (source and application of funds statement), was in advance of its time and this work has done a great deal to demonstrate the importance of a close review of the changes in financial position to investors.

The European method is extremely convenient for the assembly of data banks of company information and such data banks, compiled from figures redrafted under this method, are now being set up on the Continent. The prospects are exciting and, until a truly European company legislation emerges, which, whatever the EEC directives may say, is unlikely to be for some years, the European method offers the most concrete means of achieving international inter-company comparison.

REFERENCES

1. EFFAS Permanent Commission on Standardisation, "Project 1967" as agreed at the Noordwijk Congress, and annex including modifications resulting from the Wiesbaden Congress in 1968.
2. DAFSA was founded in 1959 by several French banks to take over the collection of their financial data. It also provides a subscription service to other interested parties. A London office was opened in 1973.
3. A book describing the European method (*Investment Analysis* by Denis Weaver) has been published by Longman in association with the British Society of Investment Analysts.

Chapter 12

The International Accounting Firms*

THE "BIG EIGHT"

The first international accounting firms began to emerge around the turn of the last century when UK accountants, following the trail of UK investment, set up offices in the United States of America. As the profession grew and expanded on both sides of the Atlantic, further offices were established throughout the world. The result was that the professions of both countries soon became dominated by a relatively small number of firms from which there evolved the "Big Eight" international accounting firms of today:

Arthur Andersen.
Arthur Young.
Coopers & Lybrand.
Deloitte, Haskins & Sells.
Peat, Marwick, Mitchell.
Price Waterhouse.
Touche Ross.
Whinney Murray Ernst & Ernst.

Although they all have extensive operations in the United States, where together, for instance, they audit 90 per cent of the companies quoted on the New York Stock Exchange, only three of the "Big Eight"—Arthur Andersen, Arthur Young, and Touche Ross—could in any way be regarded as essentially US firms. Coopers & Lybrand, Deloitte, Haskins & Sells, Peat, Marwick, Mitchell, and Whinney Murray Ernst & Ernst have resulted from mergers and associations between leading UK and US firms, while Price Waterhouse, which was originally founded in London in 1850 and opened a New York office in 1890, is now probably the most international of them all.

* The firms discussed in this chapter are not exclusively the only international accounting firms. There are, in addition to the firms mentioned here, several large UK, Dutch, German and Swiss firms (many of which are mentioned elsewhere in this book) which already have or are in the process of establishing extensive international connections.

Some of the international accounting firms have long associations with the Continent. As far back as 1911 and 1916 respectively, Peat, Marwick, Mitchell and Price Waterhouse had opened offices in Paris, but even before this Deloitte's associates, Haskins & Sells, had entered into an association in 1905 which still survives today with a leading Dutch firm, Van Dien. Following the First World War and the consequent shift in the balance of the world's economic relations as a result of which the United States became a powerful lending nation, all but two of the "Big Eight" were established in either Paris or Brussels. However, it took another world war, vast post-war US aid and investment, and eventually the foundation of the European Economic Community before the majority of firms had established themselves in most of the EEC countries (Table 12.1).

While their objectives were similar, not all of the "Big Eight" decided to open their own offices in each country. Some, like Touche Ross, preferred to associate with local firms, believing that in this way the firm "could immediately acquire the background and expertise in business practices, tax requirements, etc., that we knew our clients would be looking for in their international ventures. Further, the demands on the original three firms [George A. Touche & Co. in the UK; Ross, Touche & Co. in Canada, and Touche, Niven, Bailey & Smart in the US] for staff could be minimised."[1] Moreover, it is argued that local associates have better access to local sources of finance for clients, are better equipped to find suitable local acquisitions for clients—this is particularly important in Europe where many such companies are not openly up for sale—and have better access to local and Government authorities.

Apart from the advantages of associating with a local firm in any country, certain other considerations must be borne in mind. Many associations can run into trouble if matters such as standards of fieldwork or quality control procedures are not carefully co-ordinated beforehand. The difficulties of maintaining common high standards even within domestic offices are considerable and cannot be overstated with regard to overseas associations. Although it would seem that those international firms with associate offices are less likely to antagonise the local profession, some, such as Arthur Andersen, believe that the establishment of their own offices is the only way to ensure tight control over quality. Rather than being externally imposed from the United States or the United Kingdom, standards ideally should be developed by international debate and discussion, but it is difficult to see how this process can flourish in a loose association of national firms. It may also be argued that there is, as yet, little advantage in associating with local firms in countries such as Italy,

TABLE 12.1. YEARS IN WHICH THE "BIG EIGHT" ACCOUNTING FIRMS MOVED INTO EUROPE

	Belgium	*Denmark*	*France*	*Germany*	*Ireland*	*Italy*	*Netherlands*
Arthur Andersen	1957	1966	1957	1960	1969	1957	1961
Arthur Young	1963	1961	1923	1951	1963	1957	1962
Coopers & Lybrand	1921	1962	1930	1957	1968	1960	1949
Deloitte, Haskins & Sells	1924	1968	1920	1924	1973	1923	1905
Peat, Marwick, Mitchell	1947	1960	1911	1958	1963	1945	1959
Price Waterhouse	1921	1949	1916	1924	1973	1926	1914
Touche Ross	1959	1966	1930	1961	1972	1961	1961
Whinney Murray Ernst & Ernst	1921	1970	1920	1922	1969	1956	1957

Belgium and, to a lesser extent, France, where, as one leading UK accountant objected, "firms are virtually unknown, the idea of a profession is that it should be practised by individuals and the concepts of practice, for example the practice of auditing, are substantially different, if not contradictory".

Another area of not inconsiderable risk is the independence of the prospective associate. For example, the holdings of the German and Swiss banks in the national accounting firms might be relevant to the eventual choice of a suitable associate. Indeed it would appear that some of the international firms have experienced certain difficulty in finding associates which, in similar circumstances, could maintain and be seen to retain the same high standards of independence as are expected in the United States or the United Kingdom.

TABLE 12.2. BOOK VALUES OF US AND UK DIRECT INVESTMENT IN THE EEC 1965–1971 (in £ millions)

	US	*UK*
1965	2,252	392
1966	2,719	446
1967	3,504	551
1968	3,767	629
1969	4,273	738
1970	4,926	808
1971	5,335	985

Sources: US *Survey of Current Business*; UK *Trade and Industry*.

In keeping with the rapid growth in US and UK investment in the EEC (Table 12.2) the international accounting firms are still mainly concerned with servicing the subsidiaries of US and UK clients on whose consolidated accounts they are required to report as auditors, and may consequently be held liable. Besides this very important legal consideration, these firms are subject to considerable client pressure to provide a complete international service.

While the nationalities of the partners in the international firms reflect to some extent the client profile, they are all determined upon staffing their offices in each country with local nationals and can already claim substantial success at the most senior level (Table 12.3). On the other hand, it is not always easy to recruit high-calibre local staff in countries where the

TABLE 12.3. THE "BIG EIGHT" FIRMS: PERCENTAGES OF NATIONAL PARTNERS IN EEC COUNTRIES (March 1974)

	Belgium	*Denmark*	*France*	*Germany*	*Ireland*	*Italy*	*Netherlands*
Own office							
Arthur Andersen	22	0	75	75	100	83	75
Arthur Young	$33\frac{1}{3}$		50			20	100
Coopers & Lybrand	60		40		100		50
Deloitte, Haskins & Sells	0		20			20	
Peat, Marwick, Mitchell	40		50	60		45	40
Price Waterhouse	20	0	15	55		15	0
Touche Ross	0				0		
Whinney Murray Ernst & Ernst	$33\frac{1}{3}$		0	45		0	100
Association office							
Arthur Andersen							
Arthur Young		100		100	100		
Coopers & Lybrand		100		100		75	
Deloitte, Haskins & Sells		100		100	100		100
Peat, Marwick, Mitchell		100			100		
Price Waterhouse					100		
Touche Ross		100	85	95		100	100
Whinney Murray Ernst & Ernst		100			100		
Average	**25**	**75**	**42**	**77**	**87**	**44**	**71**

status of the profession still leaves much to be desired. Furthermore, the achievement of the above objective is greatly hampered by the many restrictions on practice rights including a nationality or residence bar imposed by some of the Member States of the EEC. There is not much satisfaction in training local staff who are frequently obliged to leave soon after they qualify. The Treaty of Rome lays down in Article 52 that "restrictions on the freedom of establishment of nationals of a Member State in a territory of another Member State shall be abolished by progressive stages in the course of the transitional period. Such

TABLE 12.4. PROFILE OF THE "BIG EIGHT" INTERNATIONAL ACCOUNTING FIRMS

	Year founded[1]	*Number of partners and staff worldwide*	*Number of countries in which firm has offices*
Arthur Andersen	1913	12,000	40
Arthur Young	1894	10,000	60
Coopers & Lybrand	1854	15,000	73
Deloitte, Haskins & Sells	1845	12,350	42
Peat, Marwick, Mitchell	1866	17,500	60
Price Waterhouse	1848	14,800	75
Touche Ross	1898	11,000	40
Whinney Murray Ernst & Ernst	1848	believed to be approximately 12,000	77

1. In each case the date given is the year in which the firm or the oldest of its predecessor or constituent firms first practised as public accountants.

progressive abolition shall also apply to restrictions on the setting up of agencies, branches or subsidiaries by nationals of any Member State established in the territory of any Member State." Although the international firms have taken a major part in the creation and development of an organised profession in many overseas countries, including Europe, only too often the local professions have become obsessed with the imposition of nationalistic restrictions. In 1964 the Institute of Chartered Accountants in England and Wales found it necessary to point out that "all forms of artificial barriers (by reference to nationality, residence, partnership association, firm names or otherwise) are detrimental to the future development of the profession and to the interests of the countries imposing such barriers".[2] Unfortunately these exhortations remain very much unheeded, and there is even a trend towards still greater restrictions in some of the EEC countries. Yet, however much they try, they will never be able to prevent the largest European companies utilising the services of the international firms—a large number have already done so—as they are increasingly forced to seek capital in centres such as London and New York. Instead, looking towards the day when their own competence and status would be unquestioned, the final decision for the local professions must be between short-sighted restrictions with meagre gains and the long-term benefits of mutual co-operation.

The rest of this section is devoted to brief biographical notes on each of the international accounting firms. The data quoted are as at March 1974.

Arthur Andersen

The firm was founded in the United States in 1913 and is therefore the youngest of the "Big Eight" international firms. Its major expansion commenced in the 1950s and it has grown rapidly since then to the extent that its 12,000 personnel are now spread throughout the world in over 40 countries. This expansion has been achieved by the establishment of its own offices rather than by merger with local firms or by associate arrangements. In this way it believes that it has been able to achieve a high degree of consistency of policies and standards throughout the world.

Arthur Andersen's aggressive independence has led to it being known as the "maverick of the profession",[3] but this has possibly been one of the main factors in its growth in recent years. Another factor may well be its success in having its offices run by national partners rather than by expatriates.

In 1973, much to the annoyance of its rivals (although the US offices of Touche Ross and Price Waterhouse are reported to have followed suit in 1974), Arthur Andersen became the first accounting firm to disclose its accounts to its staff and many of its 50,000 clients. Worldwide fees are now believed to be in excess of $300 million and the average partner's salary in 1973 was $91,400. The top 20 partners received more than $226,000 each.

In April 1974 Arthur Andersen was invited by the Russian Government to open an office in Moscow and thereby became the first Western accounting firm to operate an office in Russia since 1917.

Arthur Young

The firm of Arthur Young was founded in Chicago in 1894 by a Scottish barrister and relied very much on UK partners until the 1920s. Arthur Young's links with Europe date from 1917, when it acted as US agent for the London firm of Broads Paterson, with which it later formed a joint partnership based in Paris. The UK partnership dropped the Broads Paterson name in 1965 and merged with the largest Scottish firm in 1968 to become Arthur Young McClelland Moores.

The international firm was joined in 1944 by Clarkson Gordon of Canada and after the Second World War was further extended to include Edwin V. Nixon in Australia and E. R. Syfret in South Africa. Arthur Young International is now based in Bermuda and embraces a network of over 200 offices employing some 10,000 partners and staff in over 60 countries. It has an international service office in New York, and is administered by a Management Council drawn from the 12 major operating units.

Coopers & Lybrand

The international organisation of Coopers & Lybrand is an association of a number of firms throughout the world of which the four principal firms are in Australia, Canada, the United Kingdom and the United States. The UK firm, formerly known as Cooper Brothers and Co., was founded in 1854.

Over the years the UK firm expanded either by amalgamation or by opening offices in most of the Commonwealth and European countries. In 1948 and 1957 respectively it entered into association with the Canadian firm Macdonald, Currie & Co. (founded in 1908) and the US firm of Lybrand, Ross Bros. & Montgomery (founded in 1898), from which associations the present international firm of Coopers & Lybrand was born.

Coopers & Lybrand now has 287 offices in 73 territories and employs in total approximately 15,000 partners and staff.

Deloitte, Haskins & Sells

The firm of Deloitte & Co. was founded in London in 1845 by William Welch Deloitte, grandson of a French refugee who had settled in England. Until the Companies Act, 1862, the practice, like that of other accountants, was largely concerned with insolvency work. In the first half of the present century the international practice of the firm showed considerable expansion, although some offices in North and South America had been opened as early as the 1890s. This gained pace from the inception in 1952 of the present association with Haskins & Sells (a firm established in New York in 1895) which provided for the creation of an international practice carried on in the name of Deloitte, Haskins & Sells, and which now has a worldwide coverage.

After the merger with Harmood Banner & Co. the international organisation employs some 11,500 staff and 850 partners and has over 200 offices in 42 countries.

Peat, Marwick, Mitchell

The firm now known as Peat, Marwick, Mitchell was originally founded by Richard Fletcher in Aberdeen in 1866. W. B. Peat joined the firm in 1870, changing the name to W. B. Peat & Co. after he became controlling partner in 1891. The US firm was established in 1897 in New York City by two Scottish chartered accountants, James Marwick and S. Roger Mitchell, under the name of Marwick Mitchell & Co. Shortly before the First World War a liaison was entered into between the two firms, and in 1924 the worldwide firm became known as Peat, Marwick, Mitchell & Co.

International co-ordination is effected through a Committee whose membership comprises representatives from these two partnerships as well as from other principal partnerships throughout the world, under the chairmanship of the senior partner of the UK firm and the senior partner of the US firm alternatively.

Peat, Marwick, Mitchell now has around 300 offices in more than 60 countries throughout the world. The winter 1973 edition of the UK firm's staff magazine quoted the total number of partners and staff (excluding agency offices) at around 17,500.

Price Waterhouse

The Price Waterhouse practice was founded in London in 1848 and by 1890 the firm had opened its first overseas office in New York. Before the turn of the century it had carried out several assignments on the Continent, but it was not until 1916 that an office was opened in Paris followed by others throughout the rest of Europe, and indeed the whole world.

In 1946 the Australian, Canadian, European, South American, UK and US firms of Price Waterhouse & Co. set up Price Waterhouse & Co. (International Firm) under a partnership deed registered in the United Kingdom. In 1973 the multi-national character of Price Waterhouse was taken a stage further with the establishment of Price Waterhouse International (PWI), a partnership of over 800 partners and 14,000 staff from around 230 offices in some 75 countries. PWI co-ordinates the individual Price Waterhouse firms throughout the world; it is particularly concerned with organising interchanges of professional staff, with publishing and distributing technical material among firms, and with arranging training and professional development of staff.

Touche Ross

Touche Ross had its beginnings in the United Kingdom when George A. Touche & Co. was founded in 1898. At about the same time George A. Touche "visited the United States on numerous occasions in connection with actual or prospective British investors in American industrial securities. He also established one of the oldest accounting firms in the United States and Canada. . . ."[4] The Touche Ross International group was set up in 1959 by the US, UK and Canadian firms and now includes over 40 separate member and affiliated firms with offices in more than 200 cities around the world. The international group has approximately 1000 partners and employs some 10,000 staff. The International Executive Office, situated in New York, co-ordinates the international activities of the member and affiliated firms and has for this purpose designated regional partners for the African, Asian/Pacific, European and Latin American/Caribbean regions.

Whinney Murray Ernst & Ernst

Whinney Murray Ernst & Ernst is the international arm of Whinney Murray & Co. of the United Kingdom and Ernst & Ernst of the United States. Their association extends back to 1923, since when the international firm has been established. The international partnership has developed worldwide to meet the needs of international clients and includes closely related joint partnerships of UK and US partners with local practices. It now has offices in 77 countries. In common with the other international firms whose policy is to provide clients with services based on intimate local knowledge as well as international expertise, the Whinney Murray Ernst & Ernst organisation places great emphasis on cross-fertilisation of standards and ideas, on post-qualification training and interchange of staff.

OTHER EUROPEAN AND INTERNATIONAL FIRMS

Apart from the "Big Eight", certain other international accounting firms merit attention. Some of these firms are of particular European significance and their establishment at about the time when UK membership of the EEC became fairly certain reflected to some extent a widespread desire, especially in the case of large Continental firms, to offer a credible alternative to the worldwide services of the "Big Eight".

While the five firms referred to below are, next to the "Big Eight", probably the most significant of all the other firms operating internationally, the list is not intended to be exclusive. Indeed, as this last chapter goes to press, more and more medium-sized firms from all parts of the EEC as well as from countries such as Switzerland and Sweden seem to be rushing to form European and, with the help of the Americans, international networks.

Binder Dijker Otte (BDO)

Binder Dijker Otte was formed in 1973 as a partnership of three leading European firms: Binder Hamlyn Singleton Fabian, one of the leading UK firms; Deutsche Warentreuhand-Atkiengesellschaft, one of the 10 largest firms in Germany; and Dijker en Doornbos, which ranks number three in the Netherlands. Identical partnerships have been registered in each of the three countries which in turn own BDO-firms registered in other European countries. In the rest of the EEC area the firm operates through associates in Denmark, France, Luxembourg and Italy, and in Belgium through an existing office of Dijker en Doornbos.

The administration of the whole group is co-ordinated by an executive committee which meets every month. The three main firms have some 220 partners and employ around 2600 staff.

It remains to be seen whether progress will continue at the same pace and, more important, whether the individual firms will eventually agree to merge their separate identities in the European firm. BDO is associated with Seidman & Seidman, one of the largest US firms apart from the "Big Eight", and the combined group has correspondents throughout the world.

Klynveld, Turquands, VTDG (KTD)

Like BDO, Klynveld, Turquands, VTDG, which was also established in 1973, appears to have the potential for a genuine European partnership between three well-known firms: Klynveld Kraayenhof, the largest accounting firm in Holland; Turquands Barton Mayhew, one of the 10 largest UK firms; and Vereinigte Deutsche Treuhand-Gesellschaft, the second-largest accounting firm in Germany.

The head office of KTD is located in Brussels, where a resident Central Executive under the direction of a 12-man committee is responsible for the co-ordination and development of the new firm.

KTD now serves its clients from each office of the member firms. In cities where two or more of the member firms were already practising, including London, Brussels, Milan, Barcelona and Paris, the offices have been merged, thereby facilitating much closer professional co-operation. The member firms of KTD have between them around 4400 partners and staff in 75 offices throughout the world.

Interfides

Interfides SA was formed in the late 1960s as a European accounting firm registered in Brussels by leading professional firms in France, Germany and the Netherlands. The original members were: Fiduciaire de France, considered to be the largest accounting firm in France; Moret & Limperg, the second-largest Dutch firm; and Treuarbeit AG, the largest firm in Germany, which, incidentally, is wholly owned by the Federal and State Governments.

In 1971 Josolyne Layton-Bennett of the United Kingdom joined the group as the UK representative, and the whole group now employs some 4500 partners and staff. In contrast with the other main European groups, the member firms of Interfides are unlikely to give up their own independence for the sake of forming a truly European partnership.

McLintock Main Lafrentz

McLintock Main Lafrentz bears a similarity to some of the "Big Eight" inasmuch as it is a multi-national accounting group which has entered into joint partnerships with national firms to practise in the name of McLintock Main Lafrentz while the national firms continue to act for their own clients in their own names. The original firm was founded in 1965 when Thomson McLintock, a firm founded in Glasgow in 1877 and now one of the largest 10 firms in the United Kingdom went into partnership with Main Lafrentz, one of the largest US firms outside the "Big Eight". The partnership was later joined in 1967 by Riddell Stead of Canada, and in 1973 by Pelser Hamelberg van Til of the Netherlands and Hancock Woodward & Neill of Australia. In the EEC area the firm is associated with national firms in Denmark, France, Germany, Ireland and Italy, while the Dutch firm also has an office in Belgium. McLintock Main Lafrentz has about 4500 partners and staff working in 170 offices situated in 30 countries throughout the world.

Alexander Grant Tansley Witt

Alexander Grant Tansley Witt is an international firm which was formed in 1969 by Alexander Grant of the United States and Tansley Witt of the

United Kingdom. Since then it has entered into associations with local firms in several countries throughout the world. The firm has formed joint partnerships with established local firms in all the EEC countries apart from Ireland, where there is a separate Tansley Witt office.

REFERENCES

1. *TRB & S International: Que Para?*, June 1966, pages 10–15.
2. "Report of the Council for 1963", *The Accountant*, April 25, 1964, pages 522–534.
3. "A Fat Maverick Stirs Up the Accounting Profession", *Fortune*, December 1970, pages 97–103.
4. Mary E. Murphy, *Advanced Public Accounting Practice* (Irwin, 1966), page 514.

Appendix 1

The Principal Public Accountancy Bodies in the EEC

Belgium
Collège National des Experts Comptables de Belgique
Rue du Congres 49
1000 Brussels

Institut des Réviseurs d'Entreprises
Avenue des Arts
1040 Brussels

Denmark
Foreningen af Statsautoriserede Revisorer
Kronprinsessegade 8
1306 Copenhagen K

France
L'Ordre des Experts Comptables et des Comptables Agréés
Boulevard Malesherbes 109
Paris VIIIe

Compagnie Nationale des Commissaires aux Comptes
Rue du l'Amirel de Coligny 6
75001 Paris

Germany
Institut der Wirtschaftsprüfer in Deutschland eV
(and the Wirtschaftsprüferkammer)
4000 Düsseldorf 30
Postfach 10226

Ireland
The Institute of Chartered Accountants in Ireland
7 Fitzwilliam Place
Dublin 2

Italy
Consinglio Nazionale dei Ragionieri e Periti Commerciali
Ministero di Grazia e Giustizia
Via Arenula 71
Rome

Ordine dei Dottori Commercialisti
Via Flammia 56
Rome

The Netherlands
Nederlands Instituut van Registeraccountants
Mensinge 2 (Europa Boulevard)
Amsterdam 1011

The United Kingdom
Association of Certified Accountants
22 Bedford Square
London WC1B 3HS

The Institute of Chartered Accountants in England and Wales
Chartered Accountants' Hall
Moorgate Place
London EC2R 6EQ

The Institute of Chartered Accountants of Scotland
27 Queen Street
Edinburgh EH2 1LA

Appendix 2

Formation Dates of the Principal EEC Public Accountancy Bodies

Country	*Body*	*Date*
Belgium	Collège National des Experts Comptables de Belgique	1950
	Institut des Réviseurs d'Entreprises	1953
Denmark	Foreningen af Statsautoriserede Revisorer	1912
France	Ordre des Experts Comptables et des Comptables Agréés	1942
Germany	Institut der Wirtschaftsprüfer	1932
Ireland	The Institute of Chartered Accountants in Ireland	1888
Italy	Collegio dei Ragionieri e Periti Commerciali	1906
	Ordine dei Dottori Commercialisti	1924
Luxembourg	Ordre des Experts Comptables Luxembourgeois	1951
Netherlands	Nederlands Instituut van Registeraccountants	1895
United Kingdom	The Association of Certified Accountants	1891
	The Institute of Chartered Accountants in England and Wales	1880
	The Institute of Chartered Accountants of Scotland	1854

Appendix 3

Membership of the Main EEC Public Accountancy Bodies

Country	*Body*	*Membership*	*As at*
Belgium	Collège National des Experts Comptables de Belgique	1,525	31 December 1973
	Institut des Réviseurs d'Entreprises	227	31 December 1973
Denmark	Foreningen af Statsautoriserede Revisorer	1,012	1 January 1973
France	Ordre des Experts Comptables et des Comptables Agréés	10,029	1 October 1973
Germany	Institute der Wirtschaftsprüfer	3,133	1 April 1973
Ireland	The Institute of Chartered Accountants in Ireland	2,697	31 July 1973
Italy	Collegio dei Ragionieri e Periti Commerciali	6,321	31 December 1970
	Ordine dei Dottori Commercialisti	11,458	31 December 1973
Luxembourg	Ordre des Experts Comptables Luxembourgeois	24	31 December 1973
Netherlands	Nederlands Instituut van Registeraccountants	3,343	31 August 1973
United Kingdom	The Institute of Chartered Accountants in England and Wales	56,425	31 December 1973
	The Association of Certified Accountants	14,494	31 December 1973
	The Institute of Chartered Accountants of Scotland	8,728	19 October 1973

Appendix 4

Professional Accountants' Salaries in the EEC

Average salaries paid by two of the "Big Eight" international accounting firms at 1 January 1974

	Graduate entrant to the profession		*Three years after entry to the profession*		*Eight years after entry to the profession*
	Salary	*Approx. age*	*Salary*	*Approx. status*	*Salary*
Belgium	£3,095	24	£5,380	Still two years' experience before qualification	£10,430
Denmark	£2,385	24	£4,850	Newly qualified	£9,470
France	£4,080	24	£6,245	Newly qualified	£13,580
Germany	£4,410	24	£5,600	Still three years' experience before qualification	£10,445
Ireland	£1,250	21	£2,940	Newly qualified	£5,700
Italy	£2,015*	22	£3,655*	Has been qualified three years	£8,335*
Netherlands	£3,310	25	£5,975	Newly qualified	£11,490*
United Kingdom	£1,615	21	£3,110	Newly qualified	£5,700

NOTES:

1. The figures have been converted at the mid-market rates of exchange ruling on 2 January 1974.
2. All figures include fringe benefits.

* Figures relate only to one firm.

Appendix 5

Quoted Companies in each of the EEC Countries

	Domestic	*Foreign*	*Total*
Belgium	314	133	447
Denmark	267	1	268
France	901	228	1,129
Germany	496	123	619
Italy	184	1	185
Luxembourg[1]	24	51	75
The Netherlands	251	284	535
	2,437	821	3,258
The United Kingdom and Ireland	3,585[2]	397	3,982

1. Represents number of shares quoted.
2. Includes 151 Irish companies.

Appendix 6

Europe's Leading Companies

	Based on turnover		*Based on profitability*
	Top 500	Top 100	Top 100
United Kingdom	167.5	31.5	67.5
Germany	102.5	28.5	14.0
France	80.0	15.0	5.0
Belgium	19.5	3.0	3.0
Italy	18.5	6.5	1.0
Holland	17.0	4.5	1.5
Denmark	2.0	—	1.0
Luxembourg	1.0	1.0	—
	408.0	90.0	93.0
Rest	92.0	10.0	7.0
	500.0	100.0	100.0

Source: Vision, October 1973.

Appendix 7

Some international comparisons

Figures for 1970, unless otherwise stated

	Germany	France	Italy	Neth.	Belg.	Lux.
Area (thousand square miles)	95	213	116	16	12	1
(thousand square km)	249	551	301	34	31	3
Population (millions)	61.5	50.8	54.5	13.0	9.7	0.3
Gross national product ($000 million at market prices)	186.4	147.6	93.2	31.3	25.7	1.0
Gross national product per capita ($ per year at current prices)	3,028	2,906	1,710	2,398	2,656	2,929
Sources of gross domestic product[2] (in %)						
Agriculture	3.1[3]	6.0[3,4]	10.3	7.0[4]	4.5	4.1
Industry (including construction and mining)	54.2[3]	48.1[3,4]	40.5	41.6[4]	42.6	56.9
Services	42.6[3]	45.9[3,4]	49.2	51.4[4]	53.0	39.1
Crude steel production (million metric tons)	45.0	23.8	17.3	5.0	12.6	5.5
Primary energy production (million metric tons, coal equivalent)	175.7	68.8	33.8	42.0	10.5	0.1

1. "Net material product."
2. GDP at factor cost.
3. GDP at market prices.
4. 1969.

The Six	UK	Den.	Ireland	The Nine	USA	Japan	USSR
453	**94**	**17**	**27**	590	3,600	143	8,800
1,168	**244**	**43**	**69**	1,523	9,363	370	22,402
189.8	**55.7**	**4.9**	**2.9**	253.3	205.4	103.5	244
485.2	**121.4**	**15.6**	**3.8**	626.0	993.3	196.2	288[1]
2,555	**2,175**	**3,163**	**1,321**	2,443	4,839	1,834	n.a.
n.a.	**3.1**	**7.9**	**17.8**[4]	n.a.	3.0	8.7[4]	n.a.
n.a.	**44.4**	**40.1**	**35.2**[4]	n.a.	34.9	39.1[4]	n.a.
n.a.	**52.5**	**52.0**	**47.0**[4]	n.a.	62.1	52.2[4]	n.a.
109.2	**28.3**	**0.5**	**0.1**	138.0	122.1	93.3	116.0
330.8	**168.8**	**0.0**	**0.4**	500.2	2,151.4	71.4	1,386.1

	Germany	France	Italy	Neth.	Belg.	Lux.
International trade (extra-Community trade of the Nine)						
Imports ($ million)	14,503	8,601	8,041	4,961	3,882	
Exports ($ million)	17,840	8,062	6,824	3,336	2,990	
Trade within Community of Nine						
Imports ($ million)	15,311	10,322	6,899	8,433	7,470	
Exports ($ million)	16,348	9,677	6,385	8,431	8,605	
Merchant fleet (million tons gross)	7.88	6.46	7.45	5.81	1.06	—
Foreign aid (total net capital flow to developing countries, $ million: official loans and grants, private capital, voluntary organisations' grants)	1,487	1,808	725	457	309	—
Reserves ($ million) end-November 1971	15,469	6,726	5,862	2,314	2,326	

5. End-September.
* Does not apply.
Sources: ECSO, OECD.

The Six	UK	Den.	Ireland	The Nine	USA	Japan	USSR
*	**15,391**	**2,144**	**444**	57,966	39,963	18,881	11,739
*	**13,278**	**1,665**	**228**	54,259	43,226	19,318	12,800
*	**6,332**	**2,241**	**1,125**	58,134	*	*	*
*	**6,072**	**1,624**	**807**	57,951	*	*	*
28.66	**25.83**	**3.31**	**0.17**	57.97	18.46	27.0	14.83
4,786	**1,259**	**97**	**n.a.**	6,142	5,971	1,824	204
32,697	**5,014**[5]	**492**	**904**	39,107	10,450	14,063	n.a.

Appendix 8

Bibliography

Note: An asterisk (*) indicates publications produced for internal use and not for public sale.

FRANCE

Company law

French Law on Commercial Companies as at January 1st, 1971 (Commerce Clearing House Inc., Chicago, 1971), 345 pages. English/French edition.

Books and booklets

Arthur Andersen & Co., *Tax and Trade Guide: France* (Chicago, 1971), 187 pages.*

Coopers & Lybrand, *International Reference Manual: France* (New York, 1969), 66 pages.*

Ernst & Ernst, *International Business Series, France* (Cleveland, 1965 and 1969), looseleaf.*

Institute of Chartered Accountants in England and Wales, *Statutory Audit Requirements in France (a comparison with the requirements in the United Kingdom)* (ICAEW, London, 1973), 58 pages.

Peat, Marwick, Mitchell & Co., *International Tax and Business Guide: France* (New York, 1973), 154 pages.*

Price Waterhouse & Co., *Business Enterprises in France* (New York, 1972), 122 pages.*

Touche Ross International, *Executive Digest: France* (New York, 1970), 36 pages.*

Touche Ross & Co., *Business in France* (London, 1972), 45 pages.*

Articles and papers

Adamson, David, *French Commissaires aux Comptes and UK Auditors.* Unpublished paper presented to Paris Region of Cie des Commissaires aux Comptes, 30 May 1973, 7 pages.

Barbier, Guy (Arthur Andersen), "Accounting in France", *Accountancy* (October 1972), pp. 10–17.

Geddes, A., "Uniform accounting in Europe? French and English accounting practices compared", *The Accountant* (22 June 1972), pp. 825–827.

Harichaux, Michel (Alexander Grant Tansley Witt), "European unity is a major objective", *Accountant's Weekly* (9 November 1973), pp. 22–24.

Henrot, André, "The revision of company law in France as it concerns the audit of company accounts", *Journal UEC* (October 1968), pp. 226–227.

Lafferty, Michael J., "Changes in the French style", *Financial Times* (15 May 1973), p. 17.

Lafferty, Michael J., "Accounting for France: a case of now or never", *The Accountant* (13 December 1973), pp. 784–788.

Most, Kenneth S., "The French accounting experiment", *International Journal of Accounting Education and Research* (Fall 1971), pp. 15–28.

Sanderson, R. G., *EEC: France.* Unpublished paper presented to a meeting of the London and District Society of Chartered Accountants in 1973, 40 pages.

Wisner, Jean, "The amendment of the law relating to statutory audits of French companies", *Journal UEC* (July 1970), pp. 148–152.

GERMANY

Company law

The German Stock Corporation Law (*Aktiengesetz* 1965), translated by Dr Rudolf Mueller and Evan G. Galbraith. (Fritz Knapp Verlag, Frankfurt, 1966), 502 pages. English/German edition.

Books and booklets

Arthur Andersen & Co., *Tax and Trade Guide: Germany* (Chicago, 1968; supplement, 1972), 109 pages.*

Arthur Andersen & Co., *Dictionary of German–English Accounting and Business Terms* (Chicago, 1973), 253 pages.*

Bank Verlag GmbH, *The Banking System of the Federal Republic of Germany*, seventh edition (Köln, 1972), 30 pages.*

Coopers & Lybrand, *International Reference Manual: The Federal Republic of Germany* (New York, 1969), 58 pages.*

Ernst & Ernst, *International Business Series: West Germany* (Cleveland, 1969–70), looseleaf.*

Frankfurter Wertpapierbörse, *Principles Governing the Admission of Securities for Trading and Official Quotation* (Frankfurt, 1973), 40 pages.*

Institute of Chartered Accountants in England and Wales, *Statutory Audit Requirements in the Federal Republic of Germany* (*a comparison with the requirements in the United Kingdom*) (London, 1973), 66 pages.

Peat, Marwick, Mitchell & Co., *International Tax and Business Guide: West Germany* (New York, 1973), 129 pages.*

Peltzer, Martin, and Nebendorf, Karl, *Banking in Germany* (Fritz Knapp Verlag, Frankfurt, 1973), 248 pages.

Price, Waterhouse & Co., *Business Enterprises in Western Germany* (New York, 1970; supplement, 1972), 103 pages.*

Touche Ross & Co., *Business in West Germany* (London, 1972), 44 pages.*

Articles

Biener, H., "Legislation covering affiliated enterprises under company law in the Federal Republic of Germany", *Journal UEC* (April 1973), pp. 103–133.

Gail, Winfried, "Common features of and differences between commercial balance sheets and balance sheets for taxation purposes in the Federal Republic of Germany", *Journal UEC* (January 1973), pp. 7–12.

Goettsche, Haus. G. (Arthur Andersen), "Accounting in Germany", *Accountancy* (August 1972), pp. 24–31.

Hammer, Dieter (Alexander Grant Tansley Witt), "Practices merge to meet new challenge", *Accountant's Weekly* (19 October 1973), pp. 19–21.

Haverman, Hans, "Consolidated accounts in Germany", *Journal UEC* (April 1970), pp. 107–113.

Kafer, Karl, "European national uniform charts of accounts", *International Journal of Accountancy Education and Research* (Fall 1965), pp. 67–83.

Karoli, Hermann, "The aim of disclosure in company law", *Journal UEC* (October 1969), pp. 225–227.

Lafferty, Michael J., "Germans favour secret reserves", *Financial Times* (30 June 1973), p. 16.

Niehus, Rudolf J., "Generally accepted accounting principles in Germany and the consistency and accurate concepts", *Journal UEC* (July 1973), pp. 214–222.

Niehus, Rudolf J., "Generally accepted auditing principles in Germany", *International Journal of Accounting Education and Research* (Spring 1969), pp. 113–124.

Niehus, Rudolf J., "Stock corporation law and the public accountant", *International Journal of Accounting Education and Research* (Spring 1966), pp. 25–41.

Niehus, Rudolf J., "The public accounting profession in Germany", *The Accountant* (4 January 1973), pp. 12–14.

Scheider, Ernst, "The granting of a stock exchange quotation to securities in the Federal Republic of Germany: the question of the liability of the auditor", *Journal UEC* (January 1969), pp. 24–26.

Schoenfeld, Hans-Martin, "New German regulations for the publication of financial statements", *International Journal of Accounting Education and Research* (Spring 1970), pp. 69–88.

THE NETHERLANDS

Company law

Act on the Annual Accounts of Enterprises (Act of 10 September 1970, Gazette 414, with explanations derived from official documents) translated and published by Nederlands Instituut van Registeraccountants (Amsterdam, 1972), 140 pages.

Dutch Corporation Law translated by S. W. Van Der Upeer Zwello (W. E. J. Tjeenk Willink, 1971), 36 pages.

Books and booklets

Arthur Andersen & Co., *Tax and Trade Guide: the Netherlands* (Chicago, 1972), 135 pages.*

Ernst & Ernst, *International Business Series: Netherlands* (Cleveland, 1970), looseleaf.*

Instituut van Registeraccountants Nederlands, *Ordinance Containing Rules of Conduct and Professional Activities of Registeraccountants* (NIvRA, Amsterdam, 1974).

Price Waterhouse & Co., *Business Enterprises in the Netherlands* (New York, 1970), 33 pages.*

Touche Ross & Co., *Business in the Netherlands* (London, 1972), 43 pages.*

Touche Ross International, *Business Study: Netherlands* (New York, 1971), 167 pages.*

Articles

Netherlands Correspondent, "Establishing accounting standards", *The Accountant* (10 May 1973), p. 640.

Burgert, A., "Reservations about replacement value accounting in the Netherlands", *Abacus* (December 1972), pp. 111–126.

Knol, Alfred W. (Arthur Andersen), "Accounting in Holland", *Accountancy* (January 1973), pp. 32–38.

Lafferty, Michael J., "Perhaps the Dutch do it better", *Financial Times* (5 June 1973), p. 19.

Lafferty, Michael J., "How the Dutch adjust for inflation", *Financial Times* (4 December 1973), p. 19.

Lafferty, Michael J., "A force in European accounting: the profession in the Netherlands", *The Accountant* (31 January 1974), pp. 141–143.

Rijpstra, J. J. (Hans) (Alexander Grant Tansley Witt), "Aiming at a dynamic set of standards", *Accountant's Weekly* (5 October 1973), pp. 22–23.

Scott, George M., "A business economics approach to accounting: the Dutch experience", *International Journal of Accounting and Education Research* (Autumn 1971), pp. 309–317.

Vecht, J. M., "The public accountant's responsibility for interim financial company statements", *Journal UEC* (July 1972), pp. 217–220.

Volten, Henk, "The Netherlands: recommendations on annual accounts", *The Accountant's Magazine* (June 1973), pp. 305–306.

Wessel, P. A., "The new Dutch company law: regulations and their meaning for the profession", *Journal UEC* (July 1972), pp. 209–214.

BELGIUM

Company law

Belgian Company Laws, a translation of the *Code de Commerce, Titre IX: Des Sociétés*. Co-ordinated by the Royal Decree of 30 November 1935, and amended by the laws of 7 June 1949, 9 February 1953, 10 November 1953,

1 December 1953, 6 January 1958, 30 June 1961, 14 March 1962 and 23 July 1962. Translated by Eric Osterweil of the American law firm Coudert Brothers and reproduced in *Commerce* (September, October and December 1965), 28 pages.

Books and booklets

Arthur Andersen & Co., *Tax and Trade Guide: Belgium* (Chicago, 1967; supplement, 1972), 142 pages.*

British Chamber of Commerce for Belgium and Luxembourg, *Business Briefing for Belgium* (Brussels, 1971), 266 pages including advertisements.

Coopers & Lybrand, *International Reference Manual: Belgium* (New York, 1972), 69 pages.*

Ernst & Ernst, *International Business Series: Belgium* (Cleveland, 1970–73), looseleaf.*

Commission de la Bourse, *The Capital Market in Belgium* (Bourse de Bruxelles, 1973), 7 pages.

Commission de la Bourse, *History of the Stock Exchange in Belgium* (Bourse de Bruxelles, 1973), 13 pages.

Peat, Marwick, Mitchell & Co., *International Tax and Business Guide: Belgium* (New York, 1972), 155 pages.*

Price Waterhouse & Co., *Business Enterprises in Belgium* (London, 1972), 74 pages.*

Société Générale de Belgique, *Société Générale de Belgique* 1822–1972 (Brussels, 1972), 264 pages.*

Touche Ross International, *Business study: Belgium* (New York, 1969), 155 pages.*

Touche Ross & Co., *Business in Belgium and Luxembourg* (London, 1972), 45 pages.*

Articles

Asselman, Roger J. (Arthur Andersen), "Accounting in Belgium and Luxembourg", *Accountancy* (April 1973), pp. 10–16.

Lafferty, Michael J., "Belgians lack sophistication", *Financial Times* (15 August 1973), p. 13.

Lafferty, Michael J., "The Accountancy Profession in Belgium and Luxembourg", *The Accountant* (9 January, 1975), pp. 37–38.

Poyer, R. van (Alexander Grant Tansley Witt), "Growing fast but far too diverse", *Accountant's Weekly* (30 November 1973), pp. 22–23.

LUXEMBOURG

Company law

Law of 1915. *Loi du* 10 *aout* 1915 *concernant les sociétés commerciales,* 1915. Memorial 925 (as amended) in *Receuil des lois* (Imprimerie Victor Buck, Luxembourg, 1960).

Books and booklets

British Chamber of Commerce for Belgium and Luxembourg, *Business Briefing for Belgium* (Brussels, 1971), 266 pages including advertisements.

Dargent, Jean, *Luxembourg: an International Financial Centre* (Ministry of State, Luxembourg, 1972), 68 pages.

George, Als, *Luxembourg: Economic and Geographic Profile* (Ministry of State, Luxembourg, 1973), 48 pages.

Price Waterhouse & Co., *Information Guide for Doing Business in the Grand Duchy of Luxembourg* (New York, 1971), 56 pages.*

Touche Ross & Co., *Business in Belgium and Luxembourg* (London, 1972), 45 pages—7 on Luxembourg.*

Articles

Asselman, Roger J. (Arthur Andersen), "Accounting in Belgium and Luxembourg", *Accountancy* (April 1973), pp. 10–16.

Gerbes, Rudy (Alexander Grant Tansley Witt), "Getting those Euro-accountants together", *Accountant's Weekly* (21/28 December 1973), p. 15.

DENMARK

Company law

Danish Companies Act No. 370 of 13 June 1973 (97 pages); *Danish Anpart Companies Act* No. 371 of 13 June 1973 (84 pages): both translated by Pauline M. Katborg, translator at the British Embassy, Copenhagen, 1973.

Books and booklets

Arthur Andersen & Co., *Tax and Trade Guide: Denmark* (Chicago, 1973), 110 pages.*

Ernst & Ernst, *International Business Series: Denmark* (Cleveland 1971), looseleaf.*

Nordfinanz-Bank, Zürich, *The Scandinavian Market* (Copenhagen, 1973), 70 pages.*

Price Waterhouse & Co., *Business Enterprises in Denmark* (New York, 1970), 106 pages.*

Touche Ross International, *Executive Digest: Denmark* (New York, 1970), 40 pages.*

Touche Ross & Co., *Business in Denmark* (London, 1972), 42 pages.*

Articles and papers

Foreningen af Statsautoriserede Revisorer, *The Danish State-authorised Public Accountant's Profession* (Copenhagen, 1973), 11 pages*

Foreningen af Statsautoriserede Revisorer, *The Education of State-authorised Public Accountants* (Copenhagen, 1973), 13 pages.*

Hanner, Per V. A., "Towards a Nordic companies act", *Journal UEC* (January 1971), pp. 19–25.

Lafferty, Michael J., "Denmark raises its standards", *Financial Times* (23 October 1973), p. 21.

Lafferty, Michael J., "Small numbers, high standards: the profession in Denmark", *The Accountant* (20 June 1974) pp. 799–801.

Olesen, N. O. (Alexander Grant Tansley Witt), "New era dawns as training is streamlined", *Accountant's Weekly* (28 September 1973), pp. 20–21.

Petersen, Arne From (Arthur Andersen), "The accounting profession in Denmark", *Accountancy* (February 1974), pp. 34–42.

ITALY

Company law

Italian Civil Code. Codice Civile of 16 March 1942, translated by Mario Bettramo, Giovanni E. Longo and John Henry Merryman (Oceana Publications, New York, 1969), 787 pages.

Books and booklets

Banca Commerciale Italiana, *Vade-mecum for Foreign Investors in Italy* (Milan, 1972), 474 pages.*

Price Waterhouse & Co., *Business Enterprises in Italy* (New York, 1971), 61 pages.*

Touche Ross & Co., *Business in Italy* (London, 1972), 40 pages.*

Articles

Davis, A. D. (Alexander Grant Tansley Witt), "Waiting for the birth of the auditing profession", *Accountant's Weekly* (14 December 1973), p. 23.

Davis, A. D. (Alexander Grant Tansley Witt), "Auditing: the last dangerous profession", *Accountant's Weekly* (21/28 December 1973), pp. 14–15.

Lafferty, Michael J., "The Italian enigma", *Financial Times* (17 July 1973), p. 17.

Lafferty, Michael J., "The Italian problem: a profession yet to find itself", *The Accountant* (7 March 1974), pp. 285–287.

Pettermo, E., "The application of the first European Community directive on company law harmonisation: its consequences for the Italian company law", *Journal UEC* (October 1970), pp. 221–225.

Tenz, Walter (Arthur Andersen), "Accounting in Italy", *Accountancy* (November 1972), pp. 20–32.

THE UNITED KINGDOM

Company law

The Companies Act, 1948 (HMSO, London, 1948), 363 pages.

The Companies Act, 1967 (HMSO, London, 1967), 136 pages.

The Companies Bill, 1973 (HMSO, London, 1973), 152 pages.

Report of the (Jenkins) Company Law Committee (HMSO, London, 1962), 223 pages.

Books and booklets

Arthur Andersen & Co., *Tax and Trade Guide: United Kingdom* (Chicago, 1969), 221 pages.*

Bird, Peter, *Accountability: Standards in Financial Reporting* (Haymarket, London, 1973), 149 pages.

Cairncross, Frances, and McRae, Hamish, *Capital City: London as a Financial Centre* (London, 1973), 234 pages.

Coopers & Lybrand, *International Reference Manual: United Kingdom* (New York, 1968), 56 pages.*

Ernst & Ernst, *International Business Series: United Kingdom* (Cleveland, 1967–70), looseleaf.*

IBRO, *The Future of London as an International Financial Centre* (HMSO, London, 1973), separate chapters.

Institute of Chartered Accountants in England and Wales, *Accounting for Stewardship in a Period of Inflation* (London, 1968), 24 pages.

Institute of Chartered Accountants in England and Wales, *Companies Legislation in the* 1970*s* (London, 1969), 31 pages.

Institute of Chartered Accountants in England and Wales, *Guide to the Accounting Requirements of the Companies Acts,* 1948–1967 (London, 1967), 36 pages.

Institute of Chartered Accountants in England and Wales, *Survey of Published Accounts* 1972–73 (London, 1973), 244 pages.

Price Waterhouse & Co., *Information Guide for Doing Business in the United Kingdom* (London, 1969), 93 pages.*

Solomon, David, with Berridge, T. M., *Prospectus for a Profession* (Gee & Co., 1974), 221 pages.

Speedleberg, Richard, *The City* (Blond & Briggs, London, 1973), 264 pages.

Stamp, Edward and Marley, Christopher, *Accounting Principles and the City Code: the Case for Reform* (Butterworths, London, 1970), 202 pages.

Touche Ross & Co., *Doing Business in the United Kingdom* (London, 1973), 61 pages.*

Touche Ross International, *Executive Digest: United Kingdom* (New York, 1969), 36 pages.*

The Stock Exchange, *Admission of Securities to Listing* (London, looseleaf edition, March 1973).

Willott, R. (Editor), *Going Public* '72 (Haymarket, London, 1973), 96 pages.

IRELAND

Company law

Companies Act, 1963 (Stationery Office, Dublin), 845 pages. English/Irish edition.

Books and booklets

Arthur Andersen & Co., *Tax and Trade Guide: Republic of Ireland* (Chicago, 1972), 182 pages.*

McAleese, Dermot, *Capital Inflows and Direct Foreign Investment in Ireland* 1947–70 (Economic and Social Research Institute, Dublin, 1972), 65 pages.

Price Waterhouse & Co., *Business Enterprises in the Republic of Ireland* (New York, 1971), 67 pages.*

Robinson, Howard W., *A History of Accountants in Ireland* (Institute of Chartered Accountants in Ireland, Dublin, 1964), 485 pages.

Touche Ross & Co., *Business in the Republic of Ireland* (London, 1972), 40 pages.*

Articles

"The need for a new Companies Act", *Hibernia* (24 August 1974), p. 24.

Lang, John Temple, and Whittaker, Andrew, "Irish company law reform", *Irish Times* (28 July and 2 August 1973).

Lafferty, Michael J., "What the Irish do not have to do", *Financial Times* (18 September 1973), p. 17.

HARMONISATION OF EEC COMPANY LAW

Official documents

EEC Treaty (1962) *Rome* (HMSO, London, 1972), 183 pages.

First Council Directive (68/151/CEE) of 9 March 1968.

Commission of the European Communities, "Proposal for a Second Directive (amended) in respect of the formation of public companies and the maintenance and alteration of their capital", *Official Journal* (24 April 1970).

Commission of the European Communities, "Proposal for a Third Directive on mergers between joint-stock companies", *Official Journal* (14 July 1970).

Commission of the European Communities, "Proposal for a Fourth Directive on the annual accounts of limited liability companies (original draft)", *Official Journal* (28 January 1972).

Commission of the European Communities, "Proposal for a Fifth Directive on the structure of sociétés anonymes", *Official Journal* (13 December 1972).

Commission of the European Communities, "Proposed directive and draft council recommendations on a prospectus to be published when securities are admitted to official stock exchange quotations", *Official Journal* (13 December 1972).

Commission of the European Communities, "Proposed statute for the European company", *Official Journal* (10 October 1970).

Commission of the European Communities, "The development of a European capital market (the Segré report) (EEC 1966).

Books and booklets

American Institute of Certified Public Accountants, *Professional Accounting in Twenty-five Countries* (New York, 1964), separate chapters.

Berg, Kenneth B., Mueller, Gerhard G., and Walker, Lauren M., *Readings in International Accounting* (Houghton Mifflin, Boston, 1969), 305 pages.

Commission of the European Communities, *European Community: The Facts* (Press and Information Directorate General of the EEC, Brussels), 32 pages.

Commission of the European Communities, *Industrial Policy and the European Community* (Press and Information Directorate General of the EEC, Brussels), 17 pages.

Enthoven, A. J. H., *Accounting and Economic Development Policy* (North Holland/American Elsevier, Amsterdam, 1973), 380 pages.

Gray, S. J., *Corporate Reporting and Investor Decisions in the EEC: The Comparability Problem* (International Centre for Research in Accounting, Lancaster, 1973), 28 pages.

Gray, S. J., *Financial Reporting in the EEC and the International Economy: a Selected Bibliography* (International Centre for Research in Accounting, Lancaster, 1974), 56 pages.

Haskins & Sells, *International Tax and Business Service, Volume 5: Reporting, Accounting and Business Practices Abroad* (New York, 1972), looseleaf.*

Houghton, Charles de (Editor), *The Company Law, Structure and Reform in Eleven Countries* (Allen & Unwin, London, 1970), 394 pages.

Macbeath, Innes, *The European Approach to Worker–Management Relationships* (The British–North American Committee, Washington, D.C., 1973), 92 pages.

McLean, A. T. (Editor), *Business and Accounting in Europe* (Saxon House/Lexington Books, Hants., England, 1973), 265 pages.

Morris, R. C., *Corporate Reporting Standards and the Fourth Directive* (Institute of Chartered Accountants in England and Wales, London, 1974), 107 pages.

Mueller, Gerhard G., *International Accounting* (Macmillan, New York, 1967), 255 pages.

Noël, Emde, *How the European Community Institutions Work* (Press and Information Directorate General of the EEC, Brussels), 12 pages.

Noyes Data Corporation, *European Stock Exchange Handbook* (New Jersey, 1973), 567 pages.

Pennington, Robert R., *Companies in the Common Market*, second edition (Oyez, London, 1970), 138 pages.

Price Waterhouse & Co., *Accounting Principles and Practices in European Countries* (Institute of Chartered Accountants in England and Wales, London, 1972), 62 pages.

Price Waterhouse & Co., *Accounting Principles and Reporting Practices: a Survey in Thirty-eight Countries* (Institute of Chartered Accountants in England and Wales, London, 1974), 117 pages.

Readman, Peter, and others. *The European Money Puzzle* (Michael Joseph, London, 1973), 165 pages.

Stein, Eric, *Harmonisation of European Company Laws* (Bobbs–Merrill, Indianapolis, 1971), 558 pages.

Schmittoff, Clive M., *Harmonisation of European Company Law* (UK National Committee of Comparative Law, London, 1973), 243 pages.

Schmittoff, Clive M., *European Company Law Texts* (Matthew Buxter/Stevens, London, 1974), 322 pages.

Articles and papers

Bartholomew, E. G., "Proposed Directive on company prospectuses", *Journal UEC* (October 1973), pp. 253–258.

Benson, Sir Henry, "Harmonisation of accounting practice", *The Accountant* (14 December 1972), pp. 756–758.

Braun, Fernand, "Harmonisation of company law: the European Commission view", *The Accountant* (20 September 1973), pp. 363–366.

Davidson, David, "Fiscal influences on financial reporting", *The Accountant* (2 August 1973), pp. 150–152.

Dietrich, Wilhelm, "The European Parliament discusses the EEC Commission's draft directive relating to the right of professional accountants to establish a practice and render services freely", *Journal UEC* (January 1972), pp. 14–17.

Dietrich, Wilhelm, "The first recommendation for a directive of the EEC Commission on the freedom of the *expert comptables* to establish a practice and render professional services", *Journal UEC* (April 1971), pp. 85–92.

Elmendorff, Wilhelm, "Co-ordination of the legal accounting requirements in the various countries of the European Economic Community", *Journal UEC* (October 1967), pp. 232–239, and again in *Journal UEC* (January 1971), pp. 14–19.

Goerdeler, R., "Thoughts on a uniform European group legislation", *Journal UEC* (October 1973), pp. 281–290.

Goerdeler, R., "A true and fair view—or compliance with the law and the company statutes". Unpublished paper, presented at a *Financial Times* conference in 1973.

Greenside, J. P., "British companies and the harmonisation of EEC laws", *The Accountant* (4 January 1973), pp. 9–11.

Greenside, J. P., "Freedom of practice in EEC", *Accountancy* (June 1972), pp. 13–15.

Kaminski, Horst, "Recommendations of the EEC Commission for the Fourth Directive on the harmonisation of accounting requirements", *Journal UEC* (April 1972), pp. 122–130.

Kaminski, Horst, "Summary of the draft directives and statements published by the Commission and the Consultative Assembly of the European Commission in 1972", *Journal UEC* (April 1973), pp. 96–103.

Kaminski, Horst, "The European limited company statute", *Journal UEC* (April 1971), pp. 112–121.

Lafferty, Michael J., "Accounting in the EEC", *Financial European* (April 1973), pp. 13–18.

Lafferty, Michael J., "More flexibility is needed", *Financial Times* (19 March 1974).

Lafferty, Michael J., "Two sets of accounts is the fear", *The Financial Times* (4 June 1974), p. 15.

Lafferty, Michael J., "No EEC steamroller", *Sunday Times* (11 November 1973), p. 55.

McDougall, E. H. V., "The EEC and auditors", *The Accountant's Magazine* (July 1973), pp. 352–355.

Mueller, Gerhard G., "An international view of accounting and disclosure", *International Journal of Accounting Education and Research* (Fall 1971), pp. 117–134.

Niehus, Rudolf, "Harmonised European Economic Community accounting: a German view of the draft directive", *International Journal of Accounting Education and Research* (Spring 1972), pp. 91–125.

Parker, R. H., "A slow start to company harmonisation", *Accountancy* (June 1972), pp. 26–29.

Pittendrigh, J. C., "Accounting practices and disclosures in the EEC", *The Accountant's Magazine* (January 1973), pp. 14–19.

Schmittoff, Clive M., "New concepts in company law", *Journal of Business Law* (October 1973), pp. 312–321.

Selsdon, Lord, "One EEC stock exchange", *Financial European* (February 1973), pp. 17–19.

Stamp, Edward, "Company financial reporting in the EEC: statutory requirements and company accounts". Unpublished paper presented at a *Financial Times* conference in 1973.

Stamp, Edward, "EEC and European accounting standards: a straitjacket or a spur", *Accountancy* (May 1973), pp. 9–16.

Tempelaar, A. F., "Harmonisation of accounting practice", *The Accountant* (8 February 1973), pp. 175–176.

THE EUROPEAN METHOD

Books

Weaver, Dennis, *Investment Analysis* (Longman, London, 1971), 190 pages.

THE INTERNATIONAL ACCOUNTING FIRMS

Books

Murphy, Mary E., *Advanced Public Accounting Practice* (Irwin, Homewood, Illinois, 1966), 559 pages.

Articles

Hilton, Antony, "Making of a merger: Harmood joins Deloitte", *Accountancy Age* (3 May 1974), pp. 14–15.

Hilton, Antony, "Team flies out to meet French threat to firms", *Accountancy Age* (7 June 1974), pp. 1–2.

Louis, Arthur M., "A fat maverick stirs up the accounting profession", *Fortune* (December 1970), pp. 97–103.

Louis, Arthur M., "The accountants are changing the rules", *Fortune* (15 June 1968), p. 177 *et seq.*

Lupo, Leonard A., "Investment abroad in 1972", *Survey of Current Business* (September 1973), pp. 20–34.

Lyons, John F., "The big eight accountants", *Corporate Financing* (January/February 1970), p. 121 *et seq*.

Ragnoni, Carlo, "Putting the books in good order", *Vision*, No. 42 (May 1974), pp. 75–77.

Trade and Industry, Department of, "Book value of overseas direct investments", *Trade and Industry* (15 November 1973), pp. 368–375.

Index